Communist China and Latin America
1959–1967

Earle

CECIL JOHNSON

Communist China
&
Latin America
1959–1967

COLUMBIA
UNIVERSITY PRESS

New York
&
London
1970

Cecil Johnson is Chairman of the Department of Political Science
at Southern Methodist University.

Z 7. 46

Copyright © 1970 Columbia University Press
Library of Congress Catalog Card Number: 76-129054
ISBN: 0-231-03309-5
Printed in the United States of America

to Ruth

Preface

IN undertaking the present study I had a number of objectives in mind. First, I attempted to explain why the leaders of Communist China developed a deep interest in the remote countries of Latin America and how they have manifested their interest in the area. Second, I sought to analyze as lucidly as possible the dialectical concept of the nature of reality held by the Chinese. Third, I set out to explain the Chinese understanding of the nature of their society and their road to power. In more concrete terms, I tried to analyze their concept of people's war, which is their strategy for achieving power in the Third World. I have attempted to show precisely what the Chinese mean when they use the term "people's war." Fourth, I have sought to describe in detail the role of Cuba in the approach of the Chinese to Latin America. Fifth, I have tried to demonstrate how the Chinese have established pro-Chinese parties and movements as the "machinery" for implementing their strategy and tactics of a people's war.

The time span for the study is the period from January 1, 1959, when Fidel Castro marched into Havana, to the end of December, 1967. No attempt has been made to extend the basic research beyond the latter date. Only occasional references are made to developments occurring in 1968.

For the most part, I have depended on English and Chinese materials and translations of such materials made by agencies of the United States Government. I have, for example, relied on the translations pre-

PREFACE

pared by the staff of the United States Consul General's office in Hong Kong and those done under the auspices of the Joint Publications Research Service. I have also profited greatly from the writings of such men as Ernst Halperin, Daniel Tretiak, Kevin Devlin, and Theodore Draper.

I wish to acknowledge my indebtedness to some of those who assisted me in preparing this study. To Southern Methodist University I am indebted for a two years' leave of absence and for a faculty fellowship that financed my first year of study at Columbia University. The Contemporary China Studies Committee of the East Asian Institute and the Research Institute on Communist Affairs at Columbia generously supported the second year required for the study. I wish to express my special thanks for encouragement, advice, and financial support to Professor A. Doak Barnett, Chairman of the Contemporary China Studies Committee, and to Professors Alexander Dallin and Zbigniew Brzezinski, acting-director and director respectively of the Research Institute on Communist Affairs. I also profited from conversations with my colleagues in the East Asian Institute and the Research Institute on Communist Affairs. In particular, I am grateful for the assistance given by Professor Donald S. Zagoria, Dr. John Lindbeck, Richard Sorich, Donald Klein, Richard Diao, Kevin Devlin, and Steven Goldstein. My work was also greatly facilitated by Mrs. Christine Dodson of the Research Institute on Communist Affairs and Miss Mervyn Adams and Mrs. Mary Schoch of the East Asian Institute, who provided me with excellent office facilities and working conditions. Mr. P. J. Hsia, my research assistant, aided the project by his scanning and translation of Chinese materials. Finally, I want to express my gratitude to my wife, Ruth, who has contributed so much to this study. She has not only typed the entire manuscript but has also served as a discerning critic in matters of style and has saved me countless hours by scanning and taking notes on thousands of pages of documents.

CECIL JOHNSON

Englewood, New Jersey
May 1970

(viii)

Contents

Introduction

THE leaders of Communist China have manifested, both in word and deed, a deep and abiding interest in Latin America. There are several reasons that prompted the Chinese to turn their attention to the extremely remote countries of Latin America. In my judgment, the overriding reason was that the Chinese are convinced that the *main* "contradiction" in the contemporary world is that between the "oppressed" peoples of the Third World on the one hand and the "imperialists," led by the United States, on the other. In more concrete terms, they are of the opinion that the scene for the sharpest fighting between the two groups will be the countries of Asia, Africa, and Latin America. In fact, they contend that the entire course of history will, for the most part, be determined by the outcome of the fighting in the continents constituting the so-called Third World. The Chinese, then, regard Latin America as an integral part of that region in the world in which they are most interested.

The high priority assigned by the Chinese to the Third World is predicated on the Leninist theory of imperialism, which holds that the "monopoly capitalists" in the United States and Western Europe have been "exploiting" these countries through extracting "super-profits" from them. Those profits, in turn, have been used to delay the outbreak of "proletarian" revolutions in the "imperialist" countries. Lenin contended that members of the "labor aristocracy" had been corrupted by the class enemy, the bourgeoisie, through the payment of higher salaries, comfortable government appointments, et cetera.

He concluded that revolutions would erupt in the "mature" capital-istic countries, as Marx had predicted, once the "monopoly capitalists" were deprived of the source of "super-profits" in Asia, Africa, and Latin America. The Chinese accept implicitly Lenin's line of reason-ing. They too believe that their ultimate goal, the attainment of "victory" for "Communism" on a global scale, can best be realized through fostering revolutions in Latin America, Asia, and Africa, thereby dealing a smashing blow to the "rear" of the *main* enemy, the United States.

The Chinese maintain that revolutions in this part of the world will follow the Chinese road to power. They assume that conditions in Asia, Africa, and Latin America are essentially the same as those in China prior to 1949. This basic assumption is certainly subject to question. One of the most obvious differences is the fact that the Latin American scene has not been characterized by contending war-lords. Nor can one establish that the treaty relations between Latin American countries on the one hand and the United States and Western European countries on the other correspond to the "unequal treaty system" obtaining in China. The most serious flaw in the analogy drawn by the Chinese is the fact that no Latin American country has been involved in a war with an external foe that is even roughly comparable to the Sino-Japanese War and the bitter civil war that followed it. Despite these major differences, and others that will be developed in subsequent chapters, the Chinese still regard the countries of the Third World as "semicolonial" and "semifeudal" countries; hence they must wage, like the Chinese, an "anti-imperialist" and an "anti-feudal" revolution. Since it is an article of faith with the Chinese that the "ruling classes" never voluntarily relinquish state power, they maintain that the revolution must, of necessity, take on a violent form.

The Chinese classify these countries as "semicolonial" because the "imperialists" allegedly dominate their economic systems through their investments in the major sectors of the economy and through their control of the foreign trade of these countries. That the nations of the Third World are *politically* independent does not matter to the Chinese, who argue that nations are not truly "independent" until they have gained control of their *economic* system as well as their political

system. In practice, this means that the Chinese advocate the nationalization of all property held by aliens and the establishment of trade
with countries other than those they regard as "imperialist" states. In
short, they urge the developing countries in the Third World to limit
their foreign trade to the countries in the "socialist commonwealth,"
countries that are, according to Marxist theoreticians, incapable of
exploiting the emerging countries.

The Chinese hold that the Latin American countries are "semifeudal" in that the industrial sector of the economy is not so well
developed as the agricultural sector. A semifeudal country is also
characterized, they feel, by an excessive concentration of land ownership in the hands of a few landlords. In the Chinese view the peasants,
most of whom are landless, constitute, as in China before and after
1949, the vast majority of the population.

From their contacts with Latin Americans and from their study of
Latin America, the Chinese have learned that "anti-Americanism" is
a widespread phenomenon in the region. As is well known, the "gunboat diplomacy" and the "dollar diplomacy" policies pursued by the
United States in Latin America prior to the adoption in 1933 by
President Roosevelt of the Good Neighbor policy, generated a deep
hatred among many Latin Americans for the Colossus of the North.
In short, they bitterly resent the fact that the United States frequently
intervened militarily in a number of Caribbean countries (Cuba and
Santo Domingo, in particular) when governments there were unable
to preserve "law and order." The idea of the United States as the
"policeman" of the area still lingers in their minds. American intervention in Guatemala in 1954 and in the Dominican Republic did little to
dispel that notion. One should add that these critics visualize the
United States as the protector and defender of reactionary and corrupt
regimes throughout Latin America and as the champion of large American investors in Latin America, intervening, in various ways, to maintain the "stranglehold" of the "bloodsuckers" on the economy of the
countries concerned. Needless to say, the Chinese interest in Latin
America has been greatly enhanced as a consequence of their discover-
ing the prevalence of such ideas.

The fact that Marxist ideas are quite respectable in Latin American
intellectual circles has also stimulated Chinese interest in the area.

(3)

Most students in Latin American universities, especially those in the humanities and social sciences, are at least exposed to the basic concepts of Marxist thought. Particularly popular among them is the Leninist theory of imperialism because it provides them with a plausible explanation for the backwardness of their countries. Many are firmly convinced that the economies of the nations in the area are underdeveloped precisely because the United States government, which they regard as the "tool" of the big capitalists having investments in Latin America, has deliberately followed a policy of holding back the development of these countries. Thus, the United States is cast in the role of villain. It might also be added that they have adopted a most hostile attitude toward "capitalism" in their countries because they link it with "imperialism." They advocate a much more active role for the state than most Americans would deem advisable. One can, of course, find all shades of opinion on the Left in Latin America, but "leftists" favor, in varying degrees, state ownership of basic industries (petroleum, for example) and some type of planned economy. In Marxist terms, "subjective conditions" are favorable in such circles, but one should also note that not all those accepting Marxist concepts are willing to accept the discipline of the Communist Party.

That the Chinese think that Latin American society is basically the same as Chinese society under the old regime is reflected in their "class analyses" of Latin America. Supporting the "national democratic" revolution are the workers, the peasants, the petty bourgeoisie, and the more progressive elements of the national bourgeoisie. The main "enemy" is "imperialism," abetted by its "accomplices," the landlords and the comprador-bureaucrats. After studying Chinese "class analyses" of various countries in Latin America, I failed to discern any awareness on their part that the class structure in these nations is certainly not the same. Their dialectical analysts use the same categories in describing such vastly different social systems as those of Chile and Bolivia, a practice that casts some doubt on their claim that such analyses are based on a scientific observation of data.

In their attempt to persuade Latin American revolutionaries to follow the same "anti-imperialist" and "anti-feudal" road that they had trod many years ago, the Chinese have hammered away at the idea that they experienced, in the earlier period, precisely the same "exploitation" at the hands of the "imperialists." Furthermore, they assert that they are

(4)

still confronted with the same enemy in the Far East, an enemy who occupies Taiwan and prepares for a final onslaught against the mainland itself. That is, they try to convince Latin Americans that they and the Chinese must join forces to form a broad worldwide united front against the *common* enemy of all mankind, "U.S. imperialism and its lackeys."

Chinese interest in Latin America also increased as a result of the advent to power in January, 1959, of Fidel Castro. They responded quickly and enthusiastically to Castro's victory over Batista. While it would be an exaggeration to say that they discovered Latin America via Cuba, it is true that they had not, until Castro's triumph, fully appreciated the revolutionary potential of Latin America. For several years they attempted to harness that potential by holding up the Cuban revolution as a "brilliant example" and as a "model" to be emulated by others in Latin America intent on waging "national-democratic" revolutions. During this period, the Chinese lauded the Cuban experience more than their own. With the deterioration in Sino-Cuban relations that began in early 1965, the Chinese gradually shifted to a policy of stressing the relevance of Chinese experience. At present, they hold that Mao's theory of people's war is the *only* road to power for revolutionaries in Latin America and elsewhere, thereby rejecting the Castroite contention that the Cuban road is the only viable route to power in Latin America.

The Sino-Soviet dispute was still another factor in the arousing of Chinese interest in this part of the world. As the polemics in the international Communist movement increased in intensity, the Chinese set out to make converts in Latin America to help them in the global crusade against the "revisionists" led by the CPSU (the Communist Party of the Soviet Union). The pro-Chinese parties and movements discussed in Chapters VI to VIII were, however, regarded not only as instruments to be used against the CPSU and its allies but also as the vanguard parties for leading people's wars.

The Chinese have interests in Latin America that are not necessarily related to their revolutionary interests. For example, one of their primary goals is that of becoming a major world power. Their efforts to expand trade and cultural relations with Latin American countries are designed to realize that objective as well as to make these nations less dependent on the main enemy, the United States. Similar con-

(5)

siderations underlie their attempts to gain recognition from these countries and to gain the Latins' support for their claim that the Communist Chinese regime be seated in the United Nations as the legitimate representative of the Chinese people.

In the present study, I have concentrated on: (1) the revolutionary strategy and tactics advocated by the Chinese and said by them to be applicable to Latin America and (2) the organization of pro-Chinese Communist Parties and movements in Latin America. As a basis for analyzing the Chinese concept of people's war, their revolutionary strategy for the Third World, I have attempted in Chapter II to provide an ideological framework for Chinese foreign policy. The underlying assumption of the chapter is that one cannot understand the Chinese approach to Latin America unless one knows how the Chinese view the world and their revolution; therefore, I have tried to state as clearly as possible the Chinese concepts that are basic components of their world view and of the Chinese revolution.

In my judgment, the concept that has had the greatest impact on Chinese policy-makers is the theory of contradictions, an idea that predisposes them to assume, for example, that compromise with one's rivals is impossible. Their basic posture of hostility toward the United States and the revisionists of the CPSU has clearly been colored by the influence of this concept. Throughout the study I have pointed out other specific examples of the operative effect of this theory.

Since the Chinese contend that they base their policies on scientific "class analyses" and since they regard Chinese society prior to 1949 to have been virtually the same as that in contemporary Latin American society, I have also analyzed in Chapter II Mao's description of Chinese society under the old regime. The categories used by him in his classic analysis appear constantly in the contemporary writings of the Chinese and their supporters; hence the detailed analysis of the Chinese "model."

The Chinese understanding of their road to power and its relation to the peoples of Asia, Africa, and Latin America are other matters stressed in this chapter. Briefly stated, they present their revolution as one having progressed through two stages: (1) the "new democratic" stage and (2) the "socialist" stage. Those forming a "united front" against the "enemies" of the people in the first stage are the workers, the peasants, the petty bourgeoisie, and the national bourgeoisie. Once these classes, under the leadership of the proletariat, have accomplished the tasks of the first stage, the transition is then made to the higher stage of "socialism." The Chinese postulate that countries in the Third World will follow the path trod by them.

In Chapter III dealing with the Chinese concept of people's war, I have attempted to explain precisely what the Chinese mean when they use that term, and I have tried to show how they have sought to persuade others to use in Latin America the strategy and tactics devised by them in their rise to power to effectuate the defeat of the main enemy, the United States. Since the Chinese are urging the Latin Americans to emulate their example by waging people's wars against "U.S. imperialism," I have provided the reader with a detailed analysis of the Maoist "model." Finally, I have indicated, from time to time, some of the problems that would confront Latin American revolutionaries attempting to imitate the Chinese example.

Régis Debray, a young French admirer of Fidel Castro, in a book published in January, 1967, challenged the Chinese claim that the Chinese strategy and tactics for fighting a people's war had universal validity. Debray contended that Latin American revolutionaries should look to Havana rather than Peking for guidance in fighting such wars. In Chapter IV I compare and contrast the Cuban and Chinese positions on various aspects of the concept.

As a consequence of Debray's challenge and other factors explained below, Sino-Cuban relations reached an all-time low in 1966. In Chapter V on Sino-Cuban relations, I indicate the reasons for the Chinese enthusiasm, in the early years, for Fidel Castro and the Cuban revolution. I also demonstrate how they attempted to exploit Castro's popularity among the Jacobin Left by extolling the Cuban revolution as a "model" for the rest of Latin America. When the Chinese realized, in early 1965, that Castro could not be pressured into abandoning his position of neutrality in the Sino-Soviet dispute, their ardor for him as an ally gradually waned. Since January, 1966, Mao and Castro have regarded one another as rivals for the ideological and political leadership of revolutionaries in Latin America. As noted above, Debray's theory of people's war was a clear challenge to the Chinese concept of such a war.

The last three chapters deal with the pro-Chinese Communist

Parties and movements in Latin America which, I think, can best be described as the instruments that the Chinese use or propose to use in their struggle against the "evils" of "imperialism" and "revisionism." At the risk of being called an apologist for the Chinese, I maintain throughout the book that the use made of these groups by the Chinese has been misunderstood by some Western observers because the latter do not examine Chinese behavior in light of their long-range strategy. The critics frequently charge the Chinese with using these parties and movements solely as an instrument against the CPSU in the Sino-Soviet conflict. I certainly would not deny that the Chinese have used them for this purpose, but I do maintain that the Chinese struggle so intensely against revisionists precisely because they consider the latter as obstacles to be removed so that they can then address themselves to the main task at hand, the elimination of "imperialism" from the world. Admittedly the Chinese may be devoting so much of their time and energy to combatting the "deviationists" in the "short run" that they may never have an opportunity for destroying the "imperialists" in the "long run"! I do feel, however, that they regard the parties and movements in Latin America as the nuclei for developing people's war against the imperialists and their supporters in the region. In these chapters I trace the main developments in the evolution of these groups and point out the position taken by them on domestic and international issues. Although the stand of the parties in the various countries is quite similar, there are sufficient differences in emphasis on certain issues and in the conflicts within these parties to warrant separate treatment for each country. In short, they are not simply "carbon copies" of one another. To cite only one example, developments in the Dominican Republic are certainly quite different from those in Colombia or Bolivia. Suffice it to say at this point that the situation in the Dominican Republic is far more complex than that in the other two countries in that there are three groups that claim to be the legitimate representative of the pro-Chinese forces and there is a "pro-Castro" group, the June 14 Movement, that is as "pro-Chinese" as any of the three! Having indicated some of the reasons for the Chinese interest in Latin America, let us examine how they have manifested that interest.

(8)

I

Commercial, Cultural, and

Propaganda Activities

ALTHOUGH the present study is primarily concerned with the revolutionary strategy and tactics of the Chinese and the development of pro-Chinese parties and movements, the Chinese have also engaged in other activities which should be briefly analyzed so as to give the reader a better appreciation for the broad range of Chinese activities in Latin America. One such activity is the radio broadcasting program in Spanish and Portuguese. Chinese short-wave radio broadcasting is subject to the supervision of the Propaganda Department of the Central Committee of the Communist Party and the Administrative Bureau of the Radiobroadcasting Agency of the Council of State. The Chinese began their Spanish language broadcasts in 1957, when they were transmitting only 7 hours per week to Latin America. In 1961 they increased their broadcasting time to 28 hours per week and continued at that level through 1966. During this period, they beamed their programs for 2 hours per day to the countries of South America and 2 hours per day to those in Central America. It was not until 1960 that they initiated broadcasts in Portuguese. From 1960 to 1966 they transmitted programs in Portuguese for 10½ hours per week.[1] In 1966 they more than doubled the number of hours devoted to broadcasting in Portuguese, increasing the time from 10½ to 28

---

[1] "Communist China in Latin America," *Este & Oeste* (*East & West*), December, 1966, as translated in Joint Publications Research Service, *Translations on International Communist Developments*, No. 940, p. 73. Hereafter cited as JPRS, *TICD*.

hours per week. Thus, they devote equal time to Spanish and Portuguese language programs, thereby indicating the importance attached by the Chinese to Brazil. It is most interesting to note that the Cubans also increased their Portuguese programs in 1966 from 7 to 14 hours per week, leaving unchanged the time devoted to Spanish language programs (124½ hours per week).[2]

The New China News Agency (NCNA) or *Hsinhua*, under the direction of the Propaganda Department of the Central Committee of the Chinese Communist Party (CCP), is another agency that has been quite active in Latin America. NCNA collaborates closely with Radio Peking and *People's Daily*. Major broadcasts are reproduced in whole or in part by NCNA and vice versa.

The agency is concerned with far more than the mere collection and distribution of news. Its staff also has the responsibility for collecting magazines and other publications in foreign countries and forwarding them to Peking for analysis by the intelligence community. In countries where the Chinese have no diplomatic representatives, they frequently perform functions customarily discharged by consular officials such as handling visa and trade problems. At times they make travel arrangements and take care of cultural exchanges. They often serve as contacts with overseas Chinese, whom they try to win over as supporters. Finally, they are known to have passed money to groups having a pro-Chinese orientation, particularly newspapers and magazines that are financially weak. Doubtless they also provide much of the money required by the pro-Chinese Communist parties, movements, and front organizations in Latin America. Since Communist China is recognized by only one country in Latin America, Cuba, the staff members of NCNA are especially valuable to the Chinese. In a sense, they serve as quasi-diplomatic representatives for their country.

The Chinese gained a foothold in Latin America in 1959, when a delegation of four journalists, led by Yao Chen, toured the area in the summer of that year. Chu Mu-chih led another delegation in 1960. The agency established a bureau in Havana in August, 1960. Those working in Cuba were given credit for preparing the way for the recogni-

[2] United States Information Agency, Office of Policy and Research, "Communist Propaganda Organizations and activities in Latin America During 1966," p. 54.

tion of Communist China by Cuba in September, 1960. (In Africa a similar pattern has evolved—first the NCNA correspondents arrive and then diplomatic relations are established.) [3] By the end of 1960 NCNA was operating in the following countries: Argentina, Brazil, Colombia, Ecuador, the Dominican Republic, Peru, and Venezuela. In 1962 and 1963 the agency had also begun operations in Uruguay and Mexico.[4]

NCNA correspondents in Latin America, like those in Asia and Africa, have frequently been arrested by the police on charges of "subversion" or "espionage." For example, on the night of June 14, 1963, the Argentine police raided and closed the office of Juan Gelman, after which they arrested him. The All-China Association of Journalists sent a message to President Guido protesting his "unjustifiable arrest" and demanding his immediate release. The International Organization of Journalists also sent a message to President Guido protesting the arrest as a serious violation of the principles of freedom of the press. Gelman was freed on August 5, 1963, for lack of evidence. The police report indicated, however, that the search had resulted in the confiscation of an important deposit of propaganda.[5] Alejandro Roma, manager of the NCNA office in Ecuador, was arrested on May 23, 1963, and then released. Another correspondent, Pedro Sorro Encalada, was arrested in Ecuador in July of the same year. The police closed the Ecuadorian office of NCNA on July 18, 1963.[6] In late December, 1963, the Venezuelan police arrested Humberto Rojas, the NCNA correspondent. The All-China Association of Journalists sent President Betancourt a message demanding his immediate release. One month later, he was released.[7]

An even better known case occurred in April, 1964, involving the NCNA correspondents in Brazil, Wang Wei-chen and Chu Chi-tung, who arrived in Brazil on December 29, 1961, when the Brazilian Ministry of Foreign Affairs offered them "all sorts of facilities for

---

[3] "The New China News Agency: Mao's Messengers Around the World," *Current Scene*, April 1, 1966, pp. 4–6.

[4] "Communist China in Latin America," JPRS, *TICD*, No. 940, pp. 75–91.

[5] *Survey of the China Mainland Press*, No. 3110, p. 18 and No. 3037, p. 26. Hereafter cited as *SCMP*.

[6] "Communist China in Latin America," p. 84.

[7] *Ibid.*, p. 91.

their activities." According to the Brazilian press, their visas, issued on January 11, 1962, for one year, had not been renewed before their arrest on April 3, 1964, along with seven other Chinese, following the ouster of President Goulart by the military. They were charged with "espionage." The searches conducted by the police resulted in the production of "sabotage plans," elaborated with the assistance of the China-Brazil Cultural Institute, and a hidden cache of arms. In protest against these arrests the Chinese mounted one of their largest and most intense campaigns. Finally, the nine Chinese were expelled from Brazil.[8]

According to the latest annual report (1966) published by the United States Information Agency, the Chinese had "stringers" or local newsmen hired by the NCNA in Costa Rica, Venezuela, and Peru. Since dispatches from the Peruvian correspondent are often received in Peking four or five months after the events have taken place in Peru, one may assume that this correspondent is virtually inactive. The long delays occur even in regard to stories concerning the pro-Chinese Communist Party in Peru. Argentina is listed as having an "unofficial stringer." Countries having a correspondent and distribution of news service were Bolivia and Colombia, countries that have had a great deal of guerrilla activity. Chile and Uruguay have a bureau or office and distribution of news, while Mexico had, until October, 1966, a three-man bureau in Mexico City. The three returned to China to participate in the cultural revolution. Finally, the USIA report indicates that Guyana has an "unofficial correspondent." Obviously, then, the Chinese have made several different arrangements to provide themselves with the services rendered by the agency.[9]

The Chinese have also attempted to expand their influence in Latin America through the use of films. As early as March, 1959, they were showing Chinese films in remote Bolivia, where they were seen by crowds in La Paz, Cochabamba, and Catavi. Altogether they scheduled showings of the films in forty other Bolivian cities, including Sucre and Santa Cruz.[10] In May, 1959, a Chinese film, *Little Heroes*, was shown under the auspices of the Colombian-Chinese Friendship

[8] *Ibid.*, pp. 77–78.
[9] USIA, "Communist Propaganda Organizations and Activities," pp. 20–21.
[10] *SCMP*, No. 1981, p. 35.

Society in Bogotá, Colombia. Before the show, Alfonso Romero Buj, a lawyer who had recently returned from a visit to China, gave his impressions of China and told of the achievements of the Chinese people in their "socialist construction." He also contended that they had a right to "liberate" Taiwan and to resume China's legitimate seat in the United Nations.[11]

In China itself, the Chinese people throughout the country had an opportunity in January, 1961, to see a film entitled *Fighting Cuba*, which was a full-length color production. The Chinese photographers had made the film in Cuba, where they received the wholehearted co-operation of the Cuban authorities. Chinese audiences were shown pictures of the places where leading events in the Cuban revolution had occurred, and they were taken to "the mountain fastness of the Sierra Maestras to meet the *guerrillas* led by Fidel Castro, to Havana where miles of cheering Cubans hail the entry of Fidel Castro and the insurgent forces under his command on that memorable day of January 1, 1959; to the mass rally where Premier Castro announces the confiscation of the more than 60 U.S. companies, firms and sugar refineries. . . ."[12]

The Chinese have also sought to influence Latin Americans by translating into Chinese the works of leading Latin American writers and political figures. Hoping to flatter the Latin Americans, the People's Literature Publishing House announced in January, 1959, the publication of thirty of the poems of José Martí because they reflected "the struggles of the Cuban people against dictatorship and oppression of his time." It also announced at the same time the publication of a collection of poems entitled *Americans, Go Home* by the Chilean poet, Pablo Neruda, and other Latin American poets.[13] Since the action was taken only twenty-nine days after Castro marched into Havana, the Chinese obviously were most anxious to exploit Castro's popularity in Latin America at that time. In June, 1962, the World Knowledge Publishing House in Peking published two pamphlets containing Cuban documents. One was Castro's radio and television speech of March 26, 1962, entitled "Certain Questions on the Work-

11 *SCMP*, No. 2012, p. 30.
12 "Fighting Cuba," *Peking Review*, January 6, 1961, p. 27.
13 *SCMP*, No. 1949, pp. 2-3.

ing Methods of the Cuban Integrated Revolutionary Organizations"; the other contained the First and Second Havana Declarations of September 2, 1960, and February 4, 1962, respectively.[14]

In the wake of the Cuban missile crisis, the Chinese sought to ingratiate themselves with Castro, who was thoroughly disillusioned with the Soviets, by publishing on October 30, 1962, a number of Cuban revolutionary works. Among them were the Havana Declarations; Castro's famous speech, *History Will Absolve Me;* his address to the 15th United Nations General Assembly; and some of his other speeches.[15] The Chinese edition of Castro's revolutionary works and publications as well as films and tapes showing Chinese "firm support for Cuba" were presented on December 5, 1962, by representatives of the Chinese press, radio, and publication industries to the National Directorate of the Cuban Integrated Revolutionary Organizations, the Cuban Revolutionary Government, and Fidel Castro, "the great leader of the Cuban people." [16]

Some of Mao's works were available in Spanish as early as May, 1959, when the Cubans published in *Combate,* organ of the Cuban Revolutionary Directorate, five of his poems, including "Snow" and "Long March." [17] I was able to purchase in Mexico City in the summer of 1961 all of his major works in pamphlet form. They were published by the Foreign Languages Press in Peking. The Cubans published in 1962, 1963, and 1964 several of his essays, including "Combat Liberalism," "On the Correct Handling of Contradictions Among the People," "The Chinese Revolution and the China Communist Party," "On New Democracy," "On Protracted War," and "Problems of Strategy in Guerrilla War Against Japan." In the initial stages of the cultural revolution, the Chinese prepared Spanish editions of his *Selected Works* and, of course, the "Little Red Book" (*Quotations from Chairman Mao Tse-tung*).

Although the Chinese have labored very hard to expand trade with Latin America, Sino-Latin American trade still constitutes only a small percentage of the foreign trade of Communist China and the Latin American countries. There are several reasons for this development. First, the great distance separating the trading partners results in very high freight costs for the goods shipped. As a consequence, the

[14] *Peking Review,* June 22, 1962, p. 20.   [15] *SCMP,* No. 2852, p. 26.
[16] *SCMP,* No. 2878, p. 26.   [17] *SCMP,* No. 2011, p. 39.

Chinese prefer to sell their goods in Hong Kong. Second, the Chinese produce few of the industrial goods which the Latins must purchase from external sources; in fact, they produce very little that the Latins require. Third, they are hampered by the fact that only Cuba has extended diplomatic recognition to Communist China; all the others still recognize the Nationalist regime on Taiwan as the legitimate government of China. Fourth, the Latin Americans produce few goods which the Chinese really need, or which they cannot purchase elsewhere at lower prices. Fifth, the American embargo on trade with Communist China and its policy of discouraging "allies" from engaging in trade with the Communist regime on the mainland doubtless has had some effect on the willingness of Latin American governments to expand trade with the Chinese.

Mexico is one of the countries in which the Chinese have been most active on the commercial level. On November 24, 1963, a Chinese trade mission, led by Chang Kuang-tou, manager of the China National Chemicals Import and Export Corporation, arrived in Mexico to prepare for the first Chinese trade exhibition in Latin America. In his speech at the airport, he expressed the opinion that the display would promote friendship and trade ties between the two countries, geographical distance notwithstanding.[18] The exhibition opened on December 7 with over 5,000 Mexicans visiting on the first day, including President López Mateos. The exhibition was divided into six sections: general, heavy industries, agriculture, textile, and other light industries, handicrafts, and culture and education. It had two sales pavilions and a cinema ground. The total floor space was 2,400 square meters. Chang made a speech in which he stressed friendship and the need for trade relations based on mutual respect and benefit.[19] The exhibition closed on January 6, 1964, having drawn a total of "230,000 excited Mexicans, including a number of dignitaries like President López Mateos, former president General Cárdenas and Minister of Industry and Commerce, Raúl Salinas." [20] In January, 1964, NCNA announced that the delegation had purchased 26,000 bales of Mexican cotton, 20,000 bales of which were already on the way to China. It also announced that new cotton purchases were being negotiated under an agreement signed between the delegation and the Mexican

18 *SCMP*, No. 3110, p. 37.   19 *SCMP*, No. 3118, p. 26.
20 *SCMP*, No. 3137, p. 32.

International Compensation Stock Company.[21] In late February, 1964, the Chinese also bought 450,000 tons of wheat from the Mexicans worth approximately $30 million.[22]

An eleven-member Mexican trade delegation, led by Gustavo Solorzano, a high official in the National Bank of Foreign Trade, arrived on April 20, 1964, in Peking to promote the sale of grain and cotton. Hsiao Fang-chou, Vice Chairman of the China Council for the Promotion of International Trade, thanked the Commission for the promotion of economic relations between Mexico and China and other "Mexican friends" for their help in promoting Sino-Mexican trade and in making arrangements for the trade exhibition.[23] The importance attached by the Chinese to the mission is indicated by the fact that Premier Chou En-lai received the Mexican guests.[24] Solorzano Hernández released a written statement to NCNA in which he asserted that there were wide prospects for further expansion of trade between the two countries.[25]

Ultimas Noticias (*Latest News*), a Mexico City newspaper, published on November 6, 1964, the following chart on trade from 1961—July, 1964:

	Mexican Sales to People's China	Importation of Chinese Products
	(In Mexican Pesos)	
1961	15,778,000	13,943,000
1962	18,215,000	7,236,000
1963	22,416,000	4,135,000
July, 1964	26,653,000	2,335,000

In the four years Mexican imports of Chinese goods dropped sixfold whereas Mexican exports increased approximately 1½ times.

In March, 1965, the Chinese purchased another 32 million pesos of cotton, and on June 29, 1965, another 5,000 tons of cotton.[26]

The Chinese have manifested an interest in Argentine millet, meat,

[21] *SCMP*, No. 3139, p. 34.
[22] Daniel Tretiak, "Mexican Traders," *Far Eastern Economic Review*, May 28, 1964, p. 415.
[23] *SCMP*, No. 3205, p. 32.   [24] *SCMP*, No. 3212, p. 39.
[25] *SCMP*, No. 3221, p. 27.
[26] "Communist China in Latin America," p. 86.

and wheat. According to the Brazilian radio station Radio Tupi, they purchased in 1962 50,000 tons of millet and 28,000 tons of wheat. In 1963 they attempted to purchase 100,000 tons of meat and again in 1964 they asked to purchase 300,000 tons of meat, a request with which the Argentine authorities could not comply. In the latter year, they stepped up their efforts to purchase wheat, asking on January 23 to buy 700,000 tons from Argentina's National Grain Committee. The Argentines, after long negotiations, agreed to sell half that amount. A second agreement, however, was signed shortly thereafter covering 400,000 tons of wheat. The Chinese requested on August 24, 1964, to purchase one million tons of "agricultural products," and on September 20 they signed a three-year agreement to buy wheat. The delivery terms stipulated were: 400,000 tons in 1964, 300,000 tons in 1965, and the same quantity in 1966. In April, 1965, a Chinese mission met a delegation from the Argentine National Grain Committee to consider the purchase of 300,000 tons of wheat. Later in the year they requested a similar amount. "Finally, one million tons were sold to the Chinese, who paid in cash. And during the same year, an additional 500,000 tons of wheat were delivered to the Chinese by the Argentinians." [27]

When João Goulart became President of Brazil in August, 1961, the Chinese were quite optimistic regarding the prospects for expanding trade with Brazil as well as for gaining diplomatic recognition. Their optimism was based on the fact that he was visiting China at the very time that he became president after the unexpected resignation of President Janio Quadros. While in China, he had made statements that were most encouraging to the Chinese. In the section below dealing with exchanges of delegations, we shall discuss more fully the Goulart visit to China.

In June, 1963, the Chinese dispatched a preparatory working team to make arrangements for an economic trade exhibition in Brazil. Heading the group was Hou Fa-tseng.[28] In November, 1963, the Brazilian foreign minister denied them permission to hold the exhibition, and it was not until February, 1964, when the Goulart administration moved sharply to the left, that approval was granted.[29]

[27] Ibid., p. 74. [28] SCMP, No. 3000, p. 26.
[29] Daniel Tretiak, "China's Tough Brazil Nut," Far Eastern Economic Review, April 15, 1965, p. 126.

Shortly after the ouster by the military of Goulart, nine Chinese were arrested on April 3, 1964; this resulted in a worldwide campaign by the Chinese to force the Brazilian authorities to release the prisoners. The evidence used by the authorities to secure convictions was of questionable probative value. Suffice it to say that they depended largely on two documents, a letter allegedly written in Switzerland by a Comrade Cheng to a Comrade Wang on his way to Brazil and a diary. The Chinese contended that both documents were forgeries, pointing out, for example, that the calligraphy used in the letter was not that of a Chinese from the mainland because it used the traditional, not the simplified characters.[30] According to the letter, the Chinese had maintained "an intimate and personal friendship and very satisfactory business relations" with João Amazonas and Mauricio Grabois who were the principal leaders of the pro-Chinese group in Brazil. Comrade Cheng, the alleged author of the letter, suggested that these leaders be sent to China for training as special agents.[31]

Following the arrests, the China Council for the Promotion of International Trade, the All-China Journalists Association, and the New China News Agency sent messages to the Brazilian authorities demanding their release. The messages indicated that those arrested were: Wang Yao-ting, deputy representative of the Representative's Office of the China Council for the Promotion of International Trade in Brazil and Vice Manager of the China National Textiles Import and Export Corporation; staff members Ma Yao-tseng and Sung Kuei-pao; Hou Fa-tseng, leader of the advance group for the preparatory work of the exhibition and staff members Wang Chih, Su Tzu-ping, and Chang Pao-sheng; and Wang Wei-chen, the NCNA correspondent in Brazil and staff member Chu Ching-tung. The protesting organizations contended that the nine had entered Brazil legally to promote mutual understanding and friendship between the peoples of the two countries and to strengthen trade ties between them. There was no justification, they maintained, for the arrests because the nine had "been engaged in proper and legitimate pursuits in preparing for the exhibition, promoting trade, and reporting news."[32] A spokesman for the Ministry of Foreign Affairs made a statement on

[30] *Ibid.,* p. 127.　　　　　　　　　　[31] *SCMP*, No. 3226, p. 23.
[32] *SCMP*, No. 3196, p. 22.

April 12 in which he denounced the arrests as a serious breach of the principles of international law and requested that the arrestees be released.[33]

After a trial lasting over three months, a Brazilian military tribunal found the Chinese guilty of "subversion" and imposed on them ten-year prison sentences. The Chinese Law Association protested the "unlawful sentences" of December 22, 1964.[34] The following April the Brazilian authorities yielded to the intense pressure exerted by the Chinese and ordered the nine Chinese expelled from the country. They arrived in Shanghai on April 20 and in Peking on the following day.[35]

The Chinese did not deny in any of their numerous statements dealing with the incident that those arrested had contacted the persons specified in the incriminating documents. In fact, they argued that their representatives had had a right to engage in such relations as were necessary for discharging their legitimate assignments. Not only did they contact the leaders of the pro-Chinese Communist party, they also arranged meetings with radical nationalists such as Lionel Brizola, President Goulart's brother-in-law, and with Francisco Julião, leader of the Peasant Leagues in Brazil's Northeast, an area in which the Chinese had been deeply interested for some time.[36] Julião had visited China at least once, although the Chinese press did not report his presence.[37] On the other hand, the Chinese featured prominently the visit of his wife and two daughters. They arrived in Peking on April 6, 1962, at the invitation of the China-Latin American Friendship Association. Chu Tu-nan, President of the Association, gave a banquet in their honor. Ch'en Yi, the Foreign Minister, received them on April 12, and Mao himself received them on April 18.[38] Obviously the Chinese were most intent on winning the friendship of Julião, a member of the Chamber of Deputies from Pernambuco, and an advocate of radical land reform on behalf of the landless peasants of Brazil's Northeast.

[33] SCMP, No. 3200, p. 24.   [34] SCMP, No. 3366, p. 30.
[35] SCMP, No. 3444, pp. 31-32.
[36] Tretiak, "China's Tough Brazil Nut," p. 128.
[37] Gondin da Fonseca, *Assim Falou Julião* (2d ed.; São Paulo: Editora Fulgor, 1962), p. 80.
[38] SCMP, No. 2718, p. 31.

The downfall of Goulart made much more difficult the work of the Chinese in Brazil. His downfall was one of the most serious setbacks experienced by them in their drive to expand their influence in Latin America. Had Goulart remained in power, they might very well have succeeded in gaining one of their major objectives in the area, diplomatic recognition by a major Latin American power. Recognition by Brazil, in turn, might have influenced other Latin American nations to follow suit.

Sino-Chilean trade relations have increased in recent years. The two countries have been trading since 1959, and since October, 1961, the Chinese have maintained an Office of Commercial Information in Santiago. Those managing the office have succeeded in negotiating a number of agreements to purchase Chilean mineral products. In 1963, for example, the Chinese purchased 10,000 tons of copper at a price of $8 million and in April, 1964, they signed an agreement to buy 5,000 tons of refined copper for a reported $7 million.[39] On May 12, 1964, NCNA reported that China had decided to buy 20,000 tons of niter from Chile for 310,000 pounds sterling, with deliveries to be made from July to September of 1964. The representative of the Chilean corporation signing the agreement expressed interest in studying the possibility of importing Chinese products and said that he hoped to increase the sale of niter to China in the future.[40] Lin Ping, the commercial representative of the China Council for the Promotion of International Trade, signed, in April, 1965, a contract with Chile's Nitrate and Iodide Sales Corporation for the purchase of 40,000 tons of nitrate and 48 tons of iodine. On May 24, 1965, he signed another contract to buy 6,000 tons of electrolyzed copper.[41] He signed on May 28 still another contract with Chile's Mauricio Hochschild Company for the purchase of 1,500 tons of refined copper. Javier Lagarrique, Vice President of the Copper Department, was reported to have said that China's economic construction was developing rapidly. Chile, therefore, took "a great interest in selling its copper to this great power." Eduardo Simian, Minister of Mining, added that Chile's plans for developing its national copper industry

[39] "The Activity of Communist China in Latin America," *Est et Ouest,* July, 1966, as translated in JPRS, *TICD,* No. 878, p. 20.
[40] *SCMP,* No. 3222, p. 17.   [41] *SCMP,* No. 3468, p. 21.

"should take into account the People's Republic of China as a market." [42]

According to John Gittings, the Chinese maintained in 1966 their interest in Chilean copper. They were thought to have purchased 10,000 tons in that year, and there were reports that they would probably buy twice that amount in 1967. The Chileans, according to these reports, required payment in full in American dollars prior to the shipping date. The price paid was believed to be the equal of the best London price. Gittings also reported that the Chinese purchase of copper in Europe was double the average annual purchase for the preceding five years. The increased Chinese buying of copper in Chile and Europe was thought to be related to the Chinese war effort in Vietnam. He also pointed out that the Chilean press carried no news of these sales, presumably because the Chilean authorities did not want to endanger the close relations with the United States, nor did they want to offend the Taiwan regime. [43]

The Chinese held an economic and commercial exhibition in Chile just as they had done in Mexico and had attempted to do in Brazil. It opened on May 16, 1964, and lasted until June 7. In attendance on opening day were the chief justice of the supreme court of Chile; the director of the Research Department of the Ministry of Economic Affairs; leaders of the United Confederation of Labor; members of parliament et cetera. The leader of the delegation, Chang Kuang-tou, expressed the hope that the exhibition would promote friendship and economic and trade relations, adding that the Chinese would like to overcome the various obstacles to development of trade with Latin America on the basis of equality and mutual benefit. Guillermo del Pedregal, one of the Chilean sponsors, asserted that China would be a vast market for Chile's nitrate and copper in particular. In all, the Chinese displayed over 4,000 items, including heavy and light industry (mostly textiles), farm products, and handicrafts. [44] After three weeks, over 460,000 persons had, according to the Chinese accounts, visited the exhibition. Many visitors (62,000) packed the cinema showing

[42] *SCMP*, No. 3472, p. 26.
[43] John Gittings, "Chinese Copper," *Far Eastern Economic Review*, January 19, 1967, pp. 101–02.
[44] *SCMP*, No. 3224, p. 27.

Chinese films. The Chinese reporter stated that the visitors were most complimentary with regard to the quality of the products displayed.[45]

In June, 1965, the Chinese established a commercial mission in Chile under the direction of the China Council for the Promotion of International Trade. Lin Ping and Liu Chang-heng gave on June 10 a reception that was attended by Senator Salvador Allende; Guillermo del Pedregal, a former Vice President of Chile; Juan Gómez Millas, Minister of Education; and Jorge Cass, political adviser of the President.[46]

Since Sino-Cuban trade relations are discussed in Chapter V, only a few additional comments are required. First, one should note that the trade with Cuba exceeded that with any other Latin American country. Second, one should also note that the Cubans were quick to appreciate the fact that the Soviets were a more dependable trade partner than were the Chinese. Lastly, the Cubans resented deeply the Chinese efforts to pressure them, through manipulation of trade, into abandoning their policy of "neutrality" in the Sino-Soviet dispute.

Finally, the Chinese have attempted to increase their influence in Latin America through the exchange of various types of delegations. Space will not permit a full analysis of their efforts in this field, but a review of the principal aspects of their program will demonstrate, in still another way, that they are indeed interested in Latin America. Given the limited financial resources of the Chinese, their expenditures to bring hundreds of delegations from the remote countries of Latin America must surely be construed as strong evidence of their deep interest in Latin America. The following statistics will illustrate what they have attempted to do in this respect. For 1959 and 1960 they received well over two hundred delegations from twenty-one Latin American countries; in the same period they sent twenty-four delegations to fifteen Latin American countries. In 1961–1962 they dispatched fifty delegations to Latin America and received over ninety. The number of countries with which they had made contact increased from five in 1956 to over fifteen in 1962. Thus they had established contacts with virtually all the Latin American nations at one time or another.[47] For 1963–1964 they received one hundred and five delega-

[45] *SCMP*, No. 3237, p. 25.   [46] *SCMP*, No. 3480, p. 23.
[47] Joseph J. Lee, "Communist China's Latin American Policy," *Asian Survey*, November, 1964, p. 1123.

tions and sent sixteen delegations to Latin America. In 1965 they received forty-seven delegations from Latin America and sent only four in exchange.[48] According to the coverage provided by the *Survey of the China Mainland Press* there was a rather sharp drop in exchanges in 1966–1967. In this two-year period thirty-one delegations from Latin America visited China, while only one delegation visited Latin America. Particularly significant is the fact that only three Cuban delegations went to China in this period, while one Chinese delegation visited Cuba. In earlier years the flow of delegations between these two countries had been the heaviest of all. Argentina, Colombia, Chile, and Mexico sent as many or more delegations than the Cubans in 1966–1967. Chile, with ten, was the country with the largest number of delegations. Mexico, with five, and Colombia with four were second and third respectively.

In my judgment it would be wrong to infer from the decline in 1966 and 1967 in the number of delegations that the Chinese had lost interest in Latin America. Counterbalancing this trend, in part at least, was the increased time devoted to broadcasting in Portuguese to Brazil, with the Chinese more than doubling the number of hours per week for Brazil. One should also note that the Chinese stepped up their campaign to persuade Latin American revolutionaries that the Chinese experience in waging people's war was the *only* reliable guide. Nor should one overlook the fact that the Chinese were working harder than ever before to establish new pro-Chinese parties and movements, and in the case of those previously established they succeeded in imposing stricter ideological controls. Still another factor to be considered in interpreting the decline in the number of delegations is the impact of the Cultural Revolution. As far as the Chinese were concerned, they, no doubt, were mindful of the fact that many visitors would react negatively to the instability which they might observe in China. Moreover, they were not especially enthusiastic to have foreigners in their midst while they were attempting to eradicate the influence of "bourgeois" ideology. Finally, potential visitors would be less inclined to accept invitations to visit China in that the world press carried numerous stories recounting the persecution of foreigners by the Red Guards.

The Chinese have used various organizations to handle their ex-

48 "Communist China in Latin America," JPRS, *TICD*, No. 940, p. 92.

change program. Particularly significant are the Sino-Latin American Friendship Association founded on March 16, 1960, with Chu Tu-nan as president; the Chinese People's Association for the Promotion of Cultural Relations with Foreign Countries; the Chinese People's Institute of Foreign Affairs; the China Peace Committee; the All-China Federation of Trade Unions; the All-China Journalists Association; the All-China Youth Federation, and the All-China Women's Federation. All these organizations operate under the supervision of the Department of International Relations of the Central Committee of the CCP, a body about which we know very little other than the fact that Wu Hsiu-ch'uan is the Director and Chao Yi-min is the Deputy Director. In view of the importance attached to Latin America by the Chinese it seems reasonable to assume that there is a Latin American subdivision.

In Latin America the organizations used to perform these functions are the friendship associations and/or cultural institutes or societies which can be found in most of the Latin American countries. In Argentina there is an "Association of the Friends of Communist China," headed by Bernardo Kordon, who visited China in November, 1964.[49] The Bolivians have a Bolivia-China Friendship Center with Julio Espada and Ignacio Miashiro as president and vice-president.[50] The Brazilians established in 1954 a Sino-Brazilian Cultural Society in Rio de Janeiro; in 1956 they founded a branch in São Paulo, and in 1961 another important branch in Brasilia. In Colombia a Sino-Colombian Friendship Association was created in 1959 in commemoration of the tenth anniversary of the founding of the CPR. The Chinese have been especially active in Chile, where there is a Sino-Chilean Friendship Association and a Sino-Chilean Cultural Institute, founded in 1952.[51] On December 1, 1967, NCNA reported the establishment of another Chile-China Institute in the principal port of San Antonio. Those attending gladly accepted Mao badges![52] In Mexico there are two friendship associations: the Mexico-China Friendship Association and the more militantly pro-Chinese group known as the Associa-

[49] *Ibid.*, p. 75.
[50] Peking NCNA International Service in English, October 4, 1966.
[51] "Communist China in Latin America," pp. 77, 79, and 81.
[52] NCNA, December 5, 1967.

COMMERCIAL, CULTURAL, PROPAGANDA ACTIVITIES

tion of Friendship of People's China. In October, 1966, both organizations held rallies to celebrate China National Day.[53] There is also a Committee for the Promotion of Trade between Mexico and China. Very little is known regarding the Peru-China Friendship Association. The liaison secretary of the association, Mme. Leisa de Mathews, accepted an invitation from the China-Latin American Friendship Association to visit China. She remained in the country for several weeks, arriving on September 25, 1960, and leaving Peking for home on October 31, 1960.[54] In Uruguay there is an Uruguay-China Cultural Association and a Sino-Uruguayan Cultural Institute, which serves as one of the principal centers for Chinese propaganda in Uruguay. According to the United States Information Agency the Chinese are very active in this country.[55] The Venezuelan Friendship Society, the "Society of Friends of China," has sent some delegates to China, but has not been very active since its establishment in 1960.[56]

These organizations perform a number of functions, the most obvious one being that of making arrangements for the exchange of delegations. They also serve as centers for the distribution of Chinese propaganda. Those curious regarding developments in China may attend lectures or see Chinese films organized under the auspices of these bodies. Since officers of these organizations are among the most frequent visitors to China, one could infer that the Chinese avail themselves of the opportunity to discuss with them programs of action and provide them with funds needed in implementing such programs. In short, these representatives, along with staff members of *Hsinhua* operating in Latin America, doubtless serve as "contacts" with pro-Chinese parties and movements. Given the fact that they have no diplomatic or consular representatives in Latin America, how else could the Chinese manage their affairs?

The Chinese have extended invitations to visit China to many different types of persons, ranging from experts on leprosy to leaders of peasant organizations. They have, however, displayed more interest in some of these groups than in others. For example, they have fre-

53 Peking NCNA International Service in English, October 4, 1966.
54 *SCMP*, No. 2349, p. 40; *SCMP*, No. 2372, p. 27.
55 USIA, "Communist Propaganda Organizations and Activities," p. 16.
56 "Communist China in Latin America," p. 91.

quently invited leaders of trade unions. Less frequently, they have received representatives of peasant organizations. In their efforts to gain supporters in their drive to expand trade, they have served as host to trade delegations from Argentina, Mexico, and Chile, who have also been most anxious to increase trade with China. They have manifested a deep interest in influencing the women and young people of Latin America. Apparently they are convinced that the desire for change is especially keen among these two groups just as it was in China prior to 1949. A particularly salient characteristic of the review of the events of 1967 was the frequent reference to "revolutionary students" in Latin America. More space was devoted to analyzing student disturbances and protests than to any other group.[57] Over the years the Chinese have also indicated a profound interest in winning the support of Latin American journalists. For the tenth anniversary of the founding of the CPR (1959), they had to hold a separate reception for this group, having invited over two hundred journalists on this occasion. In the years that followed, the Chinese have spared no effort in gaining supporters in this profession. They have not slighted representatives of small and rather insignificant papers and magazines.[58] Obviously they are most anxious to receive as favorable a press as possible in Latin America. They have bestowed comparable treatment on Latin American intellectuals, including professors and presidents of universities. José Luis Salcedo Bastardo of St. María University of Venezuela, Edmundo Voscondelos of São Paulo University, and Abelardo Vielapando of Thomas Frias University in Bolivia are some of the university presidents who have visited China. Some of the professors have also been active as leaders of radical groups. Rudecindo Ortega, head of the Radical Doctrine Party of Chile and former Minister of Education, and Augustin Alvarez, a member of the Central Committee of the Chilean Socialist Party, are representative of this group.[59]

The leaders of political parties are still another group in which the Chinese have been particularly interested. They have not confined

[57] Peking NCNA International Service in English, December 31, 1967.
[58] Lee, "Communist China's Latin American Policy," *Asian Survey*, November, 1964, p. 1125.
[59] *Ibid.*, p. 1126.

their efforts to winning over the leaders of the Latin American Communist parties. The Central Committee of the CCP did make a major effort in 1956 and 1959 to enlist the support of the Latin American Communist leaders, but they have also courted representatives of the July 26 Movement in Cuba, the Socialist Parties, and many others as well. Perhaps one of the best known of their attempts to win the friendship of a non-Communist leader came in August, 1961, when Vice President João Goulart paid a visit to China. The treatment accorded him reflected the high priority assigned by the Chinese to Brazil. All Peking papers highlighted his visit with news reports, a short biography, a photograph, and editorials welcoming him. On the evening of August 13, he was the guest of honor at a banquet given by Tung Pi-wu, a Vice Chairman of Communist China. Also present were Chu Teh, Chairman of the Standing Committee of the National People's Congress, and Premier Chou En-lai.[60] The Chinese conferred on Goulart the highest honor on August 18, when Mao held a reception for him and gave a banquet in his honor.[61]

Nan Han-chen, Chairman of the Chinese Committee for the Promotion of International Trade, in an article published on August 13 in *Ta-kung Pao* asserted that both countries aspired to develop trade. In his analysis of items that the Chinese were interested in acquiring from Brazil, he stressed coffee, and in doing so indicated an awareness of one of Brazil's most troublesome problems, namely, that of finding suitable markets for the leading agricultural product of the country. He also mentioned "Brazil's monoculture economy," thereby demonstrating that he understood the frustration of Latin Americans based on the fact that so many of these countries depend so heavily on one crop or mineral product for most of their foreign exchange. He charged that the United States manipulated coffee prices in such a way as to bring economic ruin to the Brazilians, a charge that must have appealed to the Brazilian delegation. Appealing to Brazilian pride, he said that Brazil had great potential for trade not only in coffee but also in cotton, sugar, sisal hemp, grain, meat, hides, cocoa, et cetera. He lauded the Brazilian policy of developing trade with all countries, including members of the "socialist countries." [62]

[60] *SCMP*, No. 2561, p. 23. [61] *SCMP*, No. 2565, p. 27.
[62] *SCMP*, No. 2561, pp. 20–21.

At a Peking mass rally on August 17, Goulart expressed his gratitude for the warm hospitality shown him by his hosts. He must have ingratiated himself with the Chinese when he said: "People's China under the leadership of the great leader Mao Tse-tung is a reality and an example that shows how a people, looked down upon by others for past centuries, can emancipate themselves from the yoke of their exploiters." [63] He added that the Brazilians maintained a close and intimate relationship with countries having experienced the same historical plight as the Brazilians. Although most of Brazil's trade at that time was with North American and European countries, the Brazilians, he said, did not exclude the possibility of expanding contacts or developing new trade ties with all countries, "in particular with such countries as People's China, which are rising up and pursuing a policy of independence and development in order to promote the welfare of their own people." [64] He asserted that Brazil had many similarities with China, but he did not indicate precisely what he meant by that remark. He stressed the independent foreign policy then being followed by the Quadros administration, and he maintained that the Brazilians were willing to establish relations with various countries irrespective of their ideologies. In conclusion, he reasserted the traditional Latin American devotion to the principle of non-intervention: "We are opposed to any policy of interference in other countries' internal affairs. The people of any country have the right to choose the form of government which they consider to be the best suited for them and should not allow any country to carry out interference in the internal affairs of other countries." [65]

As the Chinese realized, those remarks were directed, for the most part, at the United States and its policy of intervention in Latin America in the first quarter of the twentieth century.

Having demonstrated the various ways in which the Chinese have manifested their interest in Latin America, let us turn now to a consideration of those concepts that seem to have had the greatest impact on Chinese foreign policy.

---

[63] *SCMP*, No. 2564, p. 26. [64] *Ibid.*
[65] *Ibid.*, p. 27.

II

Ideological Framework for Chinese
Foreign Policy

THE thought of Mao Tse-tung, "the highest form of Marxism-Leninism in the present era," is presented by his followers to the peoples of the underdeveloped countries, and more recently to the revolutionary peoples of the capitalistic countries as well, as the ideology to which they should look for guidance in staging revolutions and in consolidating their power in the post-revolutionary period. Marxist-Leninists everywhere are called upon to look to that ideology for "inspiration" in launching a global assault on the two main "enemies" of the day, "U.S. imperialism" and "Soviet revisionism." Although U.S. imperialism is labeled as the "main enemy of the peoples of the world," one often derives the impression from observing the behavior of the Chinese on the world scene that they in fact have assigned that role to the "revisionists" of the Soviet Union and their followers. At any rate, they have clearly repudiated the Soviet global strategy, based, in part at least, on the teachings of Marx, Engels, Lenin, and Stalin.

In this chapter an effort will be made to analyze succinctly those concepts of Mao Tse-tung which seem to have most influenced the formulation of China's global strategy and tactics. Emphasis will be given to those elements in Mao's system of thought that relate to Asia, Africa, and Latin America because these have been the areas in which the Chinese have manifested the greatest interest. It is contended here that Chinese activities in Latin America make little sense unless viewed from the global perspective of the Chinese, for it is quite clear that the Chinese do not regard Latin America in isolation from the rest of the world.

The Chinese, like their mortal enemies the Soviet revisionists, take great pride in their alleged competence in analyzing scientifically the various realms of reality. They contend that the dialectic, their sharpest and most dependable weapon, has no temporal or spatial limitations. In skillful hands, it can be used to unlock the secrets of the past, the present, or the future. Furthermore, it can be applied to the natural and social worlds as well as to the realm of thought.

Mao freely acknowledges his debt to his predecessors in the Communist movement, Marx, Engels, Lenin, and Stalin, with respect to dialectical materialism. His followers, however, have claimed that he has "developed" or "enriched" the theory in certain significant respects. Those contributions will be noted in the course of the analysis of dialectical materialism.

This theory, bequeathed to the CCP by the founding fathers of "scientific socialism," was allegedly based on scientific observation of phenomena in the natural, social, and mental spheres, and has been validated by the "practice" of the proletariat and its party. Mao's position on the matter of the relation between "theory" and "practice" is essentially that of his predecessors. He considers theory as a guide to action and quotes Lenin's statement that "Without revolutionary theory there can be no revolutionary movements," but he emphasizes that having a correct theory alone is not sufficient. Unless put into practice, a theory has no significance.[1] Revolutionaries can determine whether the theory corresponds to objective reality only by putting it into practice. If the theory, when applied to concrete problems, achieves the objectives one has set for oneself, then it is "true." Corrections are to be made in the theory until the desired results are obtained. He also concurred with Marx on another point: the most important function of theory is not to explain the world but to change the world.[2] Mao's pragmatism is most apparent in his essay entitled "On Practice" as well as in many of his other writings. Doubtless much of his disenchantment with Soviet leadership in the inter-

[1] Mao Tse-tung, "On Practice," Selected Works (Peking: Foreign Languages Press, 1965), I, 304.
[2] Ibid.

national Communist movement stems from his conviction that the Soviets have not been using fully their power to effect the revolutionary changes demanded by the Chinese.

The Chinese Communists claim that they analyze domestic and foreign problems in keeping with the laws of the dialectic. One is certainly not hard-pressed to find innumerable instances in the literature of the Chinese Communists in which the theoreticians articulate the policy of the party in dialectical terms. One of the bones of contention among students of Chinese foreign policy concerns the question of the relative weight given by Chinese decision-makers to considerations of "ideology" and "national interests." Space does not allow an analysis of the issue. Suffice it to say that, in the opinion of the present writer, some commentators have dismissed, too peremptorily, the role of ideology as a "determinant" of Chinese foreign policy. While one must certainly guard against uncritical acceptance of dialectical analyses, one should also be equally cautious in assuming that dialectical materialism and other components of the thought of Mao Tse-tung serve only as devices for the retroactive rationalization of decisions based on a study of the concrete facts in the case without regard for ideology. In short, it is argued that the Chinese Communist leaders do take quite seriously their ideology, and that as a consequence their understanding of world problems is definitely colored by it. Various instances will be cited which, in the writer's judgment, demonstrate that the theoretical assumptions of the Chinese have indeed led them to adopt policies which were not reflective of "objective reality," and an effort will be made to determine whether the Chinese, in light of their failure to assess situations correctly, have revised their theory in accordance with their view concerning the relation between theory and practice.

The Chinese Communists and their Soviet rivals are in accord with regard to the superiority of materialist dialectics over the "metaphysical" or "idealist" world outlook. In his major work *On Contradiction* Mao merely reiterates the views of all Marxists concerning the "metaphysical" and dialectical material world views.[3]

He takes the idealists to task for their "static" approach to prob-

[3] Mao Tse-tung, "On Contradiction," *Selected Works* (Peking: Foreign Languages Press, 1965), I, 312.

lems and for their inability to explain developmental processes and the interconnection of phenomena. Their explanation for the source of motion is also unacceptable to him. The basis for change lies within the thing itself, not in some external cause; that is, contradictions *within* things are responsible for the development of *all* things.[4]

Mao devotes far more attention to the *particularity* of contradictions than to the *universality* of contradictions. According to him the latter has a twofold meaning. First, contradictions exist in the development of all things. Secondly, there is a movement of opposites from beginning to end of a developmental process.[5] In his discussion of universality of contradictions, he is bringing out the points which each form of motion of matter has in common with other forms of motion. He then explains why one must concentrate on the particularity of contradictions:

But what is especially important and necessary, constituting as it does the foundation of our knowledge of a thing, is to observe what is particular to this form of motion, namely, to observe the qualitative difference between this form of motion and other forms. Only when we have done this can we distinguish between things. Every form of motion contains within itself its own particular contradiction. This particular contradiction constitutes the particular essence which distinguishes one thing from another. It is the internal cause or, as it may be called, the basis for the immense variety of things in the world.[6]

Only by studying the particularity of contradiction can one differentiate clearly between things. The "dogmatists" in his party, for whose benefit he allegedly wrote the article, did not understand the need for studying concrete things that had not been thoroughly studied before. The dogmatists, whom he called "lazy-bones," he charges with refusing "to undertake any painstaking study of concrete things, they regard general truths as emerging out of the void, they turn them into purely abstract unfathomable formulas, and thereby completely deny and reverse the normal sequence by which man comes to know the truth." [7] The same charge could be leveled at pro-Chinese analysts in Latin America. After reading scores of reports and analyses drafted by them, I am convinced that they have

[4] *Ibid.* Emphasis added.
[6] *Ibid.*, pp. 319–20.
[5] *Ibid.*, p. 316.
[7] *Ibid.*, p. 321.

failed to make a "painstaking study of concrete things." Rather they have accepted, on faith, the Chinese assertion that conditions in China before 1949 and those in Latin America today are "essentially" the same, when in fact they are not.

Mao takes such dogmatists to task for failing to observe the principle that qualitatively different contradictions must be resolved by qualitatively different methods. They fail to understand that conditions in one revolution may differ significantly from those obtaining in another, and as a consequence ". . . they invariably adopt what they imagine to be an unalterable formula and arbitrarily apply it everywhere, which only causes setbacks to the revolution or makes a sorry mess of what was originally well done." [8] One may well ask: Have the Chinese, in their analyses of conditions in Asia, Africa, and Latin America, areas in which their "model" is allegedly most relevant, distinguished conditions in those regions from those in China before and after the revolution? For that matter, have they manifested in their public statements any real awareness of the fundamental differences within each region? Do their writings, for example, suggest that there are significant differences between the truly primitive African states and the more highly developed countries of Latin America, such as Mexico? In short, have Mao and his associates consistently followed this "basic" Marxist-Leninist principle? In the chapters below dealing with pro-Chinese parties and movements, I shall provide the reader with numerous examples of their writings so that he can judge for himself whether they have discharged their responsibility as "scientific" Marxist-Leninists. In my judgment, they clearly have not done so.

Mao's major contributions to the theory of dialectical materialism were the concepts of a principal contradiction and a principal aspect of a contradiction. In the developmental process of a complex thing there must be a principal contradiction, "whose existence and development determine or influence the existence and development of the other contradictions." [9] At every stage in the developmental process "there is only one principal contradiction which plays the leading role." [10] When analyzing any complex process, one must determine

[8] Ibid. [9] Ibid., p. 331.
[10] Ibid., p. 332.

which of the contradictions is the principal one. All problems can be easily resolved once this has been done. Unfortunately, he adds, "there are thousands of scholars and men of action who do not understand it, and the result is that, lost in a fog, they are unable to get to the heart of a problem and naturally cannot find a way to resolve its contradictions." [11] The CCP, in analyzing the contradictions on the international level in its June 14, 1963, letter to the Central Committee of the CPSU, singled out as the principal contradiction of the day the contradiction between imperialism and the oppressed nations.[12] In concrete terms, the Chinese were urging the Soviets and others in the international Communist movement to concentrate their efforts on the promotion and support of wars of national liberation in Asia, Africa, and Latin America. Involved, of course, is the relative priority to be assigned by Communist strategists to the Third World and the rest of the world. The Chinese maintain that top priority must be given to the Third World because it is there, they maintain, that one finds the greatest revolutionary potential. Similarly, the theoreticians of the CCP frequently point out a certain contradiction as the chief one in the analyses of the various classes in a given society. Thus there is little doubt that the concept has genuine operative significance in the decision-making process at the highest level in the CCP.

In all contradictions, be they principal or secondary, there are two contradictory aspects which Mao insists should not be treated equally. One must be the principal aspect. As he put it:

In any contradiction the development of the contradictory aspects is uneven. Sometimes they seem to be in equilibrium, which is however only temporary and relative, while unevenness is basic. Of the two contradictory aspects, one must be principal and the other secondary. The principal aspect is the one playing the leading role in the contradiction. The nature of a thing is determined mainly by the principal aspect of a contradiction, the aspect which has gained the dominant position.[13]

11 *Ibid.*

12 Chinese Communist Party Central Committee, *A Proposal Concerning the General Line of the International Communist Movement*, as cited in John Wilson Lewis (ed.), *Major Doctrines of Communist China* (New York: W. W. Norton and Company, Inc., 1964), p. 246.

13 Mao, "On Contradiction," *Selected Works*, I, 333.

At certain times in a revolutionary situation adverse conditions out-weigh favorable conditions. Mao holds that the principal aspect (the adverse conditions) can be transformed into the secondary aspect by the efforts of revolutionaries. The converse, he feels, is equally valid: favorable conditions can be transformed into adversity if revolution-aries make mistakes, and he cites as an example the "victory" of 1924–1927 which was turned into defeat.[14] Apparently he is haunted today by the fear that the "socialist victory" in China will be "transformed" into a defeat, the restoration of capitalism, which is precisely what he contends has occurred in the Soviet Union. Such a position, calling as it does for a reversal of the wheel of history, is patently contrary to the optimistic message implicit in the dialectical analysis of history.

The theoretical relationship between the formulation of strategy and tactics and the principal contradiction and the principal aspect of a contradiction is summed up by Mao as follows: "The study of . . . principal and non-principal contradictions and of the principal and the non-principal aspects of a contradiction constitutes an essential method by which a revolutionary political party correctly determines its strategic and tactical policies both in political and in military affairs. All Communists must give it attention." [15]

With the exceptions noted above, Mao's writings on the concept of the unity and struggle of opposites add little to the corpus of Marxist-Leninist doctrine. His explanation in regard to the meaning of the "unity" of opposites is a mere restatement of the orthodox view. He states that unity involves two points: ". . . first, the existence of each of the two aspects of a contradiction in the process of the develop-ment of a thing presupposes the existence of the other aspect, and both aspects coexist in a single entity; second, in given conditions each of the two contradictory aspects transforms itself into its opposite." [16] He asserts dogmatically that such contradictions exist everywhere without exception "in the process of development of all things and in all human thought." [17] In a simple process there will be only a single pair of opposites, while in a complex process there will be many con-tradictory pairs. Continuing the analysis, he contends that the pairs of opposites are also in contradiction with one another.

[14] *Ibid.*, p. 335.
[15] *Ibid.*, p. 336.
[16] *Ibid.*, p. 337.
[17] *Ibid.*

He argues that it is not enough to say that no contradictory aspect can exist in isolation. More important than their dependence on each other for their existence is their transformation into each other. "That is to say, in given conditions, each of the contradictory aspects within a thing transforms itself into its opposite, changes its position to that of its opposite." [18]

The "struggle" going on between opposites manifests itself in two types of motion, relative rest and conspicuous change. In the first type quantitative not qualitative changes are occurring; hence it presents an outward appearance of being at rest. The second type of motion must be preceded by the proper build-up of quantitative changes until a critical point is reached, at which time conspicuous change in the form of a qualitative change occurs. Marxists usually say a "leap" occurs when the "nodal point" has been reached.

That Mao assigns a higher priority to the "struggle" than to the "unity" aspect of the theory is revealed clearly in the following passage:

Things are constantly transforming themselves from the first into the second state of motion; the struggle of opposites goes on in both states but the contradiction is resolved through the second state. That is why we say that the unity of opposites is conditional, temporary, and relative, while the struggle of mutually exclusive opposites is absolute. It is because the identity of opposites obtains only in given conditions that we have said identity is conditional and relative. We may add that the struggle between opposites permeates a process from beginning to end and makes one process transform itself into another, that it is ubiquitous, and that struggle is therefore unconditional and absolute.[19]

Theoreticians for the CCP are assigned the precarious task of deciding whether the line shall place the emphasis on the "unity" or on the "struggle" side of the concept. For example, the workers and peasants, acting under the "guidance" of the party of the proletariat, often form alliances (united fronts) with other social classes and strata. From time to time the policy-makers shift rather abruptly from a policy of rather close collaboration to one demanding struggle against the ally. Corresponding instances may be cited easily in the foreign

[18] *Ibid.*, p. 338. [19] *Ibid.*, p. 342.

policy realm as the line vacillates from a "soft" to a "militant" posture in respect to allies. Emphasis on the unity aspect enables the leader to justify a temporary alliance with the "enemy." [20]

Mao's concept of the theory of historical materialism conflicts sharply with that held by many of his associates in the international Communist movement. To generalize, Marxists hold that, in the dialectical contradiction between the productive forces and the relations of production, the former develop more rapidly than the corresponding relations of production, and they contend further that the productive forces and the relations of production, constituting the economic base of a society, develop more rapidly than the superstructure. The Chinese belief in the power of organization and ideology to effect changes in the economic base is clearly a departure from the traditional view on this relationship. In doing so the CCP has stood Marx on his head and has thus assumed a position corresponding to that of the hated "idealists," who have been condemned by Marxists for their belief that the course of history is "determined" more by ideas than by economic forces.

That the Chinese have a deeper faith than the Soviets in the power of ideas can be established from a study of the rationale offered by them in inaugurating both the Great Leap Forward and the Great Proletarian Cultural Revolution. It is argued here that the Chinese believe that the course of history, in general, is determined largely by correct thinking among the people. Apparently they are convinced that the "socialist revolution" in China itself is being jeopardized by the corrupting influence of "revisionist" and "bourgeois" ideology. Further consolidation of "socialism" is contingent upon the eradication of these poisonous weeds and the inculcation of the correct world view, the thought of Mao Tse-tung, in the minds of the people.

In this context the Chinese emphasis on "propaganda" among the peoples of Asia, Africa, and Latin America, rather than on economic assistance, takes on added significance. Admittedly the distinction between propaganda and economic aid is rather artificial in that the latter is also designed to "remold," over the long term, the thinking of

[20] Arthur A. Cohen, *Communism of Mao Tse-tung* (Chicago: The University of Chicago Press, 1964), p. 18.

the recipient in regard to its future alignment with the donor against the common enemy of all mankind, "U.S. imperialism" and its "lackeys." But it can be argued that the Chinese apparently feel that they can realize a higher rate of return, if the reader will pardon the application of the jargon of the capitalist to the CCP, from their expenditures on the translation and exportation of Chairman Mao's writings on "people's war," for example, than from providing cement factories. Obviously the Chinese would prefer being more actively involved in the granting of aid to other nations. Given the underdeveloped status of the Chinese economy, their record in this field has not been unimpressive. On the other hand, the high priority assigned to propaganda activities could be viewed as a rational recognition on their part that they are no match for the more affluent Soviets and Americans in the expensive game of international "grantsmanship." Thus there is an ideological as well as a purely rational explanation for their stressing of propaganda activities in Latin America.

The class struggle theory, the concrete manifestation of the operation of the laws of historical materialism, is, according to Marxist theory, operative in all societies, past and present, since the appearance of the institution of private property. Mao has, as observers of the Cultural Revolution know, extended the operation of the principle to "socialist" societies. Since 1926 when he wrote *An Analysis of Classes in Chinese Society*, Mao has insisted that his followers emulate his example and differentiate carefully among the various classes and strata as a basis for policy-making. The need for such "scientific" analyses and their alleged relationship to decision-making are outlined by him in his well-known essay as follows:

Who are our enemies? Who are our friends? This is a question of the first importance to the revolution. The basic reason why all previous revolutionary struggles in China achieved so little was their failure to unite with real friends in order to attack real enemies. A revolutionary party is the guide of the masses, and no revolution ever succeeds when the revolutionary party leads them astray. To ensure that we will definitely achieve success in our revolution and will not lead the masses astray, we must pay attention to uniting with our real friends in order to attack our real enemies: to distinguish real friends from real enemies, we must make a general analysis of the economic status of the various classes in Chinese society and their respective attitudes toward the revolution.[21]

The analysis of Chinese society presented in the present work does not correspond, in all respects, to others made by Mao; however, no useful purpose would be served by a tedious comparison of the minor differences in them. More important than the substantive content of the analysis is the methodology used by Mao in arriving at his conclusions. That is, Mao's chief concern was in inculcating in his followers an awareness of the need for a concrete study of conflicting classes and groups in a given society. While he admits that conditions vary in colonial and semicolonial countries, he does feel that they are essentially the same as those obtaining in China, the "model" for all such countries. To the present writer, however, it seems that he too frequently glosses over extremely important differences in the "objective conditions" existing in the emerging countries.

In his model for analyzing classes Mao differentiates among the classes largely on the basis of the varying degrees of resistance or support which they extend to the revolution. On the extreme right of the political spectrum, he perceives the landlord class, the comprador class, and reactionary intellectuals. These he regards as the most backward and reactionary groups, classes that hinder the development of the productive forces. Depending on the imperialists for their survival and growth, he deems their existence as completely incompatible with the objectives of the revolution. The comprador class, having direct connections with the capitalists of the imperialist nations and with the "feudal" landlords, have always been, along with the landlords, the prime targets for all those joining forces in the revolution.[22]

The policy of the CCP with reference to the landlord class has varied a great deal in the various stages in the history of the party. In the Kiangsi period, for example, the party adopted a radical agrarian program. Under the guidance of Communist cadres, peasants seized the lands belonging to the "enemy" of the "people" and distributed

---

[21] Mao Tse-tung, "Analysis of the Classes in Chinese Society," *Selected Works* (Peking: Foreign Languages Press, 1965), I, 13.

[22] *Ibid.*; Mao Tse-tung, *The Chinese Revolution and the Chinese Communist Party* (Peking: Foreign Languages Press, 1959), p. 27.

them among land-hungry peasants. One might also add that many landlords were executed after having been denounced by those whom they had allegedly been exploiting. After the Long March, the party, in the Yenan period, pursued a much more restrained policy with respect to this group. The agrarian policy was characterized by a reduction in rents and interest rates. The lands of the landlords were not confiscated as had been the practice in the earlier period. The shift in policy was made because the CCP was desperately trying to form a broad united front against the Japanese invaders. For the time being the Communists were willing to de-emphasize the "contradiction" between the landlords and the peasants and thus try to win as much popular support as possible by posing as the most reliable leader of the anti-Japanese forces. In the civil war that ensued after the defeat of Japan in 1945, the pendulum again began to swing to the left. Land reform took the form of confiscation of land and revolutionary terror in the villages. In the process hundreds of thousands if not millions of landlords and their families were executed by irate peasants, who acted under the guidance of CCP cadres.

Occupying the center of the political stage between the "progressive" and "revolutionary" forces was the national or middle bourgeoisie. Mao's present evaluation of this group's revolutionary potential is basically the same as his appraisal of it in the 1920s and 1930s. The Chinese national bourgeoisie at that time, like its contemporary counterpart in Asia, Africa, and Latin America, was regarded as a dubious ally because of its dual character. Insofar as it was a victim of oppression at the hands of the imperialists, the comprador bureaucrats, and the feudal forces in the countryside, it was potentially an ally for the more dependable groups. However, the national capitalists had been unable to sever completely their connection with "imperialism" and "feudalism." These ties, coupled with the economic and political flabbiness of the group, frequently manifested themselves in a lack of courage vis-à-vis the imperialists and their reactionary supporters. Mao's reservations about the group, based in part on his experience in collaborating with the group in the 1920s, were apparent in the following statement: "On account of its dual character, the national bourgeoisie can at certain times and to a certain extent become a revolutionary force, taking part in the fight against imperialism and against the government of bureaucrats and warlords. At other times it may become a menace to the revolution, acting as the accomplice of the big comprador bourgeoisie." [23]

Mao's ambivalence toward this group was reflected in the party's policy in relation to it. During the anti-Japanese war, the civil war period (1946–1949), and in the period of economic rehabilitation (1949–1952) the party treated the group as an "ally." The support of the commercial elements was especially helpful to the regime in the rehabilitation of the nation's economy in the economic reconstruction era. With the adoption of the First Five Year Plan in 1953, however, the regime moved gradually toward a socialization of enterprises previously owned by the "national capitalists." Thus the alliance was a temporary one.

Mao exhibited far greater enthusiasm for the "petty bourgeoisie," composed of such groups as master handicraftsmen, small merchants, owner-peasants, and the lower levels of intellectuals—small lawyers, students, office clerks, and public school teachers. Because of its class character and size, he felt that "this class deserves very close attention." [24] The class was divided, on the basis of their respective attitudes toward the revolution, into three sections. The first section consisted of those who were eager to become rich and thus become a part of the middle bourgeoisie. They were also characterized by their timidity in regard to government officials, suspicion of the revolution, and trust in bourgeois propaganda. Needless to say, he labeled this group the "right wing" of the petty bourgeoisie.

The second section, much larger than the first, was consumed by a desire for enrichment but was finding it increasingly difficult just to maintain their standard of living. They were rather doubtful that the revolution against the landlords and the imperialists could succeed in view of the tremendous power of the "oppressing" classes; therefore, they were hesitant about joining the revolutionary movement. That is, they were not against the revolution, but they definitely preferred remaining neutral. Mao was most interested in the third section, which was experiencing a drastic decline in standards. "They are in great mental distress because there is such a contrast between the past and

---

23 Mao, *The Chinese Revolution and the Chinese Communist Party*, p. 28.
24 Mao, "Analysis of the Classes in Chinese Society," *Selected Works*, I, 15.

their present. Such people are quite important for the revolutionary movement; they form a mass of no mean proportions and are the left wing of the petty bourgeoisie." [25] Normally the three sections would have different attitudes toward the revolution. In the event of a war with an *external* enemy, however, the middle section and even the right wing might align itself with the "progressive" forces against the common enemy.

The peasants' potential for revolution, in Mao's estimation, surpassed by far that of the preceding classes. Notwithstanding the fact that Lenin anticipated him in emphasizing the importance of the peasantry in staging a revolution in backward countries, Mao was the first Communist leader to carry out a "proletarian" revolution based, for the most part, on the peasantry. The analysis below is based upon *The Chinese Revolution and the Chinese Communist Party* rather than on his *Analysis of the Classes in Chinese Society* because the terminology used in the former approximates more closely than the latter the categories generally used today by CCP and pro-Chinese theoreticians in their discussion of this class.

In a manner not disclosed, Mao ascertained that the peasantry, at the time (1939), constituted about 80 per cent of the country's total population, and in an equally mystifying way he arrived at percentages for each of the other groups in rural areas. According to his observations, a process of radical differentiation was occurring at that time which, if true, might account for the fact that his categories are somewhat different in the two essays.

The rich peasants, the first group, constituted about 5 per cent of the rural population, or about 10 per cent if they are lumped together with the landlords. Like the landlords, they were "reactionary" in that they rented part of their land to others and thus "exploited" them; however, there was also a "progressive" aspect to be considered— most of them did farm part of their land. Mao set forth his appraisal and the policy to be followed toward them in the agrarian revolution in the following terms: "Generally speaking they may make some contribution to the anti-imperialist mass struggle and may stay neutral in the agrarian revolution against the landlords. There-

[25] *Ibid.*, p. 16.

fore, we should neither group them with the landlords nor adopt prematurely a policy of liquidating them." [26]

The CCP treatment of this group has been somewhat more lenient than that afforded the landlords. According to the land law of the Soviet Republic (November, 1931), land belonging to this group would not be confiscated. Rich peasants would be assigned land, but not of the best quality, if they did not take part in "counterrevolutionary activities" and provided further they worked the land themselves. Landlords, on the other hand, were not entitled to land allotments.[27] After the moderate Yenan period, the party manifested gradually its true attitude toward the group. As quickly as local circumstances permitted, the CCP confiscated their land and distributed it among the more politically reliable groups, the "middle" and "poor" peasants. Although the regime has published no accurate statistics regarding the number of landlords and rich peasants executed, it appears that the percentage of landlords "liquidated" was higher than that for the rich peasant.

Constituting about 20 per cent of the rural population and economically self-sufficient were the middle peasants. After a good harvest, they could lay aside some of their income. The only activities engaged in by them to which Mao took exception was the occasional practice of hiring a few hands and lending money at interest. On balance, he gave them his stamp of approval in that, generally speaking, they did not exploit others, suffering instead from exploitation at the hands of the imperialists, the landlords, and the bourgeoisie. Moreover, they enjoyed no political rights, and only the more prosperous ones had an adequate amount of land. Under these circumstances, they clearly were eligible for membership in the ranks of the revolutionaries as he stated below:

They can not only join the anti-imperialist revolution and the agrarian revolution, but embrace socialism. Therefore the whole middle peasantry can become a reliable ally of the proletariat and count among the motivating forces of the revolution. Their stand for or against the

[26] Mao, *The Chinese Revolution and the Chinese Communist Party*, p. 32.
[27] Conrad Brandt, Benjamin Schwartz, and John K. Fairbank, *A Documentary History of Chinese Communism* (New York: Atheneum, 1966), pp. 224–25.

revolution is a decisive factor in its victory or defeat, and this is especially true when they become the majority of the rural population after the agrarian revolution.[28]

The group, however, in which Mao detects the most empathy for the proletariat was the poor peasantry. They and the rural proletariat (farm laborers) constituted the largest bloc in the countryside—about 70 per cent. Their attitude toward the revolution, like that of all other groups, he explained in terms of their socioeconomic status. "They are the broad peasant masses with no land or insufficient land, the semi-proletariat of the countryside, the biggest motivating force of the Chinese revolution, and by nature the *most reliable* ally of the proletariat and the main contingent of China's revolutionary forces." [29] Without the leadership of the proletariat, however, the middle and poor peasants could never achieve "liberation," but he conceded that "the proletariat can lead the revolution to victory only by forming a firm alliance with the poor and middle peasants." [30]

Through a policy of confiscation of land owned by landlords and "rich" peasants, Mao and his associates in the Kiangsi period sought to win over the "poor" and "middle" peasants. As indicated above, they adopted a more moderate policy during the Yenan period. At that time the party won widespread peasant support in the parts of China occupied by Communist forces by reducing rents and interest rates to more reasonable levels, but so concerned was the CCP with maintaining a broad united front against the Japanese that they guaranteed the civil, political, and property rights of the landlords. In fact the party guaranteed the collection of rents and interests by the landlords. During the civil war and in the period of reconstruction (1949–1952) the CCP gradually shifted to a more radical land policy. The peasants were led to believe that the land distributed to them would be theirs. By the mid 1950s, however, agriculture had been collectivized, and in 1958 the regime moved even further to the left with the establishment of the communes.

The "leading force" and the "most progressive" class in China was, of course, the industrial proletariat, although rather small compared

[28] Mao, *The Chinese Revolution and the Chinese Communist Party*, p. 33.
[29] *Ibid*. Emphasis added.   [30] *Ibid*.

CHINESE FOREIGN POLICY FRAMEWORK

with the chief ally, the peasants. How could such a tiny group hold such a position? He accounted for their superior status in terms of their concentration, being more concentrated than any other group among the revolutionary people. Secondly, they were especially good fighters because of their lowly economic status; having been deprived of the means of production they had only their labor power to sell. The exploitation to which they were exposed exceeded that of their brothers in the more advanced countries in that they were oppressed not only by the bourgeoisie but also by the warlords and imperialists.[31]

Mao's designation of the proletariat as the "leading force" and "most progressive" class was, of course, dictated by the received tradition of the Chinese Marxists. Even though this class played an insignificant role in the Chinese Communist revolution, Mao and his colleagues, to demonstrate their fidelity to Marxist dogma, felt compelled to assign the leading role to this group.

Summing up his analysis of the Chinese class structure, he said:

Our enemies are all those in league with imperialism—the warlords, the bureaucrats, the comprador class, the big landlord class and the reactionary section of the intelligentsia attached to them. The leading force in our revolution is the industrial proletariat. Our closest friends are the entire semi-proletariat and petty bourgeoisie. As for the vacillating middle bourgeoisie, their right-wing may become our enemy and their left wing may become our friend—but we must be constantly on our guard and not let them create confusion within our ranks.[32]

Mao visualized the contradictions among the various classes in Chinese society in the 1930s and 1940s as an integral part of the class struggle on a *global* scale, a vision paralleling quite closely his present view of the relationship between the continuing Chinese revolution, now in its "socialist" phase, and revolutionary movements elsewhere. He added, however, that a qualitative change had occurred in the Chinese "bourgeois-democratic" revolution. Prior to the outbreak of World War I and the establishment of a socialist state in Russia, the Chinese revolution had been in the old category of the bourgeois-democratic world revolution, of which it was a part. Subsequent to these events it came "within the new category of bourgeois-demo-

31 Mao, "Analysis of the Classes in Chinese Society," *Selected Works*, I, 18.
32 *Ibid.*, p. 19.

cratic revolutions and, as far as the revolutionary alignment of revolutionary forces is concerned, forms part of the proletarian-socialist world revolution." [33]

He contended that the whole course of history had been changed and that a new era had begun as a result of the triumph of the Bolshevik Revolution and World War I. His assessment of the historical significance of the new era was that it was one

. . . in which the world capitalist front has collapsed in one part of the globe (one-sixth of the world) and has fully revealed its decadence everywhere else, in which the remaining capitalist parts cannot survive without relying more than ever on the colonies and semi-colonies, in which a socialist state has been established and has proclaimed its readiness to give active support to the liberation movement of all colonies and semi-colonies, and in which the proletariat of the capitalist countries is steadily freeing itself from the social-imperialist influence of the social-democratic parties and proclaimed its support for the liberation movement in the colonies and semi-colonies.[34]

Needless to say, his present estimation of Soviet willingness to extend aid to national liberation movements hardly squares with the appraisal cited above.

In the course of its development, the Chinese revolution, a new type of revolution developing in China and all colonial and semi-colonial areas, must pass through two stages, a "democratic" and a "socialist" stage. Mao noted that the CCP, and thus by implication any fraternal party that follows the "Chinese road," has a twofold task in regard to the revolution within their country. It must strive to complete the "new democratic" revolution and thus prepare the conditions requisite for a transition to a socialist revolution. To those misguided comrades who failed to grasp the connection between the two stages in the revolution he said:

Every Communist must know that the whole Chinese revolutionary movement led by the Chinese Communist Party is a complete revolutionary movement embracing the two revolutionary stages, democratic and socialist, which are two revolutionary processes differing in character, and

[33] Mao Tse-tung, "On New Democracy," *Selected Works* (Peking: Foreign Languages Press, 1965), II, 343.
[34] *Ibid.*

(46)

that the socialist stage can be reached only after the democratic stage is completed. The democratic revolution is the necessary preparation for the socialist revolution, and the socialist revolution is the inevitable continuation of the democratic revolution. The ultimate aim of all Communists is to establish a socialist society and then a communist society. We can give correct leadership to the Chinese revolution only on the basis of a clear understanding of both the differences and the interconnections between the democratic and socialist revolutions.[35]

During the first stage, the "new democratic" phase, the revolutionary forces must fight "imperialism" and "feudalism"; that is, they must carry out a national revolution to oust the foreign imperialists and a democratic revolution to vanquish the domestic landlords and bureaucratic capitalists. In his judgment the national revolution was definitely more important; however, he added that the two are interrelated. The feudal landlords could not be subdued without overthrowing the rule of the imperialists because the latter constituted the "main support" of the landlords. Conversely, the imperialists' oppression could be overcome only by mobilizing the peasantry against the landlords, the domestic ally of the imperialists.[36]

Mao's emphasis on the "anti-imperialist" aspect of the revolution reflected his awareness of the greater urgency of that facet of the revolution as compared with the domestic struggle against the "feudalistic" landlords. Doubtless he was also influenced by his perception that it was much easier to unite various relatively heterogeneous groups into a united front vis-à-vis an external enemy than to enlist the support of those same groups in behalf of agrarian reform. The Chinese have displayed a comparable perception in their attempts to influence the course of national liberation movements in Asia, Africa, and Latin America.

More specifically, the CCP has been quick to appreciate the violent hatred for the United States that exists throughout Latin America. For example, when the United States dispatched troops in 1965 to the Dominican Republic, the Chinese sought to portray American intervention there as a return to the policy of gunboat diplomacy. Thus they attempted to exploit the anti-Americanism in

---

[35] Mao, *The Chinese Revolution and the Chinese Communist Party*, pp. 42–43.
[36] *Ibid.*, p. 25.

Latin America based on our past policy of sending troops into Caribbean and Central American countries such as Cuba, the Dominican
Republic, and Nicaragua to restore "law and order" after the local
authorities had failed to discharge their responsibilities to the international community. Few Latin American countries had experienced
more direct American intervention than had the Dominican Republic.

According to Mao, the state during the first stage of the revolution
would be an entirely new type of state system. Classifying state systems on the basis of the class character of their political power, he
held that there were three basic kinds: (1) republics under the dictatorship of the bourgeoisie, (2) republics under the dictatorship of
the proletariat, and (3) those "under the joint dictatorship of several
revolutionary classes." [37]

The first was found only in the old democratic countries, where,
he alleged, democracy had virtually disappeared. The second existed
only in the Soviet Union at that time (1939), but in the future it
would be "the dominant form throughout the world for a certain
period." [38] The third was a transitional form that would be adopted by
revolutionaries in colonial and semicolonial countries. That revolutionaries in the emerging countries were expected to follow the
Chinese path is shown quite clearly in the following statement:

Each of these revolutions will necessarily have specific characteristics of its
own, but these will be minor variations on a general theme. So long as they
are revolutions in colonial or semi-colonial countries, their state and
governmental structure will of necessity be basically the same, i.e. a
new-democratic state under the joint dictatorship of several anti-imperialist
classes.[39]

According to Arthur A. Cohen, inclusion of the national bourgeoisie as part of the "people" supporting the new state, the people's
democratic dictatorship, represented a creative development by Mao
of the Marxist theory of the state. In both *The Chinese Revolution
and the Chinese Communist Party* and *On New Democracy*, he had
implied that this group would be regarded as one of the revolutionary
classes represented in the state to be established in the new democratic

[37] Mao, "On New Democracy," *Selected Works*, II, 350.
[38] *Ibid.*, p. 351.   [39] *Ibid.*

stage of the revolution. He explicitly included them in the following passage from *On the People's Democratic Dictatorship:*

Who are the people? At the present stage in China [1949], they are the working class, the peasantry, the urban petty bourgeoisie and the national bourgeoisie. These classes, led by the working class and the Communist Party, unite to form their own state and elect their own government; they enforce their dictatorship over the running dogs of imperialism—the landlord class and bureaucrat-bourgeoisie, as well as the representatives of those classes, the Kuomintang reactionaries and their accomplices—suppress them, allow them only to behave themselves and not be unruly in word or deed. If they speak or act in an unruly way, they will be promptly stopped and punished. Democracy is practiced within the ranks of the people, who enjoy the rights of freedom of speech, assembly, association, and so on. The right to vote belongs only to the people, not to the reactionaries. The combination of the two aspects, democracy for the people and dictatorship over the reactionaries, is the people's democratic dictatorship.[40]

Marx and Lenin, in their discussion of the nature of the state to be established *after the revolution* in backward countries, clearly indicated that its class basis would be restricted to the proletariat and the peasantry.[41] Both held that the bourgeoisie would cease to exist as a class after the revolution. What, then, prompted this revision in the received tradition? The "Sinocentrism" of the traditional Chinese world view (which influences Mao more than he cares to admit), a desire to enhance his standing as a theoretician in the Communist world, and a conviction that conditions in China were indeed different from those obtaining in countries described by his predecessors probably contributed to his decision.

Whatever his reason, Soviet theoreticians labored diligently to dispel the notion that Mao had contributed anything to the Marxist theory of the state. In article after article published in the Soviet Union in the early 1950s, they attempted, at least by implication, to equate Mao's "people's democratic dictatorship" with the concept advanced by Lenin that the new state in backward countries would

[40] Mao Tse-tung, "On the People's Democratic Dictatorship," *Selected Works* (Peking: Foreign Languages Press, 1961), IV, 419.
[41] Cohen, *Communism of Mao Tse-tung*, p. 83.

(49)

be based on an alliance of the workers and the peasants. As Cohen points out, the Soviets were very much concerned with the *prestige* value of the Chinese claim:

For it provided Mao with a means of appealing to Communists in Asia, Africa, and Latin America to set up not a Soviet-type "dictatorship of the proletariat" after revolutionary victory but a Maoist "people's democratic dictatorship." Were the claim to be accepted in the international Communist movement, Mao would become the mid-twentieth century maker of doctrine for backward countries just as Lenin had been decades earlier.[42]

In 1953, Mao again demonstrated his ideological autonomy by proclaiming that the CPR had begun the "transition to socialism"; that is, China was now "building socialism," using, however, not a "dictatorship of the proletariat" as prescribed by orthodox Marxist-Leninist theory but a "people's democratic dictatorship," the same state form used during the first stage. Later in that same year the Maoist line concerning the nature of the Chinese state began changing rather slowly. Chinese theoreticians now argued that a "dictatorship of the proletariat" and a "people's democratic dictatorship" were, in essence, the same. It was not until late 1956, after the Polish and Hungarian uprisings, that Khrushchev, needing desperately Chinese assistance in checking the fragmentation of the international Communist movement, explicitly acknowledged that China had a form of a dictatorship of the proletariat.[43]

The proclamation that China had made the transition to socialism no doubt shocked Communists and non-Communists both in China and elsewhere, for Mao had indicated quite clearly in his earlier writings that the "new democracy" would last for several years. In fact he had taken to task the "leftist" phrasemongers for advocating an "accomplishment at one stroke" of both stages of the revolution. Their approach was "very harmful" in that it confused the steps to be taken in the revolution and weakened the effort directed toward the realization of the current goals. He said that it was out of the question to think that the revolution could enter phase two until the task of the first, fighting "imperialism" and "feudalism," had been completed. He continued: "The Chinese revolution cannot avoid

[42] *Ibid.*, p. 88.   [43] *Ibid.*, pp. 96–98.

taking the two steps, first of New Democracy and then of socialism. Moreover, *the first step will need quite a long time and cannot be accomplished overnight.* We are not utopians and cannot divorce ourselves from the actual conditions confronting us." [44]

Even more shocking must have been the assertion that the transition to socialism had actually begun at the time of the Communist takeover in October, 1949. Prior to 1953 the official line was that China was still in the new democracy stage. In part the explanation for the startling innovation may be attributed to Mao's personal and national pride. It must have been a galling experience for him to have observed Soviet theoreticians describe the building of socialism by the Eastern European nations. China, as a new democracy, was treated by other members of the bloc as a country less advanced than they. The reader should note, however, that Mao swallowed his pride as a Chinese "nationalist" and as a Marxist-Leninist until "objective conditions" were ripe for restating the regime's position with regard to the standing of China on the dialectical stairway of history. Domestically, the revision was deferred until the regime had completed its program for the economic reconstruction of the country and was thus prepared for the adoption of a planned economy based upon the five-year system of the Soviet Union. Had Mao revealed the new line earlier, in 1950 or 1951 for example, he probably would have received less cooperation from the "national bourgeoisie," whose aid was sorely needed in the initial critical period of the party's history.

With the conclusion of the Korean War, Mao enjoyed more freedom to maneuver in policy-making. Now he could devote his attention to the domestic tasks confronting the regime. The death of Stalin, in early 1953, may also have encouraged Mao to change the line of the regime. In view of his occasional willingness to act independently of Stalin, however, one should not assert dogmatically that Mao would not have dared take such a step as long as Stalin was the foremost ideological and political leader in the world Communist movement.

Consensus exists among China watchers at least on one point—the Chinese have outstripped their Soviet rivals in the field of "thought reform." Only Chairman Mao, among the leaders and theoreticians of

[44] Mao, "On New Democracy," *Selected Works*, II, 358. Emphasis added.

the Communist world, has advanced the notion that it is possible, through systematic "study," "criticism," and "self-criticism" to effect a fundamental change in the world outlook of the national bourgeoisie as well as that of other classes. They acknowledge that the former class enemy will not voluntarily relinquish the old world view; hence they have displayed inimitable patience in their attempts to remold the thinking of "bourgeois" intellectuals, the bourgeoisie, and others. Essentially what they believe that they can do is to bring about a fundamental change in the nature of man. The old ideas ("poisonous weeds") must be plucked out of the garden where they have been coexisting with the ideology of the masses, articulated in its purest form in the thought of Mao Tse-tung.

In the Maoist writings of the Great Proletarian Cultural Revolution one senses, however, a pervasive doubt regarding the effectiveness of efforts in the past to root out the influence of competing ideologies. Whatever else it may be, the Cultural Revolution is, in a very real sense, just that—a cultural revolution. It represents an all-out effort on the part of Mao and his supporters to destroy, once and for all, the influence of ideas deemed inconsistent with his vision of what China *ought* to be.

Finally, some attention must be given to a Marxist concept which, in the judgment of the present writer, has had a most profound impact on the thought of intellectuals in the Third World—the Leninist theory of imperialism. It is common knowledge among specialists on Latin American affairs that this notion has been warmly embraced by the intelligentsia of the left. Their understanding of the past and present relations between the United States and Latin America is such as to make plausible to them the Leninist thesis that the United States has, over a long period of time, cruelly exploited the rest of the Western Hemisphere. The Chinese, the Cubans, and the Russians would have much less "influence" in Latin America had they not had this intellectual weapon. Furthermore, the Chinese concept of people's war, the subject of the next chapter, draws heavily on the Leninist theory of exploitation of Asia, Africa, and Latin America.

III

The Chinese Concept of People's War

THE prime goal of the Chinese Communists before their advent to power was the acquisition of political power. They were firmly convinced that that goal could be realized only through the use of armed force. In Mao Tse-tung's own words "political power grows out of the barrel of a gun." His approach to revolution, and that of his supporters in China and elsewhere, has been based on the assumption that armed struggle represents the only viable road to power; moreover, they are persuaded that the Chinese experience in fighting such a revolutionary war is relevant for revolutionaries throughout the world, and especially for those in Africa, Asia, and Latin America. They contend that future revolutionary wars will take the form of people's wars patterned after the Chinese model. In an effort to promote such wars in the emerging countries, they have disseminated throughout the Third World copies of Mao's articles on the subject.

The international significance claimed by the Chinese for Mao's writing on people's war can be readily seen in recent issues of the *Peking Review*. For example, on October 6, 1967, this assessment was made of his works: "Chairman Mao's works, treasured books of revolution, are the indispensable spiritual food, the compass and the sharpest weapon for the revolutionary people. Therefore, the imperialists, the revisionists, and all reactionaries fear and hate these works." [1] In the same issue, a Vietnamese commander was quoted as saying

[1] *Peking Review*, October 6, 1967, p. 34.

that Mao's military thinking was the greatest aid sent by the Chinese people to Vietnam. Victory in Vietnam could be had if the Vietnamese acted according to Mao's teachings, a "sharp weapon for defeating U.S. imperialism." [2] A fighter in the Congo (Brazzaville) said: "My first need is Mao Tse-tung's thought and my second, a gun." [3] A Latin American visitor to Chingkang Mountain, the cradle of the Chinese Revolution, expressed his opinion regarding the relevance of the Chinese model to Latin America as follows:

Chairman Mao's thought is wonderful. His theories about people's war, agrarian revolution, the seizure of political power with guns and the establishment of rural base areas also suit us perfectly. Land ownership in our country is even more concentrated than in yours during the period of the Great Revolution (1924–27), with 90 per cent of the land owned by the latifundists and more than 70 per cent of the peasants having nothing. Their miseries are beyond description and their class hatred is extraordinarily deep.[4]

These and countless other statements in the same vein demonstrate quite clearly that the Chinese at least hope that their example will be emulated by revolutionaries in Latin America and elsewhere in the Third World. How representative these statements are of revolutionary thinking in these areas is another matter.

Before proceeding further, it might be helpful to describe briefly the essence of the Chinese concept of a people's war. Such a war is, in a very real sense, a "people's" war. To generalize, victory for revolutionaries is contingent on their gaining support of the "people" against a common enemy, either a domestic "reactionary" regime (such as the Kuomintang) or a foreign aggressor (such as the Japanese). The need for political mobilization is constantly stressed by the Chinese. Organizationally, the mobilization takes the form of a broad united front against the enemy. The class on whom success most depends is the peasantry. The class struggle manifests itself primarily as *armed* struggle, with the Communist Party providing leadership throughout the revolutionary process. Militarily, the war will be protracted, developing in three stages, with the "people" trying to capitalize on the enemy's weaknesses and their strong points until

[2] *Ibid.*, p. 35. [3] *Ibid.*
[4] *Peking Review*, November 10, 1967, p. 35.

finally the balance of forces changes in their favor. The *style* of fighting is quite different from that used in "conventional warfare." Guerrilla forces and local self-defense units play an important role throughout the war. Their contribution to the war effort varies according to the stages of the war. It is contended here that some students of Chinese affairs have exaggerated somewhat the importance attached by Mao to such activities. Taking the war *as a whole*, their role is clearly supplementary to that of mobile warfare. The locale for most of the war will be the countryside. There the revolutionaries establish and consolidate bases from which to launch large scale attacks against the "cities" in the final stage of the war. In the course of the war a people's army, not to be confused with the guerrillas and local self-defense forces, is to be formed. Theory has it that this is an entirely new type of army, a claim that is not entirely without foundation. It is, for example, far more highly politicized than conventional armies. Far more attention is devoted in it to the development of close ties with the "masses," especially with the peasants. An elaborate code of behavior was developed by the Red Army in an effort to win the support, or at least avoid the hostility and resistance, of those living in and around the rural bases.

What methodology is used by the top policy-makers in the formulation of global strategy of which the idea of people's war is an important component? The official version is that policy-making is based on a "scientific" analysis of the contradictions existing among the various classes in a given country and among the classes in the various countries of the world at a given time. Theoretically, the Chinese adjust their strategy in light of changes occurring in the balance of forces domestically and internationally. The selections cited below are representative of the Chinese concept of the approach used by them in the formulation of their strategy. The Chinese position on a wide range of issues in the Sino-Soviet conflict, expressed in their June 14, 1963, letter to the CPSU, was allegedly arrived at in the following manner: "This general line proceeds from the actual world situation taken as a whole and from a class analysis of the fundamental contradictions in the contemporary world, and is directed against the counterrevolutionary global strategy of U.S. imperialism." [5] Shao

[5] CCP, *A Proposal Concerning the General Line of the International Communist Movement*, as cited in Lewis, *Major Doctrines of Communist China*, p. 40.

Tieh-chen described the process in these terms: "Marxism-Leninism makes a scientific analysis of the development of the class struggle and, on the basis of this analysis, guides the revolutionary struggles of the proletariat and of all the people striving for emancipation." [6] According to Lin Piao, the "scientific basis" of the political and military strategy used in defeating the Japanese, a strategy that constitutes the core of the Maoist theory of a people's war, was a product of the fundamental doctrines of Marxism-Leninism and an application by Mao of the method of class analysis. He alleged that Mao analyzed: "First, the mutual transformation of China's principal and non-principal contradictions following the invasion of China by Japanese imperialism, second, the consequent changes in class relations within China and in international relations, and, third, the balance of forces between China and Japan." [7]

Those charged with responsibility for making these dialectical analyses must make sharp distinctions between the principal and the secondary phases of a given contradiction. Lin Piao, to the surprise of no one, attributes to Mao the capacity for singling out infallibly the principal contradiction in a complex situation and thus prescribing the solution for the problems confronting the revolutionaries.[8] Dialectical analysts must also be able to distinguish carefully between the new emerging forces, weak at present, that will "determine" the course of history and the old decaying forces, strong at present, that represent the old order of things. In short, they must be able to foresee how history will unfold and, on the basis of that vision, they are to formulate their strategy. The "people" engaged in people's wars must prevail, provided they persevere, use the correct method, and dare to seize victory at decisive moments, because they are "newly rising forces" and "represent the direction in which history advances." [9]

Since the Chinese experience in the anti-Japanese war has had such a major impact on Mao's conceptualization of a people's war, some

[6] Shao Tieh-chen, *Revolutionary Dialectics and How to Appraise Imperialism* (Peking: Foreign Languages Press, 1963), p. 1.
[7] Lin Piao, *Long Live the Victory of People's War!* (Peking: Foreign Languages Press, 1966), p. 4.
[8] *Ibid.*, p. 11.
[9] Shao Tieh-chen, *Revolutionary Dialectics*, p. 1.

attention should be given to his analysis of the contradictions of that era. One can find many striking parallels in his thinking with regard to the relationship between Japan and China and the relationship between the United States and China today. The two basic contradictions in the mid-1930's, according to Mao, were the contradiction between imperialism and the Chinese people and the contradiction between feudalism and the masses. The Japanese invasion of China changed drastically the system of contradictions, domestically and internationally. The principal contradiction was that existing between Japan and China, while those between China and other imperialist countries such as Britain and the United States descended to a secondary position. At the same time the contradictions among the Japanese imperialists and other imperialistic nations intensified as a result of the Japanese effort to seize the whole of China, thereby affording the Chinese an excellent opportunity for exploiting these contradictions in their efforts to isolate and defeat the Japanese.[10] Similar efforts to exploit contradictions among imperialist nations can be observed today.

Since the end of World War II, the United States has been substituted in the thinking of the Chinese Communists for Japan. Their global strategy, of which the theory of people's war is the key element, represents an attempt by the CCP to apply on a global scale their experience in the earlier war with Japan. Whether this approach is a sound one will be examined more fully in the final evaluation of the Maoist global strategy.

In the Chinese view, the contradictions of the present world are concentrated in Asia, Africa, and Latin America. These are described as "the most vulnerable areas under imperialist rule and the storm centers of world revolution dealing direct blows at imperialism." [11] The "national democratic revolutionary movement" which they visualize as sweeping through the Third World and the "international socialist revolutionary movement" are "the two great historical currents of our time." The former is an important component of the "contemporary proletarian world revolution." The revolutionaries in Asia, Africa, and Latin America are pounding at and undermining

[10] Lin Piao, *Long Live the Victory of People's War!*, p. 6.
[11] CCP, *General Line*, in Lewis, *Major Doctrines of Communist China*, p. 246.

the very foundations of imperialism. In fact, the whole cause of the world revolution hinges on the outcome of the struggle between the "peoples" of these areas and U.S. imperialism; therefore, this struggle has more than regional significance. It is "one of overall importance for the whole cause of the proletarian world revolution." [12] These statements provide us with valuable insight into Chinese thinking with regard to the strategic importance of Latin America, and thus explain the overriding reason for their interest in Latin America as a part of the region to which they attach the highest priority.

The Chinese propose to resolve this "principal contradiction" through waging people's war in Africa, Asia, and Latin America. To understand the reasons for adopting this strategy, rather than one of "peaceful coexistence," one must examine their assessment of the world balance of forces. In the late summer or early fall of 1957, the Chinese concluded that a significant change had occurred in the balance of forces between the two camps as a consequence of Soviet technological victories in 1957. At the Moscow Conference held in November of that year, Mao, leading the Chinese delegation, postulated that the "East Wind prevails over the West Wind." Feeling that the socialist camp was stronger than its adversary in an overall sense, he insisted on the exertion of a far greater pressure on the "imperialists." The Soviet leadership, less optimistic in their appraisal of the significance of the Sputnik and ICBM victories, clung to their policy of peaceful coexistence in relation to the West. While the Soviets were very much interested in expanding their influence in the Third World through trade, loans, and grants, they were less interested than were the Chinese in promoting and supporting "national liberation movements" in Africa, Asia, and Latin America. After several years of fruitless efforts to persuade their Soviet ally to assume a more militant posture in relation to the Western "imperialists" and to press for and support more actively "wars of liberation" in the emerging nations, Peking has apparently given up all hope that the Soviets will discard their revisionist robes. With the "restoration of capitalism" in the Soviet Union by the followers of Khrushchev, the Chinese have arrogated for themselves the position of the sole authoritative spokes-

[12] *Ibid.*

man for the revolutionary peoples of the world and especially for the "oppressed" peoples of Asia, Africa, and Latin America, who can be "liberated" only by people's war.

In his classic analysis of protracted war, Mao visualized a war developing in three stages, a vision that served as a basis for the strategic management of the war against the Japanese and later the Kuomintang. Since the Chinese believe that people's wars in the underdeveloped world will follow the example set by them, a detailed analysis of their thinking on this point will now be undertaken. The three stages of the war are: (1) the period of the enemy's strategic offensive and the people's strategic defensive, (2) the period of the enemy's strategic consolidation and the people's preparation for the counteroffensive (strategic stalemate), and (3) the period of the people's strategic counteroffensive and the enemy's strategic retreat.[13]

During the first stage, the enemy, having overwhelming military strength, would penetrate into the interior of the country. Mao was highly critical of those who attempted to hold, at any cost, the key cities. The enemy, he argued, must be *lured* into the interior so that the forces of a people's war could be mobilized against him. In essence, he believed that China should be willing to exchange some of her vast territory in order to gain the time required for gradually building up the strength needed for changing the balance of forces, at which time the enemy would lose the strategic initiative and the people could then go over to the offensive. In the first stage, then, he felt that the enemy should be allowed to capture some of the major cities and the lines of communication. As the enemy moved more deeply into the interior, some of the regular troops of the people must infiltrate behind enemy lines to engage in guerrilla warfare. They must also take the first steps in the political mobilization of the masses, without which they could not establish rural bases or obtain the personnel required for the formation of guerrilla units. Guerrilla warfare, however, would not be the primary form of fighting in this stage. Mobile warfare, the primary form, would be supplemented by guerrilla and positional warfare. As indicated above, he was most critical of the

[13] Mao Tse-tung, "On Protracted War," *Selected Works* (Peking: Foreign Languages Press, 1965), II, 136.

Kuomintang military authorities for their assigning positional warfare the primary role in the first stage.[14]

It is quite clear that Latin American revolutionaries, who might desire to emulate the Chinese example, would be faced with some rather formidable differences between the Chinese position then and their own at the present time. When the Japanese launched their invasion of China in 1937, the Chinese Communists had already gained considerable political and military experience in fighting the Kuomintang. Perhaps most significant were the facts that they had developed the core of the Red Army and had established a relatively secure base in Shensi province after the Long March. Latin Americans, eager to follow the Chinese road, would have to begin with the formation of guerrilla bands and the establishment of rural bases in areas remote from centers of enemy strength. As in China, a great deal of time and suffering would be required before the core of a Red Army could be created. In short, the *first* stage of the Chinese model is not applicable to their situation until they have at least a core of a Red Army to engage in the primary form of warfare in this stage, mobile warfare. If one can judge from the experience of the recent Bolivian guerrilla movement under Castroite leadership, one can appreciate better the difficulty confronting those attempting to realize the requisites for making the transition to the first stage of the Chinese model.

The second stage of the Chinese model, that of strategic stalemate, would be one in which guerrilla fighting would be the primary form of warfare, supplemented by mobile warfare. Fighting would be especially ruthless, and the country would sustain severe devastation. Mao was convinced, however, that guerrilla warfare could be used successfully against the enemy. All in all, it would be a most painful and a comparatively long period. Numerous tasks confronted the people, the most important being the maintenance of a united front against the enemy, reformation of the armed forces, improvement of fighting techniques, mobilization of the masses, and preparation for the next stage.[15]

In the final stage, that of the strategic counteroffensive, the primary form of fighting would no longer be guerrilla warfare. Mobile warfare

[14] *Ibid.* [15] *Ibid.*, pp. 138–39.

(60)

will return to that position, with positional warfare rising slowly in importance toward the end of the war.[16]

As we have seen, the Chinese theory of people's war is characterized by three forms of warfare: mobile warfare, guerrilla warfare, and positional warfare. For each of the three stages, one of these is designated as the primary form of warfare. If one takes the war as a whole, it seems clear that mobile warfare, not guerrilla warfare, is regarded as the dominant form. The following statements by Mao have a direct bearing on the relative importance of these various types of warfare. Regarding guerrilla operations he said:

These guerrilla operations must not be considered as an independent form of warfare. They are but one step in the total war, one aspect of the revolutionary struggle. . . . We consider guerrilla operations as but one aspect of our total or mass war because they, lacking the quality of independence, are of themselves incapable of providing a solution to the struggle.[17]

Guerrilla warfare can be, for a certain time, the paramount feature of a protracted war, but Mao postulates that its primacy is limited in duration:

Guerrilla operations during the anti-Japanese war may be for a certain time and temporarily become its paramount feature, particularly insofar as the enemy's rear is concerned. However, if we view the war as a whole, there can be no doubt that our regular forces are of primary importance because it is they who are alone capable of producing the decision. Guerrilla warfare assists them in producing this favorable decision. Orthodox forces may, under certain conditions, operate as guerrillas, and the latter may, under certain conditions, develop to the status of the former. However, both guerrilla forces and regular forces have their own respective development and their own proper combinations.[18]

Elsewhere in his article dealing exclusively with guerrilla warfare, he explicitly rejected the view that a guerrilla strategy is the only strategy possible for an oppressed people. To those contending that

---

[16] *Ibid.,* p. 140.

[17] Mao Tse-tung, *On Guerrilla Warfare,* trans. Samuel B. Griffith (New York: Frederick A. Praeger, 1961), pp. 41–42.

[18] *Ibid.,* p. 56.

the regular forces be transformed into guerrilla units and that primary reliance be placed in the guerrillas he gave this somber warning: "If we say, 'Let us transform the regular forces into guerrillas,' and do not place our first reliance on a victory to be gained by the regular armies over the enemy, we may certainly expect to see as a result the failure of the anti-Japanese war of resistance." [19]

That Mao placed primary reliance for victory on the regular forces can be inferred from his advocacy of the need for transforming guerrilla units into regular forces. To make the transition two conditions are necessary: (1) an increase in numbers, and (2) an improvement in quality. The quantitative condition could be realized through combining small units and through mobilizing the masses to join the regular forces. Qualitatively, there must be a steeling of the fighters and an improvement in their weapons. More concretely, he indicated that guerrilla units must raise their political and organizational level and improve their equipment, tactics, military techniques, and discipline "so that they gradually pattern themselves on the regular forces and shed their guerrilla ways." [20] Politically, both the guerrilla commanders and the fighters must be made to realize the need for such a transformation. Political training was needed for the attainment of this goal. Organizationally, they must gradually establish suitable bureaucratic staffs—military and political. They must also create the necessary supply, medical, and health units. Finally, they must procure more sophisticated weapons and communication gear and master the techniques required for using them successfully in combat. [21]

Nothing said above should be taken to mean that Mao discounted the contribution that guerrilla warfare could make in a people's war. It will be recalled that he designated it as the primary form of warfare in the second stage of the war. It is equally clear that he assumed that it would play a significant role in the first stage. Even in the final stage, with mobile warfare the dominant form and positional warfare gradually rising in importance as the end of the war approaches, guerrillas have a role to play, although one gets the impression that their signi-

---

[19] *Ibid.*, p. 55.

[20] Mao Tse-tung, "Problems of Strategy in Guerrilla War Against Japan," *Selected Works* (Peking: Foreign Languages Press, 1965), II, 108.

[21] Mao, *On Guerrilla Warfare*, p. 113.

ficance declines relative to the other forms of warfare in this stage.

Lin Piao's essay of September 3, 1965, does not square completely with the position taken by Mao in the articles cited above. Lin described Chinese military strategy in the war against Japan as follows: "As far as military strategy was concerned, our policy was to be guerrilla warfare waged independently and with the initiative in our own hands, within the framework of a unified strategy; guerrilla warfare was to be basic, but no chance of waging mobile warfare was to be lost when the circumstances were favourable." [22] Mao had insisted "that guerrilla operation must not be considered as an *independent* form of warfare." [23] Furthermore, Lin seemed to be arguing that guerrilla warfare is the *basic* form of warfare if one takes the war *as a whole.* The same impression emerges from a study of the following statement by Lin: "Guerrilla warfare is the only way to mobilize and apply the whole strength of the people against the enemy, the only way to expand our forces in the course of the war, deplete and weaken the enemy, gradually change the balance of forces between the enemy and ourselves, switch from guerrilla to mobile warfare, and finally defeat the enemy." [24] Elsewhere he stated that a war of annihilation was the guiding principle of Chinese military operations "regardless of whether mobile or guerrilla warfare is the primary form of fighting." [25] Obviously he regarded mobile warfare as the primary form of warfare in the closing stage of the war, a position coinciding precisely with that of Mao, but in this article Lin does not distinguish clearly, as does Mao, between the first and second stages. Lin seems to be saying that guerrilla warfare will be the dominant form in the phase of the war that Mao would classify as the first and second stages. By blurring the distinction between the first two stages of the war, Lin attributed a larger role to guerrilla warfare than did Mao. Finally, his statement that guerrilla warfare was "basic" in the anti-Japanese war is clearly at odds with the view expressed by Mao that guerrilla operations in the war taken as a whole are supplementary to those of the regular forces, "who alone are capable of producing the decision.

---

[22] Lin Piao, *Long Live the Victory of People's War!*, pp. 17–18.
[23] Mao, *On Guerrilla Warfare*, p. 41. Emphasis added.
[24] Lin Piao, *Long Live the Victory of People's War!*, p. 32.
[25] *Ibid.*, p. 34.

(63)

Guerrilla warfare assists them in producing this favorable decision." [26] Mao gave an even more explicit explanation of his understanding of the relative importance of guerrilla warfare and mobile warfare in the war as a whole:

Among the forms of warfare in the anti-Japanese war mobile warfare comes first and guerrilla warfare second. When we say that in the entire war mobile warfare is *primary* and guerrilla warfare *supplementary*, we mean that the outcome of the war depends *mainly* on regular warfare, especially in its mobile form, and that guerrilla warfare cannot shoulder the main responsibility in deciding the outcome. It does not follow, however, that the role of guerrilla warfare is unimportant in the strategy of the war. Its role in the *strategy* of the war is second only to that of mobile warfare, for without its support we cannot defeat the enemy. In saying this we also have in mind the strategic task of *developing* guerrilla warfare into mobile warfare. Guerrilla warfare will not remain at the same level throughout this long and cruel war, but will rise to a higher level and develop into mobile warfare. Thus the strategic role of guerrilla warfare is twofold; to *support* regular warfare and to *transform* itself into regular warfare.[27]

Since Mao assigns the regular army the primary role in waging a people's war in Latin America or elsewhere in the underdeveloped world, let us examine his theory of army building. The army is described in a recent collection of Mao's writings on people's war as "an armed body for carrying out the political tasks of the revolution." [28] In 1945 Mao indicated the weight he attached to having a people's army: "Without a people's army the people have nothing." [29] Earlier he had made it equally clear that the party would control the army and not vice versa, the guiding principle being "that the Party commands the gun, and the gun must never be allowed to command the Party." [30] Moreover, the new people's army is to be a less selfish organization than armies in other societies in that it allegedly fights for

[26] Mao, *On Guerrilla Warfare*, p. 56.

[27] Mao, "On Protracted War," *Selected Works*, II, 172. Emphasis added.

[28] *Chairman Mao Tse-tung on People's War* (Peking: Foreign Languages Press, 1967), p. 23.

[29] Mao Tse-tung, "On Coalition Government," *Selected Works* (Peking: Foreign Languages Press, 1965), III, 296–97.

[30] Mao Tse-tung, "Problems of War and Strategy," *Selected Works* (Peking: Foreign Languages Press, 1965), II, 224.

the interests of the broad masses and the whole nation and not for the private interests of a small clique or a few individuals. Its sole purpose "is to stand firmly with the Chinese people and to serve them whole-heartedly." [31]

A people's army, unlike bourgeois and feudal armies, is to be more than a fighting organization. A people's war cannot be won if the army and guerrilla units supporting it neglect the vitally important political tasks. At a time (1929) when the Red Army was fighting desperately to retain its base in Kiangsi province, Mao argued that the Red Army, especially at that time, should not confine itself to fighting. The advice tendered by him when the Communists were in the strategic defensive phase would seem especially relevant for any Latin American group in the vulnerable stage of building up a base area. The army should shoulder

. . . such important tasks as doing propaganda among the masses, organizing the masses, arming them, helping them to establish revolutionary political power and setting up party organizations. The Red Army fights not merely for the sake of fighting but in order to conduct propaganda among the masses, organize them, arm them, and help them to establish revolutionary political power. Without these objectives, fighting loses its meaning and the Red Army loses the reason for its existence.[32]

Mao laid down three fundamental principles to guide the Red Army and any would-be emulator in other areas in the implementation of these political tasks. First, he stressed the need for promoting unity between officers and men within the Red Army. Officers must respect the dignity of their men; there was absolutely no room for beating and abusing them. Through "sharing weal and woe" and "building up a conscious discipline" the army could be closely united.[33] Secondly, the new army must never neglect the task of promoting closer unity with the people, a principle requiring the most scrupulous respect for the people's interests, organizing and arming them, conducting propaganda among them, lightening their economic burden by having the

---

[31] Mao, "On Coalition Government," Selected Works, III, 264.

[32] Mao Tse-tung, "On Correcting Mistaken Ideas in the Party," Selected Works (Peking: Foreign Languages Press, 1965), I, 106.

[33] Mao Tse-tung, "Interview with the British Journalist James Bertram," Selected Works (Peking: Foreign Languages Press, 1965), II, 53.

army engage in production whenever possible, and liquidating the "traitors" and "collaborators" harmful to the people and the army.[34] Thirdly, the people's army should strive to bring about the disintegration of enemy forces through lenient treatment of prisoners of war.[35]

A perusal of the Three Main Rules of Discipline and the Eight Points for Attention, prepared by Mao for the Red Army, provides one with additional insight into the weight attached by Mao to the political work of the army. One of the Three Main Rules of Discipline, having obvious political implications, was one that soldiers should "not take a single needle or piece of thread from the masses." [36] The Eight Points of Attention were designed to win over either the people or captured enemy soldiers. They were:

1. Speak politely.
2. Pay fairly for what you buy.
3. Return everything you borrow.
4. Pay for anything you damage.
5. Do not hit or swear at people.
6. Do not damage crops.
7. Do not take liberties with women.
8. Do not ill-treat captives.[37]

Lin Piao states that the essence of Mao's theory of army building was that one must give prominence to politics in building a people's army. His view on this point and the relative importance of politics and modern weapons and military techniques was that:

. . . the army must first and foremost be built on a political basis. Politics is the commander, politics is the soul of everything. Political work is the lifeline of our army. True, a people's army must pay attention to the constant improvement of its weapons and equipment and its military technique, but in its fighting it does not rely purely on weapons and techniques, it relies mainly on politics, on the proletarian revolutionary consciousness and courage of the commanders and fighters, on the support and backing of the masses.[38]

Those remarks were probably meant primarily for the Soviet leaders and their admirers in the People's Liberation Army who, in the Maoist

[34] *Ibid.*   [35] *Ibid.*
[36] Lin Piao, *Long Live the Victory of People's War!*, p. 29.
[37] *Ibid.*   [38] *Ibid.*, p. 30.

view, attach too much weight to highly sophisticated weapons and too little to the strength of the masses, but they were also doubtless aimed at another audience—revolutionaries everywhere who might be despairing about the prospect for waging successful people's wars when they had such primitive weapons compared with those of the enemy.

Latin American revolutionaries interested in the Chinese model would probably find more relevant for their immediate needs the Chinese views and experience in regard to guerrilla warfare. As indicated above, "objective conditions" are not yet ripe in Latin America for stage one of the Chinese model. First they must organize guerrilla units and establish bases in the countryside. Only if they survive this most critical period will they have laid the political and military foundation needed to wage mobile warfare, the primary form in the Chinese model.

The Chinese hold that guerrilla warfare is used by a nation weak in arms and equipment against a more powerful aggressor nation. One might add that the Communists also made effective use of guerrilla tactics against their domestic foe, the Kuomintang. It is used after the enemy penetrates deeply into the country "in a cruel and oppressive manner," at which time the victims of aggression can turn to their advantage certain conditions of terrain, climate, and society in general.[39] Mao provides a graphic description of the guerrillas' impact on such an enemy, likening them to:

. . . innumerable gnats, which, by biting a giant both in front and in the rear, ultimately exhaust him. They make themselves as unendurable as a group of cruel and hateful devils, and as they grow and attain gigantic proportions, they will find that their victim is not only exhausted but practically perishing. It is for this reason that our guerrilla activities are a source of constant mental worry to imperial Japan.[40]

Mao describes concretely and specifically what he regards as the major responsibilities of the guerrilla forces. They are to exterminate small forces and harass and weaken large forces and thus contribute to the gradual weakening of the enemy. Over a long period of time these many small victories of the guerrillas, together with those of the army engaged in mobile warfare, will result in the shift in the balance of forces needed for launching the counteroffensive in the

[39] Mao, *On Guerrilla Warfare*, p. 42.   [40] *Ibid.*, p. 54.

third phase. Attacks by guerrillas on the extended and thus vulnerable lines of communication will gradually undermine his capacity to continue the offensive as he encounters more and more difficulties procuring the supplies and personnel that he needs. Guerrillas can also make a major contribution by compelling the enemy to disperse his forces. Once he has done so, the guerrillas and the regular forces can then more easily concentrate a preponderance of force against the more vulnerable enemy units. Guerrillas, under the command of the military commander in a given area, can coordinate their activities with those of the regular forces in the area. This function will be examined more fully below. Finally, they are to establish bases capable of supporting attacks in the enemy's rear.[41]

As in the case of the Red Army, Mao manifested an appreciation for the crucial importance of political work for guerrilla fighters. According to Mao, political activities, to be truly effective, are contingent, first, on the proper indoctrination of military and political leaders "with the idea of anti-Japanism," [42] and they, in turn, will transmit the idea to the troops. He cautioned that membership in a guerrilla unit ipso facto was no guarantee of proper thinking. To win the protracted war "the anti-Japanese idea must be an ever present conviction, and if it is forgotten, we may succumb to the temptations of the enemy or be overcome with discouragement." [43] Among Latin American revolutionaries, the United States replaces Japan as the target at which they are to propel their nationalistic arrows.

The guerrilla military commanders in particular must study and understand the political objectives of the war; that is, they must perceive the intimate relationship between politics and military affairs. In no uncertain terms Mao condemns officers who say: "We are not interested in politics but only in the profession of arms." What they must understand is that "military action is a method used to attain a political goal." [44]

Officers and men must have a precise conception of the political goal of the revolution and the organization required to realize that goal. The guerrillas' discipline and organization must be at such a high level that they can discharge effectively their political responsibilities, which he describes as "the life of both the guerrilla armies and of

[41] *Ibid.*, p. 53.
[43] *Ibid.*

[42] *Ibid.*, p. 88.
[44] *Ibid.*, p. 89.

revolutionary warfare." [45] Lin Pao characterized guerrilla warfare as the only way to mobilize and apply all the power of the people against the enemy.[46]

To promote greater unity between the guerrillas and the people, a set of rules was adopted that was quite similar to those prescribed for the Red Army. Some of those having clear political implications were:

1. Do not steal from the people.
2. Be courteous.
3. Be honest in transactions.
4. Return what one borrows.
5. Do not be selfish or unjust.
6. Do not bathe in the presence of women.
7. Replace what is broken.[47]

Politically, the guerrillas must also adopt a policy with regard to enemy forces that will assist in the mission of destroying the strength of the enemy. Efforts must be made to propagandize enemy forces with a view to undermining their morale and thus their willingness to continue fighting for the cause of an "unjust war." Those captured must be treated with consideration, and care must be provided whenever possible for wounded captives.[48]

Discipline in these guerrilla forces is less severe than that obtaining in the regular army. According to Mao, it must be self-imposed, not a discipline of compulsion, because only the former enables the soldier to understand clearly why he is fighting and why he must obey. In fact, he describes this type of discipline as a tower of strength, "the only type that can truly harmonize the relationship that exists between officers and soldiers." [49] Officers must not physically beat or severely tongue-lash their men because such feudal behavior would destroy internal unity and fighting strength. There is no need for absolute equality between officers and fighters; however, their living standards should not differ too much. Only those officers living under the same conditions as their men can gain from their men the confidence and admiration so essential for waging successful warfare of all types.

45 Ibid., p. 88.
46 Lin Piao, Long Live the Victory of People's War!, p. 32.
47 Mao, On Guerrilla Warfare, p. 92.   48 Ibid., p. 93.
49 Ibid., pp. 90-91.

The two groups should be equal in accepting the hardships and dangers of war. Implicit in all these statements is a deep appreciation on Mao's part for the importance of political considerations in guerrilla operations.

The sources of manpower in China were more varied than those available today to Latin American revolutionaries who might attempt to follow the "Chinese path" to power. The Chinese depended, for the most part, on inhabitants of the base areas for recruitment of personnel. Latin Americans operating in relatively inaccessible base areas would be severely handicapped, as were the Cuban-oriented guerrillas in Bolivia, by the sparsity of population. It is true, of course, that such areas make it easier for the guerrillas to keep secret their operations, and yet they must procure an adequate number of men if the movement is to develop properly. Be that as it may, it does not matter that the "peasants," theoretically the best "social" source of personnel, have had no military training because the chief method of the Chinese is to learn warfare through warfare. As Mao put it, "Guerrilla hostilities are the university of war, and after you have fought several times valiantly and aggressively, you may become a leader of troops, and there will be many well-known regular soldiers who will not be your peers." [50] Quite frequently the Chinese temporarily assigned to guerrilla operations units of the regular army, the units being dispersed to engage in guerrilla warfare. Such action was taken in areas in which guerrilla forces had not been formed in sufficient numbers. In those regions having guerrilla formations, the regular troops, assigned temporarily to such fighting, would work closely with the guerrillas. Before leaving the area, the regulars attempted to organize sufficient guerrilla units to continue the operations locally once they returned to their regular units. At times regular troops were given, on a permanent basis, guerrilla assignments, such as severing supply lines. On other occasions the Chinese merged local guerrilla units with units of the regular army, operating as guerrillas in the locality. Since no "pro-Chinese" group in Latin America has a fighting force even roughly comparable to the Red Army in the late 1920s or 1930s, the foregoing sources of personnel are denied them. Nor can they depend upon the self-defense or home guards for manpower.

[50] *Ibid.*, p. 73.

Deserters from the enemy ranks and bandits, two additional sources for recruits in China, might also be tapped in Latin America. Bandits, however, are of dubious value because their inclusion in the guerrilla movement tends to discredit that movement in the eyes of the people, providing the enemy with the means for convincing many skeptical about the guerrillas that the entire movement is lawless and irresponsible. Provided political work among deserters is carefully implemented, they can be rebuilt into reliable military units. Equally important they often bring with them the most modern weapons and other equipment so desperately needed by guerrillas especially in the earliest stages of their development.

The "model" guerrilla commander should be resolute, sincere, loyal, and robust, with special attention being devoted to the last of these attributes. That is, he must have great powers of endurance if he is to function effectively under the extremely trying circumstances so characteristic of guerrilla activities. Moreover, he must be well schooled in revolutionary techniques, be self-confident but not reckless, be a good disciplinarian, and be able to cope with "counterrevolutionary" propaganda. But above all, he must have good rapport with the people in the area, being able to mix easily with them and being completely dedicated to their "liberation," the most important characteristic of all. Finally, he should be an inhabitant of the area in which the group is being formed because this will ". . . facilitate relations between them and the local civilians. In addition, officers so chosen would be familiar with the country." [51] The Cuban-inspired guerrilla movement in Bolivia, led by Che Guevara, failed in large part because the Indians among whom they moved failed to respond to the guerrillas' appeals and because the Cubans were ignorant of the terrain in which they were operating.

Scrupulous care must also be exercised in the selection of the men for guerrilla units. Only volunteers should be accepted. Social status and condition are not important as long as they are courageous and willing to bear the hardships of guerrilla warfare. Vagabonds and "vicious people" should not be admitted to the ranks of guerrillas, nor should those who habitually break regulations be allowed to remain in the units. The political consideration underlying these rules is

[51] *Ibid.*, p. 86.

reflected in Mao's statement that victory was contingent on "keeping the membership pure and clean." [52] Mao had had some most unpleasant experiences in the early years of the Kiangsi period with unruly elements, many of whom had formerly been bandits.

Performing invaluable services for guerrilla bands and regular troops are the so-called self-defense units who are not so highly trained nor as well armed as the guerrillas. Theoretically they should be composed exclusively of volunteers, who must first be trained and armed. They can serve as sentries for guerrillas and convey information to the latter regarding the enemy's activities. Thus they serve as a part of the intelligence network so essential to the security of guerrilla forces. Within their villages and towns they may arrest "traitors" and prevent the distribution of enemy propaganda. When the enemy launches a drive into the base area, they can assist the guerrillas by deceiving, harassing, and obstructing the enemy. In addition, they may serve as stretcher bearers for the wounded, carry food to troops, and maintain comfort stations to provide troops with rice and tea. With such organizations, traitors cannot hide, and bandits and thieves cannot disturb the peace. Mao describes their long-range significance as follows: "The organization of self-defense units is a transitional step in the development of universal conscription. Such units are reservoirs of manpower for the orthodox forces." [53] In the Sino-Japanese War, these units performed the functions outlined above in Mao's writings.

To work effectively with these local defense units specifically, and with the people in general, the guerrillas must establish rural bases, relying mainly, of course, on the peasantry as the principal class to be "aroused," "organized," and "won over" in these base areas. Mao unequivocally rejected the view that his men should fight as roving rebels and that there was no need for establishing base areas.[54] Since the more powerful enemy occupied the main cities, the revolutionaries, if they were to carry on the protracted struggle, must retreat to the backward villages and establish bases.[55] Lin Piao summed up

---

[52] *Ibid.*, p. 87.   [53] *Ibid.*, p. 81.
[54] Mao, "Problems of Strategy in Guerrilla War Against Japan," *Selected Works*, II, 94.
[55] Mao, *The Chinese Revolution and the Chinese Communist Party*, p. 23.

quite succinctly the view of the Chinese Communists regarding the importance of rural bases: "To rely on the peasants, build rural base areas and use the countryside to encircle and finally capture the cities —such was the way to victory in the Chinese revolution." [56]

According to Mao, the guerrillas rely on the base areas for the performance of their strategic tasks and for the achievement of their objective "of preserving and expanding themselves and destroying and driving out the enemy." [57] Without them, neither the aim of the war nor the strategic tasks of the revolutionaries could be realized.

First and foremost as a condition for the establishment of a base area is the development of an armed force. Guerrilla leaders must dedicate themselves to the task of building one or more guerrilla units, which must be gradually developed in the course of the war into larger guerrilla formations. Ultimately the best in these units will be incorporated into the regular army. Neglect in the formation of strong guerrilla formations will be fatal to those attempting to establish a base area. As Mao said: "The building up of an armed force is the key to establishing a base area; if there is no armed force or if the armed force is weak, nothing can be done." [58]

As a second condition for establishing a base, Mao indicated that the guerrillas must be used in coordination with the people in the common struggle against the enemy. Places under enemy control could be transformed into base areas only with the defeat of the enemy in the area, and the guerrillas, without popular support, could not achieve that objective. In short, the masses had to be aroused against the common enemy. [59] In addition to the self-defense units and the guerrilla formations, various mass organizations had to be formed among the workers, peasants, women, children, merchants, and professional people. Without these organizations the people could not give effect to their strength in the struggle against the common enemy.

Geography is also of crucial importance to those attempting to

[56] Lin Piao, *Long Live the Victory of People's War!*, p. 22.
[57] Mao, "Problems of Strategy in Guerrilla War Against Japan," II, 93.
[58] *Ibid.*, p. 98.
[59] For an analysis of the classes and their relative importance in the united front in the first stage of the revolution, the "new democratic" phase, see *supra*, pp. 56–66.

establish bases. Noting that mountainous areas are best suited for allow-
ing guerrillas to hold out for a long time, Mao added, however, that
there was a still more important consideration, "the main thing is that
there must be enough room for the guerrillas to maneuver, namely, the
areas have to be extensive." [60] Those countries lacking this condition,
and he listed Belgium as an example, have little or no chance for
waging guerrilla warfare.

These base areas must be distinguished from "guerrilla zones." A
base area is surrounded by the enemy but its central parts are controlled by the guerrillas. A guerrilla zone, on the other hand, is not
completely occupied by the guerrillas, who can only make frequent
raids into them. As Mao explained, ". . . they are areas which are
held by the guerrillas when they are there and by the puppet regime
when they are gone. . . ." [61] They can be transformed into "base
areas" through the defeat or annihilation of enemy troops there plus
arousing and winning over the people as explained above. Conversely,
a base area may revert to the status of a guerrilla zone as a result of
strong enemy pressure or mistakes by the guerrilla leaders.[62]

Shortly after the beginning of the anti-Japanese war, the Chinese
Communists adopted a policy of infiltrating behind enemy lines in
small contingents to establish bases throughout the countryside.
According to Lin Piao, they established nineteen of these in northern,
central, and southern China, and as a consequence the Japanese held
only the big cities and the main lines of communications, leaving "the
vast territory in the enemy's rear in the hands of the people." [63] Lin
asserts that the Communists carried out democratic reforms, mobilized
and organized the peasants, implemented policies of "a reasonable
burden" and "the reduction of rent and interest," which weakened
the "feudal system of exploitation and improved the people's liveli-
hood." The reader should note, however, that the Communists, in
keeping with the "united front" line emphasizing the anti-imperialist

---

[60] Mao, "Problems of Strategy in Guerrilla War Against Japan," *Selected
Works*, II, 99. The Chinese now admit that guerrilla wars can be fought successfully in small countries. The successes scored in Cuba, Vietnam, and Algeria
forced them to admit that they had revised their military strategy on this point.
Ralph L. Powell, "Maoist Military Doctrines," *Asian Survey*, April, 1968, p. 251.
[61] *Ibid.*, p. 96.   [62] *Ibid.*, p. 97.
[63] Lin Piao, *Long Live the Victory of People's War!*, p. 23.

theme, followed a more lenient policy toward the landlords and rich peasants than that adopted during the earlier Kiangsi period.

These base areas, so valuable to the Communists during the anti-Japanese war, served as springboards for their "War of Liberation" against the Kuomintang. Furthermore, the experience gained there during the course of both wars proved exceedingly valuable to them after their advent to power in 1949. They were, in fact, "a state in miniature." [64] There they built up the party and the Red Army, ran government agencies, engaged in agricultural and industrial production, and operated cultural and educational facilities.

Due attention must be devoted by revolutionaries to consolidation and expansion areas. To restrict the enemy to a few strongholds, the guerrillas must engage him in guerrilla fighting wherever possible, thus jeopardizing his existence and undermining his morale by expanding the base areas. Nor should consolidation of base areas be overlooked. The masses must be "aroused" and "organized" and the guerrillas and local defense units must be trained and armed. Maintaining protracted warfare and expanding it are contingent on such consolidation. In a protracted war, every guerrilla leader will be faced with the task of deciding, as conditions change, whether emphasis should be on expansion or consolidation. The correct solution must, of course, be based on a careful study of the circumstances; the commander must rely on his own sound judgment in such cases.[65]

The object of all forms of warfare, according to Mao, is "to preserve oneself and destroy the enemy." [66] To him, destruction did not necessarily mean the physical liquidation of the enemy's forces; rather it meant that the enemy should be disarmed or deprived of his will to resist. Both attack and defense may be used in the destruction of the enemy, but attack is the primary and defense the supplementary means of accomplishing that end. Attack is chiefly concerned with the destruction of enemy forces, but it also serves the purpose of self-preservation because if the enemy is not destroyed, he will destroy the revolutionary forces. Conversely, defense is primarily concerned

---

[64] *Ibid.*, p. 25.

[65] Mao, "Problems of Strategy in Guerrilla War Against Japan," *Selected Works*, II, 100–101.

[66] Mao, "On Protracted War." *Selected Works*, II, 156.

with self-preservation, but it is also a means of supplementing attack and preparing for the counteroffensive. Since destruction of the enemy is the primary goal of war and self-preservation the secondary, attack, the chief means of destroying the enemy, is primary, if one takes the war as a whole.

Mao's preference for attack may be seen in his advocacy of the principle of concentrating a superior force against a small force and "quick decision offensive warfare on exterior lines." These principles were based on certain facts concerning the weaknesses and strong-points of Japan and China. Japan, for example, lacked an adequate supply of troops, while China, though weak in many respects, had a vast territory, plenty of troops, and a population that was generally cooperative. As a consequence, the Japanese could only occupy the major cities, main lines of communication, and a small part of the plains, which left ungarrisoned a large area for guerrilla activities. Secondly, the numerically inferior Japanese were in fact "encircled" by the Chinese. Relying on their two advantages, vastness in territory and large forces, the Chinese could concentrate a superior force against selected enemy columns, encircling and attacking them. Every effort was made to achieve a quick victory over the enemy in campaigns and battles, a goal that could be realized by striking the enemy force while it was moving. Using their superior intelligence network, the Chinese knew which route the enemy was taking, and well in advance concentrated a large force under cover along the route that he was sure to take. While he was still on the move, the Chinese encircled and attacked him before he knew what was happening. If the plan were well executed, the entire enemy column or a large part of it was annihilated. The principle of "quick-decision offensive warfare on exterior lines" is applicable to guerrilla as well as to mobile warfare and was adjudged by Mao to be relevant for all stages of the war.

The policy of quick offensive decisions on exterior lines, and the flexibility and planning required for its implementation, is designed to give the initiative to the revolutionary forces. Mao defines initiative as "an army's freedom of action as distinguished from an enforced loss of freedom," [67] and to him it "is the very life of an army and, once it is lost, the army is close to defeat or destruction." [68] Both parties spare

[67] *Ibid.*, p. 161.   [68] *Ibid.*

no effort to gain the initiative and thus avoid passivity. For guerrillas it is even more essential to have the initiative, for they usually operate under the most difficult conditions: facing an enemy having stronger forces, lacking experience, being separated from other guerrilla units and from the regular forces, et cetera. Mao contends that they can seize the initiative by capitalizing on three of the enemy's weaknesses. First, they can exploit the enemy's shortage of troops by boldly moving into vast areas not occupied by him. Secondly, they can take advantage of the fact that the enemy, an alien following a "barbarous" policy, enables them to enlist the support of most of the people. Thirdly, they can use to the utmost their resourcefulness in response to the blunders made by enemy commanders.[69]

To survive for long in guerrilla warfare, the guerrillas must be quite adept at shifting positions. Whenever a strong enemy feels threatened by guerrilla operations, he will ordinarily dispatch converging columns to attack and destroy them. Guerrillas should fight whenever possible, but they should not be ashamed to run when confronted with unfavorable odds for fighting. At times they may have wiped out an enemy column in one place, after which they may, in pursuance of the policy of liquidating the enemy forces one by one, be shifted to another place for use against a second column. Concluding his advice to guerrilla leaders, Mao said:

If the enemy's forces in a certain place present a particularly serious threat, the guerrilla units should not linger, but should move with lightning speed. In general, shifts of position should move with secrecy and speed. In order to mislead, decoy and confuse the enemy, they should constantly use stratagems, such as making a feint to the east but attacking in the west, appearing now in the south and now in the north, hit-and-run attacks, and night actions.[70]

The basis for all these military movements by guerrillas is careful planning. With good reason, Mao asserts that victory in guerrilla warfare, as in regular warfare, is contingent on sound planning. Only ignorance of guerrilla warfare or a flippant attitude, he argues, could account for the view that guerrilla operations can be conducted hap-

[69] Mao, "Problems of Strategy in Guerrilla War Against Japan," *Selected Works*, II, 86–87.
[70] *Ibid.*, p. 89.

hazardly. Planning as thorough as possible must precede operations in a guerrilla area in general as well as for every single battle within that area. The commander must decide, after being briefed by his intelligence experts, what tasks to assign the various units, what kind and how many supplies are required, and so forth. It is true that his situation is such that he lacks the means available to the commander of forces engaged in mobile warfare for formulating intricate battle plans, but that does not relieve him, Mao opines, from his responsibility to use to the best possible advantage all intelligence data available to him.

Destruction of the enemy, the primary object of war, is to be accomplished by waging simultaneously a war of attrition and annihilation. The anti-Japanese war, the model for people's wars, was, according to Mao, both a war of attrition and a war of annihilation. He articulated the rationale underlying such a strategy in the following terms:

. . . unless we fight campaigns and battles of annihilation, we cannot win the time to improve our internal and international situation and alter our unfavourable position. Hence campaigns of annihilation are the means of attaining the objective of strategic attrition. In this sense war of annihilation is war of attrition. It is chiefly by using the method of attrition through annihilation that China can wage protracted war.[71]

Whenever possible, then, revolutionaries should fight battles and campaigns of annihilation in order to achieve the objective of strategic attrition. Lin Piao definitely expressed a preference for a policy of annihilating rather than routing enemy forces because battles of annihilation obviously produce a greater and more immediate impact on the enemy. As he put it: "Injuring all of a man's ten fingers is not as effective as chopping off one, and routing ten enemy divisions is not as effective as annihilating one of them."[72] He regarded battles of annihilation as the most effective way of striking the enemy; each time the enemy loses a brigade or regiment, he will have one less such unit to use against the revolutionaries. Winning such battles enables the latter to take captives and seize weapons, which in turn allows

[71] Mao, "On Protracted War," *Selected Works*, II, 175.
[72] Lin Piao, *Long Live the Victory of People's War!*, p. 34.

them to expand the army units and obtain more sophisticated weapons for use in the war.

To annihilate the enemy, the Chinese Communist strategists advocate a policy of luring him in deep. Lin Piao, reflecting Mao's views, advocates a voluntary abandonment of some cities and districts so as to allow the enemy to penetrate deeply into the interior. Only in this way can the people take part and exert fully their power. He continues:

It is only after letting the enemy in that he can be compelled to divide up his forces, take on heavy burdens and commit mistakes. In other words, we must let the enemy become elated, stretch out all his ten fingers and become hopelessly bogged down. Thus, we can concentrate superior forces to destroy the enemy forces one by one, to eat them up mouthful by mouthful.[73]

Regarding the question of fighting decisive engagements, Mao laid down three guiding principles. First, one should seize the opportunity to fight such an engagement in every battle or campaign whenever one is certain of winning. Conversely, one should avoid a decisive engagement when uncertain of victory. Finally, and most important, one "should absolutely avoid a strategically decisive engagement on which the fate of the whole nation is staked." [74] During the first two stages of the war, when the forces of the people are weakest, the enemy's aim is to maneuver them into concentrating their main forces for a decisive engagement. As Mao points out, the objective of the people is just the opposite; they must choose conditions favorable to them and fight only when sure of victory.

Coordination of guerrilla warfare with regular warfare is a requisite for victory in people's wars. Mao holds that guerrilla warfare, when coordinated with regular warfare, has major strategic value in all stages of the war. Every enemy soldier slain by guerrillas and every round of ammunition fired by enemy soldiers at guerrillas should be regarded as contributions to the total war effort. Their activities exert a profound psychological influence in the war, having a demoralizing effect on enemy troops and the people of the enemy and a stimulating effect on the revolutionary forces and the masses supporting them.

[73] Ibid., p. 36.
[74] Mao, "On Protracted War," Selected Works, II, 180.

Moreover, guerrillas coordinate their operations with those of the regular forces in campaigns and battles. In the campaign at Hsinkou, for example, they played a major role by wrecking a key railway and the motor roads in the area. Those guerrilla units operating close to regular forces can perform any task assigned by the commander of the regular forces. Typical duties given guerrillas would be those of disrupting enemy supply lines, pinning down some of his smaller units, acting as guides for the regular soldiers, and going on reconnaissance patrols to procure intelligence data for regular units.[75]

To coordinate successfully guerrilla activities with those of the regular army, there must be a unified strategic command. Guerrilla zones or base areas having several guerrilla units should have one or more units to constitute the main force, various other formations, of varying size, to serve as the supplementary force, and many armed units derived from the people "not withdrawn from production" (self-defense forces). Faced with an enemy which is under a unified command, the above-mentioned forces must be placed under the command of regular army commanders in the area concerned.

Mao advocates centralized strategic command and decentralized command in campaigns and battles. The former implies that the "center" (state) has power to plan and direct guerrilla warfare as a whole and to coordinate in every war zone and guerrilla zone or base area guerrilla warfare and regular warfare. Unity, harmony, and centralization are absolutely necessary in general matters; that is, in strategic matters. In such matters ". . . the lower levels should report to the higher and follow their instructions so as to ensure concerted action." [76] In tactical matters, however, those at a higher level must allow local commanders considerable discretion respecting matters of detail such as the actual deployment of forces for battle because ". . . such details must be settled in the light of specific conditions, which change from time to time and from place to place and are quite beyond the knowledge of the distant higher levels of command." [77] The guiding principle is that of decentralized command in campaigns and battles. Should those at the "top" have views regarding tactical problems, they should express them in the form of "instructions"

---

[75] Mao, "Problems of Strategy in Guerrilla War Against Japan," II, 91–93.
[76] *Ibid.*, p. 110.   [77] *Ibid.*

rather than in the form of "commands." The discretion of the local commander should be expanded in direct proportion to the greatness of the distance separating lower and higher levels, the vastness of the area, and the complexity of the situation. A policy based on the principle of decentralized command in tactical matters tends to encourage local personnel to develop their talents for working independently; it also enables them to cope more successfully with complex problems and allows them to expand more rapidly their guerrilla operations.[78]

For revolutionaries in Latin America, Asia, and Africa, the Chinese, in a recent collection of quotations entitled *Chairman Mao-Tse-tung on People's War*, now offer a number of guiding principles in all forms of warfare. These ten principles, derived from Chinese experience in fighting both domestic and foreign enemies, are based on a people's war and, according to the Chinese, can be used only by an army fighting a people's war. First, one must attack dispersed, isolated forces and then those that are concentrated and strong. Second, one should initially seize small and medium cities and large rural areas— and only then take large cities. Third, one's major objective should be the wiping out of the enemy's effective strength, not the holding or seizing of a city. The latter results from the former. Fourth, for every battle, one must concentrate an absolutely superior force, completely encircle the enemy forces, and attempt to prevent any from escaping. Battles of attrition in which one loses more than one gains or even breaks even if one is to realize gradually the absolute superiority needed for winning the war should definitely be avoided. Fifth, revolutionaries should prepare carefully for every battle, and fight only those they are sure of winning. Sixth, they should make full use of their style of fighting, featuring "courage in battle, no fear of sacrifice, and continuous fighting (that is, fighting successive battles in a short time without rest)."[79] Seventh, they should strive to annihilate the enemy when he is on the move, but they should not neglect positional attacks when conditions are favorable. Eighth, they must boldly seize fortified points and cities that are weakly defended. When

---

[78] *Ibid.*, p. 111.
[79] Mao Tse-tung, "The Present Situation and Our Tasks," *Selected Military Writings*, 2nd ed. (Peking: Foreign Languages Press, 1965), p. 349.

opportune, they should occupy those defended with moderate strength and wait until conditions are "ripe" before moving against strongly defended points. Ninth, they should depend on the enemy as a source of manpower and matériel. Their ". . . main sources of manpower and matériel are at the front." [80] Tenth, they should put to the best use the time they have between campaigns, using the time for resting, training, and consolidating their forces. These periods should be relatively short, for the enemy must not be given sufficient time to recuperate from their attacks.

In his article of September, 1965, Lin Piao provided revolutionaries with what he called Mao's "masterful summary of the strategy and tactics of people's war." [81] Since that statement is the most recent official articulation of the Chinese concept of people's war, I quote it in its entirety:

> You fight in your way and we fight in ours; we fight when we can win and move away when we can't.
> In other words, you rely on modern weapons and we rely on highly conscious revolutionary people; you give full play to your superiority and we give full play to ours; you have your way of fighting and we have ours. When you want to fight us, we don't let you and you can't even find us. But when we want to fight you, we make sure that you can't get away and we hit you squarely on the chin and wipe you out. When we are able to wipe you out, we do so with a vengeance; when we can't, we see to it that you don't wipe us out. It is opportunism if one won't fight when one can win. It is adventurism if one insists on fighting when one can't win. Fighting is the pivot of all our strategy and tactics. It is because of the necessity of fighting that we admit the necessity of moving away. The sole purpose of moving away is to fight and bring about the final and complete destruction of the enemy. This strategy and these tactics can be applied only when one relies on the broad masses of the people, and such application brings the superiority of people's war into full play. However superior he may be in technical equipment and whatever tricks he may resort to, the enemy will find himself in the passive position of having to receive blows, and the initiative will always be in our hands.[82]

According to Li Tso-p'eng, the "kernel" of Mao's thinking on the strategy and tactics in a people's war is the idea of concentrating a

[80] Ibid.
[81] Lin Piao, *Long Live the Victory of People's War!*, p. 36.
[82] Ibid., pp. 36–37.

superior force to destroy the enemy forces one by one.[83] His strategy was to "pit one against ten" and his tactics to "pit ten against one." [84] The "paper tiger" concept, the idea of despising the enemy strategically but taking full account of him tactically, is regarded by Li Tso-p'eng as a generalization on a higher plane of the idea of strategically "pitting one against ten" and tactically "pitting ten against one." The method of concentrating a superior force to destroy the enemy forces one by one is used for implementing the concept of taking the enemy seriously tactically; it also incorporates the other component of the paper tiger concept. Defending the latter proposition, Li argues that ". . . only by strategically despising the enemy and displaying a revolutionary and militant spirit of 'pitting one against ten' can we remain cool-headed in face of a powerful enemy and not be overawed by his truculence or confused by a complex situation; only in this way will we dare to concentrate our forces and deal the enemy blows." [85]

Li accurately states the psychological basis for the formulation of the paper tiger concept by Mao in 1946, when the Red Army was faced with a KMT foe that appeared to be much stronger. Mao's desire then, as now, was to counteract defeatism among his troops by assuring them that, in the long run, they would prevail over the enemy having a clear advantage at the time. The explanation given for his optimistic appraisal of the future in respect to the impending war against the KMT seems to be relevant to his evaluation of the chances for ultimate "victory" in people's war today. He said:

We have only millet plus rifles to rely on, but history will finally prove that our millet plus rifles is more powerful than Chiang Kai-shek's aeroplanes plus tanks. Although the Chinese people still face many difficulties and will long suffer hardships from the joint attacks of U.S. imperialism and the Chinese reactionaries, the day will come when these reactionaries are defeated and we are victorious. The reason is simply this: the reactionaries represent reaction, we represent progress.[86]

[83] Li Tso-p'eng, *Strategy: One Against Ten—Tactics: Ten Against One* (Peking: Foreign Languages Press, 1966), p. 2.

[84] Mao Tse-tung, "Problems of Strategy in China's Revolutionary War," *Selected Works* (Peking: Foreign Languages Press, 1965), I, 237.

[85] Li Tso-p'eng, *Strategy: One Against Ten—Tactics: Ten Against One*, p. 6.

[86] Mao Tse-tung, "Talk with the American Correspondent Anna Louise Strong," *Selected Works* (Peking: Foreign Languages Press, 1961), IV, 101.

To those despairing today because of the disparity in strength between themselves and the imperialists, the Chinese attempt to reassure them by arguing that *people, not weapons,* are decisive in war, which is more than a "contest of military and economic power"; it is "also a contest of human power and morale." [87] That is, "the richest source of power to wage war lies in the masses of the people." [88]

Prior to 1958, Mao, in his references to the American "paper tiger," seemed to despise "it" both strategically and tactically. The Taiwan crisis of that year, involving as it did a serious confrontation with the United States, and one in which the Chinese failed to get firm assurance from the Soviet Union that the latter would extend its "nuclear umbrella" to China, led Mao to revise the concept. Strategically, the people should treat the imperialists with contempt; tactically, they should treat them with respect. Dialectically speaking, the imperialists are "real tigers" and "paper tigers" at one and the same time. As real tigers they can "devour people"; hence they must be treated with respect in every concrete encounter with them on the battlefield. Concerning the other aspect of the contradiction, the people can despise the enemy strategically because he "in his essence and in the long run, is bound to perish in the end, no matter how powerful he may be for a time." [89]

On the whole, Chinese behavior vis-à-vis the American imperialists squares with this strategic concept. While encouraging others to emulate their example and dare to wage people's wars in Latin America, Asia, and Africa, they have, as far as is known, undertaken no commitments there that would indicate a lack of respect for American power in those areas.

In conclusion, let us examine the Chinese view regarding the interconnection between people's wars, the responsibility of China regarding them, and their impact on the power of the United States. Lin Piao, projecting China's experience in fighting a people's war on the international screen, expressed a world view, picturing North America and Western Europe as "the cities of the world" and Asia, Africa, and Latin America as "the rural areas of the world." As in the case of China earlier, revolutionary activity was developing more rapidly in

[87] Mao, "On Protracted War," *Selected Works,* II, 143.
[88] *Ibid.,* p. 186.
[89] Shao Tieh-chen, *Revolutionary Dialectics,* p. 16.

the "countryside" of the world than in the "cities" of the world; that is, ". . . the contemporary world revolution . . . presents a picture of the encirclement of the cities by the rural areas." [90] He added that the whole cause of the world revolution, in the final analysis, depended on the outcome of the people's wars in the emerging nations.

These struggles are closely interconnected and mutually supporting. Clearly what the Chinese hope for is the eruption simultaneously of several of these wars in widely separated parts of the world, pinning down and weakening the military forces of the United States. They are absolutely convinced, as are many observers in the United States, that the Americans cannot cope successfully with several "Vietnams" at the same time; moreover, they feel that American involvement in such wars will result inevitably in the desired strategic attrition of American military power, thereby removing from Asia the principal restraining force blocking the realization of her goals as a major world power. In short, they view these wars as a means for achieving national as well as revolutionary goals. Lin Piao provided us with an excellent analysis of Chinese expectations regarding these wars. He said:

> The struggles waged by the different peoples against U.S. imperialism reinforce each other and merge into a torrential world-wide tide of opposition to U.S. imperialism. The more successful the development of people's war in a given region, the larger the number of U.S. imperialist forces that can be *pinned* down and *depleted* there. When the U.S. aggressors are hard pressed in one place, they have no alternative but to loosen their grip on others.
>
> Everything is divisible. And so is the colossus of U.S. imperialism. It can be split up and defeated. The peoples of Asia, Africa, and Latin America and other regions can destroy it piece by piece, some striking at its head and others at its feet. That is why the greatest fear of U.S. imperialism is that people's wars will be launched in different parts of the world, and particularly in Asia, Africa, and Latin America, and why it regards people's war as a mortal danger.[91]

Speaking specifically of Vietnam, he pictured the United States as being "in danger of being swamped" in a people's war; moreover, the Americans, he said, were deeply concerned regarding the consequences

[90] Lin Piao, *Long Live the Victory of People's War!*, p. 49.
[91] *Ibid.*, pp. 56–57. Emphasis added.

flowing from defeat there. In a desperate effort to stave off a chain reaction of people's wars that would ensue from an American defeat, they had escalated the war, but these efforts, he contended, could only lead to a more disastrous defeat. Other peoples, contemplating the victory of the Vietnamese over the Americans, would realize that the Americans are not invulnerable, and thus they would dare to begin such wars. He likened the United States to ". . . a mad bull dashing from place to place, [which] will finally be burned to ashes in the blazing fires of the people's wars it has provoked by its own actions." [92]

The Chinese feel that they and all socialist countries should support wars of national liberation, but they have indicated quite clearly that primary responsibility in these wars rests on the people of the country concerned. In their own case, they have acknowledged the value of the international support given them, but they insist that victory was largely a result of their own efforts, a view that was expressed quite succinctly by Lin Piao, who said: "The peoples of the world invariably support each other in their struggles against imperialism and its lackeys. Those countries which have won victory are duty bound to support and aid the peoples who have not yet done so. Nevertheless, foreign aid can only play a *supplementary* role." [93] To wage and win a people's war, the people of the country involved must be prepared to continue the fight "even when all material aid from the outside is cut off." [94] In short, he contended that victory would be denied those not pursuing, as had the Chinese, a policy of self-reliance.

If one does not operate by one's own efforts, does not independently ponder and solve the problems of the revolution in one's own country and does not rely on the strength of the masses, but leans wholly on foreign aid—even though this be aid from *socialist countries which persist in revolution*—no victory can be won, or be consolidated even if it is won.[95]

Whether one regards the Chinese advocacy of the policy of self-reliance as a rationalization for China's inability to provide substantial material assistance to revolutionaries or as a genuine reflection of Chinese conviction regarding the inherent value of pursuing such a policy, the fact remains that the Chinese were serving notice on Latin

[92] *Ibid.*, p. 57.
[94] *Ibid.*, p. 42.

[93] *Ibid.*, pp. 41–42. Emphasis added.
[95] *Ibid.* Emphasis added.

American admirers of the Chinese "road to power" that they had no reason to expect significant material contributions from the Chinese. In the midst of the Cultural Revolution, the Chinese apparently feel that they have discharged their international duty to revolutionaries in Latin America, Asia, and Africa by making available, in the languages of the local people, books and pamphlets setting forth the thought of Mao Tse-tung. Again this might be interpreted as Chinese rationalization for their inability to provide for the concrete needs of their followers elsewhere, but it can also be argued that the Chinese policy reflects a deep feeling, ill-founded though it be in reality, that the *prime* need of revolutionaries everywhere is for the only *pure* expression of contemporary Marxism-Leninism, and, of course, they hold that only the thought of Mao Tse-tung can fulfill that need.

Thus far we have examined in detail the theory of a people's war as articulated by Mao Tse-tung, Lin Piao, and other spokesmen for the Maoist faction in the CCP. The impression that one derives from reading contemporary statements on people's war in the Chinese press is that Mao's thought on this subject possesses virtual magical power when mastered by revolutionaries in Latin America and elsewhere. A major flaw in the Chinese analysis is the absence of a systematic examination of conditions in China that enabled Mao and his associates to apply successfully their strategy and tactics. In short, their writings are somewhat divorced from the real world in which these strategists were operating. Let us turn now to an examination of that world.

The Chinese Communists' road to power was indeed an arduous and protracted one. In 1923 the CCP, under prompting from the Comintern, entered into the first United Front with the Kuomintang, led by Dr. Sun Yat-sen. After the death of Dr. Sun in 1925, Chiang Kai-shek gradually emerged as the most powerful leader in the KMT. The alliance was terminated in 1927 after the troops of Chiang slaughtered many of the leaders and cadres of the CCP in Shanghai. Doubtless the distrust of nationalist "bourgeois" leaders, a leading characteristic of the CCP leaders, stems in large part from their unhappy experience in attempting to collaborate with the KMT in the 1920s.

Following the Shanghai fiasco, the Communist leaders, again under instructions from the Comintern, shifted to a radical policy with emphasis on armed struggle by the workers in the major cities. The role of the peasants was that of supporting the urban insurrections. In attempting to carry out the new line, the Communist forces sustained severe defeats in the attacks on Ch'angsha, Nanch'ang, and other urban centers.

Mao Tse-tung withdrew the remnants of the forces under his command to Chingkangshan, in mountainous western Kiangsi, where he joined forces in April, 1928, with Chu Teh. P'eng Teh-huai arrived with a small band of men in the fall of that year. After reorganization in 1929, the Red Army had about 10,000 men but only 2,000 rifles. Mao was political commissar, and Chu Teh was military commander.

While members of the Central Committee remained in Shanghai and clung to their dream of widespread urban uprisings, Mao and his guerrilla comrades developed, through a process of trial and error, a strategy more relevant for the conditions then existing in China. It was in south-central China that they first established rural bases, and it was also there that Mao tested his estimation of the revolutionary potential of the peasants, especially the "poor" and "middle" peasants. Through a policy of radical agrarian reform, he sought to win their support. Many of those receiving land enlisted in the Red Army. In part they did so because of their gratitude to the Communists for the land that they had received and in part because they had been persuaded by local cadres that they must defend, by armed force, their newly acquired land and their families from "counterrevolutionary" elements. Since many of these peasants had taken part in "struggle" meetings that resulted in the killing of landlords in their villages, they feared speedy retribution at the hands of KMT authorities should the Communists be driven from the base areas. Thus they had compelling reasons for joining the Red Army.

In January, 1929, Chu and Mao abandoned the base in Chingkangshan and established a more secure base in the remote mountainous districts in southern Kiangsi near the Fukien and Kwangtung borders. Meanwhile, other Communist leaders were organizing guerrilla bands and creating soviets in scattered mountainous areas in central and northern Shensi province. In each case the CCP capitalized on Chiang's campaigns against warlords and dissident Kuomintang generals. Discipline, in these early years of the Red Army, was rather lax. Guerrilla bands too frequently engaged in senseless killing, burning, and plundering. In time, however, they became, as a result of intensive political indoctrination, an extremely well-disciplined army.

In November, 1931, the First All-China Soviet Congress met in Juichin, Kiangsi, and proclaimed the establishment of the Chinese Soviet Republic. It also adopted a constitution, a political program, a land law, resolutions on the Red Army, a labor law, and economic policies. Mao was selected as head of the Central Soviet Government, while Chu Teh was designated as chairman of the Revolutionary Military Council, which acted as the supervising organ over the Red Army.

The Kuomintang authorities viewed with alarm the increased influence of the Communists in several provinces; but since they were even more concerned with suppressing a series of revolts staged by ex-warlords and dissident KMT generals, they were unable to deal with the Communists until the fall of 1930. At the Fourth Plenary Conference of the KMT, held in November, 1930, the delegates resolved unanimously to exterminate the Communists, a task to which they assigned the highest priority. In their estimation, the task could be completed in not more than six months. In fact, five campaigns, extending over a four-year period, were required to dislodge the Communists from their bases in central China. In those campaigns Mao and Chu developed their tactics of guerrilla warfare.

The "First Extermination Campaign" (December, 1930) under the leadership of Lu Ti-p'ing was a complete fiasco. The Communists trapped one division and seized thousands of weapons. Only four days later they inflicted heavy casualties on another division. In less than two weeks they had crushed the enemy forces.

The "Second Extermination Campaign" (February, 1931) led by Ho Ying-ch'in, Chiang's Minister of War, met with a similar fate. General Ho followed a much more cautious policy than had his predecessor, but the Communists responded by encircling his slowly moving columns and destroying one by one the weakest units. Again they succeeded in capturing thousands of rifles and machine guns. According to a Nationalist estimate of May, 1931, the Communists had enhanced considerably their strength, having 117,400 men, 60,000 rifles, 768 machine guns, 29 cannon, and 74 trench mortars. At least 90 per cent of the weapons had been "supplied" by the KMT.

Nor could the KMT derive much satisfaction from the outcome of the third campaign begun in July, 1931. The campaign was interrupted by the Japanese invasion of Manchuria, an event that had a most disruptive impact on the KMT. Some of Chiang's associates clamored for an end to the struggle against the domestic foe and a concentration on the foreign aggressor. Realizing that his forces were no match for those of the Japanese, Chiang announced his policy of "non-resistance" and referred the matter to the impotent League of Nations for resolution.

The Nationalists were more successful in the fourth campaign launched in April, 1933. They ejected the Communists from the O-Yü-wan Soviet District and also scored some major gains against Ho Lung's men in western Hupeh, but in the most important area, the Central Soviet District in Kiangsi and Fukien, their progress was extremely slow. In February, 1933, the Communists again received indirect assistance from Japanese aggression along the Great Wall in northern Hopeh. Under these circumstances, the KMT had little choice but to call off the campaign against the Communists.

After arranging a temporary truce with the Japanese, Chiang Kai-shek resumed the crusade against his mortal domestic rival. The fifth campaign, begun in October, 1933, allegedly based on a strategy formulated by General von Seeckt, head of the German military mission, resulted in the expulsion of the Communists from their base in Kiangsi and Fukien. The strategy was to compress the Communists into a progressively smaller area. To implement their objectives, the Nationalist commanders ordered the construction of thousands of blockhouses and the excavation of hundreds of miles of trench barrier ditches. Simultaneously, they evacuated all the inhabitants in the combat zones, thereby depriving the foe of his sources of intelligence, food, and manpower. They also imposed a tight blockade around the Central Soviet District. As a consequence, the Communists suffered greatly from a shortage of vital supplies, especially salt. Faced with certain starvation and annihilation if they remained in the Central Soviet District, the Communists made on October 2, 1934, the historic decision to evacuate their main base and establish a new one in a more secure area. What followed was the epic Long March which resulted in the establishment of their primary base in Shensi province in northwestern China.

The CCP desperately needed time in which to rebuild the shattered Red Army and the CCP itself. The Japanese aggressors provided the Communists with that time and with a situation that enabled them to survive. Had the Japanese not increased their incursions into northern China and had a full-scale war between China and Japan not erupted in July, 1937, there seems to be little doubt that Chiang Kai-shek would have succeeded, in due time, in exterminating those who survived the excruciating experiences of the Long March.

At this crucial point, Chiang misjudged public opinion in the country. That is, he failed to appreciate the extent to which many of his countrymen were opposed to his policy of non-resistance to the Japanese. He proposed to wipe out the "Communist bandits," after which he could then consider how best to resist the external foe; consequently, he turned a deaf ear to the Communist suggestions that the CCP and KMT form a second United Front, this one against a foreign aggressor rather than against the numerous warlords who impeded the unification of the country.

Unhappily for the Generalissimo he chose Chang Hsueh-liang and Yang Hu-ch'eng as the commanders to exterminate the remnants of the Red Army in Shensi. Chang's Northeastern Army, composed of Manchurians who had been evacuated in 1931–1932 from Manchuria after the Japanese occupation of their homeland, was quite homesick. They concurred in the Chinese Communist argument that the civil war should be ended so that all Chinese might join forces against the Japanese. Yang Hu-ch'eng, an ex-warlord in the northwest, and Chang secretly arranged a truce with representatives of the Red Army.

The cessation of hostilities in the northwest aroused the suspicions of Chiang Kai-shek, who flew to Sian to investigate the situation for himself. He learned quite early in the long discussions with Chang and Yang that the troops in the northwest were deeply dissatisfied with their anti-Communist mission. After Chiang refused to change his military priorities, the two generals had him seized on the night of December 12, 1936. The "kidnapped" Generalissimo was not released until December 25, after he had apparently given his captors a verbal assurance that he would comply with their demands. Following the Japanese attack on July 7, 1937, at the Marco Polo Bridge near Peking, the KMT and CCP formalized the Second United Front.

At first glance it might appear that the Communists had paid a high price for the coalition agreement. They had agreed to repudiate their objective of overthrowing the KMT by force. Moreover, they had promised to abolish the Soviet Government and thus subject themselves to the authority of the KMT. Even their armed forces were placed under the command of Nationalist officers. In actuality, however, Communist generals retained control of their troops, and Communist officials and cadres were the dominant political figures in the nineteen base areas established by the Communists in the course of the long Sino-Japanese War.

There can be no doubt that that war had a most profound effect on the outcome of the struggle between the KMT and the CCP for control of the mainland. In the first place, the seriously weakened Red Army would have been wiped out by KMT forces after the Long March had not the war brought an abrupt change in Chiang's strategy. Secondly, the Japanese occupation of much of China resulted in the expulsion of KMT civil and military authority from those areas. Since the Japanese made no effort to occupy the countryside, Communist guerrillas, through skillful mobilization of the people, established and expanded a number of bases behind enemy lines. The Nationalist guerrillas, on the other hand, having failed to attain the same rapport with the people in occupied China, were far less successful than their Communist rivals. As we have seen, those Communist bases were later used as springboards by the Red Army in the civil war that followed the defeat of Japan in 1945. Thirdly, the Sino-Japanese War resulted in a serious deterioration in KMT military, political, and economic strength. The Communists, on the other hand, emerged from the war in far better condition than when they entered it.

According to the Chinese Communist version of the war, the Red Armies were primarily responsible for the defeat of the Japanese. Such a claim is clearly at odds with the commonly accepted facts of history in that it does not take into account the fact that the CCP had powerful "allies" in the war. First, the CCP account fails to give due credit to the Americans, the English, the Australians, and others that were very much involved in the Pacific war with Japan. Had the Japanese not undertaken the conquest of Indo-China, the Philippines, Malaya, and the Pacific islands, they would have had more troops for use against the Chinese. This is not to say that the Chinese Communists did not, in fact, appreciate fully the significance of the American entry into the war against Japan. Both they and the Nationalists were convinced that the Americans would, in due time, bring the Japanese to their knees; consequently, they kept to a minimum their clashes with the Japanese. Both preferred conserving their manpower and supplies for the postwar period when they proposed to settle, once and for all, the fate of the mainland.

Secondly, the Chinese Communists fail to accord to the Nationalists and the Soviet Union proper credit for their contribution to the joint effort in defeating the Japanese. The Nationalist troops bore the brunt of the Japanese offensive in the first year of the war and in the final Japanese offensive in 1944. In the period of stalemate (1938–1944) the Nationalist forces, poorly equipped and trained though they were, engaged 70 per cent of the Japanese troops in China. Thousands of Japanese soldiers were also engaged in garrison duty. Without their Nationalist "ally" the Communist forces would have been subject to far more intense attacks by the Japanese. The Soviet Union provided aid in the war by compelling the Japanese to maintain a powerful army in Manchuria, the Kwantung Army, as a counterweight to Soviet military power in the Far East. In the closing months of the war, the Soviets, after the war in Europe had ended, crushed that army and thus hastened somewhat the downfall of Japan.

The Chinese Communists scored a major psychological victory over the Japanese in the battle of P'inghsingkuan. The 115th Division, under the command of Nieh Jung-chen, ambushed the 5th Division of the Japanese Imperial Army, commanded by Lieutenant General Itagaki Seishiro. The Chinese captured many rifles, pistols, and other weapons as well as much ammunition, food, clothing, and money. It was the first victory over the Japanese. It should also be noted that it was the only time during the entire war that Communist commanders committed a unit as large as a division to battle.[96] The Communists

[96] Samuel B. Griffith, *The Chinese People's Liberation Army* (New York: McGraw-Hill Book Company, 1967), p. 63.

launched their major effort of the war, the "Hundred Regiments Offensive," on August 20, 1940. The well-coordinated operation by the guerrillas resulted in the derailment of trains, the destruction of bridges and viaducts, the severance of the Japanese railway system in hundreds of places, and the destruction of signal equipment. In addition, the Communists allegedly killed 20,000 Japanese and captured 281 Japanese officers and 18,000 puppet troops. As they anticipated, the Japanese retaliated by punishing the peasants who had harbored the guerrillas. The Japanese acts of brutality afforded the Communists an even better opportunity for portraying themselves as the most dependable champion of the Chinese people in the war against the hated Japanese.

Although the Communist forces made hundreds of guerrilla attacks on Japanese units, the fact remains that most of the work of the Eighth Route Army and the New Fourth Army was political rather than military in nature. Wherever they went, Red Army detachments spared no effort to win the support of the people. Cadres of the Political Department's "Mass Movement Branch" explained to all the people of the village the party's policy for dealing with the Japanese. They requested the able-bodied men to volunteer for the Red Army or at least to serve in the self-defense units. They attempted to persuade other villagers to join one of several mass organizations. The groups in which they displayed the greatest interest were the young people and children, but they were interested in winning the support of all groups. In addition to establishing schools for illiterates, they also provided entertainment for the people. The theme most stressed was the anti-Japanese one.[97] It should also be noted that Red Army units were most circumspect in regard to personal relations with the people. By the end of the war the Communists had succeeded in their efforts to convince the people that the Red Army was quite different from any that they had ever known. Given the extremely low social standing of the Chinese soldier in the past, their accomplishments in this respect were truly impressive. Their final victory over the KMT was due in large part to the fact that they had won the confidence and respect of the people, whereas the con-

[97] *Ibid.*, p. 68.

duct of KMT troops only reinforced the traditional image the Chinese people had of the soldier in Chinese society.

While building up the Red Army and enhancing their influence with the masses for the inevitable clash with the KMT, the Communists did not neglect the Community Party itself. According to Mao, party membership grew from 40,000 in 1937 to 1,200,000 in 1945. Most of the recruits were peasants. Many of the intellectuals and students who fled from the Japanese came to Yenan and "matriculated" in the party schools, where they were trained as cadres. Without these "bourgeois" intellectuals, the party would have had a severe shortage of well-trained and indoctrinated leaders. Mao was also most concerned about the quality of the party. To eradicate unorthodox tendencies he instituted in 1942 the first rectification campaign. He was convinced that the war could not be won without the leadership of the Communist Party. Similarly, he was most intent on having a large and politically reliable party at the end of the war to lead the people in the confrontation with the KMT. In short, he proposed to end as quickly as possible the civil war that had been raging almost without exception since 1927. As is well known, the Nationalists and the Communists clashed with one another more frequently in the Sino-Japanese War than they did with the Japanese. Each was clearly trying to enhance its position at the expense of the other because each was equally convinced that the final destiny of the country would be determined on the battlefield.

When the Japanese surrendered in August, 1945, the KMT, with its headquarters in Chungking, held the southwestern and western parts of the country. Its adversary was dominant in the northern and northeastern provinces. A race ensued to occupy the major cities then held by the Japanese. Had the United States not responded to a Nationalist appeal for air and sea transportation so that KMT troops could accept the surrender of Japanese units in northern China, the Communists would have had a clear advantage in that they already had military forces behind the Japanese lines. The result was that the Communists failed to obtain the Japanese arms which they needed for the impending full-scale civil war. American intervention also deprived them of possession of the principal cities in the region. Soviet forces in occupation of Manchuria, on the other hand, allowed Chinese Communist units to infiltrate into the countryside and to "capture" huge stockpiles of arms taken from the Japanese Kwantung Army. To this day the Chinese Communists have not forgiven the United States for interfering with the realization of their plans in the part of China in which they were most interested in 1945 and 1946.

Efforts by Ambassador Hurley and General George C. Marshall to avert a full-scale civil war were fruitless because the KMT and CCP had absolutely no confidence in one another. Furthermore, each felt that it could defeat the other on the field of battle. The Nationalists clearly had the advantage in terms of numbers and military equipment. They had air and naval power at their disposal, whereas the Communists had none. They were far superior to the Communists in regard to artillery, machine guns, and tanks. They had at least three times as many men under arms as did the Communists, but the leadership and morale of the KMT forces were woefully deficient. In the first place, many Nationalist generals were poorly trained in the strategy and tactics of modern warfare; consequently, they were professionally incompetent to command the large numbers of men under them. Second, petty jealousies and rivalries among high ranking officers often resulted in failure to coordinate effectively military operations. Chiang's favoritism toward the "Whampoa Clique" had a most deleterious effect on the morale and efficiency of officers and men not so favored. Third, Chiang often intermeddled in the tactical management of the war. Instead of granting his field commanders the flexibility required he attempted on many occasions to assume personal command down to the division level. Fourth, the Nationalist strategy placed an undue premium on the holding of major cities. As noted previously, Mao's prime concern was to annihilate enemy forces, not to hold or capture cities. He reasoned that such places could be taken when the enemy had been weakened through the destruction of his military power in numerous battles and skirmishes. The Nationalists, therefore, played right into the hands of their enemy, who was allowed to consolidate his position in the countryside from which he could encircle and thus cut off the major cities. Finally, the passive policy of the Nationalists gave the initiative to the Communists. Reduced to maintaining defensive positions, the morale of Nationalist forces frequently declined. The consequence was that large numbers of KMT troops defected to the enemy; and after they had been properly indoctrinated, they were incorporated into Communist military units.

The Communists adopted programs calculated to appeal to those classes and strata whom they regarded as part of the people. The new land reform program provided for the confiscation of landlords' land and its distribution among the peasants. To obtain the support of progressive intellectuals, the CCP called for the overthrow of Chiang Kai-shek, the establishment of a democratic coalition government, and the guarantee of such basic freedoms as freedom of speech, press, and assembly. Attractive to the "petty bourgeoisie" and the "national bourgeoisie" were the Communist assurances that there would be a place for them in the New Democracy. The only property to be confiscated was that belonging to those who had collaborated with the Japanese and that held by "comprador-bureaucrats," KMT officials who had been using their control of government-owned property to further their own interests or those of their families. The party's pledges to curb inflation and bring peace to the Chinese people appealed to many of those in the preceding groups as well as to the small working class in the cities.

When the Sino-Japanese War ended, KMT troops and officials were often greeted as liberators when they occupied territory formerly held by the Japanese. All too frequently, however, these representatives of the Nationalist regime acted as conquerors in their relations with the people. Their acts of brutality, corruption, and insensitivity quickly alienated the people. The Nationalist policy in the countryside was incredible. Not only did the KMT return land titles to the landlords and permit them to collect back rents and interests, they also authorized the returning officials to collect back taxes for the years of the Japanese occupation! Increasing numbers of the intelligentsia became disenchanted with the Kuomintang as it adopted ever more repressive measures in the universities. The outlawing of the democratic parties in 1947 and the increased use of the secret police against those critical of KMT policies further undermined the KMT's standing with the intellectuals. The regime's inability to curb the inflation which was having such a disastrous impact on all groups was still another reason for the collapse of the Nationalist regime. One should also cite the widespread corruption and inefficiency in the regime as a factor in the downfall of Chiang Kai-shek. In short, large numbers of people progressively lost confidence in the KMT to deal effectively with the most crucial political, social, and economic problems of the country. As a consequence they turned with enthusiasm to the Communists or they came to feel that the Communists could not possibly be any worse than the Nationalists. Add to this the fact that they desperately wanted peace after so many years of war and disorder.

The Chinese Communists emerged as victors over their old rivals because they were more sensitive than were the Nationalists to the political component of a people's war. In a very real sense the CCP put "politics in command." Their accurate perception of the most pressing needs of the Chinese people enabled them to transform their position of military inferiority into one of overwhelming military superiority. The outcome in the civil war (1946–1949) was, unlike the Sino-Japanese War, determined far more by internal than by external forces. The United States provided the Nationalists with $1½ billion in aid during World War II and approximately $2 billion after V-J Day. The American government also made available to the Nationalists the services of some of our best military talent to help train their troops and give them advice on questions of strategy, advice that was frequently ignored. One case in point was the case of Manchuria. Chiang Kai-shek, intent on occupying this strategic region before the Communists could move in their troops from northern China, turned a deaf ear to American warnings that he should consolidate his position in northern China before attempting to take over Manchuria. Soviet aid to the Communists in the form of Japanese arms could hardly be compared with the volume of military aid that we provided the Nationalists. Unfortunately most of the American equipment eventually fell into the hands of Communist units as a result of large scale defections and surrenders by Nationalist forces. When units of the PLA marched through the streets of Peking in 1949, many Western observers were impressed by the fact that much of the equipment carried in the victory parade was of American origin. Once again the CCP had demonstrated to revolutionaries that

(98)

one of the best sources of supply is one's enemy. Revolutionaries in Latin America, if they are ever to succeed, will have to emulate their example because the Chinese can hardly be expected to provide them with arms as long as the United States controls the seas.

Latin American revolutionaries have a number of "models" to which they may look for inspiration. The Cuban model as articulated by Fidel Castro, Che Guevara, and Regis Debray has been seriously studied by them for a number of years. In the chapter that follows we shall compare and contrast the Chinese and Cuban concepts of people's war.

IV

A Comparative Analysis of the Chinese and Cuban Concepts of People's War

THE Chinese and the Cubans share many views with regard to the nature of people's war. Both, for example, are firmly convinced that armed struggle is the only viable road to power in a vast majority of the countries in Asia, Africa, and Latin America. Each has expressed its contempt for those in the international Communist movement who advocate a "peaceful" path to power. The Castroites and the Maoists agree that revolutionaries everywhere must combine forces against their common enemy, U.S. imperialism; moreover, they concur in the view that the Third World is the arena for the most crucial struggle with that common enemy. Their world views are also parallel in that each regards its respective country as a part of a bloc—the "countryside" of the world. Victories over U.S. imperialism in any part of the emerging world are taken as victories for their own countries in this global conflict between the American imperialists and the oppressed peoples of Latin America, Asia, and Africa. As a consequence, both have explicitly called for many "Vietnams" because they are convinced that people's wars in the Third World will pin down the forces of the United States and thus will lead inevitably to the strategic attrition of that country. Once that goal has been achieved, the main obstacle, as they see it, will be removed, making possible the realization of their ultimate objectives in their respective spheres of influence.

To those who have analyzed carefully the recent book written by Régis Debray entitled *Revolution in the Revolution*, it is quite clear that Fidel Castro and his associates are determined to distinguish the Cuban "model" from others that have been studied by revolutionaries in recent guerrilla movements in Latin America. Debray's analysis of theories other than the Cuban was not limited to the Chinese. On the contrary, he attacked, at one time or another, virtually all of the potential or actual rivals in the revolutionary movement as well as "reformist" parties such as the MNR in Bolivia. His principal targets included the Trotskyites (especially those in Bolivia), the leaders of the Latin American Communist parties following a pro-Soviet line of "peaceful coexistence," and the pro-Chinese parties and splinter groups. His frequent warnings regarding the dangers inherent in the blind emulation of "Asian" models, coupled with his elaborate distinction between Latin American conditions on the one hand and Chinese and Vietnamese conditions on the other hand, reflect a deep anxiety on the part of the Cuban leaders that Latin American guerrillas have too frequently confused the Cuban and Asian models. Debray vents his spleen on the editors of the pro-Castro periodical *Monthly Review* for asserting that the guerrillas in Peru, whose efforts finally ended in failure, had been pursuing a Castroite strategy. Obviously he resents the implication that the Peruvian failure should be attributed to their following of the Cuban road. He intimates strongly that the fiasco in Peru resulted instead from an adherence to Maoist strategy. He said: "If we refer to recent episodes, such as that in Peru, it is not impossible that the Chinese system of supportive bases, as systematized by Mao Tse-tung in 1938, in *Problems of Strategy in Guerrilla War Against Japan*, has reached Latin Americans and superimposed its image on their conception of the Cuban guerrilla struggle." [1]

He contends that many of the guerrilla movements in Latin America had failed because guerrillas had attempted to apply principles, developed mostly in Asia (China and Vietnam), to Latin American conditions, which, he insisted, differed in several significant respects from those in China and Vietnam. In addition, he asserts that some guerrilla defeats transpired because guerrilla leaders had failed to grasp the

[1] Régis Debray, *Revolution in the Revolution? Armed Struggle and Political Struggle in Latin America*, trans. Bobbye Ortiz (New York: Grove Press, Inc., 1967), p. 59.

(101)

essence of the Cuban revolution. It seems, then, that his principal objectives in writing the book were to provide revolutionaries in the Third World in general and in Latin America in particular with a strategy better suited to the peculiar conditions existing in their areas and to convince them that the Cuban model, when properly understood and distinguished from strategies often confused with it, was the only road for them.

One can only speculate concerning the motivation underlying the selection of Debray as the one to articulate the Cuban concept of people's war. As Theodore Draper points out, Fidel Castro has been plagued with a feeling of intellectual inadequacy and inferiority and has tended to depend on others for systematic theorizing.[2] Certainly he has written nothing in the field of guerrilla warfare comparable to Mao's numerous major contributions in the field. In 1960 Guevara wrote a short book entitled *Guerrilla Warfare*, which was more of an operational handbook for guerrillas than a systematic theoretical analysis of people's war. There are two possible explanations for Guevara's not receiving the assignment for stating the Cuban case. First, and probably most important, he was too deeply involved in the organization and development of the guerrilla movement in Latin America to have sufficient time to examine the necessary documents and reexamine his experience and that of his colleagues during the Cuban revolution. Second, Castro and his associates may have felt that Guevara himself lacked the intellectual sophistication required for an effective presentation of Cuban views. Debray, on the other hand, was recognized in leftist circles throughout Latin America, as well as in Western Europe, as a brilliant young intellectual. Excellent training in philosophy equipped him admirably for the task. Furthermore, the fact that he was French, not Cuban, would tend to make him more acceptable to non-Communists in Latin America, and it was precisely to this group, the Jacobin Left, to which his book was primarily directed. One might also add that he is not identified in the minds of many Latin American intellectuals with any Communist party. In short, they do not regard him as a "Communist"; hence non-Communists on the left are more inclined to be influenced by him

[2] Theodore Draper, *Castroism: Theory and Practice* (New York: Frederick A. Praeger, 1965), p. 50.

than by a writer officially associated with the Castro or any other Communist regime. Finally, the Cuban officials doubtless were impressed both by his earlier articles, which were definitely sympathetic with their cause, and by his intimate knowledge of guerrilla warfare based on his extensive traveling in Latin America, where he lived with guerrilla bands.

If Debray is not an official spokesman for the Castroites, why should his book be treated as an authoritative statement of the Cuban position? Admittedly, much of the evidence is circumstantial in nature, but one can argue plausibly that the treatment given him and the opportunities afforded to him by the Cuban authorities certainly indicate that they did not view him as an ordinary foreign intellectual engaged in research on Cuban political theory. Roberto Fernández Retamar, who wrote the introduction to the Spanish edition, states that

. . . the leading circles of the Cuban Revolution . . . offered him every
facility for carrying out his investigation. During 1966 he was able to speak
with many who had participated in our revolutionary actions: among
others, with Major Fidel Castro, who conceived and led that struggle.
There were many long conversations, and Debray heard accounts
of the experiences undergone, sometimes at the very site of decisive
military actions. Furthermore, he had access to numerous unpublished
documents of that epoch which had been preserved: messages written in
combat, instructions to military leaders in the field, military communiqués,
letters, and other texts. This gave him the opportunity to obtain a most
vivid impression of those historic events. No one else who has written
about the Cuban Revolution has had access to such a wealth of material
for historical research.[3]

Since the book was published in Havana in January, 1967, one may reasonably assume that the manuscript was read and approved by responsible officials of the Cuban government. It would be implausible to argue that those officials would have allowed the book to be printed in Cuba had it failed to state accurately the views of the top leaders on matters to which the latter attach so much importance.

[3] Roberto Fernández Retamar, "Introduction to the Spanish Edition," in Debray, *Revolution in the Revolution?*, p. 12.

Leo Huberman and Paul M. Sweezy, editors of the *Monthly Review,* point out that

. . . the size of the first printing (200,000 copies) and the evident eagerness of representatives of the Cuban regime to secure the widest distribution of the work both inside and outside Cuba leave no doubt that Regis Debray . . . has succeeded in presenting to the world an accurate and profound account of the thinking of the leaders of the Cuban revolution.[4]

In the analysis below, the works of Debray and Guevara will be treated as the major theoretical statements of the Cuban position. Obviously the documentation on the Cuban side of the problem leaves much to be desired when compared with the numerous articles to which one may refer as sources for the Chinese views.

The Cubans have been claiming for several years that they have made a number of major contributions to Marxist-Leninist theory. One can detect a certain defensiveness in regard to the suggestion that *they* borrowed heavily from the military writings of Mao Tse-tung. Guevara denied at least three times that the Cubans were influenced by the Chinese example. As a matter of fact, he asserted that they knew nothing about Mao's theory of guerrilla warfare while they were actually fighting Batista.[5] But during an interview granted in June, 1959, to Chinese journalists in Havana, he admitted that guerrilla commanders had studied Mao's works. In the next chapter, we shall discuss this matter more fully. Debray maintains that it was fortunate that Castro was ignorant of Mao's writings when he landed in Oriente Province. Thus Castro could ". . . invent, on the spot and out of his own experience, principles of a military doctrine in conformity with the terrain." [6] It was only at the end of the war, after the summer offensive of 1958, that Castro and Guevara first obtained a copy of Mao's *Problems of Strategy in Guerrilla War Against Japan.* By that time they had already developed their own tactics. Debray describes their surprise when "they found in this book what they had been practicing under pressure of necessity." [7]

[4] Leo Huberman and Paul M. Sweezy, "Foreword," in Debray, *Revolution in the Revolution?*, p. 7.
[5] Draper, *Castroism*, p. 25.
[6] Debray, *Revolution in the Revolution?*, p. 20.
[7] *Ibid.*

Castro derived military inspiration from Pablo de la Torriente Brau's *Realengo 18*, some of the later writings of Engels stressing the problems posed for revolutionaries by the invention of better weapons by "bourgeois" officers and the widening of streets, and Hemingway's *For Whom the Bell Tolls*. Even here, Debray seems to be reluctant to acknowledge Castro's indebtedness to other writers. He says: "These books were not so much *sources* as they were coincidences: Fidel found in them only what he was looking for." [8]

When Castro and Guevara landed in Oriente Province in December, 1956, they had not yet formulated a theory of guerrilla warfare. Since they did not at that time regard that form of warfare as the key to victory, they had not prepared for a protracted campaign in the countryside. In fact they had not even studied the geography of the Sierra Maestra. Their strategy was based on the assumption that their simultaneous attacks on Manzanillo and Santiago de Cuba would precipitate a nationwide campaign of sabotage and agitation, culminating in a general strike. The initial attempt failed, but Castro and his supporters still clung to their strategy. It was not until after the dismal failure to stage a general strike in Havana in April, 1958, that Castro turned to guerrilla warfare. As Draper says, he "backed into guerrilla warfare after all his other plans had failed." [9] Castro's experience in this respect is essentially the same as his chief "competitor" in the theory and practice of guerrilla warfare. Mao turned to the countryside and the peasantry as his main source of support only after the failure of attempts by the CCP to seize power by launching attacks on and promoting proletarian uprisings in the major cities of China.

In 1960 Guevara wrote what came to be regarded, at least until the appearance of Debray's book, the most systematic and authoritative statement of the Cuban concept of guerrilla warfare. He does not explicitly acknowledge his indebtedness to Mao Tse-tung. Draper is of the opinion that Mao in fact influenced Guevara very little. Cuba's revolutionary tradition, characterized by guerrilla warfare in the nineteenth century, he feels was far more important as a factor in the development of Castro's and Guevara's concept of guerrilla warfare.[10] Experts on the subject, however, are inclined to regard Guevara's

[8] *Ibid.* Emphasis added. [9] Draper, *Castroism*, p. 24.
[10] *Ibid.*, p. 26.

book as a rather poor imitation of Mao's writings. One could cite as evidence the statement made by F. M. Osanka to that effect and the numerous footnotes prepared by the translator of Guevara's book as it appears in Osanka's book on guerrilla warfare. In his footnotes, the translator points out remarkable parallels between the ideas of Guevara and Mao.[11] It is the contention of the present writer that Guevara, in this book at least, contributed very little to the "Marxist-Leninist treasury" of guerrilla warfare. One might also contend, of course, that Mao Tse-tung did not "invent" guerrilla warfare and that the tactics advocated by him are essentially the same as those used by guerrillas long before he began writing on the subject. Certainly both propositions can be easily documented.[12] The fact remains, however, that there are so many similarities between the views expressed by the two men that it is difficult to avoid the conclusion that more than mere coincidence is involved. After all, Guevara, writing in 1960, had had sufficient time to familiarize himself with the literature in the field. It seems almost inconceivable that a man as intelligent as Guevara should not have consulted fully the works of Mao, the man recognized in revolutionary circles as the foremost authority on the subject; and yet he maintains, according to Theodore Draper, as late as November 23, 1964, that the Cubans were not influenced by the Chinese.[13]

This is not to say that all Cuban claims to originality are without substance, but it is argued here that they, in their eagerness to demonstrate how their views differ from those of the Chinese, Vietnamese, and others, have presented us with a rather distorted picture. In short, there are far more similarities than there are differences in the positions of these various groups. An effort is made here to present a better-balanced analysis of the views of those concerned.

If it is true, as maintained here, that Debray has given inadequate attention to the points on which the parties are in agreement and too much time to distinguishing their positions, one must still try to ex-

[11] Franklin Mark Osanka (ed.), *Modern Guerrilla Warfare* (New York: 1962), p. 323. The translation and condensation of Guevara's book was taken from *Army Magazine.*

[12] Frederick Wilkins, "Guerrilla Warfare," in Osanka, *Modern Guerrilla Warfare,* pp. 3–14; Peter Paret and John W. Shy, *Guerrillas in the 1960's* (revised ed.; New York: Frederick A. Praeger, 1962), pp. 6–11.

[13] Draper, *Castroism,* p. 25.

plain why he has done so. One theory, not altogether satisfactory to me at least, could be framed in terms of the personalities and the aspirations of Castro and Mao. Both men are exceedingly vain, and each is equally convinced that only his theory of people's war should serve as a beacon to light the way for revolutionaries in Latin America struggling for national liberation. Moreover, Castro has, for many years, regarded Latin America as his special sphere of influence in the international Communist movement; consequently, he must regard Mao as an outsider encroaching on his bailiwick! Mao, who is now called by his supporters the greatest Marxist-Leninist at the present time, must be shocked and annoyed that a man of Castro's lowly stature in the Communist world should contend, in effect, that the thought of Mao Tse-tung, the highest form of Marxism-Leninism of the contemporary period, has less relevance in Latin America than the concepts of the Cubans. Castro's pretensions to regional ideological supremacy must be especially galling to Maoists because Castro, at the time he assumed power, did not even claim to be a Communist.

Debray provides us with an alternative theory based on the consequences to the guerrilla movement in Latin America of confusing the Cuban, Chinese, and Vietnamese approaches to people's war. He noted that

. . . militants are reading Fidel's speeches and Che Guevara's writings with eyes that have already read Mao on the anti-Japanese war, Giap, and certain texts of Lenin—and they think they recognize the latter in the former. Classical visual superimposition, but dangerous, since the Latin American revolutionary war possesses highly special and profoundly distinct conditions of development, which can only be discovered through particular experience.[14]

In his judgment "theoretical works on people's war do as much harm as good." [15]

He takes the Latin American intellectual to task for assuming an "intellectual attitude toward war." That is, he is, in effect, a prisoner of the past. His approach to revolutionary problems tends to be inflexible in that he attempts to deal with them in terms of concepts derived from his readings. Thus he is "less able than others to invent, improvise, make do with available resources, decide instantly on bold

[14] Debray, *Revolution in the Revolution?*, p. 21.
[15] *Ibid.*

moves when he is in a tight spot." [16] By stressing so much the basic differences between Latin American and Asian *conditions*, Debray underplays similarities in Chinese and Cuban *concepts*, but it must be remembered that one of his prime concerns in writing the book was to alert intellectuals to the dangers associated with "bookish" application of concepts to conditions they had never examined closely to determine whether they corresponded in fact with the conditions on which their ideas were based.

Since the Chinese view on various aspects of people's war was fully stated in the preceding chapter, no useful purpose would be served in repeating fully their stand on the points on which they and the Cubans are in basic agreement. In addition to the shared views mentioned in the first paragraph of this chapter, one might also note that they agree that the basic area for the revolutionary struggle is the countryside, because there the revolutionaries can capitalize on the advantages of occupying relatively inaccessible remote areas. Naturally the social class of most importance to the guerrillas is the peasantry. To win their support the revolutionaries must adopt an agricultural policy that is calculated to satisfy their basic aspirations, the chief of which, of course, is the ownership of the land that they have been working for others. In short, the guerrilla fighters must become agrarian revolutionaries.[17]

The Chinese and the Cubans also agree that these wars between peoples of the emerging countries and "U.S. imperialism" supported by local "reactionaries" will be protracted conflicts that develop in three stages. The names used in describing the various stages are not altogether identical, although the essence of the stages seems to be the same. Mao refers to them as: (1) the stage of the enemy's strategic offensive and the people's strategic defensive, (2) the stage of the enemy's strategic consolidation and the people's preparation for the counteroffensive (strategic stalemate), and (3) the stage of people's strategic counteroffensive and the enemy's strategic retreat.[18] Debray speaks of ". . . first, the stage of establishment; second, the stage of

[16] *Ibid.*
[17] Che Guevara, *Guerrilla Warfare* (New York: Monthly Review Press, 1961), pp. 16–18.
[18] Mao, "On Protracted War," *Selected Works*, II, 136.

development, marked by the enemy offensive carried out by all available means (operational and tactical encirclements, air troops, bombardments, et cetera); finally, the stage of revolutionary offensive. . . ." [19] He is less precise than Mao in his description of these stages. There appears to be a major difference regarding the time at which the guerrillas should establish "fixed" bases in the countryside, an issue that will be fully analyzed below.

A similar lack of precision is apparent in the Cuban discussion of the various forms of warfare and the relative importance of each both in the various stages of the war and in the war as a whole. It will be recalled that Mao held that there are three forms of warfare: mobile, positional, and guerrilla. Mobile warfare was the dominant form in the first and third stages, while guerrilla warfare was the primary form of fighting only in the second stage, although it also played an important supplementary role in the other two phases. Positional warfare, he maintained, rose in importance in the final phase, but it was never to achieve primary status. Guevara and Debray speak of "wars of position," mobile warfare, and guerrilla warfare. Guevara refers to the latter as a "phase" in the "initial phases" of the war. He concurs with Mao's views that guerrilla warfare alone will not bring victory to the revolutionaries and that guerrilla forces must be transformed into a regular army:

Thus it is clear that guerrilla warfare is a phase that does not afford in itself opportunities to arrive at complete victory. It is one of the initial phases of warfare and will develop continuously until the guerrilla army in its steady growth acquires the characteristics of a regular army. At that moment it will be ready to deal final blows to the enemy and to achieve victory. Triumph will always be the product of a regular army, even though its origins are in a guerrilla army.[20]

It is apparent that Debray feels that the Chinese and Cuban concepts regarding the establishment of rural bases are, in several basic respects, quite different. Here, as in his analysis of the "Asian" view on armed propaganda, he explicitly warns that "the same dangers of imitation exist in regard to the guerrilla base." In this case, however, he addresses himself to the task of analyzing the Chinese, rather than

[19] Debray, *Revolution in the Revolution?*, p. 32.
[20] Guevara, *Guerrilla Warfare*, p. 20.

the Vietnamese, position. Indicating an awareness of the impact of Chinese thought, he says: "If we refer to recent episodes, such as that in Peru, it is not impossible that the Chinese system of supportive bases, as systematized by Mao Tse-tung in 1938, in *Problems of Strategy in Guerrilla War Against Japan*, has reached Latin Americans and superimposed its image on their conception of the Cuban guerrilla struggle." [21]

In this context he launched into a vitriolic attack on the editors of the *Monthly Review*. What occasioned the assault on Huberman and Sweezy, who have been among the most enthusiastic admirers of Fidel Castro among American intellectuals? Debray takes violent exception to their "presentation of Luis de la Puente's and the MIR's Peruvian experience as the very model of an alleged 'Cuban strategy' of armed struggle, enabling that magazine to predict its definitive failure." [22] Manifesting a deep resentment concerning a false interpretation of the Cuban strategy, he continued his scathing attack on the hapless editors of the *Monthly Review:*

In a recent issue of this "progressive" North American publication—we do not know whether such persevering naivete, bordering on the fine art of misinformation, is more sinister or ridiculous—one reads, from the pen of Huberman and Sweezy, that Fidel Castro's strategy "called for the establishment of a guerrilla-controlled 'security zone' in the mountains which would become the focus of revolutionary attraction and development, leading eventually, as in Cuba, to a full-scale war against the Peruvian armed forces." And, they add, "De la Puente's main addition was that because of Peru's greater size there should be not one or two but half a dozen or more guerrilla zones." It follows that this alleged "Cuban strategy" would make the establishment of a security zone the point of departure and the first objective of the guerrilla group. [23]

Huberman and Sweezy had not, in Debray's opinion, discharged their responsibility as serious students of revolutionary movements. "Simple honesty" would have required that they conduct "some sort of investigation among members of the Rebel Army concerning the real nature of the Cuban guerrilla movement." He also charges them with having failed to consult original sources before speaking of

[21] Debray, *Revolution in the Revolution?*, p. 59.
[22] *Ibid.*   [23] *Ibid.*, pp. 59–60.

"Cuban strategy." Such an intellectual, in effect, confuses "the very public he ought to be enlightening," and contributes "to the advantage of existing forces of repression." [24] Obviously, then, Debray, as the "spokesman" for Castro and Guevara, is most anxious to set the record straight! One may well ask: Does his outburst against Sweezy and Huberman reflect a smoldering deep resentment among the Cuban leadership because they feel that the Cubans have not been given due credit for having developed a new theory of people's war? Furthermore, didn't Debray single out the editors of the *Monthly Review* as a symbol of those who have failed to grasp the true nature of the Cuban revolution and thus extend to the Cubans the respect to which they feel they are entitled because of their "creative" development of a theory of guerrilla warfare peculiarly suited to conditions in Latin America? The viciousness of the attack would suggest that Huberman and Sweezy were not the only ones "guilty" in this regard. In short, the discussion on this point is only one part of a systematic study of people's war designed to prove that the Cuban road is the only one worthy of study and emulation by Latin American revolutionaries, Communists, and non-Communists alike.

According to Mao, no peasant war of the "roving rebel" type has ever succeeded, and yet, he says, there are always those who advocate the idea that base areas are neither necessary nor important. He holds, as is well known, that guerrilla warfare cannot last long or develop without such base areas; and as indicated above, he also makes a distinction between guerrilla zones and base areas, the latter being areas the central parts of which are controlled by the guerrillas, while the former are those "areas which are held by the guerrillas when they are there and by the puppet regime when they are gone." [25] In his presentation of the Cuban case, Debray makes no such distinction. Guerrillas, Mao contends, should make every effort to transform the guerrilla zones into guerrilla base areas, and he warns that poor leadership of the guerrillas or strong pressure from the enemy can effect the antithesis of this goal.

Using the base areas as a point of departure, the guerrilla units must

[24] *Ibid.,* p. 61.
[25] Mao, "Problems of Strategy in Guerrilla War Against Japan," *Selected Works,* II, 96.

expand these areas and thus reduce gradually the territory under the enemy's control. That is, they must strive to convert guerrilla "zones," adjacent to base areas, into "base areas," but Mao adds that they must, as a condition for *expansion, consolidate* existing bases. He explains:

If we attend only to expansion and forget about consolidation in our guerrilla warfare, we shall be unable to withstand the enemy's attacks, and consequently not only forfeit the possibility of expansion but also endanger the very existence of the base areas. The correct principle is expansion with consolidation, which is a good method and allows us to take the offensive or the defensive as we choose.[26]

In summary, he does not advocate the establishment of new bases until existing ones have been thoroughly "secured."

Since Debray has, in my opinion, misstated in some instances and omitted in other cases some conditions required for successful application of the Chinese experience, it might be well to comment on, in the order listed by Mao, the conditions postulated by him for the establishment of base areas. First, and most important, is the building up of an armed force. "The building up of an armed force is the key to establishing a base area; if there is no armed force or if the armed force is weak, nothing can be done." [27] Second, the enemy forces in the area must be defeated. "All places under enemy control are enemy, and not guerrilla, base areas, and obviously cannot be transformed into guerrilla base areas unless the enemy is defeated." [28] Third, the masses must be "aroused," that is, organized into self-defense units and mass organizations so that they can make their contribution to the common struggle. These three conditions he calls the basic conditions.

In addition he also mentions geographical and economic conditions. Under the former heading, he stresses one requirement, "that the area must be extensive." Naturally mountainous regions are best suited for such a purpose because bases there "can hold out for a long time." However, the primary consideration must be that the guerrillas have sufficient area to maneuver; hence, small countries, such as Belgium "have few or no such possibilities." [29] As for the economic condition, he suggests as guidelines the protecting of commerce and

[26] *Ibid.*, p. 101.   [27] *Ibid.*, p. 98.
[28] *Ibid.*   [29] *Ibid.*, p. 99.

the equitable distribution of the financial burden, terms defined in the preceding chapter.

Before considering Debray's critique of the China model, one should note that he defines a guerrilla base, in the Chinese sense, as a "fixed base of support." While it is true that Mao usually uses the two terms synonymously, one should observe that Mao does advocate the establishment of temporary bases for small guerrilla bands operating in the plains. In the second stage of fighting it is possible, when the enemy launches mopping up campaigns, to shift most of the guerrillas to the mountains and leave behind small bands, which create "base areas which are *not fixed*." [30]

Debray asserts that the Chinese experience "requires a combination of favorable conditions." [31] One is struck by the fact that he does not include any of the three "basic conditions" listed by Mao! Thus he has not indicated to the reader the fact that Mao (1) understands the absolute necessity for forming a strong armed force; (2) grasps the need for *defeating* the enemy forces in the area concerned; and (3) stresses the urgency for "mobilizing" the masses. The original Chinese model does, as Debray states, require "an extensive territory, which has as its corollary a lack of communications in the hinterland. . . ," [32] and it does require "a high density of rural population." Frequently Mao describes the guerrillas as "fishes" in the "water" which symbolizes the masses. Debray is certainly correct when he stresses the fact that Peru, where the guerrillas, he implies, followed the China road, has only nine persons per square kilometer. Next, Debray asserts that the Chinese road is relevant only where there are common borders with a friendly power. His point is well taken that the Vietnamese profited, during the war against the French, by the existence of a common border with China, but he neglects to point out that the Chinese Communists, during the Japanese war, received very little material aid from the Soviet Union. Furthermore, he does not, in all fairness to the Chinese, take account of the stress they have paid in recent years to the virtue of self-reliance.

30 *Ibid.,* p. 95. Emphasis added.
31 Debray, *Revolution in the Revolution?*, p. 61.
32 *Ibid.* Recent Chinese writings have revised the Chinese position on this point. Ralph L. Powell, "Maoist Military Doctrines," *Asian Survey*, April, 1968, p. 251.

The Chinese model also implies "the absence of airborne enemy troops." Debray's critique in this regard reflects a keen awareness on his part of the impact of technological change on guerrilla warfare:

These [the airborne enemy troops] constitute the counter-insurgent shock forces in almost all Latin American countries and they practice the most modern methods of repression, including encirclement by infantry combined with simultaneous landings of airborne troops in the center of the besieged zone, and small mobile pursuit units in radio contact with the rearguard, making it possible to locate and promptly communicate the position of the guerrilla fighters.[33]

Debray's final point regarding the Chinese model is especially significant. It involves "the numerical insufficiency of the enemy forces." In his appraisal of Japanese strength, Mao often emphasized the disparity between the size of the Japanese army in China and the virtually inexhaustible population resources of his country. In the same context, Debray brings out the fact that the Chinese Communists had a Red Army as early as 1927, and that they developed the regular army from 40,000 in 1937 to one million in 1945. When the Japanese launched their invasion of China in 1937, the Chinese Communists had something which Latin American revolutionaries, who might want to follow the Chinese example, do not have: "duly constituted regular units." [34]

He concludes that virtually none of the conditions indicated by him as prerequisites for a successful application of the Chinese theory regarding bases is present. The inference he wishes the reader to make is quite obvious: the Chinese model is totally irrelevant for Latin American revolutionaries. As an alternative model, he presents the latter with a "true" account of the revolutionary experience of the Cubans and Latin Americans and their theory based upon that experience.

During the first stage of the development of a guerrilla movement, Debray insists, the guerrillas should live a nomadic existence. Establishing fixed bases *at this time*, when the guerrillas are still numerically inferior to the enemy and rather poorly trained and equipped is, in Debray's opinion, not only unnecessary—it is extremely dangerous.

[33] *Ibid.* [34] *Ibid.*, p. 62.

Why? Such action would, he maintains, deprive the guerrillas of their best weapon, mobility. Furthermore, it would allow the enemy to contain them within a certain zone of operations, where it could use its most effective weapons against the revolutionaries. He warns revolutionaries not to assume that they can find spots that are absolutely invulnerable, pointing out that, if the guerrillas have been able to reach a point, so can the enemy. As a guiding principle he recommends that revolutionaries follow the rule of conduct followed by the Cubans: that is, they must always assume that the enemy knows precisely where they are and is ready to attack them.

His insight into the precarious position of guerrillas in Latin America is most impressive, and one might add, rather prophetic when examined in light of what happened in 1967 to the guerrillas in Bolivia under the leadership of Che Guevara. In the passage below, he also points up the conflicting objectives of the guerrillas and the "forces of repression" in this the most crucial phase in the evolution of a guerrilla movement.

As with infants in poor countries, the mortality rate is very high during the first months, decreasing with each passing month thereafter. To wage a short war, to destroy the *foco* in its embryonic stage, without giving it time to adapt itself to terrain or link itself closely with the local population or acquire a minimum of experience, is thus the golden rule of counter-insurgency. When a Yankee military adviser dreams, we are willing to bet that he sees his airborne troops dropping from the sky into the midst of a newly established guerrilla encampment. The dream, fortunately, is unrealizable, at least in this form. In every case, it is always a race against the clock between the experienced forces of repression and guerrilla forces: the guerrilla to gain time and the army not to lose a moment, the former to learn and the latter not to allow time for learning. The *foco* must be located as soon as possible; all methods are good ones, from silent infiltration to noisy mobilization of the infantry and air force so as to disturb and alarm a suspect zone, thus forcing the panic-stricken *guerrilleros* to move to more exposed territory.[35]

In October, 1957, Che Guevara attempted to establish the first base of the Rebel Army in the Hombrito Valley. He brought in a mimeograph machine, on which he began publishing *El Cubano Libre*. In

[35] *Ibid.*

the "permanent encampment" which he established, he also built a shoe repair shop, a hospital, and a bread oven. Although he planned carefully for the defense of the base, he and his men (sixty) were unable to defend it and had to withdraw into the interior. Had Fidel Castro's column not been in the same vicinity, "the results might have been disastrous." Summing up, Debray comments that the idea "was correct, but premature." [36]

It was not until April, 1958, that the guerrillas succeeded in establishing a firm base in the Sierra Maestra. Prior to that time, "the zone of operations was the only guerrilla base," [37] or as Fidel Castro said, the guerrilla base, during this stage, is "the territory within which the guerrilla happens to be moving; it goes where he goes. In the initial stage the base of support is in the guerrilla fighter's knapsack." [38] The characteristic "Castroite" lack of precision in conceptualization is readily apparent in these statements. Debray and Fidel Castro, it seems, have failed to distinguish between concepts that the Chinese would label guerrilla bases and guerrilla zones. Apparently they are speaking about guerrilla zones, not guerrilla bases. It seems to me that this lack of precision, in turn, has led to an erroneous assumption by the Cubans regarding the Chinese position on this matter. They assume that the Chinese model dictates the establishment, first of all, of a guerrilla base, which they clearly conceive of as a fixed camp. It seems, however, that the Chinese, when they first moved into a given area, established not a base, but rather they, like the Cubans, began guerrilla operations in a guerrilla zone. Only after a strong force had been built up in the area, the enemy had been defeated, and the masses mobilized could the area be regarded as a base area in the Maoist sense.

Debray's description of the procedure followed in Cuba, which he implies, at least, was different from that pursued in China, should also be examined in light of the Chinese concepts of "expansion" and "consolidation."

. . . it was the uninterrupted offensive, carried on beyond its borders, that succeeded in "liberating" a small part of the Sierra Maestra. The columns moved closer and closer to the lowlands, steadily expanding their

[36] *Ibid.*, p. 63.　　　　　　　　　　[37] *Ibid.*, p. 64.
[38] *Ibid.*, p. 65.

forays and preventing, little by little, the penetration of the mountain range by the repressive troops. . . . Thus it appears that the Sierra Maestra base *grew from the outside in, from the periphery toward the center.*[39]

As indicated above, the Maoists hold that "consolidation" must precede, in time, the "expansion" of base areas. That is, an area in the process of being transformed from a guerrilla zone into a guerrilla base must be thoroughly "secured" before beginning operations into adjacent areas. The interior should be made secure before moving into contiguous territory. Debray, on the other hand, is persuaded that the interior becomes secure after the periphery has been cleared of the enemy.

Concluding his analysis, Debray stressed that:

In Cuba, the occupation of a guerrilla base, however decisive it may have been, was not the Number One political and military objective of the rebels. Objective Number One was, apparently, the destruction of the enemy's forces and, above all, the procurement of weapons. Current Guatemalan, Colombian, and Venezuelan experiences appear to confirm the validity of the Cuban experience in this regard. There, the occupation of a fixed base has not been the *sine qua non* for the launching of the first offensive operations of the guerrillas: on the contrary, such a base becomes possible only after a first nomadic stage of slow entrenchment in a particularly favorable zone of operations.[40]

Whether intended or not there is an implication in this passage that the Chinese and their admirers in Latin America assign the highest priority to the establishment of bases, while the Cubans regard the destruction of the enemy as their foremost objective. This distinction will not bear close scrutiny. Mao quite clearly holds that the primary objective of war is the destruction of the enemy. It seems that he regards the establishment of bases, as soon as feasible, as an indispensable means to achieve that end, and I might add that the Cubans, in fact, view them in precisely the same way.

On balance it would appear that Debray is quite correct in maintaining that Latin Americans will experience much more difficulty in establishing bases than did the Chinese. Essentially this is due to the fact that the guerrillas are much weaker, politically and militarily,

[39] *Ibid.*, p. 64. Emphasis added.   [40] *Ibid.*

than were the Chinese in their war against Japan. In particular, they lack an "army" comparable to the Red Army and an actual war against a brutal and oppressive foreign aggressor that would enable them to assure the role of defender of the fatherland against the external enemy. The determination of the United States to prevent other Cubas in the Western Hemisphere and its policy of providing military equipment and/or advisers to those countries threatened by "Communism" is another major factor to be considered carefully by all revolutionaries in Latin America. The assistance rendered the Bolivian authorities in 1967 is an excellent case in point.

Debray expresses deep concern regarding the danger of imitating another type of Asian theory and practice. Obviously he feels that some of the setbacks experienced by guerrillas in Latin America could be attributed to the influence on them of the Asian concept of armed propaganda. In this instance, he explicitly refers to the Vietnamese line on this point and, in the process of distinguishing Latin American from Vietnamese conditions, concedes that the Vietnamese concepts have been validated by international experience. It is most interesting to note that he refers infrequently to the Chinese example in this context, although the Vietnamese, in this area as in so many aspects of people's war, have certainly been influenced more by the Chinese than by any other Communist Party.[41]

Those in Latin America who had been following the Vietnamese model called for the division of the initial *foco* into small teams to engage in "mass work." Their function is to arouse and organize the peasants living in the more remote areas. The underlying idea is that a people's war cannot be waged successfully without popular support. The guerrillas, acting as agitators and propagandists, are to hold meetings in the villages, where they are to explain the goals of the revolution and to indicate to the peasantry how they can accelerate the advent of a better world for themselves. Once peasant backing for the war has been secured, they then may be organized into self-defense units, guerrilla units, and mass organizations. Clearly, then, these guerrillas are not primarily engaged in military action against

[41] The reader need only scan General Giap's book on people's war to appreciate his intellectual indebtedness to Mao Tse-tung. Vo Nguyen Giap, *People's War, People's Army* (New York: Frederick Praeger, 1962).

the enemy. Rather they are attempting to organize the people for various types of resistance to the enemy.

Castro and his associates, speaking through Debray, feel that the extremely limited personnel available to the guerrillas in the initial phase must be used entirely for fighting. Once an area has been secured by guerrilla victories, then some of the guerrillas can be left behind to engage in political work. In short, "armed propaganda *follows* military action but does not precede it." [42]

To account for the success of the Vietnamese, Debray stresses two points, the first being the fact that Vietnam is a country having a heavy concentration of peasants in those areas in which guerrillas operate, enabling them to mingle easily with the people "like fish in water." The enemy, on the other hand, is an alien invader easily detected by the masses. Furthermore, given the numerical inferiority of the enemy, he cannot occupy effectively the entire country. On this point he does bring out that China's situation in the war against the Japanese was the same. Secondly, he notes that "the propagandists are linked with the bases of revolutionary support or with a people's army capable of backing them up or protecting them in their activities." [43] Moreover, they symbolize actual military victories, so they have more than "empty words" to offer peasants when the latter meet in villages to hear their programmatic statements, most of which are directed against the foreign invaders. In short, "Vietnamese armed propaganda has . . . developed within the framework of a war of national liberation, of a real war, being carried out everywhere and in all ways, by an established regular army against a foreign enemy. . . ." [44] Certainly what he says here regarding Vietnam was equally true of the Chinese war against Japan, although he does not, in this instance, explicitly indicate the similarity of Chinese and Vietnamese experience. Again the reader is left wondering whether Debray really understands the impact of Mao's military concepts on the Vietnamese military, even though the latter using those concepts occasionally arrive at a different evaluation from the Chinese in a specific military situation.[45]

[42] Debray, *Revolution in the Revolution?*, p. 56. Emphasis added.
[43] *Ibid.*, p. 50.   [44] *Ibid.*, p. 51.
[45] David Mozingo, "Peking and Hanoi," paper presented to the University Seminar on International Communism, Columbia University, February 15, 1967.

Conditions in Latin America, Debray insists, are so different from those in Vietnam that guerrillas must not look to that country for intellectual guidance. In the first place, Latin American guerrillas usually operate in areas that are sparsely populated; hence, they can hardly mingle easily with the people "like fish in water." Any recent arrival will be spotted instantly by the peasants, who, with considerable historical justification, regard all strangers with deep suspicion. Equally frustrating to guerrillas is the peasants' traditional fear and respect for all those who symbolize the status quo: the army, police, Rangers, and "Green Berets." To overcome the awe of the masses for those actively supporting the old order, the Cubans suggest the destruction of enemy forces by ambush to demonstrate that the enemy is not, in fact, invulnerable. The best propaganda, during the initial period, is military victory over enemy forces in the area. Peasants simply refuse to listen to the "fine words" of "outsiders" until the latter can demonstrate their capacity for destroying the enemy. Debray's obvious preference for military rather than propaganda action in this phase is apparent in the following statement: "During two years of warfare, Fidel did not hold a single political rally in his zone of operations." [46] His position is clearly at odds with that taken by the Chinese, who stressed the urgency of arousing and mobilizing the masses. Lin Piao asserts that the Red Army never failed to execute the three tasks given it by Mao: fighting, mass work, and production.[47]

Debray also emphasizes the fact that the "enemy" the Latin Americans face is quite different from that with which the Vietnamese were confronted. In the first place, the enemy is far more vigilant; hence propagandists have relatively few opportunities for operating without being noticed. Secondly, guerrillas must realize that they "are not dealing with a foreign expeditionary force, with limited manpower, but with a well-established system of local administration." [48] His insight into other difficulties facing revolutionaries is equally perceptive: "They themselves are the foreigners, lacking status, who at

[46] Debray, *Revolution in the Revolution?*, p. 54.

[47] Lin Piao, *Long Live the Victory of People's War!*, p. 29. For a detailed analysis of political work of the Red Army among the peasants, see Chalmers A. Johnson, *Peasant Nationalism and Communist Power: The Emergence of Revolutionary China, 1937–1945* (Stanford, California: Stanford University Press, 1962), pp. 84–91.

[48] Debray, *Revolution in the Revolution?*, p. 52.

the beginning can offer the populace nothing but bloodshed and pain. Furthermore, channels of communications are increasing; airports and landing fields are being built in the most remote areas, heretofore inaccessible by land routes." [49] In the passage above he pinpointed some of the principal problems that confronted the guerrillas in Bolivia. Particularly noteworthy was the fact that the Bolivian Indians failed to respond to their program because so many of the guerrillas were foreigners. Most of the leaders, for example, were Cubans.

Finally, propagandists in Latin America lack the support of organized regular or semi-regular armed forces. Since the limited manpower, under this alleged "Vietnamese" model, would be widely dispersed in an effort to reach as many villages as possible, the relation of forces everywhere would be adverse to them. They would lack the power to strike a telling blow at enemy forces bent on the destruction of small bands of propagandists. Once the enemy, through his vastly improved intelligence network, learns of their presence in a certain locality, the guerrilla-propagandists have little prospect of surviving. It should be noted that those following the Cuban model in Bolivia were destroyed even though they avoided blind emulation of the Vietnamese model.

In summary, Debray does not attack the notion of armed propaganda per se, but he does contend that the revolutionaries in Latin America at present are so weak that they cannot at this time afford to pursue this tactic. In fact, he asserts that their very existence, in the early phase of a guerrilla movement, would be jeopardized by following such a policy. In any event, he asserts, those adopting this concept of struggle have not succeeded in expanding decisively their sphere of influence. [50]

That the Cubans take seriously the impact of Asian ideas on revolutionaries contemplating or engaging in people's war in Latin America can be seen in Debray's adverse reaction to the practice there of referring to the guerrilla force as the armed fist of a liberation front and thereby indicating the subordination of the guerrillas to a patriotic front or a party. "This expression, copied from models elaborated elsewhere—principally in Asia," [51] must not be followed blindly

[49] Ibid. [50] Ibid., p. 54.
[51] Ibid., p. 67.

by Latin American revolutionaries because "it is dangerous to import organizational formulas. . . ."[52] In his analysis of the problem of the party and the guerrillas, the longest section in his book, Debray refers explicitly to the Chinese and the Vietnamese views rather than to those of Marx, Engels, Stalin, or more recent Soviet leaders. Why? The explanation appears to be that he regards the Chinese and Vietnamese revolutions, but not the Soviet revolution, as examples of people's wars. In short, he apparently regards the Soviet model as totally irrelevant to conditions existing in Latin America, whereas he perceives that the other two, simply because they are representative of people's wars, would naturally be attractive to Latin American revolutionaries. He maintains, however, that the Asian models are inapplicable to Latin American reality because there are a number of significant differences in the situations in which Latin American and Asian revolutionaries must labor. On the other hand, he maintains that they may study with profit the experience of those who participated in the Cuban revolution. The message is abundantly clear: aspiring guerrilla leaders must cast their eyes toward Havana, not Peking or Hanoi. Unfortunately, he asserts, those directing guerrilla movements in Latin America have frequently failed to follow the Cuban road, and as a consequence they have experienced a series of demoralizing setbacks. Since most of the Communist Parties in Latin America are pro-Soviet in orientation, he seems to be saying that these revisionist parties (using Chinese jargon) have, in their bungling efforts to direct guerrilla forces, been pursuing policies influenced in large measure by Asian theory and practice! He also attacks the factionalism of the Chinese in Latin America and the attitude and activities of pro-Chinese splinter groups.

Although Debray's remarks are most often related explicitly to Asian concepts, he is, of course, aware of the fact that Castro's stand on relations between guerrillas and the Communist Party is anathema to all Marxist-Leninists. One can well imagine how the venerable Mao would react to the ideas attributed by Debray to Castro! Surely the old man's original anxiety regarding the legitimacy of Castro as a true Marxist-Leninist must have been reinforced by the most recent pronouncements of the young Cuban leader.

[52] *Ibid.*

Mao's view regarding party-army relations is perhaps best expressed in the following quotation: "Our principle is that the Party commands the gun, and the gun must never be allowed to command the Party."[53] That principle, recognized by the CPSU as well as the CCP, had invariably governed, until quite recently, the relations between mountain and city in the Latin American guerrilla movements. In a word, guerrilla commanders operating in the countryside were subordinated to the political leaders in the major cities. When guerrilla leaders "descended" to the city to consult with their superiors, they were often given instructions formulated by "civilians" who knew virtually nothing about conditions in the rural areas where the fighting was going on. At times they were captured and imprisoned or executed by reactionary authorities, who appreciated the fact that they alone constituted any "real and present danger" to the status quo, events that led Castro to say that "The city is a cemetery of revolutionaries and resources."[54] Mao's relations with the Central Committee in the late 1920s and early 1930s were remarkably similar. He and his guerrilla comrades had every reason to complain regarding decisions made by men in Shanghai, who had little understanding of their problems in waging guerrilla warfare.

The city leaders, not understanding the real needs of the guerrilla force, often fail to provide them with what is required for successful operations. The fighters are dependent on the outside world for everything: guns, plans, ammunition, clothing, et cetera. When they fail to receive these items, a deterioration in morale ensues. They lose their sense of self-reliance and tend to develop an inferiority complex. Some guerrilla fronts have had to survive on as little as $200 per year, while the political leaders "spent thousands of dollars on propaganda work at home and abroad, on the support of functionaries, on setting up publications, convening amnesty congresses, etc."[55] Under these circumstances, Debray contends that it would be far better for the guerrillas to renounce completely their reliance on the "politicos" for arms and supplies. Rather they should procure these necessities through staging carefully planned ambushes of enemy columns in the area. As

53 Mao, "Problems of War and Strategy," *Selected Works*, II, 224.
54 Debray, *Revolution in the Revolution?*, p. 69.
55 *Ibid.*, p. 72.

noted above, the primary source of supply for the Chinese Communists' armed forces was the enemy's army. Mao, therefore, would be in perfect agreement with Debray on the point that guerrillas should be as nearly self-reliant as possible.

Debray asserts that the Chinese and Vietnamese applied successfully the traditional formula because conditions were ideally suited for a policy based on such a concept. First, both parties were, from the very beginning, actively involved in pursuit of political power. Both had, in fact, fought long wars to achieve their political objectives. Secondly, "international contradictions" precipitated wars of national liberation in their respective countries and enabled them to assume the highly attractive role of defender of the people against an alien army. That is, they were in a position to exploit the nationalistic aspirations of the masses aroused by the presence of a foreign army. Finally, the circumstances of these wars were such as to cause students and the worker elite to withdraw to the countryside where they merged with the agricultural workers and small farmers. The Red Army (China) and the Vietminh Liberation Forces became peasant armies under the leadership of the party. In practice, they achieved the alliance of the majority class (the peasantry) and the proletariat, thus forming the powerful worker-peasant alliance. In each of these three major respects the development of the Latin American parties varied from that of the Asian parties.[56] Hence, Debray argues, Latin American guerrillas should follow the example set by Fidel Castro and vest supreme power in the guerrilla commanders operating in the "mountains." Assuming for the sake of argument that Debray's description of the development of the other parties is correct, does it follow that military operations should not have been, as in Cuba, placed under the control of guerrilla commanders? In my judgment his distinction between the evolution of the war in the several countries does not support his argument.

The Chinese and Cuban positions concerning united fronts are quite distinct. For example, the Chinese advocated the formation of the Second United Front with the Nationalists at an early stage in the anti-Japanese war; the Cubans resist the formation of fronts until the guerrilla forces have built up their strength to the point that they can protect themselves against possible acts of treachery on the part

[56] *Ibid.*, p. 101.

of allies in the coalition. In terms of classes, the Chinese formulated a policy calculated to appeal to the peasants, workers, petty bourgeoisie—the so-called "4-class alliance." Debray explicitly condemned this concept and the Soviet concept of national democracy.[57] In keeping with the usual Castroite distaste for ideological niceties, he offers no detailed analysis of Latin American society, but elsewhere he indicates that entire political lines should not be based "on existing contradictions between enemy classes or between groups with differing interests within the same bourgeois social class."[58] Since 1960 the Cubans have rejected the "national bourgeoisie," a group which the Chinese include among the people,[59] although, in practice, they have tended to regard this group with distrust. Prior to his advent to power in January, 1959, Fidel Castro had welcomed the support of the middle class, but now he and his associates clearly rule out any possibility for forming an alliance that would include them. These differences notwithstanding, Castro and Mao are agreed that the line best calculated to hold together a front is one which emphasizes the anti-imperialist theme rather than themes revolving around domestic reform. These two men, so different in many ways, appreciate the fact that more people rally more readily to the flag than to the banner of social reform.

Castro's position on the role of the Communist Party within the united front is the antithesis of that of Mao as well as all other orthodox Marxist-Leninists. For many years the Chinese have held that the party must lead the revolution from its inception. A revolution of the new democratic variety, in their view, would be inconceivable without a Communist party to guide it from the very beginning.

Castro asserts that every revolution must have a vanguard, but he departs from Marxist-Leninist orthodoxy when he asserts that that vanguard need not necessarily be the Communist Party. For several years he and the leaders of most Latin American Communist parties have disagreed regarding the correct road to power. While the Communist leaders render lip service to the heroic example of the Cuban Revolution, most, in practice, have definitely preferred the peaceful path to power suggested by the CPSU. In a later chapter, Castro's relations with those leaders and with pro-Chinese groups will

[57] *Ibid.*, p. 87. [58] *Ibid.*, p. 103.
[59] Draper, *Castroism*, p. 87.

be analyzed in detail. At this point, suffice it to say that Castro and the Chinese agree that armed struggle is the only viable path to power in virtually all countries of the Third World, but they are not in accord in regard to what role the Communist Party is to play in these revolutions.[60]

The two parties differ also concerning *when* and under what circumstances the Communist party will be formed. As indicated above, the Chinese position is that the party's formation shall precede the eruption of the revolution. The Cuban stand, as expressed by Debray, is less lucid. A Marxist-Leninist party, in a literal sense, need not exist at the beginning or, for that matter, during the revolutionary process itself. The guerrilla *foco* constitutes the core of the people's army, which in turn is the party *en nuce*. Dialectically speaking, the guerrilla *foco*, essentially a military body, is transformed into a political body, the Communist Party. The latter appears as a distinct entity after the triumph of the revolution. In the case of the Cuban Revolution it would be more accurate to say that a new Communist party appeared after Castro's advent to power. The old party, the Popular Socialist Party, did not support the Castro revolution until shortly before the downfall of Batista.

During the Cuban Revolution, Debray maintains, an institutional differentiation between military and political functions did not exist. The same small group of men, led by Fidel Castro, were, at one and the same time, the supreme political and military leaders of the movement. The Cubans did not use, as did the Chinese, a system of political commissars in the armed forces. In Cuba, Fidel Castro was the politico-military commander of the Rebel Army, whereas in China, Debray contends, the distinction between the political and the military functions was symbolized by Mao and Chu Teh.[61] Debray characterizes the Cuban approach as a "decisive contribution to international revolutionary experience and to Marxism-Leninism." [62] In the passage below the reader can discern what appears to be an application of the dialectical idea that opposites coexist and struggle until one is trans-

[60] For a succinct analysis of the relations between Castro and Latin American Communist leaders see the excellent article by Kevin Devlin, "Castro and the Communists," Radio Free Europe, research paper.

[61] Debray, *Revolution in the Revolution?*, pp. 96–98.

[62] *Ibid.*, p. 106.

formed into its opposite (the law of the unity and struggle of opposites): "Under certain conditions, the political and military are not separate, but form one organic whole consisting of the people's army, whose nucleus is the guerrilla army. The vanguard party can exist in the form of the guerrilla *foco* itself. The guerrilla force is the party in embryo." [63]

This is indeed a "staggering novelty" that the Cubans have introduced! The Communist Party instead of creating the Rebel Army as required by the orthodox line is, in fact, created by the Army, the nucleus of which is the original guerrilla *foco*. This is not to say that the Cubans are oblivious to the significance of political considerations. To the contrary, for the military force to develop, on the military level, it must become a political vanguard. On this point Debray says: "Precisely because it is a mass struggle—the most radical of all—the guerrilla movement, if it is to triumph militarily, must politically assemble around it the majority of the exploited classes. Victory is impossible without their active and organized participation, since it is the general strike or generalized urban insurrection that will give the coup de grâce to the regime and will defeat its final maneuvers—a last-minute coup d'état, a new junta, elections—by extending the struggle throughout the country." [64]

Before the guerrillas can set the large motor (the masses) in motion, they must be recognized by the masses as the sole authority in the area concerned. They must, therefore, assume exclusive political and military authority in the guerrilla areas. He rationalizes the legitimacy of their action on the ground that the guerrillas personify the worker-peasant alliance, a concept analogous to that offered by Lenin that the Communist Party symbolized the will of the proletariat. Apparently sensing the need for explaining how "bourgeois" intellectuals, operating in the mountains as guerrillas, could symbolize the basic "worker-peasant alliance," Debray attempts to resolve this problem by postulating a transformation of the intellectuals in the course of guerrilla warfare. In effect, they must commit suicide as a class in order to be restored to life as "revolutionary workers, totally identified with the deepest aspirations of their people." [65]

[63] *Ibid.*
[64] *Ibid.*, p. 108.
[65] *Ibid.*, p. 112.

In conclusion, one may say that the Cubans seem to be doing to the Chinese pretty much the same thing that the Chinese did earlier to the Russians. The Cubans, while acknowledging the historical significance of the Chinese revolution in the international Communist movement, insist that Chinese experience is, for the most part, irrelevant for Latin America because conditions in China and those in Latin America have so little in common. Furthermore, Sino-Cuban relations, like Sino-Soviet relations, seem to be characterized by a struggle between the Cubans and the Chinese regarding which of the two shall be regarded by Latin American revolutionaries as the ideological and political leader of the area. It is not suggested that Sino-Cuban relations have deteriorated to the same extent as Sino-Soviet relations, but it is not inconceivable, given the personal vanity of Mao and Castro, that we may be witnessing the opening round in a contest between the two. It is doubtful that their relations will ever be characterized by the violent polemics of the other dispute because: (1) the Chinese and the Cubans do have far more in common than do the Soviets and the Chinese, and (2) the stakes involved in this case are not such that the Chinese would want to precipitate a bitter fight with the Cubans. That Chinese-Cuban relations are not as cordial as one might expect may be seen in the fact that the Chinese press carried no comment on the death of Che Guevara in 1967 or the activities of the guerrillas in Bolivia. Chinese silence regarding such major events in the world revolutionary movement suggests that all is not well in the ranks of the most militant members of the international Communist movement. Clearly Sino-Cuban relations were hardly as cordial as they had been in the early 1960s. Let us now consider the initial reaction of the Chinese Communists to the Fidelista triumph in Cuba.

V

Sino-Cuban Relations

THE victory in January, 1959, of Fidel Castro and his July 26 Movement over the discredited Batista regime elicited a prompt and enthusiastic response from the leaders of the Chinese Communist Party. The Chinese, who had been following closely the course of events in Cuba, seemed to perceive almost instantly in the charismatic young Cuban leader the potential for becoming their chief ally in the Latin American revolutionary movement. That he was not a professed "Marxist-Leninist" at the time of his advent to power did not appear to be a major source of concern for the strategists of the CPR. The policy adopted by them in regard to the "historical significance" of the Cuban Revolution reflected more flexibility on their part than China specialists often attribute to them. It is contended that the Chinese here, as elsewhere in the Third World, made revisions in their ideological framework in order to promote their national interests in Latin America.

Their major objective in Latin America, it seems to me, is to bring about revolutions in the area that will undermine the power and influence of the United States in its own backyard. The underlying assumption is that the United States cannot maintain its position as the leader of the imperialist camp if deprived of the surplus profits accruing to the American monopoly capitalists who allegedly dominate through their investments the economies of the Latin American countries. Once the American capitalists lose this major source of super profits, they will no longer have the capital needed for appeasing their own workers. In time, then, the contradictions between the proletariat and the bourgeoisie would become so intense that revolutions would erupt, as Marx had predicted, in the mature capitalist countries. The result would be the establishment of "dictatorships of the proletariat" in the United States and Western Europe, the citadel of world capitalism. In short, imperialism would be vanquished once and for all. The Chinese regard the revisionists in the Communist movement as standing between them and the attainment of this their maximal goal, the victory of world Communism. It was for that reason that they were to subject Castro to such intense pressure in the mid-1960s to align himself with the true Marxist-Leninists, led by the CCP, against the traitors in the socialist camp, led by the CPSU.

The Chinese came to regard Fidel Castro as the man best suited to help them implement their strategy for Latin America, although he was not to declare himself a "Marxist-Leninist" for some time. For reasons that I shall disclose below, I am convinced that the Chinese did not think of him as a "Communist" at least until the end of the first stage of the Cuban Revolution. Their attitude toward him was in sharp contrast with their attitude regarding bourgeois nationalist leaders in some Asian and African countries. As Donald Zagoria points out, the Chinese felt that leadership of the national democratic revolution could not be entrusted to them, for they could not be depended on to accomplish fully all the tasks of that revolution. Wang Chia-hsiang, a secretary of the CCP, expressed in *Hung Ch'i* the distrust of the Chinese for such leaders:

The bourgeoisie which is in power in these countries has played to a certain degree a historically progressive role. . . . It may to a greater or lesser degree go part of the way in *opposing imperialism and feudalism.* . . . But after all the bourgeoisie is the bourgeoisie. When in power, it does not follow resolute, revolutionary lines; it *oscillates* and *compromises.* Therefore it is out of the question for these countries to pass to socialism, *nor is it possible for them to accomplish the tasks of the national-democratic revolution.* What is more, even the national independence they have achieved will not be secure . . . there may emerge bureaucrat-capitalism, which gangs up with imperialism and feudalism. . . . Thus, *in the final analysis, they cannot escape the control and clutches of imperialism.*[1]

The evidence available suggests that the Chinese trusted Castro to carry the revolution forward. In the case of Cuba, then, they indicated a willingness to allow a non-Communist nationalist leader to perform the "national" and "democratic" tasks of the revolution. To realize fully the significance of their position vis-à-vis Castro's leading the revolution through the extremely crucial first stage of the revolutionary process, one must recall that Mao Tse-tung had held in the case of the Chinese Revolution itself that the first stage, the new democratic one, must be under the leadership of the proletariat: "the Chinese democratic republic which we desire to establish now must be a democratic republic under the joint dictatorship of all anti-imperialist and anti-feudal people *led by the proletariat.*"[2] In view of this longstanding insistence by the Chinese on the leadership of the first stage by the proletariat (the Communist Party), why did they make an exception in Castro's case?

Apparently they believed, on the basis of their observation of the strategy used by him in attaining state power, that his road to power was, in many ways, similar to their own. They were undoubtedly impressed by his alleged reliance on the peasantry as the main force of the revolution. Equally impressive to them was the fact that he gained state power via the path of armed struggle. Furthermore, he and his comrades established bases in the countryside, engaged the enemy in guerrilla warfare there, and finally encircled the cities from these bases in the countryside. Once in power, he assumed a militantly "anti-imperialist" posture in regard to the United States, clashing on many occasions with the "number 1 enemy of mankind," U.S. imperialism. Moreover, his domestic reforms such as land reform and nationalization of U.S. properties in Cuba and later those of wealthy Cubans as well must have persuaded the Chinese that he was committed to the implementation of the democratic tasks of the revolution. In the

---

[1] *Ten Glorious Years, 1949-1959* (Peking: Foreign Languages Press, 1960) as quoted in Donald S. Zagoria, *The Sino-Soviet Conflict 1956-1961* (Princeton, New Jersey: Princeton University Press, 1962), p. 258. Emphasis added.

[2] Mao, "On New Democracy," *Selected Works*, II, 350. Emphasis added.

realm of foreign policy, he established political and economic ties with the socialist bloc after a series of incidents led to a rupture of diplomatic and commercial relations with the United States. These and similar acts by the Cuban revolutionaries persuaded the Chinese that the Cuban Revolution was developing in the direction of a socialist revolution, the second stage in the revolutionary process, and hence could be held up by them as a model to be emulated by revolutionaries throughout Latin America.

In the meantime, the accomplishments of the Cuban Revolution attracted the attention of the CPSU and fraternal parties in East Europe. In fact, Cuba was one of the countries that inspired the concept of a national democratic state, defined in the Moscow Declaration of 1960 as a state which

. . . consistently upholds its political and economic independence, fights against imperialism and its military blocs, and against military bases on its territory; a state which fights against the new forms of colonialism and the penetration of imperialist capital; a state which rejects dictatorial and despotic forms of government; a state in which the people are assured broad democratic rights and freedoms (freedom of speech, press, assembly, demonstrations, establishment of political parties and public organizations), the opportunity to work for the enactment of agrarian reform and the realization of other democratic and social changes and for participation in shaping government policy.[3]

Soviet and East European theoreticians thought of this new state form in the underdeveloped world as a transitional one that was more progressive in nature than the bourgeois democratic one but less progressive than a socialist state. In their view, the leaders of the national democratic state would perform the national and democratic tasks in the first stage of the revolutionary process and thus lay the foundation required for making the transition to the second stage, the socialist stage, which, in their dialectical conception of history, was a higher state form.

It should be noted that these theoreticians did not insist on an explicit acknowledgment, in the Moscow Declaration of 1960, of the leadership of the proletariat (the Communist Party). By implication,

[3] *Moscow Declaration of 1960* as cited in *Fundamentals of Marxism-Leninism* (2d ed. rev.; Moscow: Foreign Languages Publishing House, 1963), pp. 421–22.

then, they were willing to allow the bourgeois nationalist leaders, such as Nasser and Nehru, to play the leading role in the first stage of the revolution. In short, they seemed to feel that such leaders, although they vacillated at times between progressive and reactionary domestic and foreign policies, were still sufficiently revolutionary in orientation to be entrusted with accomplishing the national and democratic tasks of the first stage of the revolution.

In more concrete terms, the Soviets expected such leaders to assume at least a benevolent neutrality with regard to the East-West conflict. They did not insist that nationalist leaders adhere to military pacts with the socialist bloc against the West, but they did expect that such leaders refuse to associate themselves with the West in military agreements. Aid from the Soviet Union, but not from the imperialists, was to be encouraged. Domestically, the nationalist leaders should allow the local Communist party to participate freely in the political process. Land reform, nationalization of foreign-owned holdings, and the establishment of a planned economy should be adopted. As between the nationalist (anti-imperialist) aspects and the democratic aspects of the revolution, higher priority was assigned to the former than to the latter, at least in the early phases of the revolution, because it would be easier to rally the various classes supporting the revolution against a foreign foe than to enlist their support in behalf of more controversial measures such as land reform or the adoption of a planned economy.

In its initial reaction to Castro's victory, *Jen-min Jih-pao*, in an editorial on January 4, 1959, spoke of the "national, democratic movement of the Cuban people." The title of the editorial, "Defeat of U.S. Imperialism in Cuba," provides the reader with valuable insight into the Chinese appraisal of the revolution. In this and countless later articles dealing with the Cuban Revolution, the official organ of the Central Committee of the CCP manifested its preoccupation with the national rather than the democratic aspects of the concept. To demonstrate how Cuba had been exploited by U.S. imperialism, it provided its readers with the following account of the recent history of the country:

Cuba, "the sweetest country in the world," has long been a paradise for U.S. monopoly capitalists. . . . Total U.S. investments in Cuba are more than 1,000 million dollars. The U.S. controls the sugar industry—basis of the Cuban economy—and other economic developments such as power, communications and transport and mining. In the past five years alone, the U.S. took profits amounting to 750 million dollars from Cuba. To ensure and expand this plunder of the Cuban people, the U.S. has in the past decades been putting into the "Presidency of the Cuban Republic," in the service of the interests of U.S. monopoly capital, one traitor after another to the Cuban people.[4]

Batista, the deposed dictator, was alleged to be one of those traitors to the Cuban people. During his many years in office, the Chinese editor contended, he served U.S. capitalism. American investments more than doubled in his tenure in office, resulting in resistance from all strata in Cuban society to his policy of selling out the national interests of the Cubans. Thus "two years ago the *armed struggle led by Castro* won wide support among the Cuban people."[5] Two observations should be made concerning this statement: (1) the fact that the Chinese, from the very beginning, stressed that state power was obtained in Cuba by *armed struggle;* (2) the fact that they explicitly acknowledged that Castro, rather than the Communists in Cuba (the PSP), had *led* the revolution.

P'eng Chen, Vice-Chairman of the National Committee of the Chinese People's Political Consultative Conference and a member of the Political Bureau of the Central Committee of the CCP, in a speech delivered on January 22, 1959, to a rally welcoming ex-President Lazaro Cardenas of Mexico, articulated a theme used so often by the Chinese in their anti-imperialist propaganda. He contended that the Chinese people identified with the peoples of Cuba and Latin America because they too had experienced for many years "imperialist aggression and suppression," and he reminded Latin Americans that the "U.S. imperialists" were still occupying Taiwan. He summed up the Chinese view as follows:

The Chinese people and the Latin American people have common aspirations and interests in the just struggle against imperialist aggression, in their striving for and protection of national independence and the safeguarding of world peace.

[4] *Survey of the China Mainland Press*, No. 1930, p. 26. Hereafter cited as *SCMP*.
[5] *Ibid.*, p. 27. Emphasis added.

This is precisely why the Chinese people regard the struggle of the Latin American people as our own struggle and the victory of the Latin American people as our own victory.

Every achievement by the Latin American people is a matter of rejoicing for the Chinese people and serves as a strong support and inspiration to us.[6]

From the earliest period of the Cuban Revolution, the Chinese hammered away at the theme that imperialism is the common enemy of the Cubans and others in Africa and Latin America. A Peking rally adopted on January 25, 1959, a resolution in support of Cuba and the Congo that was quite representative: "Imperialism is our common enemy. Having suffered from imperialist enslavement for more than a hundred years, the Chinese people fully sympathize with and pledge their support to the people of Cuba in their just struggle in defense of national independence and against U.S. imperialist intervention. . . ."[7]

Since the Chinese regarded the United States as the main enemy of the peoples of Asia, Africa, and Latin America, they held up the Cuban victory over that enemy as "a great inspiration to the national revolutionary movements not only of Latin America, but also of Asia and Africa."[8] Thus it can be seen that they visualized the Cuban Revolution as a part of the global struggle against U.S. imperialism. Liu Chang-sheng, a Vice-President of the All-China Federation of Trade Unions, made that point when he stated that the Cuban revolution "was a major component as well as the forefront of the world's peoples' struggle against the U.S. imperialist policy of war and aggression."[9]

In his appraisal of the significance of the Cuban victory, an NCNA commentator emphasized that Cuba was the first Latin American country in which the people emerged victorious in a protracted armed struggle, and he also noted that Castro and his supporters had waged guerrilla warfare for two years before obtaining state power.[10] His statement, made January 25, 1959, less than a month after Castro's advent to power, reveals how quickly the Chinese sensed the similarity between the Cuban and Chinese roads to power and thus provides us with additional evidence regarding the reasons for their enthusiastic

[6] *SCMP*, No. 1942, p. 32.   [7] *SCMP*, No. 1944, p. 23.
[8] *Ibid.*, p. 21.   [9] *SCMP*, No. 2302, p. 29.
[10] *SCMP*, No. 1944, p. 17.

response to him. The authoritative *Jen-min Jih-pao* in an editorial on March 2, 1960, described the Cuban victory in precisely the same terms. It stated that the Cuban people "won state power only after a bitter and arduous guerrilla war. . . ." [11]

Che Guevara granted an interview in June, 1959, to Chinese reporters in Havana, telling them that the Cuban revolutionaries had been influenced in their war against Batista by Mao's military strategy. He said:

> We all admired Comrade Mao Tse-tung very much. We studied Mao's theory on guerrilla war while we were fighting it. The mimeographed copies of [Mao's works] spread widely among commanders in the front, and were called "the food from China." . . . There were many problems, we discovered, that had already been systematically and scientifically studied and solved by Mao a long time ago. It gave us great help. [12]

No doubt Guevara's acknowledgment of Cuban indebtedness to the Chinese in the field of revolutionary strategy was conveyed to Mao and other policy-makers in Peking. If it were, one has still another explanation for the Chinese effort to persuade Latin American revolutionaries to follow the Cuban road to power.

While in Peking in November, 1960, Guevara made several statements which must have endeared him to the hearts of his Chinese hosts. He affirmed that the Cuban victory had not been achieved "by resorting to the method of the ballot-box, nor by pseudo-democratic parliaments." [13] He added that the experience of the Chinese Revolution was of genuine value to revolutionaries of Latin America because the Chinese, like the Latin Americans, had lived for many years under feudalism and colonialism. He intimated that the Cubans would be examining carefully not only the past experience of the world's largest country but also the current experience with a view to following, in part at least, the Chinese model for building socialism:

> We have also many things to learn from the achievements of the people's communes and all the other social systems adopted by China.
> It may be that one of these methods or something similar will be

[11] *SCMP*, No. 2211, p. 43.
[12] "Land Reform—the Spear-head and Banner of the Cuban Revolution," *Shih-chieh Chih-shih*, June 5, 1959, p. 22.
[13] *SCMP*, No. 2385, p. 35.

adopted by the Americas in pursuing the road of liberation when the first step has been taken—that is, the seizure of power by the workers and peasants.[14]

In another speech in Peking, he stated that the Latin Americans had discovered a new road to power by studying the "great experience of the Chinese people in their twenty-two years of struggle in the backward countryside, which is like the countryside in the Americas." [15] Small wonder that Che took Peking by storm!

To the dialectically oriented Chinese, these statements by Guevara indicated that the Cuban revolutionaries perceived that the main contradiction of the day was the conflict between the oppressed peoples of the Third World and U.S. imperialism. Furthermore, they were satisfied that Cuban practice had validated Cuban theory. In short, they felt that the Cuban leaders' revolutionary pronouncements had been followed by concrete acts that pushed forward the revolution, or to use the terminology of the Moscow Declaration of 1960, the Cuban leaders had demonstrated their willingness and ability to fulfill the national and democratic tasks of the first stage of the revolution. There is evidence to suggest, however, that the Chinese, as well as the Russians, might have thought that Castro and his associates were attempting to move into the second stage, the socialist stage, before completing the tasks of the preceding stage. Perhaps it would be more accurate to say that Soviet and Chinese policy-makers felt that the Cubans had proclaimed prematurely the advent in Cuba of socialism. Involved here is the problem of Chinese and Soviet recognition of the socialist character of the Cuban revolution.

On April 16, 1961, Fidel Castro presented the Soviets and the Chinese with the problem when he proclaimed that his revolution was now a socialist revolution. Economic and military considerations lay behind the announcement. The Cuban economy was in desperate straits, and Castro felt that, given the hostility of the United States toward his regime, he could obtain increased foreign aid only from the socialist bloc. His military needs were even more pressing because the enemies of Castro were, at the very time he spoke, in the process of attacking the island. The Bay of Pigs invasion took place the following day. Under these circumstances, he desperately needed the

[14] *Ibid.*, p. 36.   [15] *SCMP*, No. 2384, p. 27.

military support of the Soviet Union and China. He hoped that the two major Communist powers would feel an obligation to come to the aid of a fraternal socialist country.

To his surprise the Soviets were not at all keen on extending recognition to his regime as a socialist state. They appreciated the economic and military implications of such a step. They realized that once they accepted Cuba as a member of the bloc, it would be incumbent on them to render fraternal assistance to the Cubans to help in the "construction of socialism." The Russians were deterred from recognition even more by the military implications. Taking part in the defense of a socialist Cuba might very well involve them in a nuclear confrontation with the other major world nuclear power, the United States. Finally, there was a serious ideological problem for the Russians. It seemed to them that the young Cuban leader was trying to jump too quickly into the socialist system. As orthodox Marxists, the Russians could not countenance the skipping of stages in the social development of a country aspiring to become a socialist state.[16] Since our primary concern is not with Soviet–Cuban relations, suffice it to say that the Russians did not officially recognize the socialist nature of the Cuban state until April 8, 1963, when *Pravda* in publishing the May Day slogans referred to Cuba as a country "building socialism." [17]

With the Chinese, economic and military factors were of less importance than to the Russians, but they were very much concerned with the ideological aspects of the problem. To them it was absolutely unthinkable that the Cuban Revolution could enter the socialist stage under non-Communist leadership. We have seen that they acknowledged Castro's leadership in the war against Batista, and for some time after he assumed power they made no claim that the PSP was sharing leadership with him. On January 25, 1959, for example, a Peking rally adopted a resolution stating that "the people of Cuba, under Castro's leadership" would win more victories.[18] In a joint statement issued on July 16, 1960, by Chinese and Cuban Trade Union

[16] Kevin Devlin, "Castro's Place in the Communist World," Research paper, Radio Free Europe, September 21, 1967, pp. 3–4.

[17] Andrés Suárez, *Cuba: Castroism and Communism, 1959–1966* (Cambridge, Mass.: M.I.T. Press, 1967), p. 179.

[18] *SCMP*, No. 1944, p. 23.

(138)

representatives, reference was made to "the heroic struggle waged by the workers and people of Cuba under the leadership of Prime Minister Castro." [19] *Red Flag*, however, in its September 1, 1960, issue, spoke of "the patriotic, democratic forces headed by Fidel Castro and the Cuban People's Socialist Party," [20] a formula that was repeated on September 2, 1960, by *Ta-kung Pao*. Obviously, then, the Chinese were having trouble adjusting to the idea that a non-Communist such as Castro could govern without the participation of the PSP during the national democratic stage. When Che Guevara arrived in the fall of 1960 in Peking, he must have dispelled any such notion from their minds, for Vice-Premier Li Hsien-nien omitted any reference to the PSP. Using the slogan employed by the Chinese until their recognition of the socialist nature of the Cuban Revolution, he stated that "the Cuban people, under the leadership of the Cuban revolutionary government *headed by Prime Minister Fidel Castro*" [21] had won numerous victories over U.S. imperialism.

One should not infer from the *Hung Ch'i* and *Ta-kung Pao* articles that the Chinese had lost their enthusiasm for the Cuban revolution. *Jen-min Jih-pao*'s editorial on New Year's Day, 1961, stressed the worldwide historic significance of the victory of the revolution, a victory which allegedly shattered the fatalistic view that the people's revolution could not succeed in the immediate vicinity of U.S. imperialism. The paper reiterated the idea that the Cuban revolution was "a brilliant example for the Latin American peoples and has greatly inspired and advanced the national and democratic revolutionary movement on the entire Latin American continent and in Asian and African countries." [22] The significance attached by the Chinese to winning Cuban goodwill can be seen in the fact that Mao himself received on January 3, 1961, José Llanusa, the visiting mayor of Havana. Furthermore, they praised the Cuban Revolutionary Government "under the correct leadership of Premier Castro" for its achievements. It should be noted that the Chinese listed the accomplishments under the section of the Moscow Declaration of 1960

19 *SCMP*, No. 2301, p. 33.   20 *SCMP*, No. 2332, p. 34.
21 *SCMP*, No. 2383, p. 28. Emphasis added.
22 "Salute to Cuba and Latin America," *Peking Review*, January 6, 1961, p. 25.

dealing with national democratic states. According to the *Jen-min Jih-pao* version of the section all oppressed peoples wanting complete national independence

. . . must carry forward the national, anti-imperialist and democratic revolution to the end; that it is necessary to wage a determined struggle against imperialism and the remnants of feudalism and to unite all the patriotic forces of the nations in a single national-democratic front in order to accomplish the urgent tasks of national rebirth. These national tasks are: the consolidation of political independence, the carrying out of agrarian reforms in the interest of the peasantry, elimination of the survivals of feudalism, the uprooting of imperialist economic domination, the restriction of foreign monopolies and their expulsion from the national economy, the creation and development of a national industry, improvement of the living standard, the democratization of social life, the pursuance of an independent and peaceful foreign policy, and the development of economic and cultural cooperation with the socialist and other friendly countries. The Cuban Revolutionary Government and people . . . have, in the past two years scored outstanding achievements in these respects.[23]

Given the fact that this statement was made in the context of national democratic states, the implication is quite clear that the Chinese so regarded the Cuban regime, although it did not explicitly use the term to describe the "Revolutionary Government."

In their excitement over the Cubans' victory at the Bay of Pigs, the Chinese came very close to accepting Castro's claim that the Cuban revolution had become a socialist revolution. On May 5, 1961, *Red Flag* evaluated the significance of the Cuban revolution, lauding the Cuban people for having waged an unflinching struggle against the "imperialists" and for having adopted a number of social and economic reforms:

In Cuba, land reform has been realized, the large-manorial system abolished, and the entire land occupied forcibly by U.S. monopoly capital requisitioned, as a result of which the broad masses of landless and land-short poor peasants have obtained, and on this foundation built people's farms and agricultural cooperatives. The people of Cuba have confiscated all the U.S. monopoly capitalist enterprises in Cuba,

[23] *Ibid.*

all the large private enterprises and privately-owned banks in Cuba, turned them into state-owned enterprises and begun to make planned economic development.[24]

The acts singled out by the Chinese are obviously quite similar to those which Mao Tse-tung declared would be done in the first stage of the Chinese Revolution. Yu Chao-li, author of the *Red Flag* article, did not explicitly state that the Cubans had made the transition to socialism, but that was clearly implied when he noted that Castro, in his May Day speech, had pointed out ". . . that the history of the Cuban people has *already turned a new leaf*. He stated that the Cuban revolution was a socialist revolution. 'To wipe out exploitation of man by man' is 'the program and thought of socialist revolution' of the Cuban revolutionary government." [25]

Yu neither agreed with nor denied the statement made by Castro, but the fact that Castro's claim was reproduced in the most authoritative theoretical Chinese journal was significant, especially when one adds that Yu defended the right of the Cuban people to choose the social system they wanted for themselves. He continued:

Nobody can deprive them of such rights. The reason why the people of Cuba, having overthrown the dictatorial rule of Batista and liberated themselves from the slavery of U.S. imperialism and big manorial lords of the country, are unceasingly pushing the revolution forward after they have won national independence and democratic rights, is just because they want to live the life they dream of.[26]

Yu quoted, with obvious approval, a statement made by Castro regarding President Kennedy's attitude toward Cuba:

If Mr. Kennedy does not like *socialism*, we can't help it! Neither do we like imperialism and capitalism. If he held that he has a right to reject the *socialist system* existing in a place only 90 nautical miles from the U.S. coast, then similarly we have a right to reject the capitalist system which exists in a place only 90 nautical miles from the Cuban coast.[27]

[24] Yu Chao-li, "The Great Significance of the Victory of the Cuban People's Patriotic Struggle Against U.S. Imperialism," *Red Flag*, May 5, 1961, as cited in *Survey of China Mainland Magazines*, No. 262, p. 4.
[25] *Ibid*. Emphasis added.   [26] *Ibid*., p. 5.
[27] *Ibid*. Emphasis added.

In my judgment, the Chinese failure or reluctance to make at this time an explicit and unmistakable declaration to the effect that the Cuban revolution was a socialist revolution was because they could not openly make such a statement until a bona fide Communist party had assumed absolute leadership over the movement. Their unquestioning acceptance of the dogma that the Communist party is the vanguard of the proletariat and has undivided authority under socialism would not allow them to accept Castro's contention.

One can observe in an article by Chang Yeh the same ambivalence regarding the nature of the Cuban regime. Writing for *Shih-chieh Chih-shih* on May 10, 1961, Chang stressed the *nationalization* on October 14 and 15, 1960, of 382 foreign enterprises in Cuba, hailing the act as the one starting "the second stage" of the Cuban revolution. He asserted that the tasks of the second stage were to consolidate further the revolutionary regime, to strengthen revolutionary unity; to enlarge the revolutionary armed forces and militia and raise their political consciousness and fighting qualities; to promote further land reform; to expel American imperialistic economic influence and to develop the national economy; to continue the nationalization policy; to raise the people's cultural and living standards; to eliminate illiteracy; and to solve gradually the unemployment problem. Although he speaks of the second stage of the Cuban revolution, he does not expressly state that Cuba had become a socialist country.

With the deepening development of the revolution, "the polarization of class forces in Cuban society exacerbates, and the division between revolutionary and counterrevolutionary forces becomes clearer." Chang insisted that the class division did not signify a weakening of the revolutionary force; instead, he said, it was evidence of "the strengthening of the revolutionary force and the consolidation of the revolutionary regime. The Cuban revolutionary government, the revolutionary armed forces, . . . and other state agencies, continuously carry out reorganizations of a progressive nature and make this revolutionary regime represent . . . the proletariat, the peasantry, the petit bourgeoisie and the progressive section of the national bourgeoisie." [28] The "class analysis" of those represented by the "revolu-

[28] Chang Yeh, "Cuba Is Advancing Forward," *Shih-chieh Chih-shih*, May 10, 1961, pp. 9–11.

tionary regime" corresponds to that given by Mao for Chinese society in the first stage, the "new democratic" one, and yet the title of the article ("Cuba Is Advancing Forward") would suggest that the Chinese were satisfied with the accomplishments of the Castro regime.

On September 22, 1961, President Osvaldo Dorticós arrived in Peking, hoping to obtain additional economic assistance and formal recognition of the socialist nature of the Cuban revolution. In both respects, his mission must have been a source of disappointment to him and his associates, who were laboring so diligently in order to persuade the Russians and the Chinese that the Cubans were indeed most serious regarding their claim that they had made the transition to socialism. Liu Shao-ch'i, in his speech at the airport, described Cuba as "the first Latin American country where a thorough national and democratic revolution has been carried out," [29] but he did not make the statement which Dorticós hoped for; he did not say that Cuba had, after completing the national and democratic tasks of the revolution, begun "building socialism" or say that the Cuban revolution was now a "socialist revolution." At a banquet given the following evening in honor of Dorticós, Liu commented on the Cuban social and economic reforms and added that the "Cuban revolutionary cause is advancing step by step" [30] but made no reference to the matter of so much concern to Dorticós.

Dorticós, in his speech at the banquet, began by pointing out the similarities between the revolutions in the two countries:

In the stage of insurrection, the dominant features common to both our countries were the *strategy of guerrilla warfare* and the *participation of the peasants* as a *fundamental force* in the struggle. In the stage of peaceful construction, . . . China has had to overcome serious difficulties and oppose the imperialist enemies who are most cruel. Similarly, the Cuban Revolution, which is being carried out 90 miles from the North American Empire, has to carry on construction while continuing to fight against foreign espionage, sabotage, terrorism, malicious propaganda, landing of arms by air and sea, and even against the invasion of mercenaries financed and organized by the Government of North America.[31]

[29] *SCMP*, No. 2588, p. 33.   [30] *SCMP*, No. 2589, p. 24.
[31] *Ibid.*, p. 26. Emphasis added.

At a Peking rally held on September 25, Dorticós again referred to the guerrilla warfare that the Cubans had waged in the countryside. After winning political power and full national sovereignty, the Cuban people "confronted with the limitations of an under-developed economy, and the lop-sided development of their semi-feudal and capitalist economies" had had to make a choice between the roads of socialist and capitalist development and had chosen the former. In an obvious effort to convince the Chinese that the proper foundation for socialist development had been laid before choosing the "socialist" road, he recounted some of the steps taken:

The Cuban people have recovered their wealth. Today, they have taken hold of not only all the U.S. public utility services, factories and enterprises, but also all the major branches of industry in Cuba, the control of foreign trade, banking and finance; big manors have been abolished; cooperatives and people's farms have emerged in the form of collective farming; illiteracy will be completely wiped out within this year, and the *foundation for socialist development has been laid.*[32]

He also repeated to his Chinese audience Castro's statement of April 16, 1961, in which he had declared "the socialist nature of our revolution," and Dorticós added that Cuban soldiers participating in the battle Playa Girón (Bay of Pigs) had "fought for the socialist revolution of Cuba." He ended his speech by hailing Mao, "the great leader of the Chinese people" and "socialism."

The only comment made in the joint communiqué, issued on October 2, regarding the matter of socialism in Cuba was one stating that the Chinese "noted with pleasure that the heroic Cuban people, under the correct leadership of the Cuban Revolutionary Government headed by Prime Minister Castro, have chosen the road of socialist development. . . ."[33] *Kuang-ming Jih-pao* was somewhat more enthusiastic in its comment on the communiqué, saying that the Chinese people "greatly admire" the Cuban people, who "have chosen the road of socialist development."[34] *Jen-min Jih-pao* reported that "the Chinese people are especially happy to note that . . . the Cuban people . . . have *thoroughly completed the tasks of the national democratic revolution* . . . are dauntlessly and steadily *carrying forward*

[32] *SCMP*, No. 2590, p. 32. Emphasis added.
[33] *SCMP*, No. 2594, p. 27.   [34] *Ibid.*, p. 37.

their revolution *along the path of socialist development* chosen by themselves." [35]

At the farewell banquet on October 2 given by Dorticós, Liu Shao-ch'i emphasized that the Cuban people had a full right to choose their own road freely and nobody could object to the exercise of this right by the Cuban people. For these kind remarks, Dorticós, in his farewell speech at the airport, apparently could not resist the temptation to urge the Chinese to remember the Cubans as a people engaged in "building socialism." He asserted that he and his travelling companions would, on their return to Cuba, tell ". . . our workers, peasants, women and children, intellectuals and students that, on the other side of the warm Antillano Sea, where the sun rises every day, we have a giant and amiable friend who extends to us his generous hand, and is ready to join his effort with ours in the building of a world which is most just and most happy, a *socialist* society." [36] He closed with salutes to socialism and to Chairman Mao Tse-tung, leader and teacher of the great People's Republic of China.

Fidel Castro's television speech of December 1, 1961, declaring that he had always been a Marxist-Leninist and that he would remain one as long as he lived, elicited no comment from the Chinese, but they responded most favorably to his Second Declaration of Havana proclaimed on February 4, 1962. The Soviet leaders, on the other hand, reacted rather coolly to the Declaration. The contrasting reactions of the Soviets and the Chinese stemmed from the fact that the dominant theme of the statement was that the road of armed struggle represented the only viable path to power. Castro's view coincided with that of the Chinese rather than with that of the Russians, who were then advocating, whenever possible, that peaceful means be used in the effort to obtain state power.

Hailing the Second Havana Declaration as a "militant banner of unity of the Latin American Peoples," the Chinese contended that there were only two roads available for the Latin Americans: (1) the anti-imperialist and anti-feudal road advocated by the Cubans, and (2) the path of continued submission to "exploitation" by U.S. imperialism. Arguing that "the burden of U.S. imperialism and the reactionary Latin American *latifundia* weighs like two mountains on

[35] *Ibid.*, p. 39. Emphasis added.   [36] *Ibid.*, p. 35. Emphasis added.

the masses of these countries," the Chinese concurred in the position expressed in the Declaration that the struggle against U.S. imperialism and feudalism was the current militant task confronting the peoples of Latin America. They also supported the Cuban's statement that: "Today, Latin America is under the control of an imperialism more cruel, more powerful and ruthless than the Spanish colonial empire." [37]

The Chinese maintained, as did the Cubans, that the policy of exploitation by U.S. imperialism and its lackeys had generated widespread hostility among many classes and strata vis-à-vis that policy. The time was ripe, therefore, for the formation of a very broad national democratic united front. As the Chinese put it:

> Workers, peasants, intellectuals, petty bourgeoisie and national bourgeoisie—all have had their fill of enslavement, exploitation and oppression by U.S. imperialism and its lackeys. It is therefore not only necessary but also entirely possible for these classes and social strata to line up in the broadest national democratic front against their enemies.[38]

It should be noted that this class analysis did not, on the surface, correspond with that made in the Declaration:

> In the anti-imperialist and anti-feudal struggle, it is possible to unite the vast majority of the people for the goal of liberation which joins the efforts of the working class, the peasantry, the working intellectuals, the petty bourgeoisie and the *more progressive* sections of the *national bourgeoisie*. They constitute the vast majority of the population and cement the great social forces which are capable of sweeping away imperialist domination and feudal reaction.[39]

It is contended that there is no substantial difference between the Cuban and Chinese views as expressed here when one examines the Chinese formula in light of the longstanding attitude of the Chinese regarding the political reliability of the national bourgeoisie as an ally. They have long held that the people can, in the final confrontation with enemies of the people, count on the support of only a portion of this group. In short, only the "more progressive" part of this stratum will associate itself with the people. The following statement, I feel, states authoritatively the real attitude of the Chinese toward this

[37] "Militant Banner of Unity of the Latin American Peoples," *Peking Review,* February 16, 1962, p. 8.

[38] *Ibid.*   [39] *Ibid.* Emphasis added.

group: "As for the vacillating middle bourgeoisie, their right wing may become our enemy and their left wing may become our friend—but we must be constantly on our guard and not let them create confusion within our ranks." [40] When the Chinese used this phrase, they used it in this sense rather than in the literal sense of the term, believing as they do in the dual nature of the group.

It is also contended that the Chinese did not portray the Declaration as a document advocating that emphasis be placed on the formation of the united front, which would rely primarily on peaceful tactics rather than armed struggle. On the contrary, the Chinese maintained that the Cuban and other Latin American peoples had learned "from their protracted and bitter struggles" that their main enemy, "U.S. imperialism," was "utterly ferocious, savage and vicious" and that it was "an international gendarme armed to the teeth," which had "consistently resorted to military repression of the most savage type against the patriotic forces of the Latin American countries." In short, their relations with that enemy had made them realize "ever more clearly that no unrealistic illusions should be entertained about U.S. imperialism and its lackeys." Hence they must resort to "armed struggle." They quoted, with obvious approval, this statement from the Declaration:

In those places where the roads of advance of the people are blocked, where repression of workers and peasants is ruthless and where U.S. imperialist domination is strongest, the first and most important thing is to understand that it is neither just nor right to hold back the people with vain and complacent illusions that it is possible to use legal means, which do not exist at present or in the future, to deprive the ruling classes—which are entrenched in all the state positions, monopolize education, own all the means of propaganda and possess vast financial resources—of their power, a power which the monopolists and oligarchies will defend with fire and sword, with their police and armies.[41]

The Chinese concluded that "it is precisely U.S. imperialism and its lackeys who have taught the people that they must take up arms and wage an armed struggle to smash the sword of U.S. imperialism and the reactionaries of the various countries." [42]

The Chinese statements on the united front and armed struggle

---

[40] Mao, "Analysis of the Classes of Society," *Selected Works*, I, 18.
[41] *Ibid.*, p. 9.   [42] *Ibid.*

should not be read in isolation from one another. Actually the Chinese have long maintained that armed struggle cannot succeed unless accompanied by a united front. That is, they have held that victory on the battlefield cannot be realized without the thorough political mobilization of the masses, a mobilization taking on the organizational form of a united front.

In conclusion, the Chinese took note of the statement that revolution was inevitable in many of the countries of Latin America. Cuba would serve as a "brilliant example" for those taking up arms. None of these countries should think of itself as weak because "each is a part of the family of two hundred million brothers who suffer the same privations, share the same feelings, have the same enemy, aspire to the same beautiful destiny and enjoy the support of all honest men and women of the world." [43]

Fidel Castro's purging on March 26, 1962, of Aníbal Escalante, one of the former leaders of the Popular Socialist Party, on the ground that he had engaged in sectarianism, evoked a message of approval on April 17 from Ch'en Yi, the Chinese Foreign Minister, who added that Castro's struggle against sectarianism designed to promote unity in the revolution was "very helpful to Cuba's *socialist* revolution." [44] Only two days later *Ta-kung Pao*, in an editorial, continued the Chinese campaign to win over the Cuban leader, Fidel Castro, who they sensed quite early, aspired to be recognized as the leader of the revolutionary forces in Latin America. The paper paid tribute to the Cuban people, on the first anniversary of their victory at Giron Beach, for having "greatly encouraged the people of Latin America and other parts of the world in their struggle against U.S. imperialism." [45] Their victory proved that a united people was invincible in a confrontation with the seemingly formidable U.S. imperialism, thereby establishing that the latter was, in fact, a paper tiger. Within the past year the Cuban people had "embarked on the road to socialism." Liu Shao-ch'i and Chou En-lai dispatched a message of greetings to Dorticos and Castro, on the eve of the Cuban Revolutionary Day, stating that the Second Havana Declaration had pointed the correct way for

---

[43] *Ibid.*, p. 10.
[44] *SCMP*, No. 2724, p. 30. Emphasis added.
[45] *SCMP*, No. 2726, p. 29.

Latin Americans in their united struggle for liberation. More significantly, they acclaimed "the Cuban people, under the correct leadership of the Revolutionary Cuban Government headed by Premier Castro," for having gone "a step further to advance the Cuban revolution to a new stage and confidently *moving along the road to socialism*." [46] On the same day (July 25), *Ta-kung Pao* carried another article on the Cuban revolution, contending that the development of the Cuban revolution fully proved

. . . the absolute correctness of the principle that in order to achieve complete national liberation an oppressed nation must carry through the national, anti-imperialist, and democratic revolution. The Cuban people and government understand fully that the seizure of power is not the end of the revolution and that the revolution can be consolidated only by steady development.[47]

While the Chinese were lavishing praise on the Cubans and trying at the same time to guide them in their socialist development, the Cubans were finalizing their plans with the Soviets to transport missiles and bombers to Cuba. The abrupt withdrawal of those missiles and bombers, over the protest of Castro, brought Soviet–Cuban relations to their lowest point in many years. Castro felt that he had been betrayed and humiliated by the strongest socialist power in the bloc. Needless to say, the Chinese intensified their efforts to expand their influence over Castro and thus enhance their standing in Latin American revolutionary circles.

Sensing the pride which the Cubans attached to the Sierra Maestra mountains as the birthplace of their revolution, Chang Yeh wrote on December 25, 1962, an article for *Shih-chieh Chih-shih* entitled "Cuba's Sacred Place of Revolution—the Sierra Maestra Mountains." His account of Castro's road to power indicates that he felt that the Cuban and Chinese military strategy was remarkably similar. Although he did not describe the struggle as a people's war, one can detect in his version of the process many of the elements of such a war. He related how Castro had led 82 fighters in the first landing on December 2, 1956, in Cuba. After the initial skirmishes with Batista's troops, only 12 fighters with 7 rifles survived. "This small but strong group raised

---

[46] *SCMP*, No. 2790, pp. 24–25. Emphasis added.
[47] *Ibid.*, p. 30.

high the banner of *armed struggle, relied on and organized peasants to carry on guerrilla warfare* in the Maestra Mountains, *built up a consolidated base,* and put into practice the no. 3 law that *distributed land to the peasants.*" [48] To those who may have been puzzled by the Chinese failure to specify in their comments on the Second Havana Declaration that the Cuban armed struggle had taken the form of guerrilla warfare in the mountains among the peasants, Chang's article clearly indicates that the Chinese clung to that concept of the Cuban revolution.

On the fourth anniversary of the Castroite takeover, *Jen-min Jih-pao* held that the significance of the Cuban revolution lay in the fact that

. . . at the very outset, its leading force headed by Fidel Castro took the correct revolutionary line and in the face of Batista's repression by violence, relied on the masses of the people in waging an armed revolutionary struggle to overthrow the reactionary Batista regime by revolutionary violence and established the people's democratic rule. After thoroughly completing the tasks of the national, democratic revolution, it courageously led the Cuban people on the socialist path and set up the first socialist country on the American continent.[49]

The statement is significant for two reasons: (1) it categorically stated that the Cubans had established a socialist state, and (2) it referred to the state form in the first stage as a people's democratic regime. Apparently the Chinese were so eager to capitalize on Castro's hostility toward the Soviets that they accepted, without any restrictions, the Cuban contention that their state was a socialist one. It will be recalled that Soviet official recognition did not occur for several months.

Chang Yeh, in still another article for *Shih-chieh Chih-shih* on January 10, 1963, acclaimed the Cubans for setting up a "glorious model of revolutionary struggle for people throughout the world." [50] His article is especially valuable in that it provides an authoritative listing of the specific features of the Cuban revolution that indicate

[48] Chang Yeh, "Cuba's Sacred Place of Revolution—the Sierra Maestra Mountains," *Shih-chieh Chih-shih,* December 25, 1962, p. 13. Emphasis added.

[49] *SCMP,* No. 2892, p. 38.

[50] Chang Yeh, "Four Fighting and Victorious Years," *Shih-chieh Chih-shih,* January 10, 1963, p. 4.

the accomplishment of the national democratic revolution. They were:

1. The smashing of the state and military machines of the reactionary regime and the establishment of a people's democratic regime;

2. The fundamental remolding of old Cuba's semicolonial and semifeudal economic structure;

3. The penetrating reform in cultural and educational fields;

4. Great improvement in the Cuban people's living standards;

5. The adoption in foreign policy matters of an independent and peace-loving policy and the establishment of relations with socialist countries.

His useful article also contained a statement concerning the reasons for holding that Cuba should be classified as a socialist country. They were:

1. The Cuban Unity Revolutionary Organization, led by Castro, had proved itself in past years to be a *Marxist-Leninist Party*, and Castro had proved himself to be a *brilliant Marxist-Leninist* revolutionary fighter;

2. After the Cuban revolutionary regime stepped onto the stage of socialism, it became a proletarian dictatorship, i.e. a socialist democratic system;

3. Cuba's socialist revolution eliminates the capitalist ownership of fundamental productive materials and establishes all people and collective ownership. It also carries out socialist reform in agriculture;

4. There is a socialist revolution in the fields of thought and culture;

5. Revolutionary Cuba resolutely opposes the aggression of American imperialism, insists on the principle of proletarian internationalism, supports unity among socialist countries and in the international Communist movement, and supports people's liberation struggles of other countries.[51]

The reader should note the emphasis placed on the Marxist-Leninist character of the Cuban Unity Revolutionary Organization (ORI) and the Marxism-Leninism of Castro. As stated before, Chinese uncertainty regarding these matters was the underlying reason for their delay in declaring their unconditional recognition of the socialist nature of the Cuban revolution.

[51] *Ibid*. Emphasis added.

Liu Ning-i, head of the Sino-Cuban Friendship Association, established on December 29, 1962 under the joint auspices of eighteen Chinese people's organizations, in an address to the newly created Association, referred to the "leadership of *comrade* Fidel Castro" and also asserted that the Cuban people had established the first socialist country in Latin America and the Western Hemisphere. The guiding principles, he said, of Latin Americans had become: "Walking the road of the Cuban revolution" and "Defend the Cuban revolution." [52]

Lo Jung-ch'u, in an article entitled "The Victorious Road of the Cuban Revolution," advanced the proposition that the most important experience to be derived from the rich experience of the Cuban revolution was that it "once again proves the correctness of the Marxist-Leninist road to achieve revolutionary victory through people's armed struggle." [53] He then made a claim which, to my knowledge, had not been made before by the Chinese in regard to the Cuban revolution. He contended that the Cuban victory once again proved that the historical law of people's revolution generalized by Mao was a universal truth. The Russian and Chinese revolutions had followed this principle and now so had the Cuban.

It should also be noted that he quoted Guevara's three fundamental lessons of the Cuban revolution as stated in his book *On Guerrilla Warfare*. Again one detects the abiding interest of the Chinese in the guerrilla war aspect of the Cuban revolution and its relevancy for Latin American revolutionaries. Mei-hung held that Castro's road, "the glorious road of July 26," was the right road for all Latin Americans fighting for their independence, democracy, and socialism. He argued that the guerrilla war led by Castro was essential to revolutionary victory. [54]

Through such pronouncements the Chinese sought to expand their influence with Castro and his supporters in Latin America at a time when Soviet prestige and influence among them was at an extremely

[52] "Address of Liu Ning-i," speech given for the Sino-Cuban Friendship Association on December 30, 1962, as cited in *Hsin-hua Yueh-pao*, No. 220, February, 1963, p. 146. Emphasis added.

[53] Lo Jung-ch'u, "The Victorious Road of the Cuban Revolution," *Hsin-hua Yueh-pao*, No. 220, February, 1963, p. 152.

[54] Mei-hung, "The Glorious Road of July 26," *Shih-chieh Chih-shih*, July 25, 1963, pp. 10–11.

low ebb. In carrying on the campaign against the Soviets, the Chinese inaugurated in March, 1963, the publication of the Spanish language version of *Peking Review* (*Pekin Informe*) and they expanded the network of Hsinhua bureaus in Latin America. On the Communist Party level, they accelerated their factionalist activities within the Latin American Communist parties, and in those parties their followers continued to glorify the Cuban revolution and hold it up as a model for all Latin America.

In the meantime, however, Fidel Castro, the Marxist-Leninist leader in Cuba whom they were trying to win over in the Sino-Soviet conflict was, through economic necessity, moving slowly toward reconciliation with Moscow. On February 8, 1963, the Soviet-Cuban trade agreement for 1963 was published. In an obvious attempt to placate the irate Castro, the Soviets demonstrated their generosity. They granted Cuba another credit "long range, with favorable conditions" for "the imbalance in the trade with Cuba" in 1961 and 1962 and to cover the anticipated imbalance for 1963. Furthermore, they allowed Cuba to withdraw one million tons of sugar from its annual commitment to the Soviet Union and sell it on the open market, thereby realizing a larger profit in dollars. The Soviet government also announced that it had proposed "a change be introduced into the agreement in order to raise the price of the Cuban sugar that was to be bought in 1963." [55] The Chinese, by comparison, could, in the April 26, 1963, agreement, only agree to allow the Cubans to carry over the 1962 trade deficit.[56] Thus the Chinese inability to compete effectively with the Soviets on the economic level undermined the impressive gains made by the Chinese in the months immediately following the missile crisis of 1962.

Recognizing that the Soviet Union represented his only major source of economic and military support, Fidel Castro in April, 1963, accepted the Soviet invitation to visit the Soviet Union. Since he was aware of the deep Chinese animosity toward Khrushchev and Soviet revisionism, he was clearly prepared to risk offending the Chinese by visiting the country which symbolized to the Chinese the betrayal of

---

[55] Suárez, *Cuba: Castroism and Communism, 1959-1966*, pp. 178-79.
[56] Daniel Tretiak, "Mao, Castro and Khrushchev," *Far Eastern Economic Review*, November 7, 1963, p. 299.

the cause of the world revolution. The Chinese manifested their displeasure by reducing their press coverage of events relating to Cuba. They printed the joint Cuban–Soviet statement issued at the conclusion of Castro's negotiations with Khrushchev, but they ignored the speech made by Castro, an address in which he described Khrushchev as an "extraordinarily human person," "a very simple man," and "one of the most luminous intelligences I've ever met." [57] Obviously, Castro was most exuberant concerning the outcome of the negotiations in Moscow. No doubt the Chinese suspected that he had used their endorsement of him as the model for Latin America to gain more leverage in his bargaining with the Russians.

Since Castro could exploit Soviet anxiety regarding the possibility that he might side more openly with the Chinese, he was not totally at the mercy of the Soviets, even though he desperately needed their assistance. On balance, the young Cuban leader emerged with an agreement eminently satisfactory to him. In the communiqué of May 23, the Cubans accepted the Soviet interpretation of the missile crisis and peaceful co-existence, but they did not agree to condemn the Albanians. They also expressed their indebtedness to the Soviets for continued economic support. For their part, the Soviets described the Second Havana Declaration as having "historic significance for the national liberation struggles of the peoples of Latin America," a position that suffered by comparison with the ringing endorsement of the Declaration by the Chinese. At the Soviets' insistence, the communiqué provided in effect that the revolutionary vanguard in each country must decide for itself whether it wanted to emulate Castro's path of armed struggle or to pursue the peaceful path to power advocated by the Soviets. Again one can see that the Russians exhibited less willingness than did the Chinese to hold up the Cuban revolution as a model for Latin Americans. [58]

To avoid excessive dependence on the Soviets, Castro demonstrated, in word and deed, that he wanted to retain his ties with the Chinese. His refusal to ratify the test ban treaty was, no doubt, calculated to appease the Chinese, who, as we have seen, were angered and disappointed by his recent dealings with the "treacherous" Russians. In his

[57] Suárez, *Cuba: Castroism and Communism, 1959–1966*, pp. 182–83.
[58] Devlin, "Castro's Place in the Communist World," Research Paper, p. 6.

speech of July 26, 1963, on the tenth anniversary of the storming of the Moncada Barracks, a meeting attended by two large Chinese delegations, he stressed the primacy of armed struggle in Latin America. The speech must have had a salutary effect on Sino-Cuban relations. Raúl Castro, Fidel's brother, and Che Guevara expressed "solidarity" with the Chinese by attending a meeting in Havana in celebration of the 36th anniversary of the creation of the Chinese People's Liberation Army. Portraits of Mao and Castro adorned the stage. Raúl Castro, the Cuban Defense Minister, also sent a message of greeting to Lin Piao.[59] These acts and statements and countless others in the same vein by Cuban leaders indicate that they were intent on pursuing a policy of neutrality in the Sino-Soviet conflict. Che Guevara summed up the Cuban position as follows:

For us, the Sino-Soviet dispute is one of the saddest events. We do not participate in this dispute. We are trying to mediate. But as it (the dispute) is a fact, we inform our peoples about it and it is discussed by the party. Our party's attitude is not to analyze who is in the right and who is not. We have our own position, and as they say in the American movies, any resemblance is purely coincidental.[60]

Guevara published in the September, 1963, issue of *Cuba Socialista* an article entitled "Guerrilla Warfare: A Means" which the Chinese translated for their readers in China and abroad. For Chinese readers the article appeared in *Hsinhua Yueh Pao* in December, 1963; for foreign readers the Chinese disseminated the article in *Peking Review* on January 14, 1964. A close scrutiny of the document will reveal why the Chinese gave it such wide circulation. The writer was amazed when he compared the Chinese concept of people's war, as analyzed in Chapter III, with Guevara's ideas as expressed in this short article. I found little in it to which a Chinese expert in the theory of people's war could have taken violent exception and many ideas that would have met with the approval of even the most doctrinaire exponent of that concept.

Certainly the Chinese subscribed to the underlying idea of the

[59] *SCMP*, No. 3034, pp. 40–41; and No. 3035, p. 24.
[60] *Revolución*, August 2, 1963, as cited in Andrés Suárez, "Castro Between Moscow and Peking," *Problems of Communism*, September–October, 1963, p. 25.

article: guerrilla warfare should be thought of as a means or tactic for seizing state power. In fact the editor of *Peking Review*, in subheads prepared by him rather than by Guevara, entitled one as "A Means for Seizing Power." In so doing, he left absolutely no doubt that the Chinese view guerrilla warfare precisely in that light.

Our mythical Chinese analyst must also have applauded Guevara's handling of one of the criticisms that had been made in Latin America of those advocating guerrilla warfare. These critics charged that the proponents of guerrilla war had forgotten the mass struggle, insinuating, Guevara argued, that mass struggle and guerrilla warfare were opposing forms. Rejecting the insinuation, he maintained:

> Guerrilla warfare is a kind of *people's war*, a kind of mass struggle. To attempt to carry out this form of war without the support of the local population means certain defeat. The guerrillas are the people's armed, fighting *vanguards* operating in a certain area of a certain place. They aim to carry out a series of combat activities for the sole, possible strategic goal—*seizure of state power*. They have the support of the workers and peasant masses of the area in which they operate, or even of the whole territory. *No guerrilla warfare can be conducted without these prerequisites.*[61]

In short, military victory cannot be had without *political mobilization* of the masses. Elsewhere he indicated that those supporting the revolution would be the workers, peasants, revolutionary intellectuals, and some of the petty and national bourgeoisie.

Nor would the Chinese have objected to his statement that most of the fighting would take place in the countryside, where the peasantry constituting the major source of support for the revolution must be won over through the adoption of land reform. The Chinese would also concur that the peasantry as a class is not suited for leadership of the revolution. Guevara argued that ". . . the peasantry is a class which, because of the ignorance in which it has been kept and the isolation in which it lives, requires the revolutionary and political leadership of the working class and the revolutionary intellectuals. Without that it cannot alone launch the struggle and achieve victory." [62]

---

[61] Ernesto Che Guevara, "Guerrilla Warfare: A Means," as cited in *Peking Review*, January 14, 1964, p. 15. Emphasis added.
[62] *Ibid.*

It is contended here that the Chinese probably interpreted this to mean that Guevara was arguing for leadership of the revolution by a Marxist-Leninist party. Why? In the first place, Communists equate "the leadership of the working class" with leadership by the Communist Party. Secondly, Guevara refers in his article to "the leading Marxist-Leninist Party." [63] Third, it would be quite logical for the Chinese to have made this inference in light of the fact that the Cuban leaders had been laboring so hard to convince the members of the bloc that they were bona fide Marxist-Leninists. The Chinese, of course, did not think that Guevara was suggesting that leadership be entrusted to Communist party leaders in Latin America because most of the latter had, by this time, displayed total acceptance of the Soviet line of the peaceful path to power, an idea that was as obnoxious to Guevara as it was to the Chinese. Guevara's insistence that leadership of the revolutionary movement could not be entrusted to the national bourgeoisie was also in accord with Chinese strategy in the Third World.

The Chinese must have looked with favor on Guevara's implicit rejection of the Soviet contention that revolutionaries need not make revolution; they should wait for the socialist revolution because the balance of forces in the world was developing in a way favorable to the cause of revolution. In this context, Guevara quoted from Castro's July 26, 1963, speech:

It is for all revolutionaries, particularly at the present moment, to recognize and to have a good grip on the change that has already taken place in the world balance of forces, and to realize that such a change is to the advantage of the struggle of the people in various countries. *Instead of waiting for the miracle of a social revolution* in Latin America to arise from this change in the balance of forces, the task of all revolutionaries, and the revolutionaries of Latin America in particular, is to make full use of all factors favorable to the revolutionary movement in this balance of forces and *to make revolution.*[64]

In my judgment the Chinese found little to criticize in Guevara's assertion that there was a complete polarization of the various forces in Latin America, "with the exploiters on one extreme and the exploited on the other." [65] The workers, peasants, and revolutionary in-

[63] *Ibid.*, p. 18.　　　　　　　　[64] *Ibid.*, p. 17. Emphasis added.
[65] *Ibid.*, p. 19.

tellectuals could count on the support of some of the petty bourgeoisie: ". . . the mass of the petty bourgeoisie will lean to either
of these sides according to their own interests and the ability of
either side to win them over politically; to be neutral will be an
exception. Such is revolutionary war." [66] The Chinese, as we have
seen, affirm that the people will be supported by some of this group.
Regarding the national bourgeoisie, his views reflected quite well the
true feelings of the Chinese. He argued that a majority of this group
"was in league with U.S. imperialism and want to throw in their lot
with it in every country," and he added that "however revolutionary
the bourgeoisie may appear to be at one time, the alliance with it can
only be a temporary one." [67]

He defended, as do the Chinese, the line that guerrilla warfare was
the correct road on the ground that the enemy would fight to maintain power. That is, the enemy would use the repressive powers of
the state, primarily the army and the police, to avoid sharing power
with the people. Therefore, the people must eliminate this army: "But
to eliminate this army, there must be a *people's army* to oppose it.
This people's army does not come into existence by itself; it must
be armed *by the weapons presented by the enemy*." [68]

Like the Chinese, he argued that the establishment of bases was
indispensable to the waging of guerrilla warfare, constituting "the
basic factor for the continuous growth of the guerrillas." He referred
to them as "*strongholds* which the enemy cannot break into without
paying a heavy price in casualties. They are the fortresses of revolution and the havens for the guerrillas who become bolder and bolder
in launching attacks toward far-away regions." [69]

The Chinese probably interpreted the section labeled by the editor
"How to Open Up a Guerrilla Center" as Guevara's conception of
what the Chinese call guerrilla zones. The reader should note that
Guevara's discussion of guerrilla centers was separated by the editor
from his analysis of "Building Guerrilla Bases." Concerning guerrilla
centers he said:

Small units with few people in them choose some place favorable for
guerrilla activities, from where they can advance for counter-attack and

[66] *Ibid.*   [67] *Ibid.*, p. 20.
[68] *Ibid.*, p. 18. Emphasis added.   [69] *Ibid.*, p. 19. Emphasis added.

to where they can retreat for refuge, and they *begin to take actions in these places*. But one point must be perfectly clear: at the *initial* stage, when the guerrillas are still rather weak, they should concentrate on getting a firm footing, familiarizing themselves with the surroundings, establishing contact with the inhabitants, and *consolidating places which can be turned into bases*.[70]

These words, it is submitted, would suggest to the Chinese reader the idea of transforming a guerrilla zone into a guerrilla base.

Finally, Guevara's concept of a protracted revolutionary struggle of continental scope and developing in three stages certainly squared with the Chinese position on these matters.[71]

There were, however, certain points in his analysis which must have aroused some anxiety in the minds of the Chinese. For example, it seems to me that they would have felt far more comfortable in presenting his strategy as the correct road for Latin Americans had he elaborated on the relationship between the guerrilla bands and the Marxist-Leninist Party. As we noted in the preceding chapter, Debray's position on this vital issue is diametrically opposed to that of the Chinese as well as that of the Russians. Secondly, I am not at all certain that the Chinese agreed with the second of the three contributions of the Cuban revolution quoted by him from his book on guerrilla warfare. The second was "that we ought not wait for all the revolutionary conditions to become ripe, and that the center of the uprising can create such revolutionary conditions." This declaration does violence to the Communist belief that revolutions can succeed only if "objective conditions" as well as "subjective conditions" are ripe. Guevara's position, then, is far more militant than that of the Chinese; in fact, it borders on being what Communists frequently call adventurism or Blanquism.

These defects notwithstanding, the Chinese apparently concluded that his article incorporated enough of their own strategy to warrant their vigorous endorsement of it as setting forth the correct line for all revolutionaries in Latin America. This article would also account for the high esteem in which the Chinese held Guevara, at least until the breakdown in Sino-Cuban relations.

In the same month (January, 1964) that the Chinese reprinted

[70] *Ibid*. Emphasis added.   [71] *Ibid*., pp. 19–20.

Guevara's article in *Peking Review,* Fidel Castro, whom the Chinese were exalting as the model for Latin American revolutionaries, made his second visit to Moscow. On this occasion, the Cuban economy was in the midst of a severe crisis, a fact of which the Soviet leaders were painfully aware. So desperate was Castro's economic plight that he assumed a position that more nearly approached that of the Soviets than ever before or since. In exchange for a long-term sugar trade agreement and a pledge by Khrushchev to come to the aid of Cuba in the event of aggression, he made concessions to the demands of the Russians. He concurred in the communiqué's condemnation of "factionalist and sectarian activity in the ranks of the Communist and workers' parties"; and he indicated that he approved of "the steps that have been taken by the Central Committee of the CPSU" to eliminate existing differences and "strengthen the unity and cohesion" of the Communist movement. At his insistence, no doubt, the document did not explicitly single out the Chinese, but the latter certainly understood that they were the target at which these remarks were directed.[72] His presence in Moscow and his pro-Soviet remarks there must have enraged the proud Chinese, for it dramatically underscored their inability to cope satisfactorily with the financial and military needs of the Castro regime. In view of the sacrifices that they had made rather than compromise their "principles," they probably regarded Castro's actions and statements as opportunistic at best and treasonable at worst. By this time they prided themselves on being self-reliant, a virtue which they commended to all revolutionaries. The Chinese, however, did not openly vent their spleen on Castro for his betrayal of Marxism-Leninism, but some of their supporters in Latin America, in their subsequent attacks on Castro, refer to this conference as the beginning of the Sino-Cuban controversy.

Another conference that has figured prominently in that controversy was the Havana Conference of Latin American Communist Parties held in November, 1964. There were at least three reasons for convening the conference: first, the Soviets were very much disturbed over their loss of prestige and influence among Latin American Communists as a result of their failure to render firm support to Cuba during the missile crisis; consequently, they hoped to reestablish firm

72 Devlin, "Castro's Place in the Communist World," Research Paper, p. 8.

control over these parties. They were especially anxious to do so at this time because they felt the need for Latin American support at the world conference that they were promoting in order to expel the Chinese from the international Communist movement. Second, all the parties represented at the conference were deeply concerned because of Chinese factionalism. As pointed out below, the Chinese had been extremely active in most of the Latin American Communist parties since 1963 and had already succeeded in establishing pro-Chinese parties in Brazil and Peru. The pro-Soviet leaders knew that the Chinese were intent on splitting as many of these parties as possible, and they were most anxious to prevent the formation of such parties in their respective countries. Third, there was the need to effect a reconciliation between Castro and the old guard leaders of these parties. A bitter controversy had raged for some time between them in regard to: (a) the primacy of the peaceful or violent path to power and (b) the standing of Castro in the Latin American revolutionary movement. A majority of the Communist leaders accepted the Soviet thesis that, given the favorable balance of forces in the world, it was possible to obtain power by peaceful means. Castro, of course, was a proponent of the policy of armed struggle. Regarding his status in the movement, he had long considered himself as its rightful leader. While the old guard leaders paid lip service to the Cuban revolution and acknowledged his leadership of it, they were not prepared to allow him to assume control over the strategy and tactics for their respective parties, primarily because they felt that objective conditions were not ripe for a violent revolution such as he advocated.

Viewed against this background, it is obvious that the communiqué adopted represented an attempt to accommodate the conflicting interests of those participating in the conference. It contained a recommendation that the parties render active support to the freedom fighters in Venezuela, Colombia, Guatemala, Honduras, Paraguay, and Haiti. Regarding Venezuela, a country in which the Castroites were most active, it advocated that "an active movement of solidarity of all the Latin American countries with the liberation struggle of the people of Venezuela should be organized on a continent-wide scale." [73] It

[73] "Unity Is the Guarantee of Success in Our Struggle," *Pravda*, January 19, 1965, as translated in Joint Publications Research Service, *Translations on Inter-*

did not, however, prescribe the violent road as the only road to power. Presumably, then, each party was free to select its own path to power.

The communiqué, as published by *Pravda* on January 19, 1965, also dealt extensively with the problem of unity in the Communist movement. Commencing with a reaffirmation of their determination to work for that goal, the participants exhibited their anxiety about "the situation which has developed in the international communist movement in which acute differences occur, differences that are fraught with the threat of a split and that play into the hands of our enemies whose aggressiveness keeps growing in view of this." [74] They demanded an end to the public polemics and the cessation of factionalism:

. . . the Meeting demands an immediate end be put to public polemics and emphasizes the need for finding proper channels to solve the questions, which have arisen, in the spirit of fraternity which must prevail in the relations between the Marxist-Leninist Parties.

At the same time the conference holds that the unity of each party is an indispensable condition for the further development of the revolutionary process in each country. Consequently, any factional activities, no matter what their source or nature, must be categorically condemned.[75]

The above paragraph condemning factionalism and the fact that the Cubans did not see fit to extend an invitation to the Chinese to attend the conference, when twenty-three other parties were invited, must have been deeply resented by the proud Chinese.[76] Although they did not denounce the conference, their supporters, the Albanians, did in an editorial in *Zeri I Populit* on February 16, 1965. They charged the Soviet "revisionists" with having organized the conference "with diabolical aims, and in order to exploit for their own anti-Marxist plans the sympathy which revolutionary Cuba enjoys among the communists of various countries." [77]

A Bolivian writer, Martín Balanta, in an article entitled "Rupture

---

national Communist Developments, No. 695, p. 37. Hereafter cited as JPRS, *TICD*.

[74] *Ibid.,* p. 38.   [75] *Ibid.,* p. 39.

[76] George Albertini, "Communist Tactics in South America," *Corrispondenza Socialista,* August–September, 1965, as translated in JPRS, *TICD*, No. 796. p. 64.

[77] As cited in Devlin, "Castro's Place in the Communist World," p. 8.

Between Castro and Peiping," asserted that he had learned from Venezuelan sources that Mao Tse-tung was furious when he learned of the outcome of the Havana Conference. Shortly after the meeting, a committee of delegates from several Latin American Communist parties visited Peking apparently in an attempt to placate him. Mao had "one of his rare attacks of fury" and informed them that China would never accept the challenge launched by Castro, who, he contended, was depending more on Soviet than on Chinese aid in helping the Venezuelan guerrillas. He accused Castro of being so afraid of "imperialism" and the "atomic bomb," two of the three "demons" in the present world, that he accepted the third, "revisionism." Balanta also reported this extremely interesting anecdote: "When a Uruguayan delegate tried to interrupt him, Mao told him that he was 'speaking in the name of 650 million people' and asked him how many he represented. He also had a violent exchange of words with the Cuban Carlos Rafael Rodríguez." [78] Balanta reported that these details were revealed by the Venezuelans after they became dissatisfied with Castro's failure to provide aid that he had promised. The story, if true, sheds additional light on the status of Sino-Cuban relations.

The Chinese press manifested indirectly the Chinese leaders' displeasure with Castro's position in regard to the Sino-Soviet conflict. Daniel Tretiak has made a valuable survey of the Chinese and Cuban presses and their coverage of events relating to the other's country. He found, for example, that *People's Daily* in 1963 and 1964, years when they were ardently courting the good will of the Cubans, regularly carried speeches by the Castro brothers and Guevara. From January to May, 1965, the period immediately following the Havana Conference, it did not carry a single speech by these leaders. The Soviets, on the other hand, in 1965 increased their coverage of Castro's speeches, after lagging behind the Chinese in 1964. Tretiak also points out that Chinese coverage of Cuban foreign policy responses and economic developments decreased sharply early in 1965. The other party, the Cubans, displayed a corresponding coolness in their press coverage of stories concerning Chinese leaders. They provided, for example, far more coverage than the Russians of Chou En-lai's 1964

[78] Martín Balanta, "Rupture Between Castro and Peiping," *Segunda Republica*, January 30, 1966, as translated in JPRS, *TICD*, No. 810, p. 32.

tour of Africa, but they virtually ignored his 1965 trip to the same continent.[79]

In subsequent chapters numerous statements by pro-Chinese groups in Latin America will be cited to provide additional evidence regarding the Chinese response to Castro's position at the Havana Conference. Suffice it to say at this point, that these supporters charged him with having joined sides with the revisionists of the world, led, of course, by the CPSU. The evidence adduced thus far will, I believe, support the contention that Sino-Cuban relations deteriorated seriously in 1965, after reaching their high point in 1964.

The tension that had been building up throughout 1965 culminated in a violent but short open polemic in early 1966. From the several speeches and statements made during this period, we can reconstruct what transpired in the preceding months. On January 2, 1966, Fidel Castro made his first overt attack on the Chinese on the eve of the historic Tricontinental Conference, a meeting attended by almost six hundred delegates representing eighty-two countries.

At the conference guerrilla leaders from Latin America had an opportunity to compare their experiences with those of revolutionary leaders from Africa and Asia. The underlying purpose for convening the conference was to consider and adopt a strategy for these three continents to cope with the global strategy of the U.S. imperialists and their supporters; that is, an effort was made to help the revolutionaries to understand that their fighting was not in isolation but was, in fact, an integral part of the worldwide struggle against the imperialists. As a representative of the Venezuelan guerrillas put it: "The effective solidarity among the nations of our three continents must bring into practice a world revolutionary strategy which responds to the world strategy of American Imperialism." [80]

In their comments on the conference, the Chinese clearly accepted the notion that the peoples of Africa, Asia, and Latin America ought to combine forces in the effort to articulate such a strategy. They were most gratified that the conference adopted a resolution condemning U.S. "aggression" in Vietnam, and they joined with the

[79] Daniel Tretiak, "China and Latin America: an Ebbing Tide in Trans-Pacific Maoism," *Current Scene,* March 1, 1966, pp. 4–5.
[80] George Albertini, "The Conference in Havana," *Est et Ouest,* March 15, 1966, as translated in JPRS, *TICD,* No. 834, p. 22.

majority of delegates in the call for support of the Vietnamese who were manning the "main front" in the worldwide struggle against the enemy.[81] Chinese efforts to link that struggle with the struggle against revisionism failed because most of the delegates were weary of hearing the Soviets and Chinese exchange insults at international conferences. The twenty-seven Latin American delegations, who often set the tone for debate, were not at all interested in having the conference rehash the familiar arguments used in the Sino-Soviet dispute. Castro, who wanted to remain as neutral as possible in that conflict, was reported to have asked the delegates prior to the meeting not to bring their quarrels to the conference.[82]

In his speech of January 2, 1966, the day before the conference formally opened, Fidel Castro stated that the Chinese government had indicated that it could not fulfill his expectations for the 1966 trade protocol. He reported that the Cuban Ministry of Foreign Trade had just informed him that the Chinese would be unable to accept the 800,000 tons of sugar offered by the Cubans because they simply did not need that large a quantity. Regarding rice to be supplied Cuba by the Chinese, the latter said that they could not supply 250,000 tons as they had done under the 1965 trade protocol because they had an inadequate supply of rice to meet their domestic needs and also provide aid to Vietnam.

Castro replied that the Cuban people understood the need for meeting the requirements of the Vietnamese people because "for the Vietnamese people we are ready to give not just sugar, but also our own blood, which is worth more than sugar." He added, however, that Cuba had no other source for procuring rice because the American economic blockade prevented Cubans from purchasing rice from the United States, the former source of supply. As a consequence, Cuban rations of rice would be reduced by one half.[83]

A correspondent for Hsinhua News Agency held an interview with a "responsible official" in the Ministry of Foreign Trade and attempted

---

81 "The First Afro-Asian-Latin American Peoples' Solidarity Conference," *Peking Review*, January 21, 1966, p. 21.

82 Robert F. Lamberg, "Latin America and the Tri-Continental Conference," *Der Ostblock und die Entwicklungslaender (The East Bloc and the Developing Countries)*, June, 1966, as translated in JPRS, *TICD*, No. 890, p. 41.

83 "Fidel Castro on Trade Between Cuba and China," *Prensa Latina*, as cited in *Global Digest*, Vol. III, No. 4, 1966, pp. 92-98.

to ascertain the Chinese version of the controversy. The official said that Castro's remarks regarding the volume of trade for 1966 as compared with earlier years were "at variance with the facts." He disputed Castro's claim that the 1966 volume of trade was lower than that for any of the years from 1961 to 1965. He conceded that the Chinese offer to send 135,000 tons of rice in 1966 was less than the amount shipped in 1965, but he hastened to add that the 250,000 tons in 1965 was much higher than the usual shipment. The 1966 figure, he contended, was higher than for 1962 or 1963 and about the same as that for 1964. For 1966 the Cubans had requested even more than they had received in the preceding year. The Chinese could not meet the current Cuban request for 285,000 tons of rice; all they could afford to send was 135,000 tons.

Regarding the extraordinary amount furnished for 1965, he explained that the Chinese, in response to a request made in October, 1964, by Castro, agreed to supply that amount for one year. He insisted, however, that his government had not promised to provide that amount every year. The Cubans had not requested a long-term annual supply of 250,000 tons of rice; therefore, there was absolutely no basis in fact for Castro's assumption that the Chinese would continue supplying rice at that high level. Moreover, he contended that the figures for 1966 had not been finalized in that the negotiations then going on in Peking were preliminary in nature. That is, the trade protocol for 1966 had not been signed. Why, then, had Castro seen fit to make public these matters? He asked: "Why, then, has he suddenly taken such an extraordinary step on the eve of the three continents peoples' solidarity conference in Havana? This offers food for thought." [84]

Castro responded with an extremely violent attack on the Chinese leaders, charging them with having engaged in economic brutality and having displayed contempt for his country. He stated the Cuban complaints as follows:

It was no longer a matter of more or fewer tons of rice . . . though it affected that too, but a matter of very much greater importance, fundamental to the peoples, namely: whether in the world of tomorrow the powerful countries will be able to take on themselves the right to black-

[84] "Facts on Sino-Cuban Trade," *Peking Review*, January 14, 1966, p. 23.

mail, exercise extortion against, pressure, commit aggression against and strangle smaller peoples; whether there will also prevail in the world of tomorrow, which revolutionaries are struggling to establish, the worst methods of piracy, oppression and filibustering that have been introduced into the world ever since the emergence of class society. . . .[85]

That Castro should have inferred that the Chinese were manipulating Sino-Cuban trade for political purposes is perfectly understandable. In the negotiations for the 1965 trade protocol, which took place in late 1964, the Chinese doubled their commitment to ship rice to Cuba. At that particular time the Chinese were most anxious to gain additional Cuban goodwill because Khrushchev had just fallen from power and they believed the Cubans would be especially pliant at that stage. On the other hand, when negotiations for the 1966 protocol took place in late 1965, Sino-Cuban relations were much less cordial. Castro realized that the Chinese resented very much the stand he had taken at the Havana Conference of 1964. Under these circumstances, it was only natural that he should have concluded that the Chinese were, through the use of economic means, attempting to blackmail him into abandoning his policy of neutrality in the Sino-Soviet dispute.

Castro's February 6 speech revealed an even more serious source of friction with the Chinese, the propagandistic and factional activities of Chinese operating in Cuba. Castro displayed no more enthusiasm regarding these developments than did his rivals in the Latin American Communist movement, the pro-Soviet leaders of those parties. He sounded his first warning against proselytizing in his speech of March 13, 1965:

Naturally, we have the full right . . . to drive from our country, from the ranks of our people, these disputes, these byzantine feuds. And we want everyone to know that here our party makes the propaganda, that here our party shows the way, that here this question is our business; and if we do not want this apple of discord to appear here—and we don't want it—no one will be able to smuggle it in as contraband.[86]

85 "Castro's February 6 Anti-China Statement," *Peking Review*, February 25, 1966, p. 22.
86 As cited in Devlin, "Castro's Place in the Communist World," Research Paper, p. 8.

According to Castro's speech of February 6, 1966, the Chinese government had increased the delivery and distribution of propaganda materials among government civil officials as well as to "the General Staff of the Revolutionary Armed Forces, to the staffs of the armed services, to the staffs of the army corps, to divisional staffs, to the staffs of the commands of various military branches, to the leaders of the sections of the political department, and, in many instances, directly to the personal address of officers of our armed forces." [87]

His account indicates that the Chinese had indeed been active in Cuba. He expressed his outrage at these violations of "the most elementary norms of respect" among socialist countries. On September 14, 1965, the Cuban authorities filed a formal protest with the Chinese Chargé d'Affaires and informed him that they regarded such practices to be precisely the same as those of the U.S. Embassy in Cuba in "its attempts to interfere in the internal affairs of Cuba and in one form or another impose its will on this nation." Such infringement of Cuban sovereignty would not be tolerated.

Despite the protest, he added, the Chinese had continued shipping in large quantities of their propaganda. He cited figures to demonstrate how many copies of various issues of the *Bulletin* had arrived in the preceding months. The numbers assigned to the *Bulletin* correspond to those of *Pekin Informe* (*Peking Review*). In all, 58,041 copies had been sent to Cuba after the September protest. In addition, tens of thousands of copies of other materials had arrived in the same period. Castro also pointed out that the Chinese had tried to contact officers directly "to win them over, either for the purpose of proselytism or perhaps for the purpose of intelligence." [88] Castro's words reflected his determination to prevent conversion and recruitment by the Chinese of Cuban military and government personnel.

Jen-min Jih-pao, in an editor's note of February 22, 1966, responded to Castro's charges. He expressed amazement that Castro should have objected to such practices, which he called "perfectly normal, aboveboard and beyond reproach." After all, he observed, the Cuban Embassy had been circulating Cuban printed matters in China. He asked: "Why should China's printed matter be dreaded like the plague while

[87] "Castro's February 6 Anti-China Statement," p. 21.
[88] *Ibid.*

(168)

anti-Chinese propaganda material published by the leaders of the Communist Party of the Soviet Union is allowed to deluge Cuba? Why such a lack of confidence in one's own cadres and officers and in one's own people?" He indicated that his reply should not be taken for a systematic reply and that the Chinese reserved the right to do so.[89]

Thus far the Sino-Cuban conflict had not extended to the ideological level; however, with the publication of Régis Debray's book, the two countries began a debate, much less violent than the Sino-Soviet to be sure, regarding the proper strategy for Latin American revolutionaries. As of July, 1968, the Chinese had not published an explicit refutation of Debray's book. That is, they had not attacked him by name, but they have, in their recent statements on the crucial points of the concept of people's war, reflected an acute awareness of his "erroneous" views on the matter.

Given the Chinese conviction, stated explicitly in Lin Piao's article of September, 1965, that Mao's theory of people's war had universal applicability and given Fidel Castro's determination to become *the* acknowledged leader of the Latin American revolutionaries, a serious clash between the Chinese and the Cubans on the theoretical as well as the political level was inevitable. There is evidence to suggest that the Chinese, once they came to doubt the reliability of Castro as an ally, launched a campaign to present Mao rather than Castro as the mentor for Latin American and other revolutionaries. In a domestic broadcast in Mandarin on February 4, 1965, a claim was made that revolutionary peoples everywhere greatly respected Mao's ideology, and they allegedly were most eager to possess and study his works which had been translated and published in more than one hundred countries and regions in Asia, Africa, and Latin America. In Cuba, the people had shown "great enthusiasm" for Mao, having bought all of the 500,000 copies of a single-volume collection of Mao's works. Furthermore, a Cuban professor had written to China asking for all of the volumes in his selected works because he needed them to understand Marxism-Leninism. The broadcaster also asserted that during the war against Batista the Cubans had studied some of his

[89] Editor's note, *Jen-min Jih-pao*, February 22, 1966, as cited in *Peking Review*, February 25, 1966, p. 13.

(169)

military writings. Mao's work on strategic problems in anti-Japanese guerrilla war was "very popular at the revolutionary base in the Sierra Maestra Mountains." [90] It is also interesting to note that he reiterated the story concerning Guevara's statement that he and his commanders had studied Mao's writings on guerrilla warfare, "food from China," because they helped them to solve many problems.

The Cubans, however, were not the only Latin Americans to have expressed their admiration for Mao's work. An unnamed Peruvian professor "hailed Mao's works as a beacon guiding the people toward the path of struggle, pointing out the revolutionary direction, and showing them a future of victory." [91] The secretary of an Indian association in Ecuador reportedly had praised "Mao as the greatest Marxist of our time saying that Mao's theories on the peasant movement are of great significance to the revolutionary cause in Latin America. From the experiences of the Chinese revolutionaries and from the works of Mao, the revolutionary people of Asia, Africa, and Latin America have obtained the *theoretical weapons for waging revolutionary struggles.*" [92] The broadcaster also averred that a supplementary publication of the organ of the Venezuelan National Liberation Front, the *Combat Handbook*, urged that Mao's theory of "strategically despise the enemies but tactically take them seriously" should be popularized among the members of the army and other people. Finally, he alleged that a Venezuelan Communist Party member, who was also a member of the Venezuelan National Liberation Army, had said that everyone in Venezuela knew Mao and that his works had become teaching material which all Venezuelan revolutionaries must read.

The Chinese assertions that Mao's works were quite popular in Cuba and that Guevara had acknowledged the indebtedness of the Cubans to Mao for strategic guidance in the anti-Batista war probably reflected Chinese frustration based on the fact that Castro and his associates were not displaying proper respect for Mao's contributions to revolutionary strategy. The references to the Venezuelan fighters probably showed the Chinese desire to demonstrate that they were not without influence in Venezuela, a country that had experienced several years of guerrilla warfare. The Ecuadorian report would seem-

[90] Peking Domestic Service in Mandarin, February 5, 1965.
[91] *Ibid.*   [92] *Ibid.* Emphasis added.

ingly indicate that the Chinese were anxious to have Latin Americans look to China for guidance in solving the peasant problem.

This broadcast and the Chinese reaction to Debray's assault on the universality of Mao's theories take on additional significance when viewed in light of one of the indicators of Sino-Cuban relations, the periodic analyses made by the Chinese of the situation in Latin America. Prior to 1965, they had given priority to Cuban developments, pointing to that country as one blazing a trail for other countries in Latin America. In the survey of 1964, published in the January 15, 1965, issue of *Peking Review*, the anti-American demonstrations in Panama were given a higher priority than were developments in Cuba. The Cuban people were not singled out as a "brilliant example," nor did any of the terms used in the section dealing with Cuba suggest that other countries should look to that country for inspiration.[93] On May 28, 1965, *Peking Review*, in its comments on the "storm brewing in the U.S. backyard," held up the Dominican patriots as an "inspiring example" to Latin Americans. There were references to events in Bolivia, Ecuador, and Colombia, but the article did not even mention Cuba.[94] The annual survey for 1965, printed in the January 28, 1966, issue of *Peking Review*, again gave top priority to the Dominican armed struggle which showed "that the irreconcilable condition between the Latin American people and Yankee imperialism inevitably led to armed struggle." The Dominicans' armed struggle was said to have "encouraged the revolutionary people and punched a hole in Yankee imperialism." Among the other countries commented on were Peru, Colombia, Venezuela, Bolivia, Panama, Chile, Ecuador, Brazil, and Uruguay. Cuba was not even mentioned.[95] Nor was Cuba mentioned in the survey of 1966 made in *Peking Review* on January 13, 1967. The fact that was stressed in the article was that "a number of revolutionary vanguards have begun to accept Chairman Mao's great theory of people's war."[96] Finally, the analysis of the events of 1967 also failed to mention Cuba; it concentrated instead on student activities in Brazil, Ecuador, Bolivia, and several other countries. Peasant seizures of land, strikes by work-

[93] "Latin America Marches On," *Peking Review*, January 15, 1965, p. 21.
[94] "Storm Brewing in U.S. Backyard," *Peking Review*, May 28, 1965, p. 26.
[95] Fen Hsi, "The People Fight On," *Peking Review*, January 28, 1966, pp. 15-17.
[96] "Great New Era of World Revolution," *Peking Review*, January 13, 1967, p. 23.

ers, and the steady development of "Marxist-Leninist parties and revolutionary organizations in many countries" were other developments deemed worthy of note.[97] The obvious downgrading of Cuba in these significant yearly summaries of Latin American events is cogent evidence regarding Chinese evaluation of Cuba as an ally in the Latin American revolutionary movement.

Consistent with their policy of silence in regard to Cuban developments, the Chinese press has printed no articles by Chinese officials directly attacking the ideas of Régis Debray. Anna Louise Strong, an American Communist living for many years in China, presented in the February 22, 1968, *Letter from China*, a critique of his book. She asserted that he had come forward to sell what he called revolution now that the people were preparing for people's war. She charged him with advocating that there was no need "to organize the masses, to build a party, to build an army, to study theory, to organize a broad united front, to make a base area or prepare for a protracted war—*all that is needed is a few men with guns*. Such notions, if followed, lead to serious reverses for the revolutionary people." [98] The defects attributed to Debray constitute the principal acts which, in her judgment, must be performed in waging a people's war. In predicting that his ideas, if followed, would result in disaster to revolutionaries, she did not point out, as one might expect, that when those ideas had been applied in 1967 by Che Guevara in Bolivia, the result had indeed been disastrous to the Bolivian guerrillas. She contended that Debray and those like him constituted a minor trend in Latin America, the main trend consisting of proletarian revolutionaries who had learned from Mao that "a well-disciplined *party* armed with the thought of Marxism-Leninism, using the method of self criticism and linked to the masses of the people; an *army* under the leadership of such a party; a *united front* of all revolutionary classes and all revolutionary groups under the leadership of such a party—these are the three main weapons with which we have defeated the enemy." [99]

[97] Peking NCNA International Service in English, December 31, 1967.

[98] Anna Louise Strong, *Letter From China*, February 28, 1968, p. 4. Emphasis added.

[99] *Ibid*. Emphasis added.

It was not until July 26, 1968, that *Peking Review* carried an article criticizing Debray by name. The item in question was an extract from *L'Humanité Nouvelle*, the organ for the pro-Chinese French Communist Party. The title "Marxism-Leninism, Mao Tse-tung's Thought, Is Universal" suggests the prime concern of the writer. In my judgment, the clue to the underlying reason for his writing the article, and I might add for the Chinese extracting and reprinting it, can be found in the title and in these words: ". . . the role of this book is to attack Marxism-Leninism, Mao Tse-tung's thought, and to deny the universal significance of Mao Tse-tung's theories." [100] In the same vein he maintained that "Debray preposterously opposes the correct theses of Chairmain Mao Tse-tung's, alleging that this viewpoint is valid in China, but not in Latin America." In short, the Chinese and their supporters repudiate Debray's contention that the Cuban road is the road for all Latin American revolutionaries. In their view, of course, the only road for the Latin Americans and revolutionaries throughout the world is the path prescribed by Chairman Mao. It might be noted, in passing, that the editor of *Peking Review* clearly concurs in the French analysis, describing the article as one that "denounces the fallacies of Régis Debray, author of *Revolution in the Revolution*."

The specific point in Debray's book which most troubled the French analyst was Debray's "denying the leading role of the proletarian party in the national democratic revolution." The fact that the same objection has been raised by all pro-Chinese groups that have criticized Castroite strategy would suggest that the Chinese now feel that they made a serious error in their policy regarding Castro during the first stage of the revolution, the national democratic one. After their bitter disappointment with him, they probably regret having failed to "demand" leadership by the Communist Party from the very beginning. One can well imagine the self-criticism engaged in by those responsible for policy-making in Latin America in the early 1960s!

He also took Debray to task for having a "purely military viewpoint." To Debray, "the gun commands politics." Debray erred, then,

[100] "Marxism-Leninism, Mao Tse-tung's Thought, Is Universal Thought," *Peking Review*, July, 26, 1968, p. 11.

regarding the crucial relationship between the party and the army in that he advocated subordination of the party to the army. Failure to bring out that the army should not confine itself to fighting was another defect cited by the pro-Chinese writer. He held that the army also has vital political tasks. It should "shoulder such important tasks as doing propaganda among the masses, organizing the masses, arming them, helping them to establish revolutionary political power and setting up Party organizations." [101]

Debray's failure to apply the dialectical method in his book had led him into other "errors," causing him, for example, to fail to point out the interconnection between things:

He examined each point in isolation, out of the general context. He studied the situation in Latin America without linking it to the world situation; he spoke of the revisionist parties in Latin America by glossing over the situation in the international communist movement and denying the necessity of political and ideological struggle within a revolutionary organization.[102]

More concretely, what Debray's critic was condemning was the Castroites' attempt to remain aloof from the Sino-Soviet conflict, refusing to accept the Chinese thesis that one must simultaneously struggle against revisionism and imperialism. More specifically, the pro-Chinese criticized Debray for his attacking only the revisionist parties in Latin America for their failure to pursue a military policy; he should, they feel, link the local revisionists with the real source of the deviation. In short, Debray should have attacked the CPSU as well as the Latin American pro-Soviet parties. Debray's prime concern, it will be recalled, was to concentrate on the anti-imperialist struggle. The latter portion of the quotation dealing with Debray's denying the need for political and ideological struggle within a revolutionary organization related to Castroite objections to the stress placed by the Chinese on the need for having a "pure" Marxist-Leninist viewpoint as a condition for correct action. The Chinese believe that no effort must be spared in eradicating erroneous views from the thought of party members.

Jorge Isaac Arrellano, an Ecuadorian supporter of the Chinese, prepared an article in which he attempted to refute Debray's ideas.

101 *Ibid.*   102 *Ibid.*, p. 12.

He began his analysis by conceding that the book had caused such a sensation and evoked so much admiration that he found it necessary to reply as quickly as possible to clear up the confusion that the book had created in "certain Leftist circles in our country." He entitled his essay "Revolution within Revolution? or Adventure without Revolution?—A Reply to Régis Debray," thereby emphasizing that he regarded Debray's ideas as "adventuristic" in nature. In his introduction he also stressed that involved here was an offensive of continental scope based on the ideology of the Cuban revolution. As a faithful follower of Mao, he held that it was his duty to criticize these mistaken ideas, quoting the following passage from Mao's "On the Correct Handling of Contradictions Among the People":

There is no doubt whatsoever that we should criticize mistaken ideas of every kind. It is patently inadmissible to abstain from criticising wrong ideas, or to regard with indifference the manner in which they are divulged everywhere, or to allow them to monopolize the market. Every error must be criticized, just as every poisonous weed must be removed from the soil.[103]

Arrellano rejected Debray's argument that the vanguard of the revolution need not necessarily be the Marxist-Leninist Party. He, like other pro-Chinese critics of Debray, emphasized most this point and the related point concerning the proper relationship between the party and the army. He accurately characterized Debray's position as contrary to that of Communists everywhere. Debray's position was, he said, "the most unbridled anti-Communism, the most anti-Party position possible." [104] In the following statement, Arrellano mirrored the hostility felt among pro-Chinese elements for the position and the activities of Castroites:

It [the Castroite position] is the key to a series of grave events which took place in the heart of the Marxist-Leninist movement in America, and, of course, in Ecuador also. Many people, after visiting Cuba, have returned to their countries with caudillo-like airs, and pretensions to commanding guerrilla forces, scorning all party organizations. They

[103] Jorge Isaac Arrellano, "Revolution Within Revolution? or Adventure Without Revolution?—A Reply to Régis Debray," Guayaquil, Ecuador: Ediciones Liberación (Liberation Editions), 1967, as translated in JPRS, *TICD*, No. 1010, pp. 101–102.
[104] *Ibid.*, p. 123.

proceed to launch out indiscriminately in diatribes aimed against all
revolutionaries, seeking to place themselves at the head of pseudo-revo-
lutionary factions which "multiply" like wildfire, which bleat unre-
servedly about insurrection in the country but are unable *to go to the
people, to organize a revolutionary center,* much less, evidently, to go up
into the mountains and organize guerrilla movements. These people have
returned to their countries to bring together a few discontented and
disoriented Communists, in order to take advantage of the difference of
opinion between them.[105]

He concluded that the origin of these factions was the ideology of the
Cuban revolution, which was, he contended, different from that of
Marxism-Leninism. Apparently the "returnees" from Cuba had recruited a few "discontented and disoriented Communists" from the
ranks of the pro-Chinese parties and used them to form pro-Castro
factions. Arrellano was protesting this unfair revolutionary practice
of raiding genuine Marxist-Leninist parties, a practice the latter had
been engaged in for several years vis-à-vis the pro-Soviet parties and
apparently the Castroite movement as well. In a later passage, Arrellano referred to the appearance of many little caudillos, each of whom
professed to have the support of Fidel, but, he added, "it would be
too boring to begin listing and analyzing all the pro-Cuban factions
which have appeared in this country." [106]

Arrellano classified Debray with a group which Mao called the
"vain jabberers of the Left," persons who, taking their illusions for
reality, attempt to use force at present to obtain objectives that can
be achieved only in the future. "Their ideas, isolated from present
day practice, as followed by the great majority of the people, and
isolated, too, from present day realities, are converted, in practical
action, into an undisciplined, gambler-like spirit." [107] In a word, he
considered Debray an adventurer.

He filed a violent exception to Debray's arguments that the public
polemics of the Sino-Soviet dispute had delayed the decisive struggle
of the masses and that, for that reason, revolutionaries should place
themselves above existing differences of opinion. He maintained that

[105] *Ibid.,* pp. 113–14. Emphasis added.   [106] *Ibid.,* pp. 115–16.
[107] *Ibid.,* pp. 117–18.

the revolutionary cause had not been impeded by the "ideological polemics or political struggles." Those responsible were the revisionist party leaders and the leftist adventurers:

What is responsible for its tardiness, on the one hand, is the systematic curbing of progress in which the traditional Communist parties, under the influence of their revisionist leaders, have engaged for many years now. And on the other hand, there are the guerrilla adventures which have recently taken place in our countries.[108]

He charged Debray with having underestimated and deprecated the importance of theory. Using as his point of departure the Leninist viewpoint that "if there is no revolutionary theory, there can be no revolutionary movement," Arrellano argued that Debray's views would lead the revolution "into a deep quagmire." Moreover, he continued, that was precisely what was happening in Latin America. As a consequence, many "well-intentioned but disoriented revolutionaries" had been massacred; which resulted, unfortunately, in improving the lot of the imperialists against whom they claimed to be fighting. Those relegating theory to a secondary position had done the same in regard to other important matters: ". . . the vanguard party and its proletarian ideology is of secondary importance; the united front of the masses is of secondary importance; the policy of the masses is of secondary importance and so, too, is the armed struggle of the masses." [109]

The Ecuadorian defender of Chairman Mao was very much disturbed by Debray's contention that Mao's theories were not relevant to Latin American conditions; hence Latin Americans should look to the Cuban revolution for guidance because it was based on conditions that were specifically and uniquely restricted to Latin America. Arrellano's refutation of Debray's argument was not at all satisfactory. He began by conceding that the Cuban revolution had unique features, but he deemed only one worthy of note: the fact that the leaders were from the most radical element of the petty bourgeoisie. And yet he seemed to contradict himself even on this point when he asked:

Yet what in this case, what is there specifically new or unique about this aspect? What is there that has not been recorded previously, else-

108 *Ibid.*, p. 119.   109 *Ibid.*, p. 124.

where in the world? Perhaps the only uniqueness about it lies in the identity of those who took the initiative; or does it? [110]

He then made a puzzling distinction among the Cuban leaders, intimating that some, Raúl Castro and Che Guevara, had a better ideological grasp of the problems of the revolution than did others. He explained the distinction as follows:

We must not forget that among the petty bourgeoisie elements who took the initiative in the struggle, there were leaders who had a clear ideological concept of the implications of class struggle, and of the Socialistic policy to be followed, if the revolution were to succeed, if the leaders wished to be loyal to the people who called on them to take over power. (*Such is the case of Raúl Castro and "Che" Guevara.*) [111]

Was Arrellano saying that these Castroite leaders were closer ideologically to the pro-Chinese than were Fidel Castro and Debray? In any event, he was convinced that the Latin Americans did not require a revolutionary line of their own because their revolution was an inseparable part of the world revolution which, he contended, could succeed only through adherence to the strategy of Mao Tse-tung.

No Transar, the Argentine pro-Chinese publication, in an article acclaiming Mao's theory of people's war as the indispensable guide for Latin Americans, pointed out that ideas contrary to Marxism-Leninism had often appeared in the ranks of the revolutionaries. These ideas which, the paper asserted, made difficult the establishment of the leadership of Mao's thought, seem to be of Castroite origin. At any rate, complaints similar to those listed below have been frequently made regarding Castroites' ideas: ". . . to advocate that the revolution in a dependent country has no different stages, to organize premature assaults on cities, to develop a purely military line and underestimate the revolutionary ideology of Marxism-Leninism, to have no confidence in the power of the broad masses of armed peasants and *place all hope on arming just a few fighting guerrilla groups.*" [112]

Aggravating these deviations were certain "pseudo-revolutionaries" who were waving the flag of armed struggle but were retarding the

[110] *Ibid.*, p. 126.   [111] *Ibid.*, pp. 126–27. Emphasis added.
[112] Peking NCNA International Service in English, June 26, 1967. Emphasis added.

process of mastering Mao's thought by the masses; they also had opposed the establishment of a "new type Marxist-Leninist party." Those charges were evidently directed at Cuban activities.

The Chilean pro-Chinese, as early as August, 1966, were protesting against similar developments in their party, but they explicitly linked these events to the influence of the Cubans. In a political resolution adopted at the First Congress, the Chilean Revolutionary Communist Party expressed opposition to the policy adopted by certain "petty bourgeois" groups which were trying "to copy mechanically the experience of the Cuban armed struggle." The most prominent feature of that policy was "the belief that a military group going into action and initiating the armed struggle is all that is needed to arouse the masses to join this struggle to seize political power, while ignoring the necessity to create a Marxist-Leninist Party to lead the masses and eliminate the revisionist influence among the masses as an indispensable basis for developing a people's war." [113] Since this resolution was adopted before Debray's book was published, it is clear that the Castroites and pro-Chinese groups were quarrelling over strategy several months before the Debray book appeared on the market.

An excellent summary of the essence of the Chinese concept of people's war and the differences between the Chinese and Cuban approaches to such a war can be found in a story written December 30, 1967, in Peking by a Hsinhua correspondent. After alleging that Mao's concepts represented the only correct road for Latin American revolutionaries, he reiterated the Chinese arguments that only the Communist Party could lead such a war, that most of the protracted fighting would take place in the countryside because there the enemy was weakest, that the peasants constituted the main force of such a revolution, and that the political mobilization of the masses was indispensable to final victory. He quoted a Peruvian as stating that the Peruvians had learned through experience that "a *purely military organization* cannot lead a people's war, but will face the danger of becoming a *band of roving rebels* to be eventually wiped out." [114] Those remarks, no doubt, were aimed at the Castroites. An Ecuadorian revolutionary

[113] "Political Resolution of First Congress of Chilean Revolutionary Communist Party," *Peking Review*, August 26, 1966, p. 25.
[114] News from Hsinhua, Supplement (1) 1968, p. 41. Emphasis added.

added that in the past, Ecuadorian revolutionaries had not realized the "importance of mass work, thinking that they could win the sympathy of the peasants *simply by firing a few shots,* but today we realize that it is absolutely necessary to carry out thoroughgoing and meticulous mass work in order to arouse the peasants." [115] The Cuban view on armed propaganda is obviously the object of this criticism. Finally, the Hsinhua correspondent attacked Debray by quoting an unnamed revolutionary, who related the importance attached by him to the establishment of bases. After studying Mao's works he realized that in the past they had had only guerrilla zones as a rear, but no rural base areas. "We had our rear, but it was in the big cities. When the enemy came, our connections with it were cut." He had learned that the enemy would destroy the revolutionaries unless they established these base areas. He urged that they be established at the initial stage of the revolution and that they be expanded gradually.[116] These comments might be construed as the pro-Chinese explanation for the Bolivian fiasco in 1967. That is, the Castroite guerrilla movement had been crushed because its leader, Che Guevara, who had been killed by Bolivian government forces, neglected or failed to establish a firm base area in the initial stage by transforming the guerrilla zone into a guerrilla base.

As of the end of 1967, then, the Chinese and Cubans were no longer in agreement concerning (1) the strategy to be followed in Latin America, (2) the role of Cuba in the Latin American revolution, and (3) the need for establishing pro-Chinese (Marxist-Leninist) parties in Latin America.

In the chapters that follow we shall examine in detail the reasons that impelled the Chinese to establish such parties and the steps taken by their supporters in Latin America to found these parties. We shall also analyze the positions taken, from time to time, by the followers of the Chinese on such matters as (1) the status of Cuba in the revolutionary movement, (2) the strategy to be adopted to achieve power, and (3) whether strategy should vary from one country to another.

[115] *Ibid.* Emphasis added.   [116] *Ibid.,* p. 42.

VI

The Pro-Chinese Party of Brazil

THE Chinese Communist interest in the Latin American Communist parties stems from their conviction that a genuine Marxist-Leninist party is a sine qua non for the successful waging of a proletarian revolution. Like Marxists everywhere they subscribe to the view that the Communist Party is the vanguard of the revolution. Their efforts to win over the Communist parties in Latin America can be understood only if one keeps this fact in mind. Their interest in these parties is also closely related to the Sino-Soviet dispute.

The Communist parties in Latin America, courted so ardently by the Chinese since 1960, have a long tradition of subordinating their interests to those of the Soviet Union. For many years the leaders of those parties have been among the most dependable supporters of the Soviet party. Even a casual study of the activities of the Latin American parties will demonstrate the nature of the relationship between the Soviet and Latin American Communist parties, a relationship which differs so much from that obtaining between the Chinese and the Russian parties during much of their history. When the Chinese launched their global campaign to challenge the Russians' leadership in the international Communist movement, they were confronted with the simple fact that Latin American Communists were accustomed to look to Moscow for political and ideological guidance. They have experienced many setbacks in their efforts to dislodge the CPSU from its privileged position in the Communist movement in Latin America.

The Chinese manifested a serious interest in influencing leaders of the Latin American Communist parties even in the initial stage of the Sino-Soviet conflict. Mao Tse-tung and his associates were quick to perceive the unsettling effects on Communist leaders of Khrushchev's "secret" speech of February, 1956, to the 20th Party Congress of the CPSU. Stalinists throughout the international Communist movement were deeply perturbed by Khrushchev's attack on Stalin's cult of personality because many of them had been handpicked by him and had stoutly defended for many years his policies in their respective parties. They also seriously questioned the orthodoxy of some of his views as expounded to the 20th Congress. In particular they took issue with his contention that war between the socialist bloc and the imperialists, led by the United States, was no longer inevitable. His thesis that political power can be achieved by following the peaceful path to socialism was equally obnoxious to many of these leaders.

The Chinese leaders sought to exploit the widespread confusion and disenchantment which followed in the wake of the historic Congress by inviting delegates from fraternal parties to visit China after the 20th Party Congress. Accepting the invitation were delegations from eleven Latin American countries: Argentina, Bolivia, Brazil, Chile, Costa Rica, Cuba, Ecuador, Guatemala, Mexico, Paraguay, and Peru. In a speech to the 8th Congress of the CCP, Liu Shao-ch'i expressed the opinion that the anti-colonial struggle then spreading throughout Latin America would certainly encompass the entire continent. The guests from Latin America responded most enthusiastically to that statement and to the Chinese treatment accorded them.[1]

Among those who were most favorably impressed was Diógenes Arruda, the Brazilian delegate and the chief aide, at that time, of Luiz Carlos Prestes, the most prominent leader of the Brazilian Communists. After returning to Moscow, Arruda recounted to Osvaldo Peralva his feelings regarding his visit to China. He and other delegates from Latin America were especially impressed by the fact that they were personally received by Mao Tse-tung, who talked with

[1] Shen-Yu Dai, " 'Sugar Coated Bullets' for Latin America," *Current Scene*, December 23, 1961, p. 2.

them for over two hours, after which he asked whether they would like to continue the conversation. In the Soviet Union, he complained, "he had never had the honor of being received even by the most obscure member of the Central Committee."[2] The Latin Americans were also received by Liu Shao-ch'i, the second most powerful man in China at the time. That the Brazilians' respect for the orthodoxy of the CCP was enhanced as a result of this visit to China can be inferred from the fact that the Brazilians dispatched to China, shortly after the 20th Party Congress of the CPSU, a group of their cadres for six months of indoctrination.

Khrushchev, however, was not without supporters in the Communist Party of Brazil. According to a resolution adopted on July 27, 1963, by the pro-Chinese faction then calling itself the Communist Party of Brazil, "a powerful revisionist trend" appeared in the ranks of the Communist movement after the 20th Party Congress of the CPSU. Heading the revisionist trend was Agildo Barata. Prior to June, 1957, Luiz Carlos Prestes aligned himself with those resisting the efforts of the "revisionists" to gain control of the party. Following the downfall of Malenkov, Molotov, and Kaganovich in the CPSU, Prestes allegedly shifted his position to correspond with that of Agildo Barata and the "revisionists" for reasons not entirely clear to those who had been collaborating with him in the struggle against the "revisionists." A plausible explanation would seem to be that Prestes had deferred taking a pro-Khrushchev posture until he was certain that Khrushchev had prevailed over his rivals in the CPSU. Once the "anti-party" group had been smashed by Khrushchev in 1957, Prestes apparently felt that he could embrace the doctrinal innovations introduced by Khrushchev at the 20th Party Congress. At any rate, the pro-Chinese group charged that he became a "fervent defender of revisionism" and "a fanatic apologist for capitalist development in Brazil. . . ."[3]

In March, 1958, Prestes, "by dint of anti-party tactics," imposed a

[2] Osvaldo Peralva, *O Retrato* (Rio de Janeiro: Editora Globo, 1962), as cited in Ernst Halperin, "Peking and the Latin American Communists," *The China Quarterly*, January–March, 1967, p. 119.

[3] Resolution of the Central Committee of the Communist Party of Brazil, "Reply to Khrushchov," *A Classe Operária*, August 1–15, 1963, as cited in *Peking Review*, September 13, 1963, p. 39.

thoroughly revisionist line on the Central Committee, thereby openly repudiating the Party's militant tradition. The new policy engendered bitter opposition in the Central Committee as well as among the rank and file membership of the party. By 1960 resistance to the new line had developed to the point that Prestes and his associates decided to convene the 5th Party Congress for the purpose of purging their opponents from the Central Committee. Prior to the Congress, the revisionists allegedly rigged the elections in the conferences at the lower levels, assuring themselves of a safe majority in the Congress itself. Only a few of their opponents were elected as delegates to the Congress. Thus, the real purpose of the Congress, the expulsion of twelve of the twenty-five full members and several alternate members of the Central Committee, was easily achieved.[4] As a result of the machinations described above, the losers (pro-Chinese) contended that the Congress "did not reflect the will of the Party." In August, 1961, the Prestes forces, in a move designed to facilitate the "legalization" of the party, changed its name from the Communist Party of Brazil to the Brazilian Communist Party. The minority faction seized upon this action as evidence of a betrayal of the party. Making it clear that they would never consent to the abolition of the Communist Party of Brazil, they demanded that the Central Committee call an extraordinary congress. When their demand was rejected, they were then in a position to break with the "new" party in the name of legitimacy.[5] That is, they appropriated the name by which the party had been originally known; moreover, they revived the name of the former organ of the party, *A Classe Operária*. The pro-Chinese party was formalized in an Extraordinary National Congress held in February, 1962, at São Paulo. Leading the new party were Mauricio Grabois, João Amazonas, and Pedro Pomar, all of whom had been expelled from the party in 1961 after Prestes returned from Moscow where he had attended the 22nd Party Congress of the CPSU. The pro-Chinese group established its own publishing house and translated Guevara's *Guerrilla Warfare*. Ernst Halperin is of the opinion that the group received Chinese and Cuban funds until March, 1963. He

[4] *Ibid.*, p. 40.
[5] Kevin Devlin, "Boring from Within," *Problems of Communism*, March–April, 1964, p. 29.

was informed by an unidentified East European diplomatic source in Havana that Luiz Carlos Prestes visited Havana at that time and prevailed upon the Cubans to terminate their financial support of the Brazilian group. Thereafter the anti-Prestes forces have had only the CCP on which to depend.[6]

The Communist Party of Brazil opened the ideological debate in Brazil by reprinting on January 23, 1963, an editorial from *People's Daily* entitled "The Differences Between Comrade Togliatti and the Chinese CP." Its subservience to the CCP can be seen even more clearly in an article by Mauricio Grabois, published in *A Classe Operária* (July 1–15, 1963) entitled "The World Revolution's Vanguard and Leading Force." Needless to say he held that the Chinese Communsit Party was the *vanguard* and leading force of the world revolution, and he dismissed as "absolutely untenable" the charges of the "revisionists" that the CCP was guilty of "dogmatism." In his judgment the Chinese revolution marked a new stage in the world revolution since the end of World War II; and since it occurred in a country having almost one-fourth of the world's population, it was especially significant. He argued that the study of the "rich experience" of the Chinese Communist Party was particularly important for Brazilian and other Latin American revolutionaries. He stated:

The conditions of struggle in Brazil are in some respects similar to those of the Chinese people's struggle before they defeated their enemies and gained final victory. That is why in the light of Brazil's specific conditions, the road travelled by the Chinese Communist Party is a reliable chart for the Brazilian people in their struggle for national and social emancipation.[7]

He characterized as "sharp weapons against opportunism" *Long Live Leninism* and the numerous articles published in *People's Daily* expounding the Chinese position on various issues "in the great ideological debate within Communist ranks." For the guidance of revolutionaries in Brazil the June 14, 1963, reply of the CCP setting forth the general line of the international Communist movement was reprinted, along with earlier articles from *People's Daily*, in *A Classe*

---

6 Halperin, "Peking and the Latin American Communists," p. 140.

7 Mauricio Grabois, "The World Revolution's Vanguard and Leading Force," *A Classe Operária*, July 1–15, 1963, as excerpted in *Peking Review*, August 30, 1963, p. 27.

Operária. The Communist Party of Brazil had been prompted to do so because:

All these articles have a high degree of theoretical and practical significance and a profound revolutionary content. They greatly help the
struggle now being waged in Brazil against imperialism and the domestic
reactionary forces and against the opportunists who try to deceive the
people and induce them to submit to the ruling class.[8]

When the CPSU released its "Open Letter" of July 14, 1963,
responding to the Chinese letter of June 14, 1963, the Communist
Party of Brazil rushed to the defense of the Chinese. In fact the
Brazilians reacted more quickly than did the Chinese. The Brazilians'
"Reply to Khrushchov" took the form of a resolution adopted on
July 27, 1963, and published in the August 1–15 issue of *A Classe
Operária;* the Chinese initial response did not occur until September 6,
1963, when the editorial departments of the *Jen-min Jih-pao* and *Hung
Ch'i* published the first in a series of five articles commenting on the
"Open Letter." [9] Apparently the portion of the Soviet document most
responsible for eliciting the quick response from the Brazilians was the
following statement: "The leadership of the CPC is organising and
supporting various anti-party groups of renegades who are coming
out against the Communist Parties in the United States, Brazil, Italy,
Belgium, Australia, and India. . . . In Brazil Chinese comrades support
factional groups expelled from the Communist Party (as for instance
the Amazonas-Grabois group)." [10] The Brazilians singled out by the
Soviets were described in the Brazilian resolution as "members of the
leading organ of the Communist Party of Brazil." [11]

The Brazilians dismissed as "an arbitrary assertion which goes completely against the actual state of affairs" and an "outright slander"
the Soviet charge that the comrades of the CCP were responsible for
the split in the Brazilian Communist movement. Much of the resolution was devoted to explaining the emergence in Brazil of two parties,

[8] *Ibid.,* p. 28.

[9] The Chinese articles may be found in William E. Griffith, *The Sino-Soviet
Rift* (Cambridge, Mass.: The M.I.T. Press, 1964) as Documents numbers 10, 11,
13, 15, and 16.

[10] "The Soviet 'Open Letter,' " July 14, 1963, as cited in Griffith, *The Sino-
Soviet Rift,* p. 320.

[11] "Reply to Khrushchov," p. 39.

the Communist Party of Brazil and the Brazilian Communist Party. Internal factors rather than external influences were the principal cause of the split, a fact which the Brazilians alleged that the CPSU knew quite well because, they said, the latter was well aware of the events occurring in the Communist movement in Brazil since 1956.

The explanation given by the pro-Chinese group for the split was that the trend toward revisionism was essentially the result of the penetration of "bourgeois" ideas into the party, a development which followed the advance of capitalism in Brazil. The Brazilian explanation reflected the influence of the Marxist notion regarding the relationship between the economic base and the superstructure, of which ideology is one of the components. In short, capitalism as an economic system was developing rapidly in Brazil, and the leaders of the pro-Soviet Brazilian Communist Party had been "contaminated" by the ideas emerging from the capitalistic "base" so prevalent among the ruling class, the bourgeoisie. The split was also attributed to the methods used by the Prestes "reformist" leaders. Those methods, not specified in the resolution, must have been most reprehensible to the secessionists because they said such methods "deserved the severest condemnation."

External factors also contributed to the split, the chief of these being, according to the Grabois group, "the influence coming from the 20th Congress (of the Communist Party of the Soviet Union)," which created confusion and encouraged opportunists "by adopting a number of highly debatable propositions and raising the question of the cult of the individual." [12] In the context of external factors contributing to the split in the Brazilian Communist movement, it should be noted that no reference is made to the influence of the Chinese Communist Party on Brazilian Communists.

The pro-Chinese group also took violent exception to the Soviet reference to it as an anti-party group and attempted to demonstrate that it was in fact the revolutionary Marxist-Leninist party, whereas the opposition had degenerated into a reformist party like its model, the CPSU. That the Prestes group was linked to the CPSU, the leader of the revisionists of the world, while the Grabois-Amazonas group was connected with the CCP, chief defender of revolutionary

[12] *Ibid.,* p. 41.

Marxist-Leninist faith, emerged clearly from the description of their respective positions on some of the leading issues in the Sino-Soviet conflict. For example, the Communist Party of Brazil, like the CCP, held that the ruling classes had blocked the peaceful path to power; hence the people must be prepared to resort to armed struggle. The Brazilian Communist Party, following one of Khrushchev's theses pronounced at the 20th Congress, accepted the notion that the goals of the anti-imperialist and anti-feudal revolution could be achieved peacefully.[13]

The Communist Party of Brazil also revealed its pro-Chinese orientation by bitterly attacking Khrushchev for alleging that the Chinese leaders were bent on dragging the world into a thermonuclear war. It also took him to task for the manner in which he had treated a fraternal party, the Albanian Party of Labor, and for his policy of reconciliation with Tito. At the same time, it extolled the Chinese viewpoints as expressed in various articles that had been reprinted in *A Classe Operária:*

These documents are a highly valuable contribution to the struggle against modern revisionism and in defence of the revolutionary principles of Marxism-Leninism. Many theories which these documents defend completely correspond to the actual conditions in our country. They help us to understand better the struggle against opportunism and enable us to see that the ideological problems confronting us today are not confined to Brazil. These problems are phenomena which exist in the world Communist movement as a whole.[14]

The Brazilian supporters of the CCP closed their attack on Khrushchev with an appeal for unity in the international Communist movement. The Marxist-Leninist ideas of the Moscow Declaration and the Moscow Statement constituted the basis of that unity. They were of the opinion, however, that unity in the movement was feasible only on the basis of a "revolutionary political line." In the quest for unity, Communists everywhere must not compromise their principles. The differences between the CPSU and the CCP must not be concealed because the erroneous views of the revisionists could be overcome only through the vigorous struggle of opposites on the ideological level. Implicit in the statement below was the idea that, in the dialecti-

[13] *Ibid.*   [14] *Ibid.*, p. 42.

cal struggle between revisionist concepts and revolutionary Marxist-Leninist ideas, the latter will inevitably triumph: "Differences should not be concealed, let alone put aside. Differences should be overcome by the ideological struggle which is indispensable in forwarding the revolutionary movement so as to guarantee the solid unity of the Communists and uphold the purity of the great proletarian teachings." [15] Their faith in the inevitable victory of their ideas over those of Khrushchev and his followers was even more clearly stated: "The Communist Party of Brazil holds that truth must be told. Truth will triumph sooner or later. Defying all obstacles, we are determined to hold aloft the banner of Marxism-Leninism in our country and do all in our power to strive for the victory of the cause of revolution." [16]

How did the Chinese respond to these developments in remote Brazil? It seems that the Chinese were unwilling to place their stamp of approval on the newly established party until they had satisfied themselves regarding the orthodoxy of the pro-Chinese group. At any rate, the Chinese press failed to report the founding of the Communist Party of Brazil. As a matter of fact, the Central Committee of the Chinese Communist Party sent on March 24, 1962, a message of greetings to the Central Committee of the Brazilian Communist Party, describing the latter as the vanguard of the Brazilian working class and the staunch defender of the Brazilian nation and its working people. The CCP rejoiced and was inspired by the example set by the Brazilian comrades.[17] There was nothing in the message from the CCP to indicate that it accepted the distinction then being made in Brazil by the Grabois-Amazonas group between the Brazilian Communist Party and the Communist Party of Brazil.

On March 31, 1963, a two-man delegation representing the new party, Manuel Jover Telles and Jaime Mihanda, arrived at the Peking airport. Again there was no indication that the Chinese leaders were prepared to "recognize" the Communist Party of Brazil, for the delegation was characterized as a delegation of the Brazilian Communist Party. This is not to say that the Chinese attached no significance to the visit of the Brazilians. On the contrary, the scanty evidence available suggests that they assigned a very high priority to winning the

15 *Ibid.*, p. 43.   16 *Ibid.*
17 *SCMP*, No. 2708, p. 28.

goodwill of the visitors. For example, at the airport they were met by T'an Chen-lin, a member of the Political Bureau and the Secretariat of the Central Committee; Wu Hsiu-ch'uan, Director of the Foreign Affairs Department of the Central Committee and a member of the Board of Directors of the Chinese People's Institute of Foreign Affairs; and Li Chi-hsin, a "leading functionary of a department under the Central Committee of the Communist Party of China." [18] P'eng Chen, then a highly influential member of the Political Bureau and the Secretariat, and K'ang Sheng, alternate member of the Political Bureau and a member of the Secretariat, met and dined with them on April 9. Present for the occasion were Wu Hsiu-ch'uan and Li Chi-hsin.[19] The highest honor that the Chinese extend to any visitor was conferred on the Brazilians on April 19, when they were received by Mao Tse-tung himself, who met, dined, and had a friendly talk with them. Wu and Li were also present for this occasion.[20] The following day the Brazilians were seen off at the airport by P'eng Chen, Wu, and Li. It seems reasonable to assume that they informed their hosts, in the three weeks that they were in China, of the developments in the Brazilian Communist movement. No doubt they also explored the possibility for receiving Chinese assistance in their struggle against the Prestes faction. In support of their request for Chinese support, they could point to the numerous articles from *People's Daily* reprinted in *A Classe Operária* in which they had clearly aligned themselves with the Chinese vis-à-vis the CPSU. Perhaps the Chinese made available to the Brazilians additional funds with which to defray the costs of continuing the polemics against their mutual enemies, but they still refrained from recognizing the Communist Party of Brazil.

The Brazilians' drive to obtain legitimacy from Peking, the only other available center of authority now that they had broken ties with the CPSU, continued with the publication in the July 1–15, 1963, issue of *A Classe Operária* of the article by Mauricio Grabois entitled "The World Revolution's Vanguard and Leading Force." The excerpts from the article published in *Peking Review*, August 30, 1963, did not indicate to the reader that the Brazilian fortnightly was the official publication of the Communist Party of Brazil. Nor did it

[18] *SCMP*, No. 2953, p. 22. [19] *SCMP*, No. 2956, p. 20.
[20] *SCMP*, No. 2965, p. 23.

specify that Grabois was one of the leading figures in the Brazilian party. All the reader was told was that the article was written on the occasion of the 42nd anniversary of the founding of the CCP. When one notes the highly flattering terms used by Grabois in describing the position of the Chinese Communists in the world Communist movement, one is hard pressed to explain the failure or refusal of the Chinese to confer legitimacy on their admirers in the Western Hemisphere.

Recognition, however, was to be extended to the Brazilians shortly thereafter. According to Ernst Halperin, *Zeri i Popullit*, the official organ of the Albanian Communists, published on August 24, 1963, the full text of an anti-Soviet resolution adopted by the Communist Party of Brazil.[21] As we have seen, excerpts from the Brazilians' "Reply to Khrushchov," presumably the resolution referred to by Halperin, was also reprinted in *Peking Review* September 13, 1963. A slightly more abridged version of the same resolution appeared earlier in the Daily News Release, *Hsinhua*, on September 5, 1963. In both versions of the resolution, the reader was informed that the resolution was adopted on July 27, 1963, by the Central Committee of the *Communist Party of Brazil*. Apparently, then, the CCP, in the first half of September, 1963, decided to accept the verbal distinction made by its supporters in Brazil.

Additional evidence in support of this conclusion is the fact that *Hsinhua* carried in its Daily News Release of September 5, 1963, an article by Jose Duarte written for "*A Classe Operária* of the *Communist Party of Brazil* in its August 16–31 issue." [22] Duarte's article entitled "Attacking the Communist Party of China in Defence of Opportunism" attacked Luiz Carlos Prestes, "general secretary of the *Brazilian Communist Party*" and Luis Corvalan, general secretary of the Chilean Communist Party, for their assaults on the Chinese Communist Party *after* the publication of the July 14, 1963, letter of the CPSU. Prestes had written an article for *Novos Rumbos*, the official organ of the pro-Soviet group, in which he "openly sided with the revisionists." Duarte accused Prestes of having zealously repeated

21 Halperin, "Peking and the Latin American Communists," *The China Quarterly*, January–March, 1967, pp. 141–42.
22 Daily News Release, *Hsinhua*, September 5, 1963, p. 26. Emphasis added.

Khrushchev's theses of the 20th Congress of the CPSU. His accusation that the Prestes group had failed to apply "creatively" Marxist-Leninist principles in light of different conditions confronting Communist parties in their respective countries may be seen in the following passage:

They lauded the resolutions of the Congress of one party as universal laws applicable to the entire Communist movement. In their eyes, complete [sic] worthless is Lenin's behest that it is necessary to make a critical analysis of the experience of other parties and other countries. They say, "our line is based on the theory of the 20th Congress of the CPSU." Thus they had based themselves, not on reality but on something proclaimed by the leader of another Communist party. They had thus acted subjectively and departed from the Marxist-Leninist path.[23]

Duarte also criticized Prestes for "parroting Khrushchov's slander against the Communist Party of Brazil" and pinning the label of "the anti-party group" on the orthodox revolutionaries. It will be recalled that the position of the Communist Party of Brazil was that the real "anti-party group" was the Brazilian Communist Party, led by Prestes. It, rather than the Communist Party of Brazil, was responsible for the split in the Brazilian Communist movement.

Duarte vented his spleen on Luis Corvalan, General Secretary of the Chilean Communist Party, for having made a speech to the Chilean Central Committee, subsequently printed in *El Siglo*, in which he "insolently launched attacks on the Chinese comrades while fawning on Khrushchev and other leaders of the CPSU." [24] He disputed the argument made by Corvalan that the differences were between "the Chinese Communist Party and almost the entire international Communist movement." Corvalan was attempting to persuade the Chilean people that the Chinese were isolated in the debate then being waged among Communists everywhere. Duarte vigorously denied the validity of this statement, holding that the number of parties and Communists sharing the views of the Chinese was steadily growing; and even if the Chinese were isolated, as claimed by Corvalan, did that show that they were in the wrong?

Regarding the differences in the movement, Duarte acknowledged that deep differences did exist between the CCP and the CPSU,

[23] *Ibid.*   [24] *Ibid.*, p. 27.

but he insisted that the controversy was much more extensive in scope than that. He said that the differences "also exist between various parties and within some parties. This is so because the ideological struggle now going on is between Marxism-Leninism and modern revisionism." [25]

Corvalan's contention that the majority is always right was totally unacceptable to Duarte. In this context, the Chilean Communist had criticized the following passage from the June 14, 1963, letter of the CCP to the CPSU: ". . . if the leading group in any party adopts a non-revolutionary line and converts it into a reformist party, then Marxist-Leninists inside and outside the party will replace them." Duarte held that the Chinese "theory" had been validated by the "practice" of revolutionaries elsewhere. The experience of Fidel Castro and his comrades in Cuba and developments in Latin America were cited as cases in point:

The example of Cuba fully shows that if the organization regarded as the vanguard failed to play its role in the revolution, it would be replaced by some other forces. Fidel Castro and his comrades were not Communists when they waged the struggle to overthrow Batista. The developments in Latin America show that wherever the party became opportunist and proved a failure, new revolutionary forces emerged. Such militant forces have also emerged in our country and are growing in size and strength. The existence of the Communist Party of Brazil is a case in point.[26]

He censured Corvalan's attempts to prevent those in the Chilean party with views different from his own from reading and discussing documents then being circulated on a global scale by the Chinese in an effort to explain their position on the major issues to members of the international Communist movement. Clarification of the positions of the participants in the great debate and exposure of the erroneous views of the revisionists, he claimed, made necessary the free circulation of the Chinese documents among all the Communist parties of Latin America.

Duarte concluded his diatribe against the pro-Soviet Communist leaders by expressing his views regarding the future development of the debate in Latin America. The debate, far from being harmful, he argued, would redound to the benefit of the revolutionary movement.

[25] *Ibid.*, p. 28.   [26] *Ibid.*

In the end, "the great Marxist-Leninist ideology will certainly triumph on our continent." It is evident from the context of this article that the Marxist-Leninist ideology referred to was the Chinese interpretation of that ideology. He was also optimistic concerning the appearance, in the near future, of revolutionary vanguards in the various countries that would be competent to lead the masses in the struggle against opportunism and the common enemy of the people.[27] In short, parties comparable to the Communist Party of Brazil would emerge, in due time, in the other countries of Latin America.

On April 1, 1964, the Chinese and their supporters in Brazil experienced a setback of major proportions when the military ousted the Goulart government. Prior to that time, the Chinese had succeeded in expanding trade with Brazil and had established there their first trade mission in Latin America.[28] The Brazilian government had allowed *Hsinhua* to establish an office in Rio de Janeiro in the latter part of 1961. At the time of the military coup in 1964, the Chinese had nine representatives in Brazil trying to expand their influence in the largest country of South America.

The authoritative Chinese evaluation of the coup appeared in a long editorial in *Jen-min Jih-pao* entitled "What Are the Lessons from the Brazilian Coup?" As one might expect, the Chinese assigned to Washington the dominant role in the planning and implementation of the coup. The American imperialists had been allegedly colluding for several years with reactionary elements in the Brazilian military to remove the Goulart government, which had become "a thorn in the side of U.S. imperialism" because it had pursued a policy which promoted the Brazilian people's interests. In the field of foreign policy, for example, the Chinese asserted that Goulart had "adhered to the principles of non-interference and self determination and maintained diplomatic relations with Cuba." This statement regarding the most salient characteristics of Goulart's foreign policy was not without foundation. That the United States State Department was not altogether satisfied with the Brazilian insistence on their need for greater independence in foreign relations was common knowledge at the time. The speed with which the United States extended recognition to the military junta lends credence to this interpretation, but this is not

[27] *Ibid.*
[28] Tretiak, "China and Latin America," *Current Scene*, March 1, 1966, p. 8.

to say that the American government actively conspired with rightist elements to bring down the leftist Goulart administration.

On the domestic scene, Goulart's policies were, according to the Chinese, much too progressive for the Americans, and they cited several instances of actions taken by the Goulart administration that directly affected the "interests of U.S. imperialism and those of the pro-U.S. comprador forces in Brazil." [29] For example, the Goulart government had proclaimed a state monopoly of petroleum imports, restricted the remittance abroad of profits earned by foreigners, and was about to assume control over private oil refineries which were mostly owned by American investors. Thus, the Chinese reasoned, the American government, allegedly the tool of large American monopoly capitalists, connived with the Brazilian military to remove their common enemy from the political scene. While the United States government was no doubt displeased with these actions taken by the Goulart regime, it does not necessarily follow that representatives of the American government, at the behest of large investors in Wall Street, organized, with the help of Brazilian puppets, the coup that toppled the Goulart administration.

In accordance with the Marxist dogma that theory must be examined in light of practice, the Chinese attempted to extract certain lessons from the Brazilian coup. The first lesson was that U.S. imperialism was "the sworn enemy of the Latin American peoples and that they must not entertain any illusions about this most ferocious enemy." [30] In Latin America, as elsewhere in their propaganda, the Chinese hammered away at the idea that the interests of the peoples of the Third World and those of U.S. imperialism are fundamentally and inevitably incompatible. The Brazilian experience, coupled with similar experiences of other Latin American nations, demonstrated that all Latin American nations had only two alternatives in regard to the problem of "U.S. imperialism": They may ". . . either allow themselves to be ruled by lackeys of U.S. imperialism and be dominated and enslaved by the U.S. as in the case of Nicaragua and the Dominican Republic or rid themselves of the influence of the U.S. aggressors and resist U.S. intervention as in the case of Cuba. There is no third possibility." [31] Thus the Chinese contend that it is impossible

[29] *SCMP*, No. 3212, p. 27.   [30] *Ibid.*, p. 28.
[31] *Ibid.*

for the United States and Latin American countries to work out relationships that would be mutually beneficial. In short, those trading with or receiving aid from the United States are, by definition, being exploited by the Americans. The message is abundantly clear: the Latin Americans should avoid all contacts with the leading imperialist nation if they want to retain their freedom.

The second lesson was that the national democratic forces in Latin America, as elsewhere, must be fully prepared to deal with armed suppression by U.S. imperialism and strike back with armed force if necessary. The peaceful transition message being preached by modern revisionists was both an illusion and a monstrous crime. "Counter-revolutionary violence can only be answered with revolutionary violence. This is a universally applicable truth." [32] In short, there is only one viable path to power, the path of armed struggle.

The third lesson was that oppressed nations and peoples of Latin America "must form a broad national-democratic front by rallying all patriotic domestic forces and resolutely fight against U.S. imperialism and its lackeys" [33] to effectuate a national-democratic revolution and win national and social liberation. From the discussion that followed on this point it was clear that the Chinese felt that the class struggle then going on in Latin America was essentially the same as that of China in the first stage of the Chinese revolution. That is, their class analysis of Latin American society was remarkably similar to that given in Chapter II regarding Chinese society in a comparable stage of the Chinese revolution. Moreover, the revolution in Latin America, as in China at an earlier date, was an anti-imperialist and anti-feudal revolution. The Chinese quoted, with approval, the following passage from the Second Havana Declaration:

It is possible to organize the immense majority of the people in the anti-imperialist and anti-feudal struggle for the goals of liberation which unite the efforts of the working class, the peasants, the intellectual workers, the petty bourgeoisie and the most progressive sectors of the national bourgeoisie. Together these forces include the immense majority of the people and command great social forces which are capable of sweeping away imperialist domination and feudal reaction.[34]

[32] *Ibid.*, p. 29. [33] *Ibid.*, p. 30.
[34] *Ibid.*

The Chinese concept of the enemy in Latin America was also quite similar to that expressed earlier in regard to the enemy in China itself. Only a handful of feudal landowners and comprador bourgeoisie elements, constituting the most reactionary forces, would refuse to align themselves with the classes enumerated above in a joint struggle against "U.S. imperialist oppression and enslavement" in order "to win and uphold national independence." It was, therefore, entirely feasible to unite more than 90 per cent of the patriotic people against the reactionary forces and U.S. imperialism and its accomplices. The reader's attention is also called to the fact that the line recommended by the Chinese for Latin America stresses the anti-imperialism theme more than the anti-feudalism theme. The Chinese emphasized the former theme more than the latter for precisely the same reason as in China, namely, that they appreciated the fact that the former would serve as a better rallying point for more groups than would the anti-feudal theme.

In any event, the united front could not be formed without organizing the masses; moreover, the united front must have a strong leadership and be based on "an alliance between the workers and peasants, who form the overwhelming majority of the population." The Chinese view that the united front in Latin America must be based on the worker-peasant alliance was, of course, the same formula that they had used prior to the Chinese Communist takeover in 1949. The key role assigned the peasantry in Latin America was identical to that of the peasantry in the Chinese revolution:

The peasant question is a key question in the national democratic revolution of the Latin American countries. It is necessary, therefore, to make extensive efforts to develop the peasant movement, to help them organize themselves into a main force of the revolution. That is why in the Latin American countries a national democratic united front cannot be firmly established, nor can it lead the national-democratic revolution to victory, if its revolutionary program cannot provide a solution to the land problem.[35]

This passage suggests that the Chinese regard the peasantry in Latin America as the class with the greatest potential for revolution. It also indicates that the peasants' potential for revolution can be harnessed

[35] *Ibid.*

by Communists through the adoption in their program of action of land reform proposals, but two assumptions underlying the Chinese prescription for revolution in Latin America appear to be of questionable value. The first assumption was that Chinese and Latin American peasants would be equally "ripe" for mobilization by cadres of the Communist Party. They provided no data in support of this assumption. The second assumption was that the peasants in the various countries of Latin America were equally receptive to promises of "land reform." Would it not be extremely dangerous for Communists in Chile, for example, to assume that Chilean peasants are as ready subjectively as their counterpart in Guatemala? How well does the passage above square with the Chinese contention that their policies are always based on a scientific and objective analysis of the conditions confronting their policy-makers? Clearly this statement did not reflect an accurate appreciation on their part of the complexity of Latin American reality.

Returning now to the Chinese critique of the Brazilian coup, we note that the Chinese were definitely not pleased with the way in which their supporters had participated in the national democratic revolutionary movement. The setback for the movement occurred ". . . for no other reason than that it did not have a broad united front with strong leadership. It had not truly aroused and organized the broad sections of the peasants and other people." [36] The Communist Party of Brazil apparently had not, in the Chinese view, discharged properly its role as vanguard of the revolution; that is, it had failed to provide strong leadership, and it had not formed a united front, with the peasantry as the main force.

The Chinese authorities had attempted to win the friendship of Francisco Julião, leader of the Peasant Leagues in Brazil's Northeast. No doubt they were attracted by his radical land reform program in the impoverished northeastern part of Brazil. In an effort to enlist his support, they invited him to visit China at least once. Furthermore, they highlighted the visit of his wife and two daughters in April, 1962. Indicative of the high priority accorded to the Brazilian "peasant" leader and his family was the fact that they were received by Ch'en Yi and by Mao himself. From the evidence produced at the

[36] *Ibid.*

trial of the nine Chinese arrested in April, 1964, at the time of the military coup we know that those arrested had contacted Julião as well as members of the pro-Chinese party itself. Obviously the coup occurred before the local party leaders had time to organize the peasants in the northeast and thus establish a base in the countryside. Given the remoteness and the inaccessibility of the area, one can well imagine that the Chinese Communists were extremely excited about their prospects for winning a foothold in this the largest and most strategic of the republics in Latin America.

The final lesson to be learned from the Brazilian fiasco was "that the people of all the Latin American countries must form the broadest possible international front to fight their common enemy—U.S. imperialism, and support and coordinate with each other in the common struggle." [37] Once again one notes the Chinese attempt to capitalize on the anti-American sentiments so prevalent in many parts of Latin America by portraying the United States as the common enemy of all Latin Americans. The Chinese held that since the Latin Americans had so many common interests they ought to form a close alliance so as to be better able to support one another and to defend the Cuban revolution. Through such joint action they could "certainly defeat U.S. imperialist aggression and intervention and drive away the U.S. aggressive forces from the Latin American continent." [38]

Revolutionaries, however, should regard the Brazilian coup as a temporary setback from which they could heighten their consciousness and thus understand better what they must do to advance the cause of the revolution. The Chinese analysis ended on the customary optimistic note: "A second, a third or even more Cubas will undoubtedly emerge in Latin America." [39]

One final observation should be made regarding this long *Jen-min Jih-pao* editorial, and that is that it was an attempt by the Chinese to lay down a general line for the Communist movement in Latin America. Their frequent references to Latin American conditions in general make abundantly clear that their remarks were addressed to genuine Marxist-Leninists elsewhere in Latin America as well as to those in Brazil. In short, the Chinese availed themselves of this op-

[37] *Ibid.*
[38] *Ibid.*, p. 31.
[39] *Ibid.*

portunity to make recommendations regarding the strategy and tactics that Marxist-Leninists in all parts of Latin America should follow.

The Central Executive Committee of the Communist Party of Brazil adopted a resolution in August, 1964, making its own analysis of the domestic situation in Brazil and the tasks of the party after the April coup. The Brazilians felt that one of the basic causes for the defeat of the democratic, anti-imperialist movement was the idea that the revolution in Brazil could follow the peaceful path. Needless to say they associated that idea with their domestic foes, the Brazilian Communist Party, which had allegedly labored under the illusion that they could achieve reforms through collaboration with João Goulart, their main ally, and had thus allowed the "reformist bourgeois leadership," headed by Goulart, to gain the upper hand, while they trailed behind the bourgeoisie. That is, they failed to fulfill their responsibility as a Communist party to act as a *vanguard* for the proletariat. In attacking the type of leadership provided by the Brazilian Communist Party, the pro-Chinese group may have been trying to exonerate themselves from charges concerning their own shortcomings in this respect. In any event, the statement by the pro-Chinese group reflected accurately the Chinese position on the matter of leadership in democratic, anti-imperialist movements and the strategy and tactics to be used:

Reality once again proves that the democratic, anti-imperialist movement can win complete success only when it is headed by a revolutionary vanguard representing the most advanced class in society, namely, the proletariat; it can win victory only when it pursues a revolutionary instead of a reformist line; it can succeed only when it rallies all forces opposing U.S. imperialism and its supporters in our country to form a broad united front; it can win victory only when it is prepared politically and ideologically to wage the most resolute and powerful struggle or even resort to revolutionary violence of the masses to answer the violence of imperialism and domestic reaction.[40]

Of particular significance was the statement by the party concerning the peasant question. The coup was caused, in part, by the

[40] Resolution of the Central Executive Committee of the Communist Party of Brazil, "The Domestic Situation in Brazil and the Tasks of the Communist Party of Brazil," as excerpted in *Peking Review*, May 28, 1965, p. 21.

neglect of the peasant movement, the mainstay of the revolutionary forces. Apparently the party devoted too much of its efforts to winning popular support in the cities only to discover that the strength of the enemy was greatest there. For that reason, rural work, in the future, must be assigned a higher priority than work in the cities. The Brazilians' acceptance of the urgency for strengthening their position in the countryside appeared in the following statement:

The worker-peasant alliance is the foundation on which the democratic, anti-imperialist united front should be built. . . . Therefore, the greatest possible efforts must be made to organize and develop the peasant movement. The importance of rural work is easily understood when one realizes that the national-liberation struggle is bound to be arduous and protracted and in the main be waged in the hinterland. All signs indicate that the first centers of revolt against the enemy of our people will emerge in the countryside. Thus, it can definitely be said that the question of the peasantry is the crucial question for the Brazilian revolution.[41]

The above quotation incorporated, as the reader will recall, several of the basic ideas of a people's war, although the Brazilians did not use that expression.

In a resolution adopted in June, 1966, the Communist Party of Brazil stated its views on East-West relations, the Sino-Soviet conflict, and the domestic situation in Brazil. The document prepared after Lin Piao's historic essay on people's war in September, 1965, called on the Brazilian people to prepare for people's war; but because it was drafted before the Cultural Revolution had become characterized by excessive praise of Mao, it did not bestow on Mao's thought the magic qualities it was later said to possess. It was also significant for the stand it expressed on the matter of neutrality in the Sino-Soviet conflict. The supporters of the CCP held that there could be no reconciliation or halfway stand in the global struggle between Marxism-Leninism and revisionism.

The Brazilian analysis of international developments merely repeated the familiar themes of the Chinese. Their image of the world was one in which the peoples of the world were engaged in mortal combat with U.S. imperialism allegedly bent on establishing its world hegemony. They condemned the Johnson administration for

[41] *Ibid.*

escalating the war in Vietnam and for its active preparation for war with China. In their judgment the main aim of the United States was to isolate and attack China, which they called "the most powerful base of the world revolutionary movement." [42] In this context, it is significant that the Brazilians singled out China, Albania, and the Democratic Republic of Vietnam as specific examples of "socialist countries" that were giving "firm and resolute support" to the people of the world struggling against U.S. imperialism. The omission of the Soviet Union, the East European regimes, and Cuba clearly reflected the Chinese influence on the Brazilians. The latter's concept of the dominant role played by China in the world revolutionary movement and the contribution China was making to the movement was apparent in the following selection:

China is the *most powerful base* of the world revolutionary movement. . . . Because of the revolutionary and internationalist position of People's China, the U.S. imperialists take it as their *principal enemy* and are *concentrating their forces against it.* . . . By drawing against itself vast military resources of the United States, China gives inestimable help to the peoples struggling for liberation.[43]

Especially significant was the claim that the Chinese were assisting, indirectly at least, revolutions in Latin America and elsewhere by pinning down much of the military power of the United States, which now regarded China, not the Soviet Union, as the principal enemy and for that reason was "concentrating their forces against it." The Soviet Union, on the other hand, could not be counted on by those engaged in national liberation movements because it was pursuing "a policy of collaboration with the United States, with a view to dividing the world into their spheres of influence." [44]

Within this international framework the Communist Party of Brazil had a number of tasks to perform. Top priority was assigned to the active support of the Vietnamese who were "bearing the brunt of U.S. aggression." Protests should be made against the Brazilian Government's sending of grain and medicine to "the Saigon puppets."

[42] "Political Resolution of the 6th National Conference of the Communist Party of Brazil," *Peking Review*, December 16, 1966, p. 28.
[43] *Ibid.* Emphasis added.   [44] *Ibid.*

Support should be given to those engaged in armed struggle against imperialism and the reactionaries. Similarly, support should be given to the CPR's efforts to form a world united front to defeat U.S. imperialism's plan for global domination, and no effort should be spared in exposing the scheme of the American and Russian leaders to divide the world into their respective spheres of influence. In Latin America itself, efforts must be made to protect the various countries against exploitation by U.S. monopoly capitalists and to oppose the establishment of a "so-called Pan-American peace force." [45]

With regard to the Sino-Soviet split, the Grabois group displayed an intransigent posture vis-à-vis revisionism. Ideological struggle was given a very high priority. In fact, the "struggle against *ideas* alien to the interest of the proletariat and to defend unremittingly the theories of Marx, Engels, and Lenin *is the most important task* of the world working-class movement." [46] This statement on the absolute necessity for combatting erroneous ideas, so typical of Chinese thinking, provides us with a key to understanding why so much of the time and efforts of the Chinese and their supporters have been devoted to defeating revisionist ideas. It should be stressed that, in the Chinese view, the struggle against revisionism is intimately connected with the struggle against imperialism: "The struggles of the peoples of the various countries against U.S. imperialism are inseparable from the relentless struggle against modern revisionism." They are convinced that the revisionists ". . . must be unmasked, isolated and struck down. If this is not done, it will be impossible to defeat U.S. imperialism and carry the revolution forward." [47]

These passages support the thesis advanced in Chapter II that the Chinese regard correct thinking as a prerequisite to correct action. More concretely, they feel that the battle against the main enemy, U.S. imperialism, cannot be won until the ideas of the renegades in the international Communist movement have been liquidated. It seems to me that those analysts of Chinese behavior who have criticized the Chinese for providing very little material assistance to those engaged in national liberation movements have failed to see that the Chinese regard their ideological campaign against revisionism as in-

[45] *Ibid.*, p. 29.   [46] *Ibid.*, p. 30. Emphasis added.
[47] *Ibid.*

dispensable preparation for the final onslaught against the imperialists. In short, ideological victory over revisionism is a condition precedent to military and political victory over imperialism.

Given these assumptions, the Chinese and their supporters, such as the Brazilian group, must reject proposals calling for unity between Marxists and revisionists. Reconciliation is out of the question. Nor is there any room for an intermediate position in the struggle between the two diametrically opposite points of view. Communists must choose between the conflicting lines as expounded by the CPSU and the CCP. The Brazilians cited Fidel Castro's attempt to pursue a policy of neutrality as proof of the impossibility of standing aloof in the Sino-Soviet controversy. They insisted that sooner or later such individuals must, like Castro, align themselves with one of the superpowers in the movement:

What happened in Cuba is very illustrative. In the polemics between the Marxist-Leninists and the modern revisionists, Fidel Castro for a certain period of time tried to refrain from defining his attitude, arguing that this could better safeguard the unity of the Communist movement. But this attempt to take a middle-of-the-road position completely failed. Fidel swang [sic] into open and unjustifiable attacks on the Chinese Communist Party and all Marxist-Leninists of the world. Although he proclaims his intention to combat U.S. imperialism, he in fact already stands on the side of the CPSU and other revisionist parties.[48]

Several points made in the resolution with regard to the domestic situation require brief comment. First, the Brazilians visualize a two-stage revolution comparable to the Chinese revolution as described in Chapter II. The terminology used is not precisely the same, but the essence of the two stages in both cases appears to be identical. The Brazilians did not speak of their first stage as a new democracy; rather they spoke of a "national, democratic, agrarian, and anti-imperialist revolution" in which they called for an end to U.S. imperialist plundering and the evil latifundia. That is, the revolution must be "anti-imperialist" and "anti-feudal" in character. This revolution "will give birth to a true people's government and a democratic and progressive system of government." [49] Furthermore, it would provide the country

[48] *Ibid.*, p. 31.   [49] *Ibid.*, p. 29.

with a new economic structure, and it would eliminate foreign plundering and monopoly in land. Lastly, it would bring freedom, culture, and happiness to the people. Assuming leadership for this stage was the proletariat (Communist Party), which would form the basic alliance with the peasantry. Explicitly rejected was the view expressed by some that the national bourgeoisie could serve as the leader in the first stage. The allies of the workers and peasants were the petty bourgeoisie, progressive intellectuals, and the more progressive members of the national bourgeoisie. All in all, this class analysis was identical to that found in Mao's writings dealing with the first stage. The second stage, the socialist stage, will be entered when "the tasks of democracy and national liberation are completed," a task that can be completed only under the leadership of the proletariat. That the Communist Party of Brazil regarded itself as the leader of the revolutionary movement was beyond doubt. It explicitly referred to itself as holding the vanguard position in the Brazilian people's struggle for national and social liberation.[50]

Second, the resolution stressed that the revolution in Brazil must take the form of a people's war, but the reader should note that the resolution did not expressly refer to the revolutionary experience of China in this respect. Nor did it enjoin Marxist-Leninists to study and master the military writings of Chairman Mao Tse-tung. The impression that emerges from a careful scrutiny of the analysis under this heading is that the Brazilians were merely paying lip-service to the Chinese literature which laid so much stress on the absolute need for mobilizing all the people in a people's war. Certainly the statement below did not reflect mastery of the complexities of the Chinese concept of people's war:

The Brazilian people must make preparations for a people's war. In all parts of the country, and especially in the countryside, discussions must be held on the question of armed struggle, and practical measures for the preparations of armed struggle must be taken in accordance with the principles of secret work. By uniting their own force to form a broad united front, unfolding energetic political activities and using different forms of struggle, the Brazilian people will certainly be able to achieve victory.[51]

[50] Ibid., p. 32.   [51] Ibid., p. 30.

By mid-summer of 1967 the Maoists in Brazil had inaugurated a campaign to study Mao's works and to exalt the Cultural Revolution. They, like pro-Chinese groups around the world, were enjoined to study Mao's works to educate the party members in the spirit of Marxism-Leninism and to gain a better understanding of problems affecting the revolution in Brazil. Such study would "help us to analyze the reality in Brazil more profoundly and apply the universal truth of Marxism-Leninism correctly to our revolutionary practice." [52] The Cultural Revolution was of major importance to all peoples because it was occurring in the country having one-fourth of the world's population, but more importantly because the problems being "solved" there were directly related to the world revolution. It would be, as a more advanced stage of the socialist revolution, of inestimable assistance to all peoples. China would be enabled to play an even greater role as the principal base of the world revolution.[53]

By the end of 1967 the Communist Party of Brazil was deeply involved in the revolution that was affecting the ranks of Maoists around the world. As in China itself, the Brazilian supporters of Chairman Mao were busily engaged in the study of his works, especially his writings on people's war. The scanty evidence available does not indicate whether there was in Brazil a split in the party comparable to that existing in China. That is, we have no evidence that some of the Brazilian comrades were supporters of Liu Shao-ch'i, Teng Hsiao-p'ing, and other opponents of Lin Piao and Chairman Mao. It seems reasonable to assume, however, that the Brazilians must have been most adversely affected by the intense struggle going on in China. With the final outcome of that struggle still very much in doubt at the time, one can well imagine that the Brazilians would be most hesitant with regard to starting a people's war in Brazil. After the leaders of the CCP have resolved their major differences, the Brazilians may intensify their attempts to go to the countryside and establish rural bases in the vast hinterland of the country. Certainly Brazil has some of the major ingredients for waging a people's war. It is, for example, a country with a vast amount of space in which

[52] "Brazilian Communists Must Study Mao Tse-tung's Works," *Peking Review,* June 30, 1967, p. 41.
[53] *Ibid.*

guerrillas could maneuver. The peasantry, constituting a majority of the population, is ripe for revolution, especially in the northeast. The military dictatorship's policy of outlawing virtually all political opposition has generated widespread dissatisfaction. The pro-Chinese forces have not, as far as I have been able to determine, even begun a guerrilla movement. Nor have they succeeded in forming a broad united front against the domestic reactionary forces and U.S. imperialism. Clearly, then, they have many tasks to perform before they are ready to engage their enemies in mortal combat.

When evaluating the revolutionary accomplishments of this and similar groups in Latin America, one must also take into account two other considerations. First, these parties are quite young. In the case of the Chinese Communist Party itself, victory over the KMT came only after a struggle of over twenty years (1927–1949). In short, the Latin American parties are still in their formative stage of development. Second, the strategy of people's wars is, in essence, a cautious one. Lin Piao, as one of the spokesmen for the Maoists, made perfectly clear in his famous article that revolutionaries should not fight until they have a good chance for winning. Chinese comments on guerrilla movements in Latin America, led by Castroites, explain their setbacks in terms of poor preparation in a military and political sense. One can hardly level the same charge of adventurism at the pro-Chinese groups. One can, of course, fault them for being so slow in the political mobilization of the masses and in the development of strong and well-disciplined parties to serve as vanguards for the revolution.

VII

The Pro-Chinese Parties of Peru, Bolivia, and Colombia

I N 1964 and 1965 the Chinese stepped up their campaign to organize pro-Chinese parties in Latin America. In those two years their
followers succeeded in forming such parties in Peru, Bolivia, and
Colombia. The Peruvian party, first of these to be established, was to
become the largest and most influential of all the Latin American
parties looking to Peking for guidance.

PERU

The pro-Chinese party in Peru was established almost two years after
the Communist Party of Brazil. Like its Brazilian predecessor it was
founded by a conference rather than by a party congress, but, unlike
its Brazilian counterpart, the name chosen by this group was exactly
the same as that used by the pro-Soviet group, both parties being
called the Peruvian Communist Party. Another basic difference between developments in Peru and those in Brazil was the fact that the
pro-Chinese in Peru expelled in their conference the pro-Soviet group
from the Peruvian Communist Party. Those expelled refused to recognize the authority of their domestic rivals to oust them from the
party. As a consequence, each party asserts that it alone is the legitimate Communist party in Peru. Complicating the picture even more
is the fact that the pro-Chinese group itself split, in January of 1966,
into two factions, one headed by Saturnino Paredes Macedo and the

other led by José Sotomayor Pérez. The Chinese, for reasons that are not entirely clear, have recognized only the Paredes faction.

The evidence concerning the initial split in January of 1964 is in sharp conflict. The accounts provided by pro-Soviet and pro-Chinese sources have little in common other than the fact that the split occurred in January, 1964, at a conference called the "Fourth Conference" by the pro-Chinese group.

The pro-Soviet version, as given by Jorge del Prado, a member of the Politbureau and Secretariat of the Central Committee of the pro-Soviet party, was that the pro-Chinese members of the Communist Party leadership began their drive to seize control of the party early in 1963. On January 5 of that year the police staged a raid, which resulted in the arrest of several of the national leaders of the party, among whom was Raoul Acosta, secretary-general of the party. Taking advantage of the imprisonment of the top pro-Soviet leaders, the new factionalists, assisted and supported by the leadership of the CCP, stepped up their efforts to take over the top organs of the party. Remnants of old factionalist tendencies joined forces with the new factionalists, succeeding at the 17th plenary session of the Central Committee in replacing several members of the Politburo on the ground that they could not, while in prison, provide leadership for the party. This action was allegedly taken by the factionalists at a time when they knew that the leaders were about to be released. After their release from prison, the pro-Soviet leaders clashed with the factionalists at the 18th plenum of the Central Committee. On this occasion they blocked efforts by their antagonists to exclude from the Central Committee "the most steadfast comrades," meaning, of course, the pro-Soviet leaders. At this point, the pro-Chinese group decided to break openly with the party by walking out of the assembly, thereby rejecting its decisions. Shortly thereafter they decided to hold their National Conference at which they excluded Acosta and other pro-Soviet leaders from the party and attempted to elect a new leadership and usurp the name of the party.[1]

At its own Fourth National Conference, the pro-Soviet forces drafted a statement entitled "Opportunist Divisionism of the Left,

[1] Lazitch, "Repercussions of the Sino-Soviet Dispute on the Latin American Communist Parties," JPRS, *TICD*, No. 693, pp. 19-20.

Uncovered and in Defeat" which provided additional evidence on the origin of the split. It contained the charge of open complicity between the police and the fractionalists, providing the latter "with the best opportunity to show their true colors." [2] This conclusion was based on the different treatment given by the police to the arrested leaders of the two groups.

As is known, the heads of this group—Sotomayor, Paredes, Alvarez and Cunti—were as well-known for their Communist affiliation as other national and regional leaders. But the Governing Military Junta, having failed with their raids to decapitate and immobilize the Party, decided to free precisely the above individuals while keeping in prison the most important members of the Central Committee and of the Regional Committees. Subsequent events proved that this discrimination was not accidental. As soon as Sotomayor, Paredes and company were freed they began to launch against the imprisoned leaders the very slanders which the Peruvian Investigative Police and the officials of the Military Zone used in their attempt to justify the raids and the monstrous trial which followed. [3]

Raoul Acosta Salas, secretary-general of the pro-Soviet group, echoed the charge of police complicity. He noted that the pro-Chinese leaders had been released from prison several months before the pro-Soviet leaders because the police evidently knew about the former's factional activity and decided to use them to undermine the party. [4]

In his article, Acosta also alleged that the "anti-party group" received "the direct assistance and support of the leadership of the CPC," a contention which neither the Chinese Communist Party nor its supporters in Peru has seen fit to deny. As we shall see, however, they did join issue with the pro-Soviet party on the question of whether the pro-Chinese Fourth National Conference was truly representative of the Communist movement in the country. As one would expect, Acosta held that the conference represented only the

[2] Statement of the Fourth National Conference of the Peruvian Communist Party, "Opportunist Divisionism of the Left, Uncovered and in Defeat," *Unidad*, as translated in JPRS, *TICD*, No. 658, p. 55.

[3] *Ibid*.

[4] Raoul Acosta Salas, "Whom Do the Chinese Leaders Support in Peru?" *Pravda*, May 22, 1964, as translated in JPRS, *TICD*, No. 616, p. 26.

schismatics, who had, he contended, adherents only in Lima but no representatives in the departmental and zonal party committees.

The pro-Chinese account of the origin of the split was that the Fourth Party Conference of January, 1964, was preceded by a period of intense and prolonged struggle especially since the convening of the Fourth National Congress held in 1962. According to their version, the contradictions in the party originated at least a year earlier than the pro-Soviet account would indicate.[5]

The Chinese coverage of the controversial Fourth National Conference indicated that they recognized the Peruvian group much earlier than the Communist Party of Brazil. By early 1964 the CCP was fully committed to pursuing a policy of splitting Communist parties on a global scale, hence the speedier response to developments in Peru. In the case of the Peruvian group, recognition was extended within less than a month, while in the Brazilian case, Chinese recognition came in September, 1963, almost eighteen months after the founding of the party.

The Chinese cited statistics in support of their contention that the Fourth National Conference, the founding conference, was, in fact, a representative body. They contended that it had been convened by a majority of the Central Committee and representatives from thirteen of the seventeen regional committees, a contention that hardly squared with the account given by Acosta! After analyzing the situation in the party, the more than seventy representatives voted unanimously for the expulsion from the party of a number of leaders. Their names and the grounds for their expulsion were:

. . . Jorge del Prado, Juan Barrios de Mendoza, Victor Raul Acosta Salas, Ruben Molleopaza Bilbao, Alfredo Abarca, Carlos Vega, Rodolfo Dias, Felix Arias Schreiber and Cesar Levano La Rosa because of their betrayal of Marxism-Leninism, their political degeneration, their misuse of party funds, their recourse to splitting the party and creating parallel organizations in a truly sectarian and divisive manner.[6]

[5] "The Peruvian Communist Party Down the Path of Mariátegui," *Bandera Roja* (Red Flag), as translated in JPRS, *TICD*, No. 910, p. 3.

[6] "Revisionist Leading Group Expelled from Peruvian Communist Party," *Peking Review*, February 14, 1964, p. 23.

Chinese theoreticians analyzing the political report adopted by the Fourth National Conference must have been most gratified by the correct analyses of the international and domestic situations made by the Paredes-Sotomayor group. First, on the international scene, the Peruvian analysts perceived a situation "favourable to the people of the world fighting for national liberation." They accepted Mao's idea, articulated at the Moscow Conference of 1957, that the "East Wind prevails over the West Wind," and they adhered to his instructions to select, as a basis for policy-making, the principal contradiction of the present historical era. They did not, however, refer to the contradiction between the oppressed peoples of Asia, Africa, and Latin America and U.S. imperialism as the principal contradiction, but they did assert that this contradiction was "the *focus* of contradictions in the postwar years." [7] It was in these "storm centers of world revolution," where imperialist domination was weakest, that the world's contradictions were concentrated. In this discourse on contradictions, the analysts also cautioned the comrades to be on guard regarding several "erroneous formulations," such as the idea that "all problems of the world are reduced to contradictions between the socialist and capitalist camps." The list was really nothing more than a paraphrasing of the position on this subject by the Chinese in their June 14, 1963, letter to the CPSU.

Similarly, the stand taken by the Peruvians on questions of war and peace coincided precisely with that of the CCP. They insisted, for example, that imperialism, not the bellicosity of People's China, was the source of modern war. Emulating their Chinese mentor, they also rejected the Soviet understanding of "peaceful coexistence." Suffice it to say, that the Peruvians held that revolutionaries must not be awed by the nuclear power of the United States. If they were, their will to struggle for national liberation would be paralyzed.

As a basis for policy-making in domestic affairs, the Peruvians made an analysis of Peruvian society. It is quite apparent that they felt that the social system of Peru was virtually identical to that of China during the first stage of the Chinese revolution, a similarity stemming from the fact that Peru was, like China in the earlier period,

[7] "Fourth National Conference of Peruvian C.P. Denounces Revisionism," *Peking Review*, May 22, 1964, p. 17. Emphasis added.

a "semi-feudal and dependent society." Their revolution was in its first stage and was described as an "anti-imperialist, national democratic, agrarian revolution or as Mao Tse-tung said, a bourgeois democratic revolution of a new type." [8] The terminology used departed from that used by the Chinese, who spoke of the "new democratic" revolution that was in essence an anti-imperialist and anti-feudal one, but it seems that the substance of the Peruvian formula was the same as the Chinese. In discussing the classes and strata participating in the first stage of the revolution, the Peruvians provided the reader with a more detailed class analysis than that furnished by the Brazilians, but their class analysis was a far less elaborate one than that found in Mao's writings:

In the anti-imperialist agrarian revolution, the proletariat should give leadership through its political vanguard, the Communist Party. Standing together with the proletariat should be poor peasants (natural allies), middle peasants, urban petty bourgeoisie (professional people, students, handicraftsmen, petty traders, progressive intellectuals and so on) as well as the national bourgeoisie at a certain time and under definite conditions. This is to say, the party of the working class should, through an operationally flexible, bold and firm policy, form a broad anti-imperialist, anti-feudal united front with all the forces that can be united. It is particularly important and of decisive significance to pursue a correct united front policy, in the struggle against imperialism and feudalism.[9]

Missing from this class analysis were precise statements regarding which classes constituted the enemy and which of these groups was the main enemy. Nor did the Peruvians explicitly refer to the worker-peasant alliance described by the Chinese as the basis of the united front. They could also have been faulted for failing to explain the interconnection between the domestic and external enemies of the people.

The Peruvians' statements regarding the importance of the peasantry and the relative weight to be attached to work in urban and rural areas were in perfect accord with Maoist concepts. The report explained the importance of the role played by the peasantry in the first stage of the revolution in terms of their numerical importance and their poverty and exploitation. Under these circumstances, the revo-

[8] *Ibid.,* p. 18.   [9] *Ibid.,* p. 19.

lution must extend from the countryside to the cities, and the party must devote its main energy to work in the countryside.[10]

Equally orthodox, if one takes Maoist thought as the model, were the rejection of the peaceful road to power and the refusal to compromise with the revisionists, led by the CPSU leaders, because they had allegedly betrayed Marxism-Leninism and revolutionary principles by adopting a line of peaceful coexistence, disarmament, and negotiations with the enemy. In a word, revisionism had become a grave danger to the unity of the international Communist movement. The Peruvians stated that they had found quite helpful in the struggle against revisionism certain Chinese documents for the light they shed on the issues dividing the movement.[11]

The political report of the Political Commission, adopted at an enlarged session on September 28, 1965, dealt almost entirely with international problems. In a party as responsive as the Peruvian party to policy statements from Peking, one would expect to find in the document a reference to the need for waging a people's war. Perhaps the Peruvians had not had sufficient time to digest Lin Piao's essay of September 3, but they did display greater sensitivity concerning the matter of contradictions of that time. One part of the report explicitly adopted the Chinese view that the "principal contradiction" was that existing between the "oppressed nations" and U.S. imperialism. The Chinese influence was also reflected in the stress placed on the contribution being made by the Vietnamese in the struggle against imperialism. Peoples elsewhere would advance "along the glorious road of the Vietnamese people in their struggle to rid themselves of imperialist oppression." [12] In the struggle against the number one enemy of mankind, U.S. imperialism, the report repeated the need for forming a broad, worldwide united front. To emerge victoriously from that struggle, the Peruvian Communists insisted that Communists everywhere must also "wage a struggle against revisionism, because to unite with revisionism in the struggle against imperialism is unimaginable." [13] They did not expressly refer to China as the leader

---

[10] *Ibid.*   [11] *Ibid.*
[12] "Political Report and Resolution of the Peruvian C.P.," *Peking Review,* January 7, 1966, p. 20.
[13] *Ibid.,* p. 21.

of the anti-revisionist forces, but one can infer from the following statement that the Chinese, in their opinion, should be so regarded: "The Communist Party of China has contributed greatly to the general development of Marxism-Leninism and the other Marxist-Leninist Parties of the world have also made their contributions in the light of the specific conditions in their own countries." [14] China, in fact, was the country most praised by the Peruvians as one of the socialist countries having achieved brilliant successes under the leadership of Marxist-Leninist parties. Others in this category were Albania, the Democratic People's Republic of Korea, and the Democratic Republic of Vietnam. Missing from the list were the Soviet Union, its East European allies, and Cuba. Apparently the Peruvians were as displeased with the Cubans as were the Chinese for their refusal to align themselves with the enemies of revisionism, still led by the CPSU, although Khrushchev had been replaced by Kosygin and Brezhnev.

The Political Commission adopted a resolution in October, 1965, (the exact date is not specified) responding to the Chinese call for people's wars throughout the Third World. It expressly held that the only way to achieve "emancipation from the rule of domestic and foreign oppressors and exploiters" was "to wage a hard and protracted armed struggle," which would take "the form of, and by the method of, a revolutionary people's war, that is, by cooperation and co-ordination between the armed struggle and the political struggle of the masses." [15] These and other remarks made in the resolution concerning the concept of people's war did not reflect a sophisticated understanding of the idea. Guerrillas, then beginning armed struggle in Peru, would find little concrete guidance in the resolution as to how one should go about waging such a war.

The class analysis was more detailed than that provided by the participants in the Fourth National Conference. The enemies of the Peruvian revolution singled out for attack were the "latifundists, U.S. imperialists and their henchmen." On this occasion the Peruvians also explicitly urged the creation of a united front "on the basis of the worker-peasant alliance," thereby approximating more closely the Chinese model for a united front.

Saturnino Paredes, general secretary of the pro-Chinese party, sub-

[14] *Ibid.*   [15] *Ibid.*, p. 22.

mitted to the Fifth National Conference held on November 15 and 16, 1965, a report entitled "The Political Situation and the Tasks of the Peruvian Communist Party." The conference also adopted a document entitled "The Conclusions and Resolutions of the Fifth National Conference of the Peruvian Communist Party."

The document and the report contained fresh data regarding the twenty-two Latin American Communist Parties Conference held in Havana toward the end of November, 1964. Obviously the pro-Chinese elements in Peru as elsewhere in Latin America were offended by Castro's description of the Sino-Soviet polemics as "Byzantine discussions." They rejected the idea that the conference was held on the initiative of some Latin American parties. On the contrary, they charged that these parties had merely acted under instructions from the CPSU. The joint statement by Castro and Khrushchev made in January, 1964, was a prelude to the Havana Conference in that the two leaders had affirmed their "identity of views on the course of the world revolution and some questions concerning the international communist movement at present." [16] In short, Castro had allegedly aligned himself with the revisionists in January, 1964. After the Havana Conference in November, 1964, observers had noted that "the Cuban Communist Party has further slid to the wrong stand of modern revisionism headed by the leaders of the CPSU." [17] The Peruvians vowed to continue the simultaneous struggle against revisionism and imperialism, "for it is inconceivable that anyone can seriously oppose imperialism without opposing revisionism at the same time." Thus they rebuked Castro for laboring under the illusion that he could ignore revisionism and devote himself wholly to the anti-imperialist struggle.

In his report to the Fifth National Conference, Paredes paid tribute to the CCP for its contributions to the struggles against imperialism and world reaction. He expressly acknowledged the centrality and the leadership of the Chinese in the following terms:

The glorious *centre* propelling the development of Marxism-Leninism *has shifted from Europe to Asia, from the Soviet Union to China.* The

[16] "Fifth National Conference of Peruvian Communist Party," *Peking Review*, March 18, 1966, p. 21.
[17] *Ibid.*

(216)

proof of this is that this life and death struggle against imperialism and world reaction is *led* by the Communist Party of China. The Communist Party of China has made tremendous contributions to the *overall* development of Marxism-Leninism, while the other Marxist-Leninist Parties of the world have also made their contributions according to the concrete conditions of their respective countries.[18]

The "Sinification" of the Peruvian group can be detected from the description of Peruvian society and the stage of the revolution at that time. The Peruvians asserted that, in the first stage of the revolution, an "anti-feudal, anti-imperialist democratic and national-liberation revolution," the primary motive force was the working class, playing a leading role through its own political party. The peasantry constituted the main force that had to be closely united with the workers. Another motive force was the "impoverished and radical petty bourgeoisie." Finally, there was the least dependable group, the national bourgeoisie, having a dual character which enabled it to join the other classes under certain circumstances. Opposing all these groups were the enemies of the revolution—U.S. imperialism, the latifundists (landlords) and the big bureaucrat-comprador bourgeoisie.[19] Obviously the Peruvians had accepted the Chinese contention that Chinese society, before the revolution, was essentially the same as that of all societies in the Third World. The inference to be drawn, then, would be that the peoples of Asia, Africa, and Latin America should emulate the example of the Chinese and designate armed struggle as the main form of struggle.

For reasons that are not altogether clear, the Peruvians did not use the term people's war in either of these documents, although they had used it just a month before. The terminology used, however, in describing the armed struggle, the "main form of struggle," suggested that they had been diligently studying Mao's military writings. For example, they stated that the armed struggle was, "in essence, a peasant revolution, spreading from villages to cities." Moreover, the conference decided that the party's main task was the organization and development of its own armed forces, "with the peasants as the main force and the working class (through its party) as the leading force." The document also provided: "As Comrade Mao Tse-tung said, the build-

18 *Ibid.*, p. 22. Emphasis added. 　　　　19 *Ibid.*, p. 24.

ing of the Communist Party, the united front and armed struggle are the three principal magic weapons of the revolution." [20]

With reference to the building of the party, the document pointed out that the revolution could not be carried out to the end without accelerating the development of the party "ideologically, politically, and organizationally." Revolutionary perseverance depended on the education of party members so they would develop the habit of "studying Marxist classics and have a clear knowledge of the content of the struggle against modern revisionism." Paredes, in the portion of his report dealing with party building, condemned the erroneous tendency of setting the leader against the masses. Leaders, he said, did not emerge overnight; they had to prove themselves in the course of struggle. They certainly could not appoint themselves as chiefs or leaders. He held up Mao as a model and referred to him as the undisputed leader of the world revolution: "Because he is good at integrating the universal truth of Marxism-Leninism with the specific conditions in China and has greatly enriched the experience and deepened the study of Marxism-Leninism and carried Marxism-Leninism forward, Comrade Mao Tse-tung has become—not because he himself wants to or proclaims to be such—the undisputed leader of world revolution." [21] He also maintained that the cause of party building would be enhanced by the launching of a broad rectification campaign to correct and overcome all shortcomings.

The document concluded with a statement regarding the tasks confronting the party:

Our Party's present objectives are: uphold Marxism-Leninism, persist in the struggle against U.S. imperialism, persevere in the struggle against modern revisionism and its partners in Peru, rally the whole people round a broad united front for liberation, reorganize and unify our ranks, carry on the revolution in order to destroy the principal enemies of the Peruvian people and establish a democratic, popular and revolutionary new state serving the interests of the working class and the broad masses of the people. It is the duty of our party to make every effort to fulfill these historic tasks.[22]

To the present writer, the references to China as the glorious center of Marxism-Leninism and to Mao as the undisputed leader of the

[20] *Ibid.*   [21] *Ibid.,* pp. 22–23.
[22] *Ibid.,* p. 24.

world revolution were the two most significant aspects of the report and the document. Both statements were evidence of the increased influence of the CCP on the leaders of the Peruvian Communist Party.

Bandera Roja, in an article entitled "Our Tribute to the Chinese Revolution," stated that China had become "a powerful base" for supporting all nationalist and revolutionary movements. For years it had served as "the shock brigade" of the world Communist movement and the revolutionary proletariat around the world, and as a consequence "Yankee imperialism and their allies, the modern revisionists and their followers, have unleashed a veritable offensive of lies, calumnies, and provocations against the CPR." [23] The article also stressed the special significance of the Chinese revolution for the peoples of Asia, Africa, and Latin America. That is, China was held up as a model for these peoples. The rationale given was that they were suffering from the same exploitation and oppression that the Chinese had experienced prior to their "liberation"; hence "the lessons of the Chinese revolution constitute a great contribution which should be assimilated and made use of in light of concrete reality in each country." [24] The article concluded with an expression of total solidarity with the CCP, the Chinese people, and "their great leader Comrade Mao Tse-tung." The glorification of Chinese experience and Mao Tse-tung were much more apparent here than in the preceding publications of the Peruvian party.

Shortly before this laudatory article was written, the pro-Chinese party experienced a split. Whether the split resulted from genuine differences over policy or was essentially a power struggle among corrupt and ambitious party leaders is not clear. I am persuaded, after studying the scanty documentation available, that the schism had little ideological content.

According to the Paredes group, which was later recognized by the Chinese, an intense struggle among the pro-Chinese forces began a few months after the Fourth National Conference. It occurred mostly on the national level, that is in Lima, and was especially sharp after the Fifth National Conference of November, 1965.[25] The "anti-

---

23 Peking NCNA International Service in English, March 30, 1966.
24 *Ibid.*
25 "The Peruvian Communist Party Down the Path of Mariátegui," JPRS, *TICD*, No. 910, p. 4.

party" group, headed by José Sotomayor, sought to overthrow "the national leaders with great experience." [26] For an unspecified time, the group gained control of "certain important positions in the party's national administration." [27] The Sotomayor forces also allegedly repressed the Lima Regional Committee and all other regional committees that refused to accept "the introduction of bourgeois ideological contraband into the political line of the party." [28] There was also a bitter struggle between the two factions over control of the Peruvian Communist Youth Union.

The National Commission of Controls and Cadres, controlled by the Paredes group, responded on January 31, 1966, to these power moves by the Sotomayor faction. It adopted a resolution proclaiming itself the temporary supreme organ in the party, assigning as justification the grave crisis in the party that had resulted from the traitorous acts of the other group.[29] Within a week, the Lima and Cuzco Regional Committees, supposedly repressed by the enemy, issued statements in support of the National Commission of Controls and Cadres. According to the periodical *Perú Juvenil* (*Young Peru*) the crisis was resolved by "the expulsion of José Sotomayor, Jorge Valdez Salas, and the group of rightist traitors who conspired against the Communist Party, against the Peruvian Communist Youth, against the Peruvian revolution." [30]

The victorious faction sought to discredit its foes by asserting that the viewpoints of "the broken-down group of Sotomayor" coincided completely with those of the revisionist group led by Jorge del Prado, both groups having allegedly become agents of imperialism and the oligarchy. The charge of nepotism was levelled at both groups as was the accusation that they had been spreading lies and slanders about the Paredes group. Moreover, the Sotomayor clan was charged

[26] "Regional Committee of Lima," *Bandera Roja*, March 4, 1966, as translated in JPRS, *TICD*, No. 829, p. 188.

[27] "Regarding the Fifth National Conference of the Peruvian Communist Party," *La Voix du Peuple*, October 7, 1966, as translated in JPRS, *TICD*, No. 903, p. 33.

[28] "Regional Committee of Lima," p. 188.

[29] "Resolution of the National Commission of Controls and Cadres of the Peruvian Communist Party," *Bandera Roja*, March 4, 1966, as translated in JPRS, *TICD*, No. 829, pp. 184–85.

[30] "Regarding the Fifth National Conference of the Peruvian Communist Party," p. 34.

with having furnished the police with certain information regarding cadres, secrets, and party organizations. The ideological deviations attributed to Sotomayor's group were not clearly defined, but apparently their line, which they allegedly tried to impose on the party, was erroneous in its position regarding the national bourgeoisie and the character of the existing regime. On the latter score, the Paredes group alleged that Sotomayor's view was that the Belaunde regime was representative of the interests of the national bourgeoisie, a stand which, incidentally, coincided precisely with that taken at the Fourth National Conference. He was also attacked for advocating a policy of unity and struggle in relation to the national bourgeoisie, a policy which was certainly consistent with Mao's teachings on the subject. Perhaps the source of friction was that he was placing too much emphasis on the unity aspect of the dialectical relationship of unity and struggle. Lastly, the Paredes group alleged that Sotomayor had become an advocate of the peaceful road to socialism, the usual charge made against revisionists. How such a man could have held, for several years, a top position in the pro-Chinese movement in Peru was not explained. All in all, it appears that power considerations rather than ideological differences produced the rift between Sotomayor and Paredes.

In January, 1967, *Bandera Roja* announced that the pro-Chinese party and its periodical were going underground. The rationale advanced in support of the new line was couched in terms of the idea that the Communist Party was the organized vanguard of the proletariat, and as such it was inevitably the prime target of the repressive machinery of the state. Supposedly the favorite dream of the enemies of the people was to defeat "the revolution by annihilating the party of the proletariat, the only party that is capable of carrying the revolution forward to its conclusion." [31] The editorialist postulated that the party must create a secret organization if it were genuinely sincere about intending to win power.

The decision to go underground represented a "milestone" in the development of the party. At the same time, the writer acknowledged that the clandestine publication of the journal would give rise to cer-

[31] Editorial of Political Committee of the Central Committee of the Peruvian Communist Party, "The PCP and Secret Work," *Bandera Roja*, January, 1967, as translated in JPRS, *TICD*, No. 962, p. 82.

tain problems, such as those concerning a smaller number of copies for distribution, but offsetting these disadvantages would be the fact that the periodical would gain in clarity and greater precision in that it would be designed primarily for the guidance of the militants. That is, it could be used to make the militants more aware of the increasing urgency for diligent studying, not just reading the journal. Thus they would be better prepared to discharge their duties as members of the vanguard.

The leader of the vanguard party dispatched, on October 1, 1967, a message to the Central Committee of China on the 18th anniversary of the CPR, a message reflective of the spirit of the Cultural Revolution. It extolled the thought of Mao as "the Marxism-Leninism of the present times," and it defined, in terms reminiscent of the Stalin era, the duty of all revolutionaries vis-à-vis China:

People's China, as the *vanguard* of the world proletarian revolution and as the *basis* of world revolution, as the *rearguard* of the peoples fighting wars of national liberation, must be *defended to the death by all of us, everywhere, by every revolutionary throughout the world*, making revolution in each of our countries. The struggles and wars of national liberation mutually support and defend one another. Proletarian revolutions mutually support one another.[32]

On behalf of the Peruvian Communists, Paredes promised the Chinese that they would not permit a repetition of the Indonesian fiasco because they were determined to maintain the purity of their Marxism-Leninism and were resolved to prevent contemporary revisionists from corrupting their ranks. In this context they spoke of the "painful experience of the brother Communist Party of Indonesia." [33] Paredes seems to be assuring the Chinese responsible for the management of the pro-Chinese parties in Latin America that his party was determined not to engage prematurely in armed struggle. Obviously he accepted the Chinese thesis that the first order of business was the development of a "Marxist-Leninist" party thoroughly indoctrinated in the thought of Chairman Mao. In keeping with the spirit of the Cultural Revolution, his group was following a line that

[32] Lima Correspondent's Dispatch in Spanish to NCNA, October 10, 1967. Emphasis added.
[33] *Ibid.*

assigned the highest priority to the maintenance of ideological purity. In brief, the Peruvians are convinced that they must take part in the global struggle against revisionism, a struggle in which they look to Peking for strategic guidance. In their view, final victory over the imperialists on a worldwide scale, their maximum global objective, is contingent on their eradication of the renegades in the ranks of the international Communist movement.

Before proceeding further with our analysis of Chinese efforts to organize parties in the Andean countries, let us consider the probable major factors that prompted them to do so. First, they were most interested in contesting the leadership of the Soviet Union in the world Communist movement. To that end, they fostered the establishment of parties in Latin America and elsewhere that would look to Peking just as Communists, in the Stalin era, looked to Moscow for guidance. Second, the terrain of Peru, Bolivia, and Colombia was such as to be highly attractive to Chinese strategists wedded to the idea that guerrilla warfare was the only viable tactic for the attainment of political power. Those who have studied carefully a physical map of South America know that much of the territory of these three countries is extremely mountainous in nature, terrain that must remind the Chinese of their own experience. Third, these were countries that were semifeudal in a literal sense. Most of the population was composed of the peasantry, a major portion of which was the largely unassimilated Indians. The relations between landlords and peasants were analogous to those that had existed before the Communist takeover in China. Suffice it to say that there was an undue concentration of land ownership in the hands of the landlords and that the peasants had to pay exorbitant rents and interest rates to the landlords. Furthermore, they were compelled to render without compensation numerous personal services to the *patrón* and his family. Only in Bolivia had a meaningful land reform program been adopted, a fact that seems to have eluded the guerrillas led by Che Guevara. In any event, the Chinese no doubt concluded that their experience was especially relevant in the Andean countries, where the peasantry was the principal social class. Finally, the Chinese were attracted to the three countries because guerrilla activities were so widespread there. As noted above, Debray alleged that some of the guerrillas in Peru had apparently been

(223)

influenced by a number of Chinese concepts. Given the Chinese pre-occupation with guerrilla warfare, one can easily understand the fascination these countries held for the Chinese.

 BOLIVIA

Until mid-April, 1965, pro-Soviet elements controlled the Communist movement in Bolivia. At that time pro-Chinese sympathizers held an "Extraordinary First National Congress" and expelled the pro-Soviet faction.[34] The Chinese press failed to take note of the creation of the new party. Shortly after the establishment of the party, armed struggle erupted in Bolivia, an event that evoked comment from the Chinese, and yet they did not, in any way, relate the new party to these promising events. Their silence was quite mysterious in view of the fact that they had responded so quickly just the year before when the Peruvian pro-Chinese party was established.

The explanation seems to be that the Chinese leaders were not at all satisfied with the stand taken by the Bolivians on the Sino-Soviet dispute. The anti-party group, as it was called by the supporters of the Soviet Union, sought to pursue a neutralist policy regarding the differences in the international Communist movement. For example, they insisted that Chinese documents as well as Soviet documents be allowed to circulate among party members, a demand which their Bolivian opponents found totally unacceptable. To the pro-Soviet elements, they were trying to play the role of impartial judge in the controversy between the two major Communist powers. In short, they, like the Castroites, were refusing to take a position.[35] If the pro-Soviet forces were dissatisfied with their posture on the Great Schism, one can well imagine how the Chinese must have reacted to their neutralism.

[34] Edgar Millares Reyes, "Pro-Chinese and Trotskyite Communists Wage World-Wide Ideological Struggle," *Este & Oeste*, April, 1967, as translated in JPRS, *TICD*, No. 980, p. 129.

[35] "Statement of the Political Committee on the Existence of an Anti-Party Group in Our Ranks," *Unidad*, August 15, 1964, as translated in JPRS, *TICD*, No. 650, pp. 38–39.

In late 1966, the pro-Chinese group launched a major ideological assault on revisionism, led by the CPSU. The document was entitled "Let Us Raise High the Banner of Marxism-Leninism" and bore the caption: "Position of the Communist Party on the Differences Within the International Communist Movement." The reader's attention is called to the fact that the pro-Chinese prefaced their remarks with a statement which seemed rather apologetic or defensive in nature: "If our party to date has not clearly established its position with reference to the ideological problems in dissent it is because that position must be the result of the conviction of all our militancy." [36] The latter part of the statement suggests that the group experienced considerable difficulty in achieving a synthesis regarding the stand the party should take.

By taking a stand that was clearly pro-Chinese, the Bolivians must have ingratiated themselves with their "sponsors." In their analysis of the contradictions of the contemporary world, they lashed out at the Soviet Union's alleged underestimation of the strategic significance of the national liberation movements in the Third World. The Soviet contention that the principal contradiction was that between the two blocs would have the effect, if followed, of "reducing the role of the people to mere spectators of history who are waiting for the outcome of the peaceful competition" between the Soviet Union and the United States. Again, taking a Chinese position, they announced their willingness to use violence, although they expressed regret that this was necessary. By implication they repudiated the revisionist notion that Communist parties may achieve state power by peaceful means. On the matter of the consequences of a nuclear war, they selected certain portions of the Moscow Statement of 1960 to refute the pessimistic appraisal of the revisionists that such a war would mean the end of mankind. To the contrary, they argued, the consequence would be the inevitable victory of communism over capitalism. They attempted to discredit their domestic rivals by subjecting to scorn the pro-Soviet faction's policy of peaceful coexistence with Yankee imperialism; such a policy apparently meant, they contended, that the "most active way which the Bolivian people have to fight against

[36] Millares Reyes, "Pro-Chinese and Trotskyites Wage World-Wide Struggle," p. 130.

Yankee imperialism is to coexist with it." [37] In their judgment, one could not make a more absurd statement without committing treason. They concluded with a condemnation of the League of Communists of Yugoslavia, and the leaders of the CPSU, and all of their "small followers," and a pledge to continue their fight to preserve the purity of Marxism-Leninism.

At this time the fledgling party received an extremely serious blow with the death of its most gifted and powerful leader, Federico Escobar Zapata, first secretary of the party and strong man of the Siglo XX mines. We know little about the activities of this mysterious figure from the time of his departure from Bolivia in 1965, following the repression by the military of the miners' uprisings at the mining centers of Siglo XX and Catavi, to his death in late 1966. Escobar announced that his destination, after his arrival in Chile in 1965, was Peking. The Chinese press did not report his presence in China for the period in question, but, of course, it is entirely possible that Chinese policy-makers may have deemed inadvisable the reporting of his presence in the country. It might also be noted that Escobar had previously gone to Havana as a guest of Castro, and that he, after his return to Bolivia, adopted the Cuban fad of wearing a guerrilla cap, a practice that was emulated by others working in the mine areas.[38]

The Barrientos regime dealt the Bolivian pro-Chinese still another heavy blow in January, 1967, when it arrested Oscar Zamora Medinacelli, Escobar's successor as first secretary of the party. Zamora's arrest, along with that of some of the leaders of the Nationalist Revolutionary Movement (MNR) and the Revolutionary Party of the Nationalist Left (PRIN), followed university students' strong protests and demonstrations against the authorization of the establishment of a private university.[39] That the Chinese were following these developments and were interested in them can be seen in the statement issued by the Political Science and Law Association of China condemning the Bolivian dictatorship for its unjustifiable arrest of Zamora

[37] *Ibid.*, p. 131.
[38] "Exodus of Communists from Bolivia," *Este & Oeste*, October 15-30, 1965, as translated in JPRS, *TICD*, No. 789, pp. 63-64.
[39] La Paz Radio La Cruz del Sur, January 19, 1967.

and other party leaders. The association praised the Bolivian Communist Party for having carried out a staunch heroic struggle against U.S. imperialism and its Bolivian lackeys and modern revisionists.[40]

Additional arrests of leaders and active members of the pro-Chinese party occurred on February 22. Justiniano Ninavia, a member of the Secretariat, issued a statement recounting the latest harassment of the group. Among those arrested were Reinago Cabalt, Luciano Duran, and most importantly, Jorge Echazu Alvarado, correspondent for NCNA. The homes of several other members were raided, while still others were being kept under strict surveillance or were being persecuted.[41] NCNA dispatched, on February 27, a cable to President Barrientos strongly protesting the arrest of its correspondent in La Paz. The cable called for his speedy release and for the effective guarantees of all his rights as a newsman. His arrest, the agency charged, was a complete violation of the principle of freedom of the press.[42]

The Central Committee of the Bolivian Communist Party issued another statement on March 31, denouncing the wave of arrests and persecution against trade union leaders, university students, and the activists of the party for the purpose of silencing the general protest against poverty, hunger, and the illegal enrichment of the regime. To the growing list of names of party members arrested were added the names of Justiniano Ninavia (author of the preceding statement), Casiano Ammurio, Carlos Escalier, Mario Ortuno, Rodolfo Ninavia, Carlos Yanez, Nataniel Ninavia, and leaders of other "popular groups." Ricardo Romero, author of this statement, charged that the government was planning to murder or physically eliminate Oscar Zamora and Guillermo Lora, a prominent Trotskyite leader.[43]

These adverse developments elicited a commentary from *People's Daily* denouncing the persecution of the Bolivian Communists. The paper alleged that the Bolivian regime was acting at the instigation of U.S. imperialism in stepping up its persecution of Bolivian Communists and in its outlawing on April 11 of the party. The persecution was being accelerated because the "Bolivian Communist Party is a

[40] NCNA, February 1, 1967.   [41] NCNA, February 27, 1967.
[42] *Ibid.*
[43] La Paz Correspondent's Dispatch to NCNA Peking, March 31, 1967.

genuine revolutionary party holding high the revolutionary banner of national liberation and firmly opposing the traitorous policies of the dictatorial regime, and opposing U.S. imperialist domination and enslavement." [44] The paper also assigned as reasons for the persecution the "facts" that the Bolivian people were awakening and revolutionary struggles were developing. (It was true at the time that there was more unrest and disorder than usual in the landlocked country.) The commentator closed with an appeal to the people of Bolivia and to the peoples of Latin America and the world to unite in opposition to the suppression of the Bolivian Communist Party. That is, they were to agitate for the lifting of the ban on the party and for the freeing of Oscar Zamora.

In the meantime, Che Guevara and his guerrillas were attempting to build up a viable guerrilla movement in the mountains of southeastern Bolivia. Neither the pro-Soviet party nor the pro-Chinese party provided any significant help to the movement. According to Che Guevara, the leader of the pro-Soviet group, Mario Monje, visited him in the mountains in late 1966, but he refused to accept Monje's terms for the active participation of the pro-Soviet forces, an event which, no doubt, contributed to the increasing tension between the Castroites and similar groups in Latin America. If the accounts given by the Chinese and their Bolivian supporters are true, most of the leaders of the pro-Chinese group had been imprisoned by late February, 1967, rendering most difficult any effective collaboration with the Castro-dominated guerrilla movement, assuming, of course, that there was a mutual desire to join forces against the Barrientos regime. I have been unable to find any evidence that either side made an effort to cooperate in the movement.

But this does not mean that the Chinese and their supporters in Bolivia expressed no awareness of the guerrillas. Both NCNA and *Peking Review* carried stories concerning a "recent appeal" (April, 1967) by the Political Committee of the Bolivian Communist Party calling on the people of that country to rise up and struggle resolutely against U.S. imperialism and its local agents. Both accounts stressed the Bolivian Party's statement that the emergence of guerrillas signified that the Bolivian people could "stand it no longer," referring to the

[44] NCNA, April 19, 1967.

intolerable conditions then existing in the country.[45] The NCNA account related that the Bolivian Communist Party maintained "that the only way to liberate the people is to make revolution by armed struggle." [46] In conclusion, the Bolivians urged the people engaged in the struggle to "organize themselves and form a broad people's front in order to set up an anti-imperialist people's government which is capable of solving the problems of their own country." [47] The reader should note that the pro-Chinese group and the Chinese did not explicitly support the guerrilla movement. Given the sharp ideological differences separating the pro-Chinese and the Castroites, one can understand why there was no such call for active support of the Castroite-controlled movement.

Oscar Zamora, in an exclusive interview for NCNA, expressed his sincere thanks to Mao, the CCP, and the Chinese people for their militant solidarity with his party and their support for him during his unjustified imprisonment. He added that his party consistently guided itself by Marxism-Leninism and Mao's thought.[48]

On the occasion of the anniversary of the Chinese revolution, Zamora sent a message to Mao and Chou En-lai. Commenting on the significance of that revolution, he said:

The Chinese people have had the glorious role of initiating the victorious struggle of colonial and semicolonial peoples against the imperialists. The peoples of Asia, Africa and Latin America, among them the Bolivian people, feel and are aware of the meaning of the Chinese people's struggle and victory, both of which constitute the bright beacon that illuminates socialism and Communism. The Chinese people, side by side with the other peoples of the world, are fighting unselfishly against U.S. imperialism.[49]

This quotation is the epitome of the spirit of total submission to Peking so characteristic of the Latin American Communists of Chinese persuasion after the advent of the Cultural Revolution.

The Barrientos regime crushed the guerrilla movement of 1967, killing its military and political leader, Che Guevara, and imprisoning

---

[45] "Armed Struggle: the Only Path," *Peking Review,* April 28, 1967, p. 38.
[46] NCNA, April 23, 1967.   [47] *Ibid.*
[48] NCNA, July 18, 1967.
[49] La Paz Correspondent's Dispatch to NCNA Peking, October 2, 1967.

its ideological mentor, Régis Debray. It seems to me that the pro-Chinese forces or any other would-be guerrilla forces can derive several important lessons from the disastrous experience of the Castro-dominated movement. First, they must be better prepared to deal more effectively with the Indians in the Andean countries. After all, the Indians do constitute a significant portion of the population of these countries. In dealing with them, any future guerrilla leader must bear in mind the simple fact that the Indians have, after many centuries of exploitation at the hands of the Spaniards and their successors, developed a profound distrust for the white man and his way of life. Winning their confidence and support, an indispensable element for waging a successful people's war, is an exceedingly difficult task for any non-Indian to perform. It is quite clear that Guevara and his guerrilla associates were never accepted by the peasants. The fact that so many of the leaders were Cubans only made more difficult the establishment of the necessary rapport with the local populace. In the future, therefore, guerrilla bands in the Andean countries must have an adequate number of leaders and men of Indian origin to enable them to gain the confidence of the peasantry. Second, guerrilla leaders, in the future, must perfect tactics that will enable them to cope more effectively with the counterinsurgency techniques which enemy officers have learned from the Americans. The Bolivian troops who snuffed out the 1967 guerrilla bands were trained by American instructors flown to Bolivia. Guevara, it seems, made an extremely serious error in his underestimation of the enemy's capacity to fight. As the Maoists would put it, he did not take the enemy seriously on the tactical level. Third, future guerrilla commanders must take more seriously the land reform programs that have been adopted by some Latin American governments. Guevara and his associates did not give proper weight to the program instituted in Bolivia in 1953. The apathy of the peasants can be attributed in part to the fact that their desire for revolution was not nearly as keen as Guevara had assumed. Most of the land that can be cultivated had been distributed as smallholdings among the peasants. Similarly, the Venezuelan government had distributed over 8½ million acres of land by 1966. The pro-Castro guerrillas in that country have made little progress because the Venezuelan authorities have responded to the basic demands of the peasants.

Finally, if the pro-Chinese forces are to succeed in Latin America, they must adhere to one of their fundamental tenets, namely, they must make painstaking studies of the real world in which they are operating. They cannot assume, for example, that strategy and tactics that succeed in Peru will work in Bolivia because "concrete conditions" in the two countries are by no means identical, one major difference being that the Peruvians, as of 1967, had not adopted a significant land reform program comparable to that of the Bolivians.

 COLOMBIA

Colombia, like Peru and Bolivia, has been the scene of significant guerrilla activity in the past few years. Given the Chinese emphasis on guerrilla warfare, one would naturally expect them to have manifested an interest in this country comparable to that shown in the other two countries. Such has, in fact, been the case.

According to José Cardona Hoyos, a frequent contributor to the pro-Soviet journal, *Problems of Peace and Socialism,* Chinese efforts to establish ties with the Colombian Communist movement began in July, 1963, when they attempted to win over the three-member delegation of the Central Committee of the Colombian Communist Youth organization then visiting China by openly criticizing an article written by Gilberto Vieira White.[50] On their return flight, their plane crashed in Irkutsk on July 13, 1963, killing all three of the delegates. In honor of the first anniversary of their death, *Voz Proletaria* (*Voice of the Proletariat*), the weekly organ of the pro-Soviet Colombian Communist Party, published an article on July 16, pointing out that one of them, Ricardo Lozano, had mailed several letters from China "in which he denounced the attacks of the Chinese comrades against the Colombian CP." [51] The failure of NCNA, in its coverage of the crash, to list the names of the three youth leaders among the victims lends credence to the pro-Soviet version of the incident.

[50] José Cardona Hoyos, "Divergencies in the International Communist Movement," *Documentos Políticos,* February, 1966, as translated in JPRS, *TICD,* No. 829, p. 166.
[51] "Communist China in Latin America," *Este & Oeste,* December, 1966, as translated in JPRS, *TICD,* No. 940, p. 79.

That the Chinese had not lost interest in cultivating the goodwill of young Communists in Colombia is evident from the speedy manner in which they responded to the news of a split in the Colombian Young Communist movement. It should be noted that the division in the Communist Party followed the schism in the youth movement. The initial rift occurred at the Fifth Plenum of the Central Committee of the Young Communists held from February 21–23 in Bogota. Agreement was reached rather easily on a resolution calling for the expression of solidarity with the self-defense movement in Colombia and requesting that the combatants shift to the offensive. Nor was any difficulty experienced in passing a resolution hailing the heroic exploits of young guerrillas in Venezuela. On the last two items on the agenda, participation in the elections and approval of the "peaceful coexistence policy," several Central Committee members and plenum delegates indicated their total opposition by walking out of the room.[52] A militant, Pedro Vasquez, was expelled on a charge that he had been organizing pro-Chinese elements in the party.[53]

Following the split at the Fifth Plenary session, the pro-Chinese youth met and established their own Communist Youth Union. In a resolution condemning the Central Committee of the Communist Party for "rightist revision," the youth leaders charged that the leaders of the party no longer regarded as the basic strategic objective the seizure of power. Instead the party leaders had "distorted realities in the country, created illusions, conjured up the possibilities for improved living standards for the masses under bourgeois rule, and adopted economist and reformist policies in the proletarian struggle." [54] As an alternative policy, the pro-Chinese group called for the youth "to wage revolutionary struggle," through a "patriotic, anti-imperialist popular revolution," to achieve the fundamental objective, the seizure of political power. To this end, they stressed the urgency of undertaking preparatory and organizational work among the masses. The resolution also condemned "certain people" for "resorting to

[52] Lazitch, "Repercussions of the Sino-Soviet Dispute on the Latin American Communist Parties," p. 16.

[53] "Present Situation of the Colombian Communist Party," *Este & Oeste*, December 1–15, 1965, as translated in JPRS, *TICD*, No. 806, p. 85.

[54] "Revisionist Line of Colombian CP Leadership Denounced," *Peking Review*, May 15, 1964, p. 24.

tactics incompatible with a revolutionary organization, such as persistent sabotage of internal democracy and democratic centralism, spreading lies and slanders, and informing against others, all for the purpose of hampering the development of the Communist Youth Union." [55] Furthermore, the pro-Chinese youth resolved to stop inquisitorial methods that had been used by the leaders of the party. The reference here was to the restrictions that had been placed by party leaders on the dissemination of Chinese materials in the party and the youth organization:

> . . . such measures prevented the membership from studying freely the different views on the strategy and tactics in the international communist movement. The restrictions were designed to obstruct the development of ideas and the ideological struggle, and to prevent necessary debates within the Party and the Union on the revisionist and tailist lines followed by the leaders. All this made it impossible to help resolve these differences in the best way on the basis of respecting the principles of Marxism-Leninism.[56]

Doubtless these developments must have been most encouraging to the Chinese, who had just begun, on a global scale, their campaign to establish splinter parties to support them in their struggle against revisionism.

By that time it was clear to the Chinese that they could not win over the leaders of the Colombian Communist Party. Since late 1962 Gilberto Vieira had publicly expressed his support for the CPSU. The Colombian delegation attending party congresses in Hungary, Czechoslovakia, Bulgaria, and East Germany in late 1962 and early 1963 aligned itself with the Soviet Union. After his return to Colombia in February, 1963, Vieira submitted a report on the situation in the international Communist movement to the 28th Session of the Central Committee, endorsing the principal Soviet themes, such as the convening of a conference of all Communist parties. The resolution adopted by the Central Committee even more clearly reflected a pro-Soviet bias in that it explicitly praised the program of the CPSU and the pro-Soviet *Problems of Peace and Socialism,* both of which were, at the time, special targets for pro-Chinese supporters everywhere.

In 1964 pro-Chinese elements began their campaign to oust Vieira

[55] *Ibid.*   [56] *Ibid.*

and other revisionists from the party and the youth organization. Leading them was Pedro Abel, a former militant in the party, who had considerable financial resources at his disposal. Pro-Soviet supporters promptly charged that he was being subsidized by the Chinese, an allegation that was probably true. As indicated above, the first major step taken by the pro-Chinese forces was the attempt to gain control of the youth organization. When that effort failed, they formed their own youth union. Next they attempted a coup in the party itself on September 6, 1964, in the Bogotá Federation. Heading the "pro-Chinese fractionists," according to the pro-Soviet *Voz Proletaria*, were Daniel Díaz, Humberto Salamanca Alba, Napoleon Martínez, Alejandro Soto, and Victor Julio Ramos, all of whom were disciplined by expulsion from the party.[57] The extent of Chinese influence was indicated by these expulsions and those allegedly involving complete regional organizations, such as those in Magdalena and North Santander, which had "been disintegrated," as well as zones like Barrancabermeja and No. 6 zone of Bogotá which "were also liquidated." The purge also "decimated" the ranks of the party in Valle de Cauca, Antioquia, North and South Santander, Cundinamarca, Boyacá, and Atlantico.[58]

Those affected by these acts responded by convening in the fall of 1964 (the exact date is not specified in the available documents) the "First Extraordinary Conference of the Regional Committees" of the Colombian Communist Party. It is not clear precisely how many regionals this conference actually represented. A resolution adopted by the body specifically mentioned the Regionals of Magdalena, Guarjira, and North Santander, and "the public declarations of many zones and cells throughout the country." [59] The editorial in the first issue of *Tribuna*, referred to above, obviously a pro-Chinese publication, stated that "the Colombian Communist Party (Marxist-Leninist) has recently been organized with the will to hold, shortly, a Marxist-Leninist Congress that all revolutionaries look forward to attending."

[57] "Split in the Colombian CP," *Est et Ouest*, October, 1965, as translated in JPRS, *TICD*, No. 776, pp. 41–42.
[58] "A Great Example," *Tribuna*, November, 1964, as translated in JPRS, *TICD*, No. 694, p. 157.
[59] "For Our Revolution: Preparations for a Major Marxist-Leninist Congress," *Tribuna*, November, 1964, as translated in JPRS, *TICD*, No. 694, p. 168.

Since the editorial was devoted to a discussion of the "First Extra-ordinary Conference," the implication seems to be that the pro-Chinese party was founded at that conference. It will be recalled that a precedent for such action could be found in the experience of the pioneer of pro-Chinese groups, the Communist Party of Brazil. In this context, it might be helpful to note that *Peking Review* did not report these developments as evidence of the founding of a new party as it had done earlier in the case of the split affecting the youth movement. On the other hand, *Peking Review* did carry an article excerpt-ing a statement from the political resolution of the 10th Congress of the Colombian Communist Party. The conclusion seems to be that the Chinese were not prepared to accept the work done at the confer-ence as proof that a new Marxist-Leninist party had been formed at that time.

An especially noteworthy feature of the editorial appearing in *Tribuna* was the fact that it prefaced its international and domestic analysis with a statement that "the Colombian Marxist-Leninists, within and without the party, should adopt . . . a clear and definite position on the divergencies that have developed in world com-munism." [60] Apparent here was the Chinese insistence that recipients of their aid make explicit commitments to the anti-revisionist crusade. A closely related theme, regarding which the Chinese were equally insistent that pro-Chinese groups openly espouse was the idea that "the struggle against revisionism in Latin America is inseparable from the fight against imperialism and all exploitative forces." [61] In a word, the struggle against the main enemy, U.S. imperialism, was being ob-structed by the revisionist leaders of the various Latin American Communist parties. The attitude of the Colombian pro-Chinese regard-ing the role of Cuba in the anti-imperialist struggle was to change drastically in the next few months. Suffice it to say at this time (1964) that the people of Latin America were said to be led by the heroic Cuban people in this struggle.

Aside from the usual allegations that the Vieira group had violated the principles of internal democracy in the party and had made a faulty analysis of the classes in Colombian society, there was little worthy of comment in the editorial. It should be noted, however, that

[60] *Ibid.*, p. 161.   [61] *Ibid.*, p. 162.

the pro-Chinese were especially harsh in their criticism of the leadership's attitude and policy toward the bourgeoisie. They belabored the revisionists for failing to understand that the government was dominated by the bourgeoisie. They subjected to scorn the notion that a "progressive bourgeoisie" existed. In reality, they insisted, the progressive bourgeoisie had "no existence outside the minds of the revisionists." [62] Unfortunately, they said, this error in class analysis had resulted in the adoption of a policy whereby the party was forever riding the coattails of the bourgeoisie. In my judgment, the stand taken by the "pro-Chinese" on the policy to be followed vis-à-vis the bourgeoisie was not strictly Chinese. The Chinese hold that this class had a dual nature, and they have always contended that there is a progressive element in this class that makes possible its participation for a time in the first stage of the revolution. The Colombian position, it seems to me, was actually much closer to that of the Castroites. According to Theodore Draper, the Cubans had been denying since 1960 the existence of a progressive bourgeoisie; they held that the entire group was under the tutelage of imperialism.[63] While I feel that Draper has overstated the case for the Cubans, I would agree that they have seemed to be less optimistic than the Chinese regarding the feasibility of working temporarily with the national bourgeoisie. It is possible that the Chinese were dissatisfied with the class analysis of their supporters in Colombia and that their disappointment on this score contributed, in part, to Chinese failure to report the first "extraordinary conference."

In early 1965 the relations between the pro-Soviet and pro-Chinese forces had degenerated to the point that Vieira felt compelled to convoke the 31st Session of the Central Committee to consolidate his position and strengthen the morale of the rank-and-file members of the party. In the meantime, the opposition forces were continuing their preparations for a "Marxist-Leninist" Congress to consider the international and national issues that were splitting the Colombian Communist movement. Unlike their Brazilian predecessors, they did not choose a name for their party that differed from that used by their domestic rivals. On the occasion of the 35th anniversary of the

---

[62] "A Great Example," p. 155.
[63] Draper, *Castroism: Theory and Practice*, p. 87.

founding of the party, they convened their "10th Congress of the Colombian CP." Soaca was the place selected for the meeting, which was attended by several dozen people, *including representatives of pro-Chinese persuasion from Peru, Ecuador,* and *Venezuela.* Most of those present were armed. Neither the press nor the authorities were able to discover anything about what transpired in the Congress.[64] The Congress decided to expel from the party the principal leaders of the pro-Soviet faction: Gilberto Vieira, Manuel Cepeda, Vargas Alvaro Vasquez, Joachim Moreno, and Manlio Lenfort, manager of *Voz Proletaria.*

The political resolution adopted by the Congress lacked several of the characteristic features of a Chinese analysis of world and domestic problems. Its analysis of the world situation made no reference to the various contradictions in the contemporary world, and consequently did not expressly state that the main contradiction was that of the oppressed peoples of the Third World and U.S. imperialism. It did state that the peoples of that area were in the "forefront of the anti-imperialist struggle" and that there was "a high tide in the worldwide anti-imperialist struggle, and particularly in Asia, Africa, and Latin America." [65]

Compared with the Chinese class analysis, that presented in the resolution was certainly inadequate. Nowhere in the document, as reproduced in *Peking Review,* can one find the "scientific" analysis allegedly required for decision-making by Communists. There was no statement regarding the national bourgeoisie or the policy to be followed in regard to this class. Several months before, the pro-Chinese position, as indicated above, was that this class could not be treated as a part of the united front.

One would also have expected the Colombians to have described Colombia as a semifeudal and semicolonial country. Nor was there any indication that the revolutionary process would consist of two distinct but closely connected stages.

Notwithstanding all of these deficiencies, the stand taken by the

[64] Luca G. Montenovo, "The Situation of the Colombian CP," *Corrispondenza Socialista,* December, 1965, as translated in JPRS, *TICD,* No. 800, p. 225.
[65] "Political Resolution of the 10th Congress of Colombian CP," *Peking Review,* August 20, 1965, pp. 21–22.

Colombians on the international issues of the day must have delighted the Chinese. Regarding U.S. imperialism, it was characterized as the "most ferocious enemy of the world's people," "the wicked international gendarme, and the main danger to world peace." It was, however, truly only a paper tiger that was being defeated in South Vietnam. With that enemy, peaceful coexistence was impossible.[66]

Like their Chinese sponsors, the Colombians displayed a profound abhorrence for the ideological traitor in the Communist movement. They attributed the origin of revisionism to the infiltration of bourgeois ideology into the ranks of the Communist parties. To them the anti-revisionist struggle was a "matter of life and death for the parties" because revisionism, in their judgment, was "the biggest hurdle in the way of revolutionary struggle." [67] The insidious infiltration of bourgeois ideology had already resulted in the restoration of capitalism in Yugoslavia; and in the Soviet Union itself, former undisputed head of the movement, certain features of capitalism had already begun to appear.

The Colombians strongly denounced a neutralist stand in the struggle against revisionism. From the context it would appear that Fidel Castro was the principal target that the Colombians had in mind. When the 10th Party Congress of the Colombian party was held in July, 1965, the Chinese had conveyed their displeasure with Castro to their followers in Latin America. The fact that the Colombian resolution did not even mention Cuba in its discussion of the revolutionary movement in Latin America would seem to support this interpretation. Only a few months before, the "First Extraordinary Conference" of the same party had declared that the Cuban people were leading the revolutionary forces of Latin America. That conference was held shortly before the Havana Conference; hence it can be concluded that Castro's stand, at the Havana Conference and in the months following, had brought about a basic change in the Chinese attitude and policy toward him.

The strategy and tactics for seizing political power reflected quite clearly the influence of Chinese thought on the Colombians. Using as a point of departure the civil war in the Dominican Republic and the American intervention in that war, they argued that civil wars in Latin

[66] *Ibid.*   [67] *Ibid.*, p. 22.

America could, like the Dominican case, develop speedily into an "out and out national-liberation war against U.S. troops." [68] That struggle would be "hard and protracted," and under present conditions, the "village is the natural battleground for a people's war." [69] Chinese influence was also apparent in the following selection: "The struggle will be mainly in the countryside and it will be waged by relying on the strength of the people. Sooner or later it will spread to the whole of the country and involve all social strata." [70]

The failure in 1964 by pro-Soviet parties to take power in Brazil and Chile was cited as evidence of the invalidity of "seizing power through elections" and "peaceful revolution." Experience, then, had established that "the only way out for the Colombian people is to seize power by revolutionary means, or in other words, to destroy the state machinery and replace it by a people's political power to be formed on the basis of the Patriotic Front for Liberation and with the support of the armed people." [71]

The reader's attention is called to the fact that the Colombians' reference to a people's war in Latin America preceded, by about six weeks, Lin Piao's historic article on that subject. The essential aspects of such a war as described by the Colombians were, of course, ideas long held by Chinese military strategists.

Revolución, organ of the pro-Chinese group, in an article praising Chinese experience in seizing power by armed struggle, urged genuine revolutionaries everywhere to study carefully the "marvelous experiences of China," summed up by Mao Tse-tung. In particular, the readers should master Mao's theory of army building, which was described as one which affirmed the *"absolute leadership of the party over the people's army* and the enforcement in the army of the three great democracies—democracy in military, political, and economic affairs." The article also emphasized "his revolutionary theory on building revolutionary bases and on waging a protracted struggle with rural areas encircling urban lands." These were called the greatest achievements of the Chinese revolution. The article concluded with a statement that the Colombian Communist Party badly needed the lesson taught by the Chinese.[72] One can observe here an increased ap-

---

[68] *Ibid.*   [69] *Ibid.*   [70] *Ibid.*   [71] *Ibid.*
[72] Peking NCNA International Service in English, January 3, 1966.

preciation by the Colombians for the subtleties of the Maoist concept of people's war.

Nuova Unità, organ of the pro-Chinese Italian Communist Party, carried an article on January 14, 1967, which provided evidence of the increasing dependence of the Colombians on the Chinese for ideological inspiration. The Second Plenum of the Central Committee of the Colombian Communist Party condemned a number of leftist deviationist tendencies that had manifested themselves in regard to the conduct of a people's war in Colombia. The Castroite deviations were discussed previously in the chapter dealing with Sino-Cuban relations.

On the international level, the Colombians indicated their awareness of the importance attached by the Chinese to explaining international tensions in terms of contradictions. They also displayed their orthodoxy by labelling as the principal contradiction that which involved the oppressed peoples of Asia, Africa, and Latin America and imperialism. The statement that U.S. imperialism in these continents was "encircled" by a "ring of fire" echoed Lin Piao's views on the nature of the global struggle between the imperialists and the oppressed peoples of the Third World. The impact of Lin's principle of self-reliance and the Colombians' ideas concerning the nature of the duty of revolutionaries to help one another as much as possible was apparent in this statement:

We are relying on our own forces in this great battle, but not only on our own forces: the struggle of the oppressed peoples is an aid to those who are fighting for liberation in Asia, Africa, and Latin America; we are counting on the aid of the proletariat of the capitalist countries, on the incontestable forces of the socialist camp, which are the best contribution and the best aid to the struggle for liberation.[73]

The latter portion of this quotation seems to suggest that the Colombians were expecting more assistance than they had been receiving from the socialist camp in their struggle against the common enemy.

---

[73] "Carrying the War by the Colombian People Through to Victory—Extract from the 'Political Conclusions of the Military Front' of the Second Plenum of the Central Committee of the Communist Party of Colombia (m.l.)," *Nuova Unità* (New Unity), January 14, 1967, as translated in JPRS, *TICD*, No. 953, p. 6.

VIII

The Pro-Chinese Parties and Movements
of Other Countries

I N T H I S final chapter we shall examine pro-Chinese parties and movements in several countries. Of these the Chilean and Dominican parties are the most significant. The supporters of the Chinese in Mexico and Argentina have organized Marxist-Leninist movements. There is some evidence to suggest that the Argentines may have advanced to the status of a party. The first of these parties, the Ecuadorian party, established in 1966, has had an extremely interesting but complex development.

ECUADOR

The Sino-Soviet dispute had its initial impact on the Ecuadorian Communist movement in 1963 and 1964. The leaders of the party, during this period, aligned themselves with the CPSU by making attacks on the factionalist activities of the Chinese. In an article published in *New International Review* in June, 1964, the Ecuadorian Central Committee charged the Chinese with attempting to split the party by encouraging Chinese supporters to attack the party and slander its leaders; moreover, the Chinese had instigated attempts by their Ecuadorian followers to seize the party's leadership. These and related charges appeared in the following selection:

(241)

All the energies and resources of the factionalists and schismatics, of the supporters of the "Chinese revolutionary line" have consisted, from the time of the setting up of the dictatorship in Ecuador, in attacking the Party, in slandering its leaders, who have taken refuge in clandestineness to pursue the struggle, to attempt to seize the Party's leadership. They have in this way helped the military dictatorship in fighting against the Party. . . . The CP of Ecuador can affirm that all that which was undertaken to isolate it from the general line of the world Communist movement, all the maneuvers which have aimed at decapitating it in order to seize upon its leadership organs, all the attempts at schism, have obtained the direct support of the Chinese leaders.[1]

If one can believe the pro-Soviet account, the pro-Chinese elements were indeed trying very hard in 1964 to take over the leading organs of the party.

Early in July, 1964, in an article appearing in the Soviet review *Party Life*, an Ecuadorian, using the pseudonym of Hernández, accused the Chinese of resorting to any means to achieve their goal of splitting the party and imposing their line: "In order to break the unity of our Party's ranks and to impose at any price their hegemonist and nationalist line, the leaders of the Chinese CP do not hesitate to use blackmail, corruption, and other similar ignoble methods."[2] He gave several examples to support his charges against the Chinese. First, he cited the case of José María Roma, an exmember of the Central Committee, who was arrested in May, 1963, at the airport after his return from a visit to China. The police found $25,000 in cash on him, which Peking's International Library had given him to finance the publishing of Chinese books and propaganda in Spanish for distribution in Ecuador. No doubt the Chinese expected him to make sure that some of these publications would be purchased and read by members of the Ecuadorian Communist Party. Such a development would have been as undesirable to the pro-Soviet leaders in Ecuador as it was to their counterparts elsewhere in Latin America. As we have seen, one of the bones of contention among pro-Soviet and pro-Chinese forces was the "discriminatory" policy followed by the former regarding Chinese documents. Second, Hernández revealed

[1] Lazitch, "Repercussions of the Sino-Soviet Dispute on the Latin American Communist Parties," JPRS, *TICD*, No. 693, pp. 18–19.
[2] *Ibid.*, p. 19.

that José Rafael Echeverría Flores, a member of the Central Committee, and Jorge Arrellano and Carlos Rodríguez had been expelled from the party on March 31, 1964, for pro-Chinese activities. Third, he accused the Chinese of being involved in an armed uprising by Rivadaneira, who was a leader of the young militants of the UJRD (Revolutionary Union of Ecuadorian Youth).[3]

The plenary session of the Central Committee of the Ecuadorian Party in a "Resolution on Organization" published in El Pueblo on November 5, 1965, ratified unanimously the "expulsion from the ranks of the Party of the divisionist traitors Rafael Echeverría and Carlos Rodríguez."[4] It also unanimously expelled from the party César Muñoz Mantilla, a member of the Central Committee, and Bolívar Sandoval Méndez, an alternate member of the Central Committee. Cicernos Robles, another alternate member of the Central Committee, was also expelled (the resolution did not indicate that this was done unanimously). Finally, three alternate members of the Central Committee, who were not named, were discharged from their posts and instructed "to become militants and to comply with their tasks."[5] Presumably Arrellano was among those in the latter category who was so disciplined, although the Hernández report indicated that he, as one of the pro-Chinese leaders, had been dismissed from the party on March 31 in the preceding year. That the disciplinary sanctions imposed by lower party organs were ratified by a plenary session of the Central Committee indicated the gravity of the situation in the party. It should also be noted that these measures were taken "to safeguard the national leadership of the Party."[6]

In 1966 those expelled from the party for factionalism combined forces to establish a new Communist party. Those involved apparently included pro-Castro supporters as well as pro-Chinese elements. It should be recalled that relations between the two countries had become quite strained by this time. Those tensions were reflected in the ranks of the newly formed Ecuadorian Communist Party, culminating finally in a split between the followers of Arrellano and those

---

[3] Ibid.
[4] "Resolution on Organization," El Pueblo, November 5, 1965, as translated in JPRS, TICD, No. 788, p. 91.
[5] Ibid.   [6] Ibid.

of Echeverría. It seems, then, that there was an ideological as well as a personal basis for the split that was to develop.

The Ecuadorians, unlike their colleagues elsewhere in Latin America, apparently did not convoke an "extraordinary conference" in 1966 to discuss the differences in the international Communist movement or to agree on the strategy and tactics to pursue in their drive for power. As far as I have been able to determine, they did not "found" the party at a "regular" party congress in 1966. Apparently what happened was that the pro-Chinese forces instituted the practice in 1966 of referring to themselves in their organ, *Espartaco* (*Spartacus*) as the "Marxist-Leninist" Communist Party of Ecuador. Had the group held either an extraordinary conference or a congress and issued a report or resolution, the Chinese press would doubtless have reported the establishment of the new party. Their practice in Latin America at the time was such as to lead one to believe that they would have recognized the new party in Ecuador had it been created in keeping with customary procedure and had it assumed a posture acceptable to the Chinese. In the case of the Chilean Revolutionary Communist Party, *Peking Review* reported its establishment within two months after it had been founded in May of 1966. The Chilean party adopted the usual political resolution, which was excerpted by *Peking Review*.[7] The Chinese policy at that time of carrying articles summarizing resolutions and reports adopted by Latin American supporters can be easily documented. In 1966 the Communist Party of Brazil at the Sixth National Congress adopted a political resolution calling on the people to prepare for people's war. *Jen-min Jih-pao* carried the full text.[8] In August of the same year the Peruvian Communist Party made a statement concerning the Chinese Cultural Revolution and Mao's thought.[9] In an article entitled "Advance Like Waves," *Jen-min Jih-pao* stated that the anti-imperialist struggle was advancing in wave fashion. On the same date, it excerpted the political report of the Peruvian Communist Party.[10] Given these practices of the Chinese, it would appear that the Ecuadorians did not hold a founding congress

[7] "Chilean C.P. Founded," *Peking Review*, August 5, 1966, p. 27.

[8] *Jen-min Jih-pao*, December 5, 1966, p. 5.

[9] *Jen-min Jih-pao*, September 10, 1966, p. 5.

[10] Ho Chiang, "Advance Like Waves," *Jen-min Jih-pao*, March 9, 1966, p. 4. The report is found on page 3.

or conference in 1966; and if they did, the reports or resolutions adopted must have been unacceptable to the Chinese. If the Ecuadorians had taken a strong stand on the differences in the Communist movement, the Chinese would have been eager to publish the attacks on the Soviet revisionists.

The Echeverría-Arrellano pro-Chinese party fell apart in February, 1967. Shortly thereafter, two articles appeared in the periodical *Política*, one dealing with the Saad pro-Soviet group, the other with the anti-party group in the Ecuadorian Marxist-Leninist party itself. In the first article an attempt was made to refute the "false claims" made against the party by "the opportunistic clique headed by Mr. Pedro Saad." [11] The Saad group had allegedly accused leaders of the Marxist-Leninist party of corruption, of advocating the idea that power could be achieved in a peaceful manner, and of failing to struggle against the dictatorship. The charge, however, which was most relevant to the impact of the Sino-Soviet dispute in Ecuador was that which alleged that the Saad forces had plunged into slander when it said that the revolutionaries "in order to achieve their goals of corruption and enrichment, made a pact with international forces promoting schism, the leaders of the Communist Party of China." [12] The reaction to this "slanderous" charge was particularly revealing:

Here we see the deserters from the revolution as they really are. People without principle, knowing that in any ideological base they will be completely revealed, they have recourse to the most grotesque and disgraceful calumny to defame their political adversaries. This is an old and rotten weapon, one always used by the reactionaries and the police to deceive the unwary and to discredit the revolutionaries.[13]

The impression that one gets from reading this angry retort is that the spokesmen for *Política* resented very much the claim that they had connived with the leaders of the CCP. The position taken by those controlling the editorial policy of *Política* was clearly not an orthodox pro-Chinese one. In the entire article there was not a single reference to the role of the CCP nor to the need for struggling against "revisionism" on a worldwide basis. On the other hand, there was a

---

[11] "Reply to the Opportunistic Clique of the False Ecuadorian Communist Party," *Política*, March–April, 1967, as translated in JPRS, *TICD*, No. 984, p. 39.
[12] *Ibid.*, p. 43. [13] *Ibid.*

comparable absence of remarks concerning the CPSU and the need for combatting the forces of dogmatism. The Saad clique was not linked to the CPSU as one would expect to find in a pro-Chinese analysis. The conclusion that emerges is that this document was a pro-Castro statement, not in the sense that it held up Cuba as the model for Latin America, but in the sense that its posture on the Sino-Soviet dispute was a neutral one. Such a statement would hardly win the respect and/or support of the Chinese. Doubtless that was the reason the Chinese press made no reference to it.

The second *Política* article purported to be an analysis of the activities of the anti-party group. Many of those in the group entered the party in the early stage of its development when party leaders were admittedly inexperienced and most anxious to enroll as many members as possible. In their anxiety to expand the new party, the leaders did not pay sufficient attention to the need for admitting to the party only those of the highest caliber. Taking advantage of the laxity in standards, a number of unprincipled opportunists entered the party and began their campaign to destroy it. They became increasingly open in their efforts to divide the party. Having "guilty consciences," they refused to attend the February plenary session of the Central Committee to state their views and make their charges against the executive leaders. After thorough deliberation of the "facts" in the case, the Central Committee determined that an anti-party group had indeed emerged in the party. It decided unanimously to expel those implicated in the conspiracy. One of these who "had managed to climb to leading posts" in the party was exposed and expelled along with the others. The name of the arch-criminal was not revealed in the article, but we now know that he was Jorge Isaac Arrellano.

In the introduction to his essay attacking Debray's book, Arrellano pointed out that *Política* had reprinted Debray's book and had stated that Debray "has distinguished himself, in the recent past, by his devotion to the study of Latin America's revolutionary process, with the aspirations of which he identifies himself." Elsewhere he spoke of "the adventurous faction led by Echeverría." [14] The pro-Soviet news-

[14] Arrellano, "Revolution Within the Revolution? or Adventure Without Revolution?—A Reply to Régis Debray," pp. 100–01.

paper, *El Pueblo*, on July 8, 1967, in an article entitled "The Perfect Jorge Arrellano" reported that "the dissident Jorge Arrellano has set up a subgroup within the factionalists, a small adventurous group which is in the process of breaking apart." [15] A careful scrutiny of the Chinese press for the remainder of 1967 disclosed no reference to either of these groups, a rather surprising development in view of Arrellano's spirited attack on Debray's book and his defense of the Chinese concept of people's war. It is not clear, then, which of the groups is "recognized" by the Chinese. Perhaps the Chinese are awaiting further developments in Ecuador before choosing between the two groups.

 CHILE

Prior to 1963 relations between the Chinese Communist Party and the Chilean Communists, led by Luis Corvalan, had been at least cordial if not friendly. It is true that the leaders of the Chilean party had consistently taken positions in the Sino-Soviet dispute that coincided with those of the CPSU, but they had not charged the Chinese leaders with attempting to impose its erroneous line on the Communist movement or with trying to split the individual parties. But before the end of the year, the leaders of the two parties were engaged in the polemical exchanges that were so characteristic of the Sino-Soviet conflict.

Playing a key role in the degeneration of relations between the parties was a small group of Chilean intellectuals, the Spartacus group, formed in March, 1963. They staffed a firm, Espartaco Editores Ltda., which shared an office in Santiago with the New China News Agency. The overt responsibility of the firm was the publication and distribution throughout Latin America of Chinese materials in the Spanish language. Perhaps its most popular item was *Pekin Informe*, the Spanish equivalent of *Peking Review*. The surreptitious distribution of these Chinese documents among party militants elicited a prompt and angry response from the party leaders, who initiated the practice of

15 "The Perfect Jorge Arrellano," *El Pueblo*, July 8, 1967, as translated in JPRS, *TICD*, No. 990, p. 90.

reprinting anti-Chinese articles from the publications of other Communist parties. In an effort to protect the naive and unwary in the party, they notified the rank-and-file members on March 30, 1963, that the line of the CCP was incompatible with the general line of the international Communist movement as expressed in the Moscow Declarations of 1957 and 1960.

The Chinese did not see fit to protest this act of "proletarian discrimination"; however, its most dependable ally, the Albanian Party of Labor, and a Socialist newspaper *Última Hora* took the Chilean leaders to task for attempting to prevent the free circulation of *Pekin Informe* and other Chinese documents. After these attacks, the Chilean leaders cast aside all restraint and subjected the Chinese position and activities to incessant attacks in the party's ideological journal, *Principios*. Luis Corvalan, secretary-general of the party, delivered a long speech on June 6, 1963, before a plenary session of the Central Committee dealing with "The Differences of Opinion with the Chinese Comrades." He alleged that only one party, the Albanian Party of Labor, supported the Chinese. For our purposes, his complaint regarding the Chinese recruiting practices in the party was most pertinent. Not only had they propagated their erroneous concepts among party members, they had, in pursuit of their goals, ". . . sought the collaboration of party members, recruited individually and against our Central Committee's will, which had been expressly made known to the Chinese comrades." [16]

The conflict escalated when dissidents in the party decided to hold meeetings in the Baquedano and Esmeralda theaters in Santiago to celebrate the 14th anniversary of the Chinese revolution. On learning of these plans, the Political Commission of the Chilean Communist Party issued a declaration, setting forth its views concerning the motivations of those sponsoring the proposed meetings:

The objective pursued by the promoters and organizers of these events was *not* the commemoration of the Chinese revolution but the intention of exploiting the differences of opinion between the Chinese CP leadership

[16] Luis Corvalan, "Differences of Opinion with the Chinese Comrades," *Principios*, September–October, 1963, as cited in Ernst Halperin, *Nationalism and Communism in Chile* (Cambridge, Mass.: The M.I.T. Press, 1965), p. 103.

and the Chilean CP in an effort to use these disagreements against the Chilean CP and the popular movement to whose orientation they are opposed. In other words, these are diversionist [*sic*] activities intended to weaken the popular struggle and especially the candidacy of Salvador Allende.[17]

The Political Commission concluded its alert message to the militants of the party and the popular movement by urging them to attend a celebration in honor of the Chinese revolution organized "in a non-political fashion" by the Chilean-Chinese Cultural Institute. The rally was to be held at the University of Chile on September 30.

The meeting in the Esmeralda Theater was sponsored by Vanguarda Revolucionaria Marxista, while the meeting in the other theater was organized by the Spartacus group and a number of the prominent FRAP leaders such as Socialist Senator Alejandro Chelen and Clodomiro Almeyda and Carlos Altamirano, members of the Socialist Party in the Chamber of Deputies. Representatives of the Communist Party presented a copy of the declaration to the Socialist Party headquarters. Party leaders also warned Communists, who were listed as sponsors of the Baquedano meeting, not to attend the meeting. The Socialist Central Committee informed its ally in FRAP that Socialists had been forbidden to attend either meeting.[18]

The Baquedano meeting on September 29 was attended by a crowd of two or three hundred persons, most of whom seemed to be students. Communist militants, stationed at the entrance, took down the names of all those whom they recognized. Senator Alejandro Chelen and Deputy Clodomiro Almeyda attended in defiance of their leaders' instructions.

Speaking from a rostrum decorated with the portraits of Mao, Lenin, Fidel Castro, Ben Bella, and Lumumba, Armando Cassigoli, a member of the Spartacus group and a writer and professor of philosophy at the University of Chile, echoed the Chinese views on peaceful coexistence and the peaceful road to socialism. To further the revolution in Chile, he advocated the establishment of a broad move-

---

[17] "Documents on Divisionist Activities," *Principios*, November–December 1963, as translated in JPRS, *TICD*, No. 550, p. 58. Emphasis added.

[18] Halperin, *Nationalism and Communism in Chile*, pp. 107–09.

ment to support all anti-imperialist revolutions, which he proposed to call MARA (Movimiento de Apoyo a la Revolución Anti-Imperialista).[19]

Corvalan, in a speech on the same day in a park only two blocks from the Baquedano cinema, attempted to belittle the efforts of the pro-Chinese elements:

There is no danger of a split in the party. They will not be able to split one single cell, a single one of our three thousand basic organizations. Once more those who try to split our party will break their teeth as if biting on a rock. What causes us to worry is the harm which these elements may cause in the people's movement, deceiving or confusing groups or individual persons in order to create distrust among FRAP parties and to stir up arguments among them.[20]

That his sole source of concern was the maintenance of the integrity of the FRAP coalition does not square entirely with the facts that the party leaders had taken such pains to prevent the rival meetings, that they expelled seven party militants, and that they published a series of articles denouncing bitterly the Chinese and the factionalists supporting them in Chile.

The Political Commission ratified on October 12 the expulsion by the North and South Regional Committees in Santiago of seven militants from the ranks of the party. They were Jorge Palacios, Rafael Barahona, Armando Cassigoli, Adolfo Berchenko, David Benquis, Oscar Vásquez, and Raúl Venegas. The charges by the North Regional Committee against Palacios, Barahona, Cassigoli, Berchenko, Benquis, and Vásquez were:

1. The clear and public violation of party discipline and the malicious use they made for their own pernicious ends, of their positions as militants.
2. The duplicity with which they acted for a prolonged period of time and the subversive activities which they pursued in the party.
3. The fractionalist effort which they engaged in and which was characterized by their holding meetings among themselves and entering into collusion with other members in order to fight against the party line and

[19] *Ibid.*, p. 110.
[20] *El Siglo*, September 30, 1963, as cited in Halperin, *Nationalism and Communism in Chile*, p. 110.

the decisions of their regular organizations—attitudes which constitute an attack against the party as a whole.

4. The flagrant violations of the norms established in the statutes and the violation of democratic centralism, which occurred when they publicly opposed the agreements and resolutions of higher organizations.[21]

The charges brought against Vásquez were:

1. Proven fractionalist activity culminating in his active participation in the events of Sunday, 29 September at the Baquedano Theater.

2. Distribution of literature contrary to the party line.

3. International contacts with adventurous elements.

4. Constant friendly contacts with individuals who have been thrown out of the party.[22]

The Political Commission and the National Control and Cadre Commission of the Communist Party issued a declaration on October 19, 1963, dealing at great length with the activities of the expelled militants, the Spartacus group, and those of other groups allegedly engaged in a conspiracy against the party and the popular movement (FRAP). The leaders had deemed a full statement of the "facts" to be necessary because

. . . everything that has happened in the past indicates that somebody is launching a conspiracy against the party and the popular movement. The rebellion and expulsion of only seven militants—none of whom was a cell secretary—would be a secondary matter if the other Trotskyite and pro-Trotsky groups were not operating in the same direction and if they were not all directed and politically and materially supported by the same source. No one can fail to see that we are dealing with a conspiracy.[23]

The Chilean Communists were, no doubt, of the opinion that the leaders of the CCP were acting as the coordinator of the activities of these various dissident forces because they stated elsewhere in the declaration that the international and national lines of the Chilean party were incompatible with those of the CCP. They also rejected the allegation of the expelled militants that they, the dissidents, had revolted against the party line because it was not sufficiently aggressive. The leaders insisted that the party line was, in fact, a revolutionary

21 "Documents on Divisionist Activities," pp. 59–60.
22 *Ibid.*, pp. 60–61.   23 *Ibid.*, p. 66.

line. Doubtless, the fact that weighed most heavily in the pro-Soviet leaders' thinking was the well-known fact that those expelled had been engaged in work for the firm known as Espartaco Editores Ltda., whose work has been explained above.

At the end of January, 1964, some sixty Marxist-Leninists of the Chilean Communist Party met in Santiago, not, it should be noted, for the purpose of creating a new party, but to discuss international and domestic developments. It seems that they were only ready, at this time, to form a well-organized "faction" within the party. In view of the reluctance of the Chinese to recognize the existence of some newly established parties, it is most significant that they saw fit to report this meeting, even though it was not labelled a party congress or an extraordinary conference. To my knowledge, this was the first time that the Chinese had acted so prematurely.

In a resolution on the international situation, top priority was given to the denunciation of the CPSU: "In view of the fact that the group now controlling the Central Committee of the CPSU has thrown overboard Marxist-Leninist principles, [this meeting] decides to denounce this as incompatible with the revolutionary struggle of the Party." [24] The CCP, on the other hand, was the "true heir to the revolutionary organization, which should never be abandoned." [25] It hailed the Cuban revolution as "the pioneer of socialism in the Americas," a living example that repudiated the notion of class compromise. Finally, in a move reflecting the idea underlying MARA, it declared support for all anti-imperialist struggles in the dependent countries.

On the domestic front, the group was most concerned with the repudiation of the Peaceful Road, the line being followed by the pro-Soviet Chilean Communist Party. Clearly the pro-Chinese elements had given up all hopes for winning over the party's leaders to the armed struggle line; hence they urged all party members not corrupted by reformism to struggle ideologically and in practice "to transform the basic organizations of the Party into revolutionary organizations." [26] Should the leaders resist, it would then "be necessary

[24] "Marxist-Leninists of Chilean CP Repudiate Party Leadership's Revisionism," *Peking Review,* May 6, 1964, p. 26.
[25] *Ibid.*   [26] *Ibid.,* p. 27.

to win over the majority of the comrades by repudiating the decisions of the leadership aimed at disparaging the struggle." [27] That is, they must defeat revisionist ideas advocated by party leaders and assume leadership themselves. As one representative said: "The time has obviously come for us to disregard the leaders and set ourselves the task of conducting underground action with a view to organizing armed struggle." [28] At the time, there were, according to the dissidents, two major shortcomings in the development of the revolution: (1) the failure to organize the peasantry, and (2) the absence of a leading organ really dedicated to the cause of armed struggle.

Missing from this analysis was a systematic class analysis. There was an appeal to the workers and peasants to follow the leadership of a "revolutionary Communist Party," and there was a statement indicating that the group was willing to collaborate "with certain sections of the bourgeoisie at a certain stage."

There was also a rather long section dealing with the problem of working with Trotskyites. In Chile, a Trotskyite organization, Vanguardia Revolucionaria Marxista, had sent in October, 1963, a long letter to the Central Committee of the Chinese Communist Party expressing a desire to cooperate with and support the CCP. Apparently, the Chinese were not at all interested in collaborating with the followers of Leon Trotsky, the bête noire of revisionists and Maoists alike. We also know that the same organization had attempted to join forces with the Spartacus group in Chile. In fact the group had sponsored one of the two meetings in celebration of the 14th anniversary of the Chinese revolution. It should also be recalled that the Corvalan group had charged that Trotskyites were working with the expelled militants. It is against this background that one must appraise the stand taken by the Chilean Marxist-Leninists in their January, 1964, meeting. The caption for the section summed up their feelings quite well: "Beware of Trotskyites." One unnamed representative said: "I think we must adopt the first stand of not having anything to do with the Trotskyites," [29] By reprinting the Chileans' remarks, the Chinese were indicating to their followers in Chile and elsewhere in Latin America what policy they should follow vis-à-vis

[27] Ibid.   [28] Ibid., p. 28.
[29] Ibid.

the Trotskyites, who quite frequently have expressed their admiration for some Chinese views.

El Siglo, the newspaper of the dominant pro-Soviet group, scored the Chinese for creating paid parties, consisting of "charlatans" and "provocateurs" for the purpose of "insulting, slandering, and attacking the respective Communist and Socialist parties, and anti-imperialist forces in general." [30] The editor then confirmed the fact that the Chinese had been engaged in factionalism in several other Latin American countries; he mentioned Peru, Ecuador, and Brazil. As expected, he asserted that their efforts in Chile had completely failed, being limited "to putting a few slippery individuals on the payroll." [31]

Following the sound trouncing of Salvador Allende, the FRAP candidate for president, by Eduardo Frei's Christian Democratic Party in the September, 1964, general election, the pro-Chinese Belgian *La Voix du Peuple* carried an article on the lessons to be learned from the attempts to pursue a policy of peaceful transition to socialism. In Brazil, "a military putsch put an end to the flirtation between the leaders of the revisionist communist party and President Goulart." [32] After the Brazilian fiasco, Latin American revisionists, the Belgian said, should have realized the folly of following Khrushchev's thesis on the "Peaceful Road," but the Chilean leaders failed to profit from the Brazilian experience. Surely, he argued, there should no longer be any illusions about the possibility for achieving a peaceful takeover through collaboration with bourgeois leaders. No doubt the pro-Chinese supporters in Chile derived as much satisfaction as he from the "validation" of the line of armed struggle which they claimed as a result of these two setbacks suffered by the adherents of the "electoral road."

In May, 1966, the pro-Chinese forces organized the Chilean Revolutionary Communist Party at their First Marxist-Leninist Congress. Those participating in the creation of the party were the Espartaco organization, the Communist Rebel Union, and revolutionary militants who had broken with the revisionist party. Prior to the congress, many

[30] "The Unity of the Communist Movement and Anti-Imperialist Cohesion," *El Siglo*, April 9, 1964, as translated in JPRS, *TICD*, No. 603, p. 12.
[31] *Ibid.*
[32] Article signed "A.H." "On Peaceful Pursuit of Socialism in Chile," *La Voix du Peuple*, September 18, 1964, as translated in JPRS, *TICD*, No. 655, p. 23.

regional congresses and branch party meetings had been held to discuss draft documents for the congress. The congress also elected its national leaders. It is interesting to note that *Peking Review* did not disclose any of their names.[33]

The political resolution reiterated the Chinese views regarding the international situation: the U.S. was the No. 1 enemy of the peoples of the world, the modern revisionists had become the bourgeois agents of the imperialists, the Vietnamese were standing in the forefront of the people's struggles against imperialism, et cetera. Reflective of the status of Sino-Cuban relations, it contained a strong denunciation of neutralism in the struggle between Marxist-Leninists and the revisionists:

This is not only an erroneous attitude very harmful to the interests of the revolution but also means complicity with the revisionists. Those who preach this "neutralism" hypocritically utilize the sentiments of the peoples for unity, in an attempt to make people follow the slogans of the revisionists and lead them to an unprincipled "unity," and to prevent the revolutionaries from opposing and exposing these slogans.[34]

As the Chileans fully realized, Fidel Castro was the foremost exponent of neutralism in the Western Hemisphere. On this occasion, the Chileans explicitly denounced the Cuban leaders for their increasing complicity with the revisionists as witnessed by:

. . . their attempts to deny and undermine the Marxist-Leninist Parties and groups, by their conspiratorial meetings and agreements with known revisionists, by their defence of the opportunist views of the revisionists in joint communiqués and at international meetings, by their perfidious and unjust attacks on the People's Republic of China, which dovetail with the manoeuvres of U.S. imperialism to isolate and commit aggression against this great socialist country, and by their active propagation of "neutralism" in the struggle of the Marxist-Leninists against revisionism, so as to facilitate an unprincipled "unity." [35]

The Chileans held that the road to power was that indicated by the Chinese model. The revolution would develop in two stages, the first

[33] "Chilean Revolutionary CP Founded," *Peking Review*, August 5, 1966, p. 27.
[34] "Political Resolution of First Congress of Chilean Revolutionary Communist Party," *Peking Review*, August 26, 1966, p. 25.
[35] *Ibid.*

being a people's democratic revolution. Using the worker-peasant alliance as a basis, the Revolutionary Communist Party would organize into a united front the various strata of the urban middle and petty bourgeoisie against the enemies of the people: the imperialists, the the latifundists, and monopoly and financial capitalists. The state to be formed after the seizure of power would be a people's democratic government, a variant of the proletarian dictatorship.

According to the resolution, there was only one road to power, and that was the road of armed struggle in the form of a people's war, the essential features of which would be a protracted armed struggle mainly in the countryside under the firm leadership of the party. As indicated in the preceding chapter, the Chileans, as early as May, 1966, were uttering highly critical remarks regarding the attempt by certain "petty bourgeois" groups who tried to copy mechanically the Cuban concept of people's war rather than that of the Chinese.

In accordance with the spirit of the Cultural Revolution, the Central Committee dispatched, on May 12, 1967, a letter to Chairman Mao expressing its firm support of the new revolution, calling it "the greatest political and revolutionary social event in our times, to which only the October Revolution and the Chinese Revolution itself are comparable." [36] Chairman Mao, according to his Chilean supporters, was the "great leader of the revolutionary peoples of the whole world," under whose "leadership the Chinese people are marching ahead as the vanguard of the revolutionary peoples." [37] In conclusion, they stoutly defended him and the Cultural Revolution against the attacks of both the imperialists and the revisionists. All in all, the letter was a typical example of the work of those practicing the Maoist cult of personality.

Comparable adulation was expressed by the Chileans in their declaration written on the occasion of China's exploding its first hydrogen bomb. The event was interpreted by them in virtually the same way as by other Latin American followers of China. That is, it was portrayed as a "hard blow to U.S. imperialism and its Soviet revisionist partners," as a powerful assistance to the Vietnamese and Arab peoples

[36] Peking NCNA International Service in English, May 12, 1967.
[37] *Ibid.*

fighting Yankee imperialism, and as a powerful weapon in the hands of the peoples of the world, and, of course, as a resounding victory for Mao's thought.

 THE DOMINICAN REPUBLIC

The Dominican civil war beginning in April, 1965, accompanied as it was by the intervention of U.S. troops, elicited a quick and a strong response from the Chinese leaders. The situation had enough in common with that obtaining in Vietnam at the time to suggest to the Chinese that the civil war in the Caribbean republic might, if organized properly, be transformed into a people's war, although they did not use that expression at the time. To accomplish that objective, they sought to exploit the anti-Americanism so prevalent in the island. They knew that few countries in Latin America had had more direct experience with dollar diplomacy and gunboat diplomacy than had the Dominicans prior to the adoption in 1933 of the Good Neighbor policy. In their propaganda utterances, therefore, the Chinese stressed the right of all countries to choose their own political system without regard to the wishes of their more powerful neighbors; thus they emphasized a theme so valued by Latin Americans, the principle of nonintervention.

The Chinese were excited by the developments in the Dominican Republic because they felt that the Dominican revolution might spark similar uprisings throughout Latin America. In that event, the policeman of the world, U.S. imperialism, would have his forces pinned down in many "Vietnams," thus reducing the troops available for deployment in areas adjacent to China itself. There is no doubt that the Chinese Communists have felt encircled by United States military power in the Far East. They sought, therefore, to convince the Dominicans that their struggle against the United States was a part of the worldwide struggle against the common enemy of all peoples, U.S. imperialism, and they called upon the Dominicans to join the broad united front against that enemy.

Reflecting the importance attached by the Chinese to the Dominican uprising, Mao Tse-tung himself issued a statement on May 12, 1965, pledging the firm support of the Chinese people to the Dominicans "in their patriotic armed struggle against U.S. imperialism." [38] He maintained that the dispatch of American troops made a mockery of American dedication to the principle of nonintervention, a contention accepted by many Latin Americans at the time. He ridiculed the American explanation that the troops had been sent to defend freedom:

What kind of freedom is this? It is the freedom to use airplanes, warships and guns to slaughter the people of other countries. It is the freedom to violate the sovereignty of other countries at will, the freedom to invade and occupy their territory at will. It is the freedom of pirates to loot and kill. It is the freedom to trample underfoot all the countries and people of the world. This is what the U.S. imperialists are doing in the Dominican Republic, in Vietnam, in the Congo (Léopoldville) and in many other places.[39]

He concluded with a plea for the formation of a worldwide united front against U.S. imperialism: "The people in the socialist camp should unite, the people of the countries of Asia, Africa, and Latin America should unite, the people of every continent should unite, all peace loving countries and all countries subjected to U.S. bullying, control, interference and aggression should unite, and form the broadest united front to oppose the U.S. imperialist policies of aggression and war and to safeguard world peace." [40] This statement by Mao translated into many languages is regarded by the Chinese as one of his most important statements on Latin America.

In an attempt to convince the Dominicans of their support, the Chinese held giant demonstrations throughout the country. In Peking alone, a crowd of more than 300,000 reportedly surged into the streets and squares, shouting such slogans as "U.S. imperialism get out of the Dominican Republic" and "People of all the world unite to defeat U.S. imperialism." Parades and mass rallies of more than 700,000 were held in Shanghai, Canton, and Shenyang. All Peking papers on May 13 gave top prominence to news reports and photographs of the Dominican revolution.[41] Attending a huge rally of 100,000 in Peking on May 12 were some of the most powerful men in China: Liu Shao-

---

[38] *SCMP*, No. 3457, p. 28.
[40] *Ibid.*, p. 29.

[39] *Ibid.*
[41] *SCMP*, No. 3459, pp. 26–27.

ch'i, Chu Teh, Chou En-lai, Teng Hsiao-p'ing, and many other Party and State leaders.[42] The huge rallies and the prominence accorded the Dominican insurrection in the Chinese press indicate the high priority assigned to developments in the tiny Caribbean republic.

As indicated above, the Chinese believed that the Dominican revolution might trigger similar movements in other Latin American countries. In an article entitled "Dominica" published in June, 1965, the Chinese journal *Shih-chieh Chih-shih* articulated the Chinese expectations:

The significance of the Dominican people's struggle far exceeds the border of Dominica. It has become a signal for a new tide of national democratic revolution in Latin America. The people of Latin American countries have all been under American imperialist oppression and exploitation. Any people's struggle in one Latin American country will light the fire of anti-American struggle in all of Latin America.[43]

When the belligerents of the two groups signed in September, 1965, a document of reconciliation to prevent the expansion and continuation of the civil war, the Chinese denounced the "cunning North Americans," who were allegedly responsible for the act, for trying to place Santo Domingo "under their boots." A *Jen-min Jih-pao* commentator contended that this move must surely fail because reconciliation between U.S. imperialism and the Dominican people was impossible. In fact, he argued, the American intervention had "sharpened the contradiction between the broad masses of the Dominican people and U.S. imperialism,"[44] a contradiction that could be resolved, he maintained, only by armed struggle. To carry on the requisite prolonged struggle, "many patriotic troops and people have already gone to the mountains and villages, taking their weapons along." What the article did not indicate was that some of the rebels going to the mountains were supporters of Fidel Castro, who probably outnumbered the pro-Chinese elements.

Apparently the Chinese followed with great interest the activities of these Dominican guerrillas in the hills. At a time (March, 1967) when the Chinese press was virtually ignoring similar activities of

[42] *SCMP*, No. 3458, p. 27.
[43] "Dominica," *Shih-chieh Chih-shih*, June, 1965.
[44] *SCMP*, No. 3535, p. 26.

the Bolivian guerrillas because they were under Cuban control, it is most significant that *Peking Review* in its article "Armed Struggle to the Hills" saw fit to report the developments in the Dominican Republic. The explanation seems to be that the Chinese felt that the groups involved in the fighting in the Caribbean island were guided more by the Chinese than by the Cuban strategy. After stating that the revolutionary forces, after much planning and preparation, had resumed their armed operations, the Chinese writer concluded: "This shows that in their battle against the rule of Yankee imperialism and the reactionary government at home, the Dominican people are moving ahead in the direction charted in Chairman Mao's May, 1965 statement supporting the Dominican people's resistance to U.S. armed aggression." [45]

The authoritative *Jen-min Jih-pao* also commented on the report that the Dominican people were engaged in guerrilla activities in the mountains. The paper in a comment entitled "The Only Road to National Liberation" argued that the suppression of the armed uprising by 30,000 aggressor troops represented only a temporary setback for the Dominican revolutionaries, who had kindled the sparks of people's guerrilla war in the countryside. Needless to say, the commentator held that Mao's strategy for fighting a people's war was the only road for Dominicans and other Latin Americans, Africans, and Asians.

The China Peace Committee, in a statement issued on the second anniversary of Mao's statement, echoed the same themes. According to the committee, the Dominican rebels had learned from their own experience that Mao's strategic concepts were "the only really powerful ideological weapon with which to struggle and win victory" and that people's war was "the only way to secure national liberation." In its judgment the "prairie fire of people's war" would inevitably reduce to ashes the U.S. aggressors and their supporters.

The competition among the forces on the Left for leadership of this revolutionary movement has been extremely intense and complex. The Dominican Republic enjoys the dubious distinction of having not two but four Communist parties, each contending, of course, that it alone is the legitimate representative of the working

[45] "Armed Struggle to the Hills," *Peking Review*, March 31, 1967, p. 29.

class. Peru and the Dominican Republic are the only two countries in which the pro-Chinese forces are thought to be more powerful than the pro-Soviet forces; however, the division of these forces in both countries would probably offset any advantage which they might enjoy over their revisionist rivals.

Since the Chinese displayed little interest in the Dominican Republic prior to the April, 1965, civil war, we know very little about their efforts to win supporters before the 1965 revolution. The group with which they came to be associated, the Dominican Popular Movement, staged a guerrilla uprising in 1963, but it failed. Apparently the Chinese were favorably impressed by their attempted coup, for they invited Máximo López Molina, president of the party, to visit China in early November, 1964. He was given an especially warm reception by the sponsoring body, the China Peace Committee, which, incidentally, was to send several messages of support to the Dominican rebels after the April, 1965, uprising.

The pro-Chinese party, the MPD, was founded in 1956 by López Molina while in exile in Havana. Prior to the two splits that were to occur in the party, *Freedom Journal*, the organ of the party, published an article praising Mao for his contribution to military strategy, the theory of people's war. It credited him with being the first person to have advanced the people's war theory.[46] Concerning the world significance of the victory of the Chinese revolution, it said: "The victory of the Chinese people has breached the imperialist front in the Orient, changed the balance of power, and encouraged the revolutionary movements of the people of all countries in the world."[47] Its stand on the role of the CCP and Chairman Mao in the global struggle against revisionism was that they had served as the vanguard of that movement. In fact, "the Mao Tse-tung viewpoint, loyal to Marxism-Leninism, destroyed the scheme of modern revisionism to dominate the international Communist movement."[48]

Shortly after this broadcast to the Chinese people of these excerpts from the Dominican pro-Chinese publication, the MPD experienced the first of two splits in 1966. In April, Máximo López Molina was discharged from his position on the Central Committee, a post that

[46] Peking NCNA Domestic Service in Mandarin, February 12, 1966.
[47] *Ibid*.   [48] *Ibid*.

he had held for years. He and several of his former comrades in the party, who had withdrawn from the party, created the Orthodox Communist Party (PCO). Apparently they established the party before the June 1 presidential election because López Molina alleged that his party was the only one to label the "elections as colonial" and as a "crime against the homeland." The second rift developed in July and resulted in a split of the six-man Central Committee, four siding with those who had been expelled (Antonio Lockwood, Narciso González, and Luis Montas), while the other two sided with the other group. In an effort to clarify the extremely confusing situation in the MPD, Florangel Cárdenas, a reporter for *Ahora*, attempted to arrange interviews with representatives of the three groups. Her well-intentioned efforts were not altogether satisfactory for two reasons: first, one of the groups chose as its representative a young worker who, although a member of the Central Committee, had only the vaguest notions regarding the nature of the ideological basis for the divisions, and second, the third group refused to select a representative to appear for the interview; instead they decided to send the reporter a letter, which, unfortunately, was solely a denunciation of the leaders of the other two groups. As a consequence, one can obtain at best only a fragmentary picture of the issues that brought about the splits.

The responses given by Máximo López were the most lucid by far. The reader is left in absolutely no doubt regarding his position on several of the major issues in the Sino-Soviet dispute. All in all, his replies reflected an unquestionable acceptance of the views characteristic of pro-Chinese groups in Latin America. In response to a question concerning the fundamental causes of the division in the party, he answered by saying that revisionism was the root cause. Since the party had been open to all classes, elements of classes other than the proletariat had entered the party bringing with them "erroneous ideas" which they tried to use to divert "the proletariat from the revolutionary Marxist-Leninist line." [49]

Elsewhere he indicated that the struggle in the party was part of the worldwide struggle between Marxist-Leninists and revisionists:

[49] Florangel Cárdenas, "The Crisis in the Dominican Popular Movement: Division among the Dominican Communists," *Ahora*, August 15, 1966, as translated in JPRS, *TICD*, No. 879, p. 88.

The differences in the MPD are profoundly principled; it is the difference between Marxism-Leninism and revisionism, the same which divides the Socialist Camp and the world proletariat, it is the difference between the thinking of Mao Tse-Tung which constitutes the Marxism-Leninism of our epoch and the counterrevolutionary line of revisionism headed by the CPSU . . . and followed by various parties who have disowned the revolutionary Marxist-Leninist line.[50]

The Marxist-Leninist Community Party, he continued, regarded China as the "bulwark of the World Revolution" and the CCP led by Mao as "the Vanguard of the Revolution"; that is, a Marxist-Leninist was one who was "on the side of China and the thoughts of Mao Tse-tung." [51]

He lashed out at the policy of Cuban neutralism in the global battle between the two camps. He indicated quite clearly that he regarded Fidel Castro and his supporters as revisionists in that they had failed to pass the tests as Marxist-Leninists—they had refused to stand on the side of China and the thoughts of Chairman Mao. Earlier he had sent a letter to Fidel Castro from Paris berating him for abandoning "proletarian internationalism" and for "not assisting the Dominican people in the Patriotic War." [52] He, like many other militant revolutionaries in Latin America, was keenly disappointed when Castro failed to dispatch troops to help the Dominican rebels against the Yankee imperialists. For his failure to consult with the Central Committee before sending this letter, López was removed from the Central Committee.

Alfred Toussent Jean, the representative of the second group, had been a member of the MPD since 1962 and alleged that he was a member of the Central Committee when the July crisis erupted. He served as the spokesman for the group headed by Narciso González, Antonio Lockwood, and Luis Montas. According to Cayetano Rodríguez del Prado, all of the leaders in this faction, except Narciso González, had come into the party from the June 14 Movement just a few months before the split, an allegation, which, if true, might explain the fact that Toussent's statements were not as strongly pro-Chinese in orientation as were those of López Molina. Perhaps the

[50] *Ibid.*, p. 90. [51] *Ibid.*, p. 93.
[52] *Ibid.*, pp. 90-91.

young worker did not appreciate the need for articulating more pre-cisely the position of his group on such matters as neutralism in the Sino-Soviet dispute. On the other hand, perhaps he was acting on in-structions from his associates not to assume a strong pro-Chinese stand because some of them had not, after only a few months in the party, completely renounced the views they had held as members of the pro-Castro June 14 Movement. At any rate, Toussent did not denounce Castro as a revisionist, nor did he condemn the policy of neutralism in the polemics of the Sino-Soviet conflict. He did contend that the acts of the opportunists debased the name of the CCP, with whose position his group asserted solidarity. He added: ". . . it is not enough to say one is a partisan of the Marxist-Leninist concepts maintained by the glorious Communist Party of China but one must practice one's teachings, making use of the scientific experiences contributed by Comrade Mao Tse-tung." [53] He upbraided his opponents for de-valuing the experience of the international proletariat, but he made clear that his group, in borrowing from the experience of others and especially that of the CCP, would "identify with the true Marxists, *with those who truly struggle to bury imperialism and the other exploiters.*" The italicized words could be construed to mean that this group was willing to learn from the Castroites, who had repeatedly proclaimed their determination to defeat the imperialists. In any event, his failure to denounce vigorously the revisionists would certainly raise serious questions regarding the sincerity of his commitment to the Chinese global campaign against that group.

Cayetano Rodríguez del Prado, the spokesman for the third group which, like the second, called itself the MPD, refused to appear for the interviews with the other men because, he said, this would con-tribute to strengthening the erroneous view that the MPD was divided into three groups.[54] In his letter he insisted that there was only one MPD Party, the others having been expelled. Instead of addressing himself to the issues, he launched into vitriolic personal attacks on the leaders of the other groups. Rodríguez ridiculed López Molina for being so bold as to say that he headed a party, which, he claimed, existed in fact only in López' head. He charged López with trying to

[53] *Ibid.*, p. 94.   [54] *Ibid.*

conceal, through the use of Marxist-Leninist language and the invention of a series of fantasies, the real reasons for his expulsion from the party. Those reasons included:

. . . violations of democratic centralism and discipline . . . lying to the party, false self-critical positions and violations of the principles of communist morality, including a disorganized life and poor use of party funds to live better than his comrades and many other faults which we will not bring to light. López Molina committed many of his errors in Paris together with Ylander Selig, ex-leader of the MPD at the same time that the rest of the leaders and militants of our organization risked our lives here or fell, like Baldomero Castro, on the altar of the Revolution.[55]

Although he rebuked Toussent for trying to appear as the leader of the MPD, Rodríguez was not nearly as severe with him as he had been with López. He characterized Toussent as a comrade of past merit who, along with several other comrades, had been temporarily confused by a group of petty-bourgeois leaders in the anti-party group. He singled out as the ring leaders of the group that had been expelled from the party on July 12, 1966, Pin Montas, Antonio Lockwood, Narciso González, Hector Liqui Florentino, and Julio Peralta. All of these except González, he asserted, had come over from the June 14 Movement shortly before the rift. He criticized these leaders for using Toussent and the other "confused comrades" as a "proletarian screen" behind which to hide. He indicated a willingness to attempt a reconciliation with Toussent and the confused comrades; moreover, he stated his group would speak with the bourgeois leaders, on the condition that they use one of their own real leaders as a spokesman and that they make clear that their group was independent from the MPD and hence should choose another name.

The Chinese press has had few stories since July, 1966, concerning the MPD. *Peking Review* in an article on September 29, 1967, entitled "Studying Chairman Mao's Works Movement in Latin America" reported that the "Dominican People's Movement has reprinted Chairman Mao's 'three constantly read articles,' four philosophical essays and other brilliant works for its members to study so that they will get rid of their selfishness and be always devoted to the interests

[55] *Ibid.,* p. 95.

(265)

of the people." [56] In November, 1967, the MPD expressed its unflinching support for the Cultural Revolution. It attributed the "revolutionary upsurge" in the Dominican Republic to the intensive study of Mao's *Quotations* and other works. The readers were allegedly impressed by his idea that political power grows out of the barrel of a gun.

These stories did not indicate that the Chinese are aware of any of the rifts in the MPD, so there is no way to determine to which of the groups the Chinese are referring. In both instances the group was described as the "Dominican People's Movement." Perhaps the Chinese have been a bit dismayed if not disgusted with all of the squabbling among their supporters in the Dominican Republic.

The Chinese have discovered another revolutionary group in which they have manifested as much, if not more, interest than in the MPD. That group is the June 14 Revolutionary Movement, commonly described as a pro-Castro group. In 1965, shortly after the civil war began, the Chinese journal *Shih-chieh Chih-shih* featured an article on the movement which it called a revolutionary party, composed primarily of revolutionary intellectuals, college students, and petit bourgeoisie. There were also some peasants and workers. The party did not restrict its activities to the legal level; "it also created underground a military organization and sent cadres to mobilize and organize the peasants in the countryside." [57] The social composition of the party and the strategy adopted by it, no doubt, explain the reason for the Chinese interest in the organization.

Chinese approval of the movement's views was manifested in their frequent quoting of statements made by its representatives. For example, *Jen-min Jih-pao* commentator placed his stamp of approval on the group's statement concerning the lessons to be learned from the American intervention. The incident ". . . has helped the people to raise their revolutionary consciousness and enriched their fighting experience. The people of our country learned from their own experience that without struggling resolutely in various ways, mainly in

[56] "Studying Chairman Mao's Works Movement in Latin America," *Peking Review*, September 29, 1967, p. 24.

[57] Ho Li, "The June 14th Revolutionary Movement in Dominica," *Shih-chieh Chih-shih* (*World Knowledge*), June 25, 1965.

the form of armed struggle, it will be impossible to achieve social progress as long as U.S. imperialism is not defeated." [58] *Peking Review* in its January 1, 1966, issue quoted the National Committee's statement which urged the people to "push forward successfully the great mass struggles which are in the offing: strikes of workers, mobilization of peasants, struggles of students and demonstrations and rallies of the people." These acts "would end in a people's war for the liberation of the Dominican Republic." [59]

On the occasion of the first anniversary of the uprising on the island, the China Peace Committee sent a message of greetings to the June 14 Movement as well as to the MPD.[60] At a rally following a Week of Solidarity with the Dominican People, Ernesto Pimental, a representative of the June 14 organization, spoke on behalf of the Dominican people. He described the commemoration of the event as an acclamation of the triumph of people's war. The reason for the Chinese selection of him as spokesman appeared in the following:

The Dominican people have formally merged with the historical current which is encompassing the contemporary world. Such a historical current is not to be called an "atomic era" but an "era of people's war." We say this because we are convinced that neither the shameful traces left over by atomic bombs, nor the revisionist policies of peaceful coexistence, competition and transition can change the world. The world can really be changed only when the peoples of the world have defeated imperialism with people's war.[61]

It seems most significant that the Chinese printed, not a statement from the MPD but rather one from the June 14 Revolutionary Movement, on the occasion of the 18th anniversary of the founding of the CPR. The document contained statements which one would ordinarily find only in the remarks of the pro-Chinese parties that had advanced far along the "Chinese road": "On 1 October 1949, after a tenacious, prolonged war supported by the fighting Chinese People's Liberation Army, and under the correct leadership of the glorious Chinese Communist Party and the guidance of the brilliant

---

[58] *SCMP*, No. 3535, p. 26.
[59] "Dominican Republic Unreconciled," *Peking Review*, January 1, 1966, p. 24.
[60] *SCMP*, No. 3686, p. 29. [61] *SCMP*, No. 3687, p. 28.

thought of Mao Tse-tung, the industrious Chinese people proclaimed the founding of the Chinese People's Republic." [62]

The extent of the Chinese influence on the group was even more evident in the Dominican's statement that "in order to fight against a handful of party persons who were in authority and taking the capitalist road, the broad masses of the Chinese people and the proletarian revolutionaries, under the far-sighted direction of Chairman Mao Tse-tung, had carried out the great proletarian cultural revolution." It concluded by extolling the contribution made by the Chinese: "The correct path followed by the Chinese people today has completely proved the correctness of the assertions advanced by Comrade Mao Tse-tung in his works on class struggle, proletarian political power, and the struggle against imperialism and revisionism." [63]

The "Sinification" of the movement appeared to be virtually complete by November, 1967. An unnamed leader of the movement, described as a revolutionary organization, was reported to have said that Mao's thought was the Marxism-Leninism of the era and a powerful weapon of the people everywhere. He summed up the three "magic weapons" of Chinese experience as (1) the Marxist-Leninist Party must serve as the leading body, (2) a people's war must be waged, and (3) a policy of unity and struggle toward the national bourgeoisie must be followed if the revolution was to succeed. The first and the third propositions were definitely not consistent with Castroite policy. "The many defeats in the Dominican Revolution resulted from the absence of a party that was built, developed, and consolidated according to Marxism-Leninism. The revolutionaries must follow the thought of Mao Tse-tung if the revolution were to succeed." These remarks might be interpreted as a Chinese rebuke to the MPD for not exploiting a situation which the Chinese deemed to be revolutionary. The alleged activities of the June 14 Movement, on the other hand, could not have failed to bring joy to the hearts of Chinese policy-makers for Latin America.

The correspondent for NCNA in the Dominican Republic reported that those in the June 14 Movement now realized that the peasants constituted the main force and were the most dependable ally of the

[62] Peking NCNA International Service in English, October 4, 1967.
[63] Ibid.

proletariat. Victory was impossible without peasant participation; hence they had been sending their finest cadres to the rural areas. These cadres, applying class analysis in their social investigation, had relied on the poor peasants and the farmhands, had educated the peasants in the ideas of people's war, taught them the principle of self-reliance, and led them in their struggle to seize the land. They had also carried out a campaign of criticism and self-criticism from top to bottom with a view to eradicating bourgeois and petty bourgeois ideological and especially erroneous views on the matter of armed struggle. As a basis for their criticism and self-criticism, they had been reading "On Practice," "On Contradiction," "Protracted War," "Serve the People," and "Problems of Strategy in Guerrilla War Against Japan." I have been unable to find evidence to corroborate these vague reports of the NCNA reporter. In any event, there has been no significant guerrilla activity on the island.

The conclusion seems inescapable that the Chinese, as of the end of 1967, were far more interested in the revolutionary potential of the pro-Castro June 14 Revolutionary Movement than in the pro-Chinese MPD. It also seems clear that the former had become more pro-Chinese than pro-Castro if one can believe the statements attributed to them by the Chinese press.

By 1967 relative peace prevailed in the previously troubled Dominican Republic. President Joaquín Balaguer, who had defeated his more radical opponent, Juan Bosch, in the presidential election of 1966, enjoyed the general support of the people. His improved political standing was due to a number of factors. First, he profited from the fact that all the Communist forces (pro-Soviet, pro-Castro, and pro-Chinese) had declined in influence among the people. Doubtless one of the reasons for this development was that many Dominicans were disgusted with the incessant squabbling among and within these groups. As we have seen, the pro-Chinese movement, reported to be stronger than its pro-Soviet rival, spent much of its time and energy debating the domestic and international issues of concern to the world Communist movement. Second, Balaguer's acceptability to rightist elements in the military was certainly another reason for his improved position. Finally, widespread popular weariness contributed to the relative tranquility on the island.

⚘ ARGENTINA ⚘

The proponents of the Chinese line in Argentina were active by 1964, although they were overshadowed by the pro-Soviet Communist Party of Argentina, led by Victorio Codovilla. The Stalinists of the Pampas, as Robert Alexander calls them, continued to accept without question the views advanced by Moscow. As a loyal supporter of the CPSU, the Argentine Communist Party felt constrained to denounce the Chinese factionalist activities in Latin America and elsewhere. The Central Committee, in an article in *The New International Review*, disparaged the achievements of the Chinese campaign:

> The principal result of these divisive activities of the Chinese is to have attracted a few unstable elements especially from petty-bourgeois circles, to have united with them counter-revolutionaries who were excluded from the ranks of Communist Parties for anti-Party activity, with nationalist bourgeois intellectuals, and with Trotskyites.
> Although up until now these individuals have not succeeded in inflicting injury on our Party and although they are supported by only a few elements who were excluded from the ranks for anti-Party activity, since they are accentuating their divisive activity, it is therefore necessary to remain vigilant and not to allow them to harm us.[64]

The low esteem in which the party officials held the pro-Chinese followers was apparently justified in that the Chinese had influence with few persons besides those in the academic community and certain subversive groups. Although Codovilla and his associates were far more powerful than the dissident forces, they still labored very hard to prevent the emergence of an organized pro-Chinese tendency.[65]

Leading the pro-Chinese forces was Elías Seman, Political Secretary of the Communist Vanguard of Argentina. At the invitation of the China Peace Committee, the agency that was so active in the affairs of the Dominican Republic, he visited China in 1965, arriving in Peking

[64] Lazitch, "Repercussions of the Sino-Soviet Dispute on the Latin American Communist Parties," JPRS, *TICD*, No. 693, pp. 11-12.
[65] "The Present Situation of the Argentine Communist Party," *Est et Ouest*, May 15-30, 1966, as translated in JPRS, *TICD*, No. 857, p. 25.

on September 20, shortly after the publication of Lin Piao's famous essay. Ho Lin, a member of the secretariat of the host organization, was among those meeting him at the airport. Contrary to their usual practice, the Chinese did not report on the highlights of his stay in China. In fact they did not even report the date of his departure, so we have no way of knowing how long he remained in China. Nor do we know with whom he conferred while in the country.

Shortly after his arrival in Peking, the Chinese press featured on the 16th anniversary of the founding of the CPR a statement from public figures of Buenos Aires and other provinces, including trade union leaders, writers, and artists. They greeted the Chinese people and the CPR for being the "vanguard in the struggle against control by imperialism" and for "rendering inestimable support to the peoples fighting for liberation." They also praised China's economic and scientific achievements. "It is absurd to try to exclude China by maintaining no trade, diplomatic and cultural relations with it because the importance and the prestige of China, which has the largest population and the longest cultural tradition, are increasing with each passing day." [66] Since it would be beneficial to Argentina to strengthen ties with China, the unnamed Argentines concluded that it was the duty of every Argentine to work toward that goal. The message of greeting indicates that the Chinese leaders were very much interested in the improvement of commercial, diplomatic, and cultural relations with Argentina.

After his return from China, Elías Seman, in a pamphlet entitled "China in the Fight Against Imperialism and Revisionism" denounced the CPSU for allegedly working in collusion with U.S. imperialism and praised the CCP for being in the forefront of the global battle against U.S. imperialism and modern revisionism. The Chinese, he said, had made great contributions in the achievement of the fundamental task of the day—the development of the national democratic struggle in Asia, Africa, and Latin America, a struggle aimed at smashing the rear of the imperialists in those three continents.[67]

He commended to his readers the study of Mao's "On Practice" and "On Contradiction" for the light they shed on the Marxist theory

[66] NCNA, October 4, 1965.
[67] Peking NCNA International Service in English, April 5, 1966.

of knowledge. Those mastering these works could analyze situations in a dialectical way and could better understand the relationship between theory and practice. To my knowledge, he was the first of the pro-Chinese leaders to have explicitly urged his followers to study these two highly theoretical works of Mao.

His evaluation and analysis of Mao's concept of people's war was essentially the same as that found in the writings of other pro-Chinese leaders with one exception. He devoted more attention than most to a discussion of the principle of self-reliance, which Lin Piao had stressed in his September, 1965, article. This principle

. . . embodies proletarian internationalism and raises to the utmost the capabilities of the people of every country to develop their own productive forces and defeat the enemy. In this sense, the support given to each other by the socialist countries is a contribution to the socialist construction in each country; yet, such support cannot be a substitute for the revolutionary mission of the peoples to build up their own socialist economies.[68]

While the primary thrust of these remarks was directed at the Soviet Union for its unilateral withdrawal in 1960 of aid to the CPR, Seman, it seems to me, was also reminding Argentine followers of Mao that the primary responsibility for achieving national liberation was theirs and not that of the Chinese.

As the Cultural Revolution unfolded, *No Transar*, the organ of the Communist vanguard, like comparable pro-Chinese publications around the world, hailed the new developments in China and, of course, the thought of Mao Tse-tung. It held that the Cultural Revolution was a new victory for Mao's thought.[69] Mao's thought was the "Marxism-Leninism of our era," and for that reason, revolutionaries everywhere were "looking toward Peking, the center of China." The paper alleged that many Marxist-Leninist organizations, and especially those in the Third World, were "carrying out ideological revolutions to remold the thinking of revolutionaries and apply Mao Tse-tung's thought to their political line."[70] The paper concluded that Mao's

[68] *Ibid.*
[69] Peking NCNA International Service in English, February 18, 1967.
[70] NCNA, October 29, 1967.

thought was educating revolutionaries and leading them on to the road of people's war.

The Argentine organization was one of several groups mentioned in an article in *Peking Review* (September 29, 1967) entitled "Studying Chairman Mao's Works Movement in Latin America" as studying his works to attain a correct world outlook. According to this report, the Argentines attached a high priority to ideological training. One of their leaders allegedly said: "The study and application of Chairman Mao Tse-tung's works in a creative way should become a regular activity in our organization. This is the principal means to prevent the growth of revisionism and to guard against it in our organization." [71] The total subordination of this group to the CPR emerges when one notes that he made clear that the members of the organization "should first study the 'three constantly read articles' ["Serve the People," "In Memory of Norman Bethune," and "The Foolish Old Man Who Removed the Mountains"]." [72] Those who have followed events on the mainland itself know that these three works were required reading for all those participating in the Cultural Revolution. If this report from Argentina is true, then it is clear that the Argentines were emulating the example set by the Chinese and were busily engaged in the eradication of erroneous bourgeois ideas from their minds. In short, they were going through their own little Cultural Revolution. As we have seen, other parties released reports indicating that they too were involved in ideological remolding.

The orthodoxy manifested by the Argentines may account for the fact that the organization was called the Argentine Communist Vanguard Party. References in the past to the group had not used the word party as a part of its name. Since the Chinese are customarily most precise in their usage of such important terms, one could argue that this action constituted recognition by them that the group had advanced from the status of a movement to that of a party.

The scanty evidence available suggests that the Argentine group is one of the weakest of the pro-Chinese groups in Latin America. In

[71] "Studying Chairman Mao's Works Movement in Latin America," *Peking Review*, September 29, 1967, p. 23.
[72] *Ibid.*

my research I have encountered references only to the name of Elías Seman, who visited China at a time when Mao Tse-tung and Lin Piao were finalizing their plans for launching the Cultural Revolution against their opponents in the CCP, the state bureaucracy, and the PLA. Apparently Seman and his colleagues have been unable to establish ties with the followers of the deposed dictator, Juan Perón. Should they succeed in the future, they would have as an "ally" one of the most powerful of the alienated groups in Argentina. The present military dictatorship, led by President Juan Carlos Onganía, is vigorously anti-Communist and anti-Peronista in orientation. In August, 1967, the regime introduced a law providing for the registration of known Communists and imposing stringent restrictions on their activities. Thus the Argentine supporters of Chairman Mao are confronted with a formidable military dictatorship as are their associates in Brazil, Peru, Ecuador, and Bolivia.

 MEXICO

The factionalism of the Chinese first became apparent in Mexico in late 1963. In its 14th Party Congress, the Mexican Communist Party expelled from the party a certain Camilo Chavez "for his unprincipled fractionist and anti-Soviet position." [73] According to a resolution of the Presidium of the Central Committee of the pro-Soviet Communist Party, he had succeeded in uniting an "insignificant number of supporters." Those joining forces with him were described as a "small group of adventurists and renegades," who had been trying for years to split the "worker's democratic and anti-imperialist movement." The Mexican leaders explicitly charged that the Chinese leaders were supporting these elements, but they contended that those efforts had failed:

Clear proof of the failure of the Chinese dissidents in our country is the number and character of their supporters. In fact the position of the Chinese leaders is advocated in Mexico primarily by the Trotskyite

[73] "Actions of the Chinese Dissidents Are Doomed to Failure," *Pravda*, June 6, 1964, as translated in JPRS, *TICD*, No. 619, p. 38.

groups. The Chinese leaders and their provocative actions are also popular in the so-called "Workers' Front." They also use groups of renegades to spread their propaganda including the so-called "Bolshevik Party" and opportunists of all shades.[74]

In January, 1964, Hsin Fu, an expert in political propaganda, arrived in Mexico, heading a large Wuhan delegation of acrobats and artists. In China he had excelled as an active propagandist while serving as an assistant to Chang Kuang-tu, propaganda director of the Wuhan section of the Party's Central Committee. After his arrival in Mexico, Chinese propaganda activities increased appreciably, and he apparently paved the way for the signing of an agreement with Mexico to exchange films on a regular basis, the first of its kind in Latin America. While in Mexico he freely contacted the leaders of pro-Chinese organizations.[75] It does not seem unreasonable to assume that he consulted with these leaders regarding the promotion of Chinese views in their respective organizations, and it is also possible that he attempted to persuade them to establish a pro-Chinese party or at least a movement. At any rate, it is clear that pro-Chinese forces had become sufficiently active by June of 1964 to elicit the resolution of the presidium of the CP condemning them for factionalist activities.

The Mexican supporters of Chairman Mao must have experienced difficulty in establishing a Marxist-Leninist Movement, for it was not until November 3, 1967, that one finds in the Chinese press any mention of the Marxist-Leninist Movement of Mexico. Appropriately enough, the first article of the movement to be reproduced by the Chinese was entitled "Mao Tse-tung's Thought Is Marxism-Leninism of our Era." Mao, hailed as the greatest Marxist-Leninist of our era, was credited with the development of a new strategy, based on the fact that the principal contradiction in the contemporary world was that obtaining between imperialism and the peoples of Asia, Africa, and Latin America. In opposition to his "invincible thought" was a new "holy alliance," composed of the modern revisionists and the imperialists, headed respectively by the CPSU and the United States. Predicting the final outcome of this great battle, the Mexicans said:

[74] *Ibid.*
[75] "The Activity of Communist China in Latin America," *Est et Ouest*, July 16–31, 1966, p. 26.

"This new 'holy alliance' is aimed at preventing the people of all countries from mastering Mao Tse-tung's thought and forging ahead in revolution. However, just as those who opposed Marxism-Leninism were toppled in the past, all those who oppose Mao Tse-tung's thought today will be overthrown by the action of the revolutionary masses." [76] Thus one finds in the very first pronouncement of the organization evidence of its adherence to the cult of Mao.

Only two days later, the Chinese press featured an article "To the Revolutionary Students" written by the Federal District Committee of the Mexican Marxist-Leninist Movement. To obtain victory, the students were told that they must follow the thought of Mao, the "indisputable leader of the world revolution of the era." The main points of his theories were:

1. To build a new type Marxist-Leninist party, completely different from the revisionist party ideologically, politically, in style of work and closely linked to the masses.

2. To create a people's army under the absolute leadership of the party.

3. To establish solid rural bases, develop people's war, and use the countryside to encircle the cities.

4. To pursue a policy of the united front of all anti-imperialist and anti-feudal classes and sections under the leadership of the proletariat.

5. To establish a people's democratic dictatorship as a foundation for the development of socialism.

Those drafting this statement had obviously mastered the Maoist concept of people's war; moreover, the language used suggests that they appreciated the need for distinguishing the true road from that advocated by the Castroites.[77]

The provisional national leadership advanced further along the path leading to complete "Sinification" when it contended that Mao's thought must be applied in the building of the Communist Party, in combatting reactionary trends of thought, in closely integrating with the revolutionary masses (especially the poor peasants), and in the constant study of the conditions of the peasants. "This is the

[76] "Chairman Mao Is the Greatest Marxist-Leninist of Our Era," *Peking Review*, November 7, 1967, p. 22.
[77] NCNA, November 5, 1967.

only correct way to become true proletarian revolutionaries and to create a true Marxist-Leninist organization which is to be the revolutionary vanguard of our people, leading them onto the road of people's war until national liberation and socialism are won." [78] Using this as their guiding principle, the members of the movement were to study Mao's works so as to be able to draw a clear line of demarcation between them and the revisionists and reactionaries. Finally, they were urged to put political and ideological work in first place. Again one observes the Chinese stress on the importance of correct thought.

The Mexican Government released a statement on July 19, 1967, in which it implicated the CPR in an alleged plot to overthrow the government of Mexico. The Attorney General's office announced that the Chinese had financed the operations of thirteen persons just arrested by the police. The group was charged with preparing for subversive actions both in Mexico City and several provinces. They were also accused of having dynamited an army truck on a rural road in order to procure weapons. The officials asserted that acting as the financial channel for the group was the branch of *Hsinhua* in Mexico City, which was charged with providing $1,680 per month to finance the operation. The authorities stated that Javier Fuentes Gutiérrez, a civil engineer and a former leader of the Mexican Communist Party, the Independent Farmer's Central, and the Electoral People's Front, was the top leader of the group. At the time the arrests were made, he was not in Mexico, having left for China on June 30, with Federico Emery Valle, another pro-Chinese leader. His bookstore was supposedly the headquarters for the conspirators.[79]

Among those arrested were two foreigners, Silvestre Enrique Martino, a Salvadoran, and Daniel Camejo Guenchi, a Venezuelan. The former allegedly had had much experience as a guerrilla leader in Nicaragua. In Mexico he had worked in Gutiérrez' bookstore and had taught a training course in the mountains for Mexican guerrillas. The Venezuelan, a member of a Trotskyite faction, had agreed to provide medicines, propaganda, and instruction for the group. The Mexicans involved were Adán Nieto Castillo, one of the intellectual leaders of the movement; José Luis Calva Tellez, charged with planning a holdup of a branch bank in Mexico City to provide additional funds for

[78] NCNA, January 13, 1968.   [79] *The New York Times*, July 20, 1967.

the movement; Pablo Alvarado Barrera, an unemployed teacher and supposedly the number two leader of the group; Hugo David Uriarte; and Gil Bonilla alias David Rojo, an employee of the financial secretary and general coordinator of the Communist movement in Mexico.[80]

The arrestees were accused of having established a guerrilla training camp in the relatively inaccessible state of Chiapas. The authorities also alleged that they had sent recruiters to various parts of the country in an effort to recruit personnel for urban and rural guerrilla operations. Those to be recruited would have been taken to the training camp, where they were to have received instruction in guerrilla warfare based on the writings of Mao Tse-tung. In short, the arrested men, members of the Mexican Marxist-Leninist Movement, which, as we have noted, had not yet been mentioned in the Chinese press, envisioned the creation of insurrectional centers in the critical areas of Mexico.

The Mexican police announced on July 20 that it had confiscated twelve tons of books, film, and printed materials, including some of Mao's writings on guerrilla tactics. They also conducted intensive investigations in the universities and secondary schools in a search for students who had promised to enroll for the guerrilla training course in Chiapas.[81]

Pien Cheng, chief correspondent of NCNA in Mexico, released a statement protesting the Mexican government's statement. He angrily denied that he and his colleagues, who had gone to Mexico in July, 1963, had ever engaged in subversive activities. Admittedly they supported the revolutionary struggle of the people everywhere, but it was U.S. imperialism, not they, that had "always carried out subversive activities" and "arbitrarily interfered in the internal affairs of other countries." [82]

With regard to the charge that he had been providing the engineer Fuentes with 600 pounds sterling per month, he contended that he and his colleagues had never had "any financial dealings with engineer Fuentes"; moreover, they had never used British pounds to defray their expenses in Mexico.

[80] San José Radio Reloj Network in Spanish, July 20, 1967.
[81] *The New York Times*, July 21, 1967.
[82] *SCMP*, No. 3994, p. 37.

He then addressed himself to the motivation underlying these "anti-China slanders." Prior to their departure for China in November, 1966, to participate in the Cultural Revolution, the Mexican authorities had raised no objection to their operations in Mexico, but suddenly, some eight or nine months later when they were in China, they had been implicated in an alleged plot to overthrow the Mexican government. Why? His explanation was:

U.S. imperialism, Soviet revisionism and a handful of Mexican reactionaries are mortally afraid of and bitterly hate the all-illuminating Mao Tse-tung's thought, the world-shaking great proletarian cultural revolution in China and the growing friendship between the Chinese and Mexican people. The "Statement" engineered by U.S. imperialism is a big political plot with the real purpose of trying to hamper the dissemination of Mao Tse-tung's thought in Mexico, undermine the friendship between the Chinese and Mexican people, obstruct the return of the correspondents of the NCNA branch office in Mexico to their posts to carry on their normal press work and prevent them from exposing the U.S. imperialism policy of aggression against Mexico. At the same time, it is aimed at diverting the attention of the Mexican people so as to facilitate the suppression of the people's revolutionary movement.[83]

A responsible member of *Kuo-chi Shu-tien*, the supplier of Chinese materials for *El Primer Paso* (The First Step) bookstore owned by Fuentes, made a statement on August 15, 1967, to NCNA refuting the slanders against his agency. He pointed out that it was common knowledge that the *Kuo-chi Shu-tien* was a center for the distribution throughout the world of China's publications and that it had agents in Mexico as well as in many other countries. There was, he argued, certainly nothing illegal about its having an "inter-American distributor of publications" in Mexico, for all of the works on sale there were for public distribution throughout the world. He characterized as a fabrication and the vilest slander the Mexican authorities' labeling of these books, periodicals, and other printed materials as evidence of subversion. Such materials, he added, had been on sale for over ten years without the Mexican government's once objecting to them. The explanation given by him was couched in the same conspiratorial terms as that advanced earlier by the representative of NCNA.

[83] *Ibid.*, p. 38.

With reference to the status of Fuentes in the case, the responsible member maintained that the China Publication Center's practice of inviting its agents to visit China to discuss trade matters was entirely consistent with the usual commercial practice. It was, therefore, ridiculous to treat the invitation of Fuentes as evidence of subversion. According to this statement, Fuentes had not, as reported in the Mexican government's statement, visited China several times. "Apart from his recent and first visit to China on a trade-talk mission, he had never been to China before." [84] In checking through *SCMP* for stories concerning a possible visit by him to China, I found no reference to his having been in China prior to the incident, but I did find an NCNA article dated June 23, 1966, concerning a reception given by Kuo Mo-jo, for a "well-known Mexican engineer, Adolfo Orive Alba, ex-secretary of irrigation work, his wife and seven other members of his family." [85] Fuentes was described by *The New York Times* as a civil engineer and former leader of the Independent Farmers' Central.[86] Whether the two men are one and the same is not clear.

In view of the lateness in the appearance of a Marxist-Leninist movement in Mexico, it is too early to determine whether it will be more successful than the impotent Mexican Communist Party. Thus far the pro-Chinese elements have manifested the greatest interest in radical university students, especially those at the National University in Mexico City. Fierce fighting between government forces and the students erupted in the autumn of 1968 on the eve of the Olympic games in the national capital. The Díaz Ordaz regime, through the use of specially trained riot forces, restored order after a long and bloody battle with the students. It is most doubtful, however, that the authorities crushed the desire for revolutionary change of the more militant elements in the student movement. One can, therefore, anticipate that the Chinese will attempt, as in the United States, to win over those who are most alienated from their social and political order. In both countries the followers of Chairman Mao have had to compete with the heroes of the Cuban revolution, Fidel Castro, Che Guevara, and Régis Debray.

84 *SCMP*, No. 4003, p. 36.   85 *SCMP*, No. 3727, p. 24.
86 *The New York Times*, July 20, 1967.

🌿 OTHER COUNTRIES 🌿

Although the Chinese undoubtedly have supporters in other Latin American countries, they have been unable to muster sufficient support for the formation of true Marxist-Leninist parties and movements. In Paraguay, it was thought for a time that Oscar Creydt, the secretary-general of the party, had formed a pro-Chinese faction in the party. As Ernst Halperin brings out in his article, Creydt was really denounced by some of his pro-Soviet colleagues, not for his pro-Chinese tendencies but for his resistance to the new Soviet policy, adopted at the Havana Conference of 1964, of encouraging cooperation between Castroites and Latin American Communist parties. If he has succeeded in forming a pro-Chinese faction in the exile party, it has not been reported by the Chinese.[87]

The Chinese must be most depressed with the course of events in Venezuela, a country in which guerrillas have been extremely active for many years. Naturally, then, they have displayed a deep interest in the revolutionary movement of the country that has had so many advocates of the superiority of the road of armed struggle to all other paths to power. They must be given credit for having tried very hard to win over members of the Politburo of the Venezuelan Communist Party. For example, they attempted to gain the support of Eduardo Gallegos Mancera when he visited China in August, 1964, and they, no doubt, were very much encouraged by the remarks he made at a press conference. He said:

Armed struggle is the main form of struggle today in Venezuela, which is in bondage to U.S. imperialism. Our Party has reached a definite decision on this question. We are using revolutionary violence against counter-revolutionary violence. We are determined to gain liberation. The legal ways to liberation have all been blocked up, and we have to take up arms and carry on the struggle. Only through the barrel of the gun can we

---

[87] Halperin, "Peking and the Latin American Communists," *The China Quarterly*, January–March, 1967, pp. 147–48.

(281)

compel U.S. imperialism to give up Venezuela, which it regards as a fat prize.[88]

The Chinese, however, were to learn that Gallegos did not speak for all of his colleagues in the Venezuelan Politburo. In the dialectical contradiction between the hard and soft lines, proponents of the so-called soft line or the peaceful path to socialism, emerged victorious in 1966.

In the meantime, relations with Castro and his followers in Venezuela had also cooled. As a consequence, the Chinese find themselves in the embarrassing situation of having no pro-Chinese party or movement in a country having had so many years of guerrilla activities.

The Uruguayan Communist Party, headed by Rodney Arismendi, has succeeded in holding in check efforts by dissident elements to split the party and establish a party with a Peking orientation. The policy of obstructing the circulation of Chinese materials among the rank and file members of the party, adopted in 1963 by the Uruguayan pro-Soviet party as well as by those in other parts of the world, was designed to preserve the integrity of the party. The independent Socialist newspaper *Época* on November 21, 1963, scored that policy in an article entitled "International Polemic Within the Uruguayan Communist Party." It charged that: "the present leadership of the CP has systematically and insistently concealed the Chinese publications and materials and other subject matter pertinent to the debate. Absolutely all of the materials which the Chinese comrades have sent to the CP of Uruguay have disappeared mysteriously, with the single exception of the 25-point letter sent by the Chinese CP to the CPSU. . . ." [89]

As in the case of Chile, then, the Chinese have had some ardent supporters in the Socialist Party. Pro-Chinese groups have also been active in the Revolutionary Leftist Movement, the Leftist Liberation Front, and the Peasant Action Movement, but the Chinese have been unable to unify all these groups into a single party or movement.[90]

Guatemala is, like Venezuela, a country that has experienced guer-

[88] "Armed Struggle—the Main Form of Struggle in Venezuelan Revolution," *Peking Review*, September 4, 1964, p. 28.

[89] "International Polemic Within the Uruguayan Communist Party," November 21, 1963, as translated in JPRS, *TICD*, No. 550, p. 69.

[90] "Communist China and Latin America," *Este & Oeste*, December, 1966, as translated in JPRS, *TICD*, No. 940, p. 91.

rilla warfare for several years. The Guatemalan guerrillas began their operations in 1962 under the leadership of Yon Sosa, a Chinese-Guatemalan, known as el Chino or the Chinese. *Peking Review* was quick to respond to the outbreak of guerrilla warfare in Guatemala. In an article entitled "Guatemala's Struggle Against Tyranny," the Chinese publication mentioned the November 13 Movement, led by Yon Sosa, and was obviously pleased with its endorsement of the doctrine of armed struggle and its promise to institute agrarian reform.[91] Shortly after the publication of Lin Piao's article of September, 1965, *Shih-chieh Chih-shih* carried an article dealing with Guatemala, stressing, of course, the fact that guerrilla activities were on the increase. It listed first, as an example of the "major people's guerrilla forces," those participating in the November 13 Movement.[92] Fidel Castro, in his closing speech to the Tricontinental Conference, denounced Yon Sosa as a Trotskyite, and demanded that he be replaced as commander of the Rebel Armed Forces by Luis Turcios Lima. As the Castroites and the pro-Soviet Guatemalan Labor Party gained control of the guerrilla movement, the November 13 Movement dwindled in importance. It seems to me that the Chinese might have taken steps to transform that movement into a movement comparable to the Communist Vanguard Movement in Argentina or the Mexican Marxist-Leninist Movement had they had more confidence in the political reliability of its leader. Ernst Halperin contends that the organization was probably Trotskyite in its orientation, pointing out that the terminology used in its 1965 manifesto was clearly Trotskyite. The Chinese, being rather Stalinist in their outlook, have a deep antipathy for the followers of the late Leon Trotsky and have enjoined their followers in Latin America to beware of the Trotskyites.

In this and the two preceding chapters, I have attempted to analyze the efforts of the Chinese to enlist the support of Latin Americans, the third key element in their proposed united front in the Third World. In retrospect, it seems that the Chinese finally gave up hope in the summer of 1963 that the Soviet leaders would regain their revolutionary zeal. After that date they intensified their attempts to

[91] "Guatemala's Struggle Against Tyranny," *Peking Review*, March 30, 1962, p. 8.
[92] "Guatemala," *Shih-chieh Chih-shih*, November 10, 1965, pp. 18–19.

establish parties in Latin America that would support them in the global struggle against the renegades in the world Communist movement and the imperialists led by the United States. As the polemics in the Sino-Soviet dispute increased in intensity, the nature of the relationship between the CCP and its Latin American followers changed appreciably. Prior to the advent of the Cultural Revolution, the pro-Chinese groups in Latin America subscribed to views that were clearly patterned after those of the Chinese. As the Cultural Revolution unfolded, one can detect an increasing trend toward the "Sinification" of these groups. That is, they made far more explicit references to the relevance of Chinese experience and they joined with Maoists around the world in the exaltation of China as the base for the world revolution. The exorbitant praise heaped by them upon Mao Tse-tung and his thought exceeded even that bestowed on Stalin. His thought, hailed as the highest form of Marxism-Leninism, was held to be the only reliable guide for revolutionaries around the world. Thus the pro-Chinese groups in Latin America were an essential part of the new Comintern that the Chinese were attempting to form. At present the Maoists quite clearly demand of their Latin American supporters the same type of subordination of their national interests to those of China as was demanded of foreign Communists in their relations with the Soviet party in the Stalin era. In an effort to enhance their position in the struggle with the CPSU, the Chinese Communists have frequently reproduced or excerpted resolutions or reports adopted by their Latin American supporters. By so doing they hope to persuade others that the CCP enjoys more support than it actually has in that struggle.

In addition to relating the evolution of the pro-Chinese parties to the Sino-Soviet dispute, an effort has been made to show how these parties have mirrored the views of the Chinese in their relations with the Castroite movement in Latin America. Until the closing months of 1964 Sino-Cuban relations were most cordial, as can be easily determined by studying the references to Cuba in the Chinese press and in the documents emanating from Latin America. Fidel Castro's refusal to abandon his policy of neutrality in the Sino-Soviet conflict was the basic reason for the Chinese change of attitude toward him. Whereas Cuba had been held up as a brilliant example to be emulated by all

Latin American revolutionaries, now the Chinese, in their treatment of Cuba, either explicitly condemned it for adhering to its policy of neutrality or they omitted any reference at all to Cuba in their annual surveys of significant events in Latin America. Eventually the pro-Chinese elements became embroiled in the polemics between the Cubans and Chinese regarding the proper strategy and tactics to follow in Latin America, a dispute fully analyzed in Chapters IV and V. The feud with the Cubans has only contributed to the further isolation of the Chinese and their supporters in the Latin American revolutionary movement.

Conclusion

To EVALUATE the activities of the Chinese in Latin America, one must take into account the conditions under which the Chinese have been working in that area. When one considers that the unfavorable conditions have far outweighed the favorable conditions, their achievements in the nine-year period have been greater than one might anticipate.

In my judgment, the principal asset of the Chinese has been the prevalence of anti-imperialist sentiments in Latin America, feelings based on the experience of Latin Americans in their dealing with the United States and Western European countries. There are still many Latin American intellectuals who think of the United States in terms of policies followed by this country vis-à-vis Latin America prior to the adoption in 1933 of the Good Neighbor Policy. That is, they are extremely suspicious of all acts of the United States in Latin America because they are convinced that the Colossus of the North has not really abandoned the policy of intervention in the domestic affairs of the Latin republics. The anti-imperialism of the Latins could facilitate the formation of the united front of various classes against the external enemy, the United States. As we have seen, the establishment of such a united front is an integral part of the Maoist concept of people's war.

A closely related asset on which the Chinese may draw is the respectability of Marxist concepts among Latin American intellectuals. The latter frequently espouse the Leninist theory of imperialism because it provides them with a plausible hypothesis for explaining the underdevelopment of their countries. Since Latin American intellectuals often associate capitalism with U.S. imperialism, they also reject capitalism as a model for the development of their economy. Moreover, they advocate the use of state power to mobilize the limited resources of the nation. In brief, they prefer a planned economy. Insofar as they have an antipathy for capitalism and a preference for a planned economy, they are more receptive to the economic proposals advanced by the Chinese, the Soviets, and the Castroites. In all fairness to these intellectuals, however, one should point out that many of them have rejected the totalitarian methods employed by the Communists in building socialism. The socialism they favor has more in common with the democratic socialism found in a number of Western European countries than with the totalitarian socialism found in Eastern Europe, China, and elsewhere.

The propensity of Latins to settle their political differences by resorting to armed force is a part of their political culture that could redound to the benefit of the Chinese. Since winning their independence from Spain and Portugal in the nineteenth century, they have often managed their political affairs in accordance with the principle that political power grows out of the barrel of a gun. In making the latter statement, I am not suggesting, of course, that they have consciously followed the famous Maoist maxim, but I am contending that their frequent use of armed force in the political realm would predispose them to follow the path of armed struggle advocated by the Chinese. Certainly they would be more inclined to do so than are some other peoples, such as the Dutch or the Scandinavians.

The political radicalism of university students is another aspect of Latin American political culture that the Chinese could turn to their advantage. As a political force, Latin students have been far more active in the political sphere and more influential than their North American counterparts. They have also displayed a greater receptivity to Marxist ideas than have students of the United States, and they have been far more willing than American students to engage in revolutionary activities. In this context, the victory of the pro-Chinese candidate for president of the Student Federation at San Marcos University takes on added significance. In fact the pro-Chinese candidate has won for the last four years the elections held at San Marcos University, the leading university in Peru. The reader will recall that the Chinese press has devoted much space since the advent of the Cultural Revolution to coverage of radical student activities.

The concentration of land ownership in the hands of a relatively few families in some of the Latin American countries is a condition subject to manipulation by those of pro-Chinese persuasion. Under these circumstances, the Chinese advocacy of land reform would have tremendous appeal to landless peasants. As a consequence, the Chinese, in their analyses of Latin American conditions, constantly emphasize the need for land reform. One should note, however, that other parties have been as quick as they in perceiving the popular appeal of such a slogan. The Venezuelan and Bolivian regimes in particular have undertaken significant land reform programs, thereby depriving rural revolutionaries of one of their most potent weapons in relation to the peasantry.

The desire among many Latin American statesmen for greater diplomatic and economic flexibility affords the Chinese still another opportunity for expanding their influence in Latin America. They have sensed that Latin political leaders look with disfavor on their countries' being too closely tied to the United States. Brazilians, for example, believe that they must seek other markets for their coffee because they are convinced that failure to do so will render them completely subject to the mercy of "ruthless" American buyers. The Quadros regime in Brazil was an excellent case in point. The Chinese sought to capitalize on his desire to pursue an independent foreign policy. One can observe the same desire for greater flexibility in foreign policy among the Mexicans, who have demonstrated their sovereignty by refusing to sever diplomatic relations with the Castro regime. Again the Chinese have sought to exploit this attitude by purchasing Mexican cotton and wheat.

The obstacles confronting the Chinese as they attempt to expand their influence in Latin America are truly formidable. The distance separating China and Latin America is immense, which makes transportation and travel between the two regions most difficult and expensive. Given the underdevelopment of Communist China and the fact

CONCLUSION

that the United States controls the seas, it is clearly beyond the capacity of the Chinese to provide arms and other material means of waging people's wars to their admirers in Latin America. The same considerations would rule out the dispatch of Chinese troops to the Western Hemisphere. Equally significant is the cultural gulf dividing the Chinese and the Latins. The Oriental culture of the Chinese has little in common with that of the Latins, which is derived, for the most part, from Western European culture. It is extremely difficult for me to imagine how a Peruvian Indian, for example, could relate to Chairman Mao and the Chinese Communist experience when he has traditionally regarded with such suspicion, if not hatred, the "white" man and his way of life which is so alien to his own. Prior to 1949 there were few contacts of any kind between Latin America and the Far East. There had been some trade during the colonial period between the Spanish in Latin America and the Far East, but very little after the wars for independence. There are Chinese colonies in Peru, Cuba, and other Latin American countries but the overseas Chinese seem to have manifested little enthusiasm for identifying with Communist China in their respective countries. Thus there are no large cultural or religious groups among whom they can proselytize as in parts of Asia.

The attitude of the United States government and the Latin American military regarding Communist activities in the area is another major obstacle confronting the Chinese. For well over a hundred years the United States has tended to regard Latin America as its "backyard." During much of the nineteenth century and the first third of the present century, the United States, in the name of the Monroe Doctrine, challenged any and all attempts by external forces to intervene in Latin America. Since the advent of the Cold War in 1947, the American government has led the fight against the extension of Communist influence into Latin America and attempted to hold in check efforts by the Soviets, the Cubans, and the Chinese to increase their influence in the region. American vigilance has been especially keen in regard to Chinese and Cuban activities. In a very real sense, then, the Chinese are faced with the fact that its main enemy, the United States, is firmly committed to a policy of combatting Chinese influence in Latin America. The emergence of a guerrilla movement with pro-Chinese ties would surely elicit a prompt and strong response from the United States.

Latin American military leaders, many of whom have close ties with the United States, have also quite frequently adopted a militantly anti-Communist posture. Since military dictatorships exist in Brazil, Argentina, Peru, Ecuador, Bolivia, and several other countries, the Chinese would, if they initiated a major guerrilla movement, be faced with a foe that is generally well armed and trained by military advisers from the United States. As is well known, the United States has established schools to give special instruction in guerrilla warfare to Latin American military personnel. In the case of the 1967 Bolivian guerrilla movement, for example, American representatives helped train Bolivian troops to wipe out the Cuban-led guerrillas.

The underdevelopment of the Chinese economy has placed the Chinese at a severe disadvantage with the Soviets in the competition for the support of Latin American Communists. Castro's Cuba is an excellent case in point. For economic reasons alone, the Chinese, then, would be hard-pressed to provide substantial economic or military assistance to pro-Chinese guerrillas in Latin America. In their recent pronouncements on people's war, they have taken the position that their primary responsibility to supporters elsewhere is the providing of ideological and strategic guidance, not arms or troops. Throughout these statements, one finds references to the virtue of self-reliance. Thus, they have put the Latin Americans on notice that each guerrilla leader has the primary responsibility for procuring from enemy forces, as did the Chinese, the weapons and supplies required for waging a people's war. They are not to expect the Chinese to provide these necessities for them.

It should be noted that the Chinese are better equipped to compete with the Cubans as long as the latter follow their present policy in regard to the Soviets. That is, if the Cubans continue to attack the Soviet peaceful road to socialism and persist in their vitriolic attacks on the Soviet leaders and some of the established leaders of the Latin American Communist movement, they surely cannot expect to receive from those attacked funds, weapons, or supplies with which to support their guerrilla movements in Venezuela, Guatemala, and elsewhere. The Cubans will, however, still have three advantages over the Chinese: (1) they are Latin Americans and thus they have a far greater attraction for Latins, (2) the distances involved are not so great for them as for the Chinese, and (3) they are members of LASO (the Latin American Solidarity Organization) founded in 1967. The pro-Chinese parties were excluded from the initial LASO Conference just as they had been barred from attending the Tricontinental Conference in 1966. Without support from the Soviet Union and the Eastern European powers, LASO may not, however, prove to be nearly as effective as the Cubans and their associates anticipated.

After the Bolivian fiasco and the death in October, 1967, of Che Guevara, the would-be supreme commander of the Castroite-dominated continental revolution, the Chinese had a better opportunity for seizing the initiative among the guerrillas in Latin America. The Castroite strategy for waging a people's war as outlined in Debray's book had been somewhat discredited in the eyes of Latin American revolutionaries. With their Castroite rivals rather confused and demoralized after their setback in Bolivia, pro-Chinese leaders in Colombia and Peru, for example, had a chance to move into the revolutionary vacuum. There is, however, no reliable evidence that these leaders availed themselves of the opportunity.

What have the Chinese done by way of preparing for people's wars in Latin America? To answer this question effectively, one must review the requisites for the successful fighting of such a war. The Chinese hold that there must be a Marxist-Leninist party to direct the organization of the people's army and the political mobilization of the masses. The party must be composed of individuals that are thoroughly imbued with the Marxism-Leninism of the present era, the thought of Mao Tse-tung. If the reports received from the pro-Chinese parties in Latin America are correct, no effort has been spared in raising the political consciousness of party members. Recent documents from these parties indicate that they have undertaken "thought reform" in order to eradicate erroneous ideas from their minds. The pro-Chinese elements have also been waging ideological struggle

(291)

against revisionist (pro-Soviet) and petty bourgeois (pro-Castro) forces in their respective countries to prepare themselves ideologically for engagement in people's war.

Several points should be made regarding these parties. First, their dogmatism has resulted in their isolation from other revolutionary groups. Their insistence, for example, that a guerrilla movement can be led only by a genuine Marxist-Leninist party has alienated not only the Castroites but also the Trotskyites and members of the Jacobin Left. By the latter term I have reference to non-Communist groups that have lost all faith in political democracy and thus are committed to programs of action that call for the radical restructuring of the social and political order. Until the "pro-Chinese" parties became such servile practitioners of the cult of Mao, they enjoyed appreciable support among such groups.

Second, the sectarianism of the pro-Chinese forces has resulted in schisms within such groups in some countries. As noted previously, such has been the case in both Peru and the Dominican Republic, countries in which the Maoists were reported to be more powerful than the pro-Soviet parties. Obviously the internal squabbling among the followers of the CCP has reduced the effectiveness as well as the influence of those concerned. Doubtless the Peruvians and the Dominicans could have made more progress had they not dissipated their strength through such internal bickering.

Third, in their zeal to eradicate bourgeois and revisionist ideas from their thought, they have neglected one of the major tasks of the party, namely, the mobilization of the masses in the form of a united front. They did attempt in Brazil to enlist the support of Francisco Julião, the most influential leader of the peasant movement, but it appears that Julião was equally attracted by the Cuban model. In any event, the pro-Chinese forces lost this potential ally when the Brazilian military overthrew the leftist Goulart regime in 1964. Javier Fuentes Gutiérrez, one of their supporters in Mexico, was a leader of a farm organization. The establishment by college students of peasant associations among the Peruvian Indians, an event verified by the respectable British publication, *The Economist*, indicates that the Maoists in Peru took seriously the organization of the peasantry, the main force in a Maoist revolution. Similarly, there is evidence that the pro-

CONCLUSION

Chinese forces in Bolivia enjoyed in the mid-1960s some support in the powerful tin-miners' union. There is also some evidence that they have had even more success in gaining a foothold in the university student movement in Peru, Mexico, and Chile. Finally, they have won over as allies the more radical elements in the socialist parties in Uruguay and Chile. These successes notwithstanding, pro-Chinese leaders have only begun to approximate the united front so skillfully put together by the Chinese Communists.

Another major task confronting the pro-Chinese forces is the building of a people's army in accordance with Mao's theory on the subject. Without such an army, victory cannot be realized. Recent writings of the Chinese indicate that their supporters will have to develop their armies from small guerrilla bands. That is, the guerrilla forces will be gradually transformed into an armed force capable of engaging in mobile and positional warfare. The establishment of bases in the countryside, where the peasantry constitutes the main force, is absolutely necessary for the survival and development of the people's armed forces.

The Chinese supporters in some countries may have taken the first step toward implementing these objectives. According to a dispatch of January 20, 1968, from the NCNA correspondent in Colombia, the people's liberation army (EPL) "made up of revolutionary peasants, workers, soldiers, and students" had begun fighting the "Colombian oligarchy and U.S. imperialism." Informing the Colombian people that they were assuming defense of the peasants of Alto Sinu and Alto San Jorge, they announced their determination to persist in the struggle in the northeast until they had "completely liberated" the area from the "clutches of Yankee imperialism and the oligarchy." They insisted that they were not outlaws but revolutionary fighters operating under the control of the patriotic junta formed on November 11, 1967, under the chairmanship of Major Julio Guerra. Obviously the group wanted the Colombian people to know that they were different from the "bandits" that have terrorized for so long many parts of rural Colombia. The Francisco Garnica detachment captured and executed on January 6, 1968, a landlord who allegedly had seized land belonging to hundreds of peasants and had employed for ten years hired murderers to kill dozens of peasants in the area. The same detachment had annihilated a police detachment and seized many weapons and much ammunition. The NCNA correspondent ended his report with the following slogans: "Long live the people's war"; "Long live the people's liberation army." [1] The reporter did not maintain that the pro-Chinese guerrilla band had succeeded in establishing a base in the countryside.

Hsinhua reported on November 17, 1967, that the Dominican June 14 Movement had sent its finest cadres to the rural areas, where they were applying class analysis in their social investigations. They were reported to be relying on the poor peasants and the farmhands and were educating the peasants in the ideas of people's war, stressing the principle of self-reliance. Furthermore, they were leading the peasants in their struggle to seize land. Finally, the cadres had been studying Mao's major works on people's war. The report did not indicate how far the pro-Chinese forces had progressed in their preparation for a people's war. In view of the propensity of *Hsinhua* reporters to exaggerate the influence of Chairman Mao among Third World revolutionaries, I sought to corroborate these reports. I found no reliable evidence (of a non-Chinese nature) that would confirm or rebut these reports.

In Peru, college students in early 1966 were reported by NCNA to have gone to the hills to organize peasant associations so as to enable the peasants to reclaim their rights to the land held by latifundists. The report was based on an article of January 29 in the British weekly, *The Economist,* which stated that young Latin American students liked to read Mao's works because they were so easy to read. The British paper asserted that many student leaders at Cuzco College were solidly behind Mao's theories.[2] It should be recalled that the pro-Chinese candidate has won the last four years the election for the presidency of the student federation of San Marcos University in Peru. Should these university leaders at Cuzco College and San Marcos University be truly dedicated to the Maoist concept of people's war, they could provide leadership in the future for such a movement. Nor

[1] Bogota Correspondent's Dispatch in Spanish to NCNA Peking, January 20, 1968.
[2] Peking NCNA International Service in English, February 12, 1966.

should one forget that the pro-Chinese party in Peru is the largest in Latin America.

In addition to the conditions described earlier as creating significant problems for the Chinese as they undertake any type of activity in Latin America, several others relate specifically to the implementation of their strategy of people's war. It seems to me that a crucial assumption in their strategy is the idea that the United States would eventually intervene, in a direct military fashion, in a people's war involving Marxist-Leninists and oligarchies in Latin America, assuming, of course, that the latter were unable to cope with the revolutionary threat. The Chinese are apparently convinced that the United States would not tolerate the establishment by revolutionary means of another Communist state in Latin America. In a word, they assume that the United States would respond to such a situation in precisely the same way that it reacted in the Dominican Republic in 1965, in Cuba in 1961 at the Bay of Pigs, and in Vietnam in the 1960s. Clearly they would welcome such interventions because the presence of American troops would make easier the mobilization of the anti-American sentiments so prevalent in Latin America. Thus their supporters in the invaded country could form a united front of several classes and strata against the hated Yankee imperialists. Their study of Chinese experience during the anti-Japanese war and that of the Vietnamese in the war against the French and later the Americans demonstrated to them the potential for utilizing the nationalistic feelings of many groups other than those of the Communist Party. They realize that without the presence of an external enemy on the sacred soil of the motherland, the tremendous force of anti-imperialism cannot be effectively harnessed. The Chinese, therefore, will use their limited influence to bring about civil wars in Latin America that will eventuate finally in American intervention.

The question arises, then, will the United States intervene as the Chinese postulate? In support of the Chinese contention, one could cite the specific instances referred to above in which the United States has intervened in recent years when faced with revolutionary situations involving or thought to involve Communist activities. One could also find numerous statements by recent American Presidents which are tantamount to saying that this country will not fail to act unilaterally as it did initially in the Dominican Republic, if absolutely necessary, to prevent the establishment of other "Cubas" in this hemisphere. My own impression is that the United States government would greet with even greater revulsion the establishment of a pro-Chinese Communist regime in Latin America. My point is this: given the intense hostility existing between Peking and Washington, there would be a strong temptation on the part of the United States to fall into the Chinese trap by intervening militarily in a civil war between Communists and anti-Communists. Counterbalancing any such temptation to intervene militarily would be our most painful experience in Vietnam. Given the widespread opposition to our involvement in the Vietnam war, it is most unlikely that any administration would be anxious to become involved in a similar war in Latin America. It is clear, however, that the Chinese are most hopeful that their supporters can create several Vietnams in Latin America and thus bring about the strategic attrition of the United States by luring American troops into several of these countries. It is equally obvious that they are most favorably impressed with the damage inflicted on the American imperialists by the Vietnamese. American involvement in similar wars in several Latin American countries would drain away even more of the strength of the overextended enemy.

But the coin has another side. Can the Chinese convince their followers in Latin America that they ought to be willing to bear most of the burden of the struggle against the oligarchy and its ally, U.S. imperialism? Can the pro-Chinese elements, without some material assistance from China, survive long enough to precipitate American intervention? That is the crucial question. If they can, their chance for emerging victorious would probably be enhanced by direct American military involvement. In my judgment, then, the type of aid rendered to the Bolivian government would be far more effective in dealing with people's wars than would direct military intervention. Whether Latin American regimes will be able, with indirect military assistance from the United States, to cope effectively with guerrilla threats is not clear, but their record in suppressing Castroite guerrilla movements in Venezuela, Bolivia, and elsewhere has been quite impressive.

Chinese strategists trying to apply their experience in the Sino-Japanese War to Latin America are faced with the fact that a guerrilla movement in a Latin American country would most likely not occur within the context of a world war as was the case in the Sino-Japanese War. As noted in our analysis of the Chinese experience, the Chinese Communists had powerful allies in that war. Among those allies were the Kuomintang forces, led by their mortal enemy, Chiang Kai-shek. It is true, of course, that the KMT and CCP alliance was an alliance of expedience, but the fact remains that the Nationalists did play a far more significant role in the war than the Chinese Communist account would indicate. In conclusion, it is most difficult for me to visualize a configuration of international and domestic forces in a Latin American country that would correspond to that obtaining in China during the period in question. It seems to me that the experience of the CCP during the Kiangsi period would be far more relevant for pro-Chinese revolutionaries in Latin America, who are allegedly preparing for people's war. Doubtless the reason that the Chinese have paid so little attention in their propaganda statements in Latin America to this period in their history is that the period ended in the expulsion of the Communists from their bases in Kiangsi and surrounding provinces. Should they not openly acknowledge that they sustained major defeats at the hands of the enemy and still prevailed over him in a protracted war? In my view, this posture would be far more reasonable and thus attractive to guerrilla leaders coping with the problems of the real world in which they are operating. What they need most from the Chinese in the formative stage of their development is guidance in regard to the formation and development of guerrilla bands and the establishment of rural bases for use against a domestic foe. The successes and the failures of the CCP during the Kiangsi period could provide them with lessons they so badly need at this time.

Can the supporters of Chairman Mao succeed where the followers of Fidel Castro have failed? It seems to me that the Chinese have not attached sufficient weight to several considerations. Have they, for example, considered that Latin Americans could be repelled by the Maoist cult of personality? I have found no evidence to suggest that they perceive that Latin sensibilities might be offended by the deification of the thought of Mao Tse-tung. Obviously they have failed to perceive that nationalism is a force that can also work against their interests. In this context, they should have learned from the mistakes of the Latin American Communist leaders in the Stalin era, leaders that followed, without question, every shift in policy emanating from the Kremlin. The Stalinists in Latin America and elsewhere were taught that Joseph Stalin was the greatest Marxist-Leninist, that the Soviet Union was the base of the world revolution, and that their most sacred duty was that of defending Mother Russia against all her enemies. This obvious subordination of Latin American interests to those of a foreign power was most repugnant to the nationalistically-oriented Latins. The influence of the Communist parties dropped sharply in the post-World War II period as non-Communists realized that the Communists were not bona fide nationalists. Surely the servile repetition of Chinese Communist slogans and excessive exaltation of Mao and his contributions to Marxism-Leninism must have been even more offensive to sensitive Latin American nationalists. Thus, greater emphasis on the creative application of Marxist-Leninist principles in accordance with the peculiar conditions of each Latin American country is absolutely essential.

Closely related to this point is the fact that the Chinese have not reflected in their analyses of Latin American society an acute awareness of the major differences among the several Latin American countries. They seem to assume that the same strategy and tactics will work in all these countries. They would be well advised to ponder the fate of their Cuban rivals in the Bolivian disaster. The Cubans, for example, erred in that they failed to take into account the fact that the Bolivians had had a meaningful revolution in 1952 and the fact that many of the peasants were relatively satisfied with the land reform effectuated by that revolution. The Cubans took it for granted that Cuban experience was relevant to conditions in Bolivia as well as to the rest of Latin America. As a basis for realistic planning of people's war, the Chinese must familiarize themselves with the differences as well as the similarities in the Latin American countries. Only in this way can they reasonably hope to stage successful people's wars. They certainly cannot assume that their experience is automatically applicable to all the Latin countries.

For purposes of illustration, let us compare Argentina and Bolivia. The composition of the population is quite different. In Bolivia over 50 per cent of the people are Indians, 13.8 per cent are "white," 27.5 per cent are mestizo, and the remainder of the population is unclassified. In Argentina, on the other hand, the native Indians have almost died out and there are fewer persons of mixed blood than in any other Latin American country with the possible exception of Uruguay. In addition to those of Spanish extraction there are many Italians and Germans.[3] In Bolivia most of the people live at very high altitudes in the Andes Mountains; in Argentina most live in the vast plains known as the pampas. Of the two countries Bolivia is much more mountainous in nature, an especially significant fact for those interested in guerrilla warfare. Economically, Argentina has the more fully developed economic system. Although agriculture is a key industry in Argentina, its relative standing in the economy is not as high as that of agriculture in Bolivia. That is, Argentina has a much larger urban working class (in a relative sense) than Bolivia. Conversely, the peasantry in Bolivia is larger in a relative sense than the agricultural working class in Argentina. Educationally, Argentina has one of the best developed educational systems in Latin America, whereas Bolivia, due for the most part to the large number of Indians and mestizos, has one of the most underdeveloped in South America. These are only a few of the most obvious differences between these two countries. Equally illuminating comparisons could be made between Mexico and Uruguay, Paraguay, and Uruguay, et cetera. The point is that the Chinese and their followers in Latin America must address themselves to a systematic concrete study of actual conditions in the various countries in which they are interested. Scientific class analyses based on stereotyped Marxist concepts will not suffice as a basis for successful policy-making.

Chinese and pro-Chinese leaders do not appear to be aware of the fact that the peoples in many of the Latin American countries have, unlike the Chinese people in the 1940s, an acceptable democratic alternative to rule by a totalitarian regime. Several parties have adopted programs of action that appeal to a broad range of the electorate.

[3] "Argentina," *Encyclopaedia Britannica*, 1953 ed., Vol. II; "Bolivia," *Encyclopaedia Britannica*, 1953 ed., Vol. III.

Their programs are especially attractive to the urban working class, the peasantry, the white collar workers and, to a more limited extent, the commercial and industrial leaders. The National Revolutionary parties are those that seem to hold the most promise for the development of a more democratic political order in the region. Representative of this group are such parties as the Aprista Party in Peru, the Democratic Action Party of Venezuela, and the MNR (the National Revolutionary Movement) of Bolivia. These parties, unlike the Jacobin Left, have not lost faith in democracy. They are perfectly willing to compete with others in the political arena, and equally important they are prepared to accept the will of the people as reflected in electoral returns. In the social realm, they are pledged to social reform in the basic sense. Agrarian reform, in the form of the distributing of land and the rendering of technological and economic assistance to the peasantry, is a matter to which they attach the highest priority. For the urban working class they advocate the adoption and vigorous enforcement of laws that protect and promote their interests. Rapid economic development is another item to which they are very much devoted. In the economic realm, they also constantly stress the importance of diversification in agricultural and industrial production. They deplore the situation in which the economic well-being of a country is too dependent on a small number of industries. As nationalists they insist that their countries' sovereignty shall be respected by foreign enterprises operating therein, and they advocate the establishment of economic ties with as many different countries as possible. Thus they hope to eliminate undue reliance on any one country as a trading partner. In practice, this usually means that they want to avoid excessive dependence on the United States. Finally, these groups have a distinct advantage over the Chinese, the Soviets, and the Cubans in that their ideology is an indigenous one based upon Latin American conditions and experience. Nationalists in Latin America applaud their insistence that their problems be solved in light of concepts based on actual conditions confronting policy-makers. If these parties and others in Latin America such as the Christian Democratic parties in Chile and Venezuela are successful in the implementation of their programs of social reform, social justice and political democracy will become realities in Latin America. Should they fail, those committed to the theory that social progress is not feasible within a democratic framework will be provided with a better opportunity to harness the frustrations and expectations of powerful groups in the countryside as well as in the modernized cities.

Nor have the Chinese, in my judgment, given sufficient consideration to the impact of technology on the fighting of people's wars. Debray, on the other hand, manifested an awareness of the need to take into account the importance of airborne troops in planning guerrilla operations. Better communication and transportation give the enemies of the guerrillas distinct advantages which the Japanese did not enjoy vis-à-vis the Chinese in the war that has so colored Chinese strategic thinking.

The sparsity of population in a number of the Latin American countries is in sharp contrast to the situation in China in the anti-Japanese war. Unlike China and Vietnam, countries having dense populations, some of the Latin countries are sparsely populated. Under these circumstances, it would be most difficult to drown the enemy in the sea of the people. How much assistance could the masses render the guerrillas, assuming that the latter could mobilize a large percentage of them? As we have seen, the Chinese model assumes that a people's war will be fought in a country having a large population that could be mobilized against an enemy that is numerically inferior as were the Japanese.

In summary, supporters of the Chinese are confronted with formidable obstacles as they *prepare* for people's wars in Latin America. In view of their limited successes to date, one is tempted to write them off as members of the lunatic fringe in Latin America. They should not, however, be dismissed merely on the basis that most of the pro-Chinese parties are rather small when compared with the pro-Soviet Communist parties and with the even larger reformist parties. The success of Fidel Castro's July 26 Movement in the war against Batista and the success of the Bolshevik revolution of 1917 should cause one to be cautious about predicting dogmatically the failure of small extremist groups.

I would also add that one must not ignore the proverbial patience of the Chinese. It is true that their impact on Latin America has been far less than that of the United States or even that of the Soviet Union, but one must bear in mind that these nations have been active for a much longer time in Latin America than have the Chinese. To the

Chinese, who think more in long-range terms than either the Russians or the Americans, their achievements in establishing the beginning of trade and cultural relations and in forming Communist parties and movements committed to genuine Marxist-Leninist principles, represent a foundation on which they can build in the future.

Although the present work is concerned only with the period from 1959 through 1967, the reader, no doubt, is curious regarding the policy of the CCP after the 9th Party Congress. Does the Mao-Lin group indicate that it intends to continue a strategy of people's war in Latin America? Sufficient time has not elapsed since the adjournment of the congress in April, 1969, to allow us to answer that question with certainty. A perusal of recent articles in *Peking Review* regarding their supporters in Latin America suggests, however, that the pro-Chinese parties are clinging to the strategy articulated by Lin Piao in his article of September, 1965.

Representative of the position taken in the period after the 9th Party Congress by these parties is a Draft Peasant-Agrarian Programme prepared by the Communist Party of Bolivia. The class analysis differs in no way from that described countless times in preceding chapters. People's war was depicted as *the* road to liberation. Only two items in the analysis merit special comment. (1) The party, for the first time, manifested an appreciation of the significance of the land reform law of 1953 and labored hard to demonstrate that this "so-called land reform in 1953" was designed to protect big landed property. The law also allegedly protected "the feudal relations in the form of reclamation and partnership systems." (2) The Bolivians quoted "Comrade Lin Piao" who stressed the necessity for relying mainly on the peasants in the waging of successful people's war. In this context the Bolivians explained the failure of the Castroite guerrilla movement in Bolivia: "The experience of the guerrilla movement in the southeastern part of Bolivia has fully confirmed this Marxist-Leninist thesis on the importance of the peasants, for the principal error of the guerrilla force was that it neglected the role of the peasant, failed to win their support and did not carry out intensive political work among them." [4]

[4] "Rallying Peasant Masses for an Anti-Imperialist, Anti-Feudal Revolution," *Peking Review*, June 6, 1969, p. 22.

CONCLUSION

The Communist Party of Brazil, the pioneer party for pro-Chinese forces in Latin America, in a Central Committee document entitled "People's War—the Path of Armed Struggle in Brazil" reiterated the concepts that we have encountered so frequently in the present analysis. The Brazilian armed struggle "will be a people's war." [5] The principal theater of the liberation war would be the interior, not the big cities. The war would be a "protracted one and no rapid victory should be expected." The people would "rely mainly on their own strength to carry on the war. No illusions about external logistics should be encouraged." [6] "Guerrilla warfare" would be the "principal form of struggle in the initial stage of the war." The tactics to be followed would be those summed up by Comrade Mao Tse-tung: "The enemy advances, we retreat; the enemy camps, we harass; the enemy tires, we attack; the enemy retreats, we pursue."

The crucial problem in developing a people's war "is the establishment of bases of support in the countryside. . . ." The Brazilian account indicated quite clearly that the Brazilians have accepted the Maoist concept of a protracted war that develops in three stages:

In view of the fact that the enemy is strong and we are weak, the people's fighters have to develop their struggle within the framework of the strategic defensive in the initial stage of people's war so as to accumulate and gain strength. But the strategic defensive does not mean passiveness. The revolutionary armed forces should have maximum initiative. Only when a change has taken place in the balance of strength between the two contesting sides, that is, when the revolutionary forces have become strong, will the war enter the stage of stalemate, and then the stage of the strategic offensive, when the people's forces have gained military superiority and have the conditions to deal the enemy fatal blows. [7]

The final point to be noted is the following statement which indicates that the Chinese and Castroites are still feuding regarding the proper strategy to be pursued by revolutionaries:

Repudiating the so-called theory of guerrilla "centre" which has been in circulation in recent years, the document points out: The advocates of this theory maintain that by means of the brave actions of a small group

[5] "Unfold a People's War to Overthrow Pro-U.S. Dictatorial Regime," *Peking Review*, June 20, 1969, p. 21.
[6] *Ibid.*, p. 22.   [7] *Ibid.*

of persons alone, they can attract new combatants and lead the revolution to victory. They also hold that a revolutionary party of the proletariat is unnecessary since the guerrilla is in itself the party. They do not believe that the masses can grasp revolutionary ideas and plunge themselves into the struggle. They divorce themselves from the masses and engage solely in armed actions. They hold a purely military viewpoint. This theory has been proved in practice to be entirely false. It has failed in Peru, Argentina, Bolivia and other countries.[8]

Comparable reports emanating from Mexico, Ecuador, and other Latin American countries confirm the conclusion that the Mao-Lin group, which has allegedly prevailed over its enemies in the Cultural Revolution, is at the time of writing (August, 1969) still propagating the idea that Latin Americans can be liberated only by people's war. In view of reports that the Soviet Union and Communist China might possibly be involved in a war because of their disputes over boundaries and the proper global strategy to be followed, one can reasonably predict that the Maoists will continue their bitter attacks on the revisionists in Latin America. Should the Soviet Red Army invade Sinkiang, Mongolia, or Manchuria the PLA, led by Lin Piao, will have its best opportunity to validate in practice the theory of people's war.

[8] *Ibid.*, p. 23.

Bibliography

BOOKS

ALEXANDER, ROBERT J. *Communism in Latin America*. New Brunswick, N.J.: Rutgers University Press, 1957.

BARNETT, A. DOAK. *Communist China and Asia: A Challenge to American Policy*. New York: Vintage Books, 1961.

BOYD, R. G. *Communist China's Foreign Policy*. New York: Frederick A. Praeger, 1962.

COHEN, ARTHUR A. *Communism of Mao Tse-tung*. Chicago: The University of Chicago Press, 1964.

DEBRAY, RÉGIS. *Revolution in the Revolution? Armed Struggle and Political Struggle in Latin America*. Translated by Bobbye Ortiz. New York: Grove Press, Inc., 1967.

DRAPER, THEODORE. *Castroism: Theory and Practice*. New York: Frederick A. Praeger, 1965.

DUTT, VIDYA PRAKASH. *China and the World: An Analysis of Communist China's Foreign Policy*. New York: Frederick A. Praeger, 1966.

FITZGERALD, C. P. *The Chinese View of Their Place in the World*. New York: Oxford University Press, 1964.

DA FONSECA, GONDIN. *Assim Falon Julião*. 2d ed. São Paulo: Editora Fulgor, 1962.

Fundamentals of Marxism-Leninism. 2d ed. rev. Moscow: Foreign Languages Publishing House, 1963.

GIAP, VO NGUYEN. *People's War, People's Army*. New York: Frederick A. Praeger, 1962.

(305)

GRIFFITH, WILLIAM E. *The Sino-Soviet Rift.* Cambridge, Mass.: The M.I.T. Press, 1964.

GUEVARA, CHE. *Guerrilla Warfare.* New York: Monthly Review Press, 1961.

HALPERIN, ERNST. *Nationalism and Communism in Chile.* Cambridge, Mass.: The M.I.T. Press, 1965.

HALPERN, A. M. (ed.) *Policies Toward China: Views from Six Continents.* New York: McGraw-Hill Book Co., 1965.

HINTON, HAROLD C. *Communist China in World Politics.* New York: Houghton Mifflin Co., 1966.

HSIEH, ALICE LANGLEY. *Communist China's Strategy in the Nuclear Era.* Englewood Cliffs, N.J.: Prentice Hall, Inc., 1962.

JOHNSON, CHALMERS A. *Peasant Nationalism and Communist Power: The Emergence of Revolutionary China, 1937–1945.* Stanford, California: Stanford University Press, 1962.

MAO TSE-TUNG. *Chairman Mao Tse-tung on People's War.* Peking: Foreign Languages Press, 1967.

——. *On Guerrilla Warfare.* Translated by Samuel B. Griffith. New York: Frederick A. Praeger, 1961.

——. *Selected Military Writings.* 2d ed. Peking: Foreign Languages Press, 1965.

——. *Selected Works.* 3 vols. Peking: Foreign Languages Press, 1965.

——. *Selected Works.* Vol. IV. Peking: Foreign Languages Press, 1961.

OSANKA, FRANKLIN MARK (ed.) *Modern Guerrilla Warfare.* New York, 1962.

PARET, PETER, and SHY, JOHN W. *Guerrillas in the 1960s.* Revised ed. New York: Frederick A. Praeger, 1962.

PASSIN, HERBERT. *China's Cultural Diplomacy.* New York: Frederick A. Praeger, 1963.

SCHRAM, STUART R. *The Political Thought of Mao Tse-tung.* New York: Frederick A. Praeger, 1963.

SUÁREZ, ANDRÉS. *Cuba: Castroism and Communism, 1959–1966.* Cambridge, Mass.: The M.I.T. Press, 1967.

ZAGORIA, DONALD S. *The Sino-Soviet Conflict 1956–1961.* Princeton, N.J.: Princeton University Press, 1962.

ARTICLES

ACOSTA, RAOUL SALAS. "Whom Do the Chinese Leaders Support in Peru?" *Pravda* (May 22, 1964), Joint Publications Research Service, *Translations on Communist Developments*, No. 616.

"Actions of the Chinese Dissidents Are Doomed to Failure," *Pravda* (June 6, 1964), JPRS, *TICD*, No. 619.

"The Activity of Communist China in Latin America," *Est et Ouest* (July 16–31, 1966), JPRS, *TICD*, No. 878.

ALBERTINI, GEORGES. "Communist Tactics in South America," *Corrispondenza Socialista* (August–September, 1965), JPRS, *TICD*, No. 796.

——. "The Conference in Havana," *Est et Ouest* (March 15, 1966), JPRS, *TICD*, No. 834.

ARRELLANO, JORGE ISAAC. "Revolution Within Revolution? or Adventure Without Revolution?—A Reply to Régis Debray." Guayaquil, Ecuador: Ediciones Liberación, 1967, JPRS, *TICD*, No. 1010.

BALANTA, MARTÍN. "Rupture Between Castro and Peiping," *Segunda Republica* (January 30, 1966), JPRS, *TICD*, No. 810.

CÁRDENAS, FLORANGEL. "The Crisis in the Dominican Popular Movement: Division among the Dominican Communists," *Ahora* (August 15, 1966), JPRS, *TICD*, No. 879.

CARDONA, JOSÉ HOYOS. "Divergencies in the International Communist Movement," *Documentos Politicos* (February, 1966), JPRS, *TICD*, No. 829.

"Carrying the War by the Colombian People Through to Victory—Extract from the 'Political Conclusions of the Military Front' of the Second Plenum of the Central Committee of the Communist Party of Colombia (m.l.)," *Nuova Unità* (January 14, 1967), JPRS, *TICD*, No. 953.

CENTRAL COMMITTEE OF THE COMMUNIST PARTY OF BRAZIL. "Reply to Khrushchov," *A Classe Operária* (August 1–15, 1963), in *Peking Review*, September 13, 1963.

CENTRAL EXECUTIVE COMMITTEE OF THE COMMUNIST PARTY OF BRAZIL. "The Domestic Situation in Brazil and the Tasks of the Communist Party of Brazil," in *Peking Review*, May 28, 1965.

CHANG YEH. "Cuba Is Advancing Forward," *Shih-chieh Chih-shih* (May 10, 1961).

———. "Cuba's Sacred Place of Revolution—the Sierra Maestra Mountains," *Shih-chieh Chih-shih* (December 25, 1962).

———. "Four Fighting and Victorious Years," *Shih-chieh Chih-shih* (January 10, 1963).

"Communist China in Latin America," *Este & Oeste* (December, 1966), JPRS, *TICD*, No. 940.

DEVLIN, KEVIN. "Boring from Within," *Problems of Communism* (March–April, 1964).

———. "Castro and the Communists," Radio Free Europe, research paper.

———. "Castro's Place in the Communist World," Radio Free Europe, research paper, September 21, 1967.

"Documents on Divisionist Activities," *Principios* (November–December, 1963), JPRS, *TICD*, No. 550.

"Dominica," *Shih-chieh Chih-shih* (June, 1965).

"Exodus of Communists from Bolivia," *Est et Ouest* (October 15–30, 1965), JPRS, *TICD*, No. 789.

"Fidel Castro on Trade Between Cuba and China," *Prensa Latina*, in *Global Digest*, Vol. III, No. 4, 1966.

"For Our Revolution: Preparations for a Major Marxist-Leninist Congress," *Tribuna* (November, 1964), JPRS, *TICD*, No. 694.

FOURTH NATIONAL CONFERENCE OF THE PERUVIAN COMMUNIST PARTY. "Opportunist Divisionism of the Left, Uncovered and in Defeat," *Unidad* (September 17, 1964), in JPRS, *TICD*, No. 658.

GITTINGS, JOHN. "Chinese Copper," *Far Eastern Economic Review* (January 19, 1967).

GRABOIS, MAURICIO. "The World Revolution's Vanguard and Leading Force," *A Classe Operária* (July 1–15, 1963), in *Peking Review*, August 30, 1963.

"A Great Example," *Tribuna* (November, 1964), JPRS, *TICD*, No. 694.

"Guatemala," *Shih-chieh Chih-shih* (November 10, 1965).

GUEVARA, ERNESTO CHE. "Guerrilla Warfare: A Means," in *Peking Review*, January 14, 1964.

(308)

HALPERIN, ERNST. "Peking and the Latin American Communists," *The China Quarterly* (January–March, 1967).

HO LI. "The June 14th Revolutionary Movement in Dominica," *Shih-chieh Chih-shih* (June 25, 1965).

LAMBERG, ROBERT F. "Latin America and the Tri-Continental Conference," *Der Ostblock und die Entwicklungslaender (The East Bloc and the Developing Countries)* (June, 1966), JPRS, *TICD*, No. 890.

"Land Reform—the Spear-head and Banner of the Cuban Revolution," *Chih-chieh Chih-shih*, (June 5, 1959).

LAZITCH, BRANKO. "Repercussions of the Sino-Soviet Dispute on the Latin American Communist Parties," *Est et Ouest* (January 1–15, 1965), JPRS, *TICD*, No. 693.

LEE, JOSEPH J. "Communist China's Latin American Policy," *Asian Survey* (November, 1964).

LIU NING-I. Speech given to the Sino-Cuban Friendship Association (December 30, 1962), in *Hsin-hua Yüeh-pao*, No. 220.

LO JUNG-CH'U. "The Victorious Road of the Cuban Revolution," *Hsin-hua Yüeh-pao*, No. 220 (February, 1963).

MEI-HUNG. "The Glorious Road of July 26," *Shih-chieh Chih-shih* (July 25, 1963).

MILLARES, EDGAR REYES. "Pro-Chinese and Trotskyite Communists Wage World-Wide Ideological Dispute," *Este & Oeste* (April, 1967), JPRS, *TICD*, No. 980.

MONTENOVO, LUCA G. "The Situation of the Colombian CP," *Corrispondenza Socialista* (December, 1965), JPRS, *TICD*, No. 800.

"The New China News Agency: Mao's Messengers Around the World," *Current Scene* (April 1, 1966).

"On Peaceful Pursuit of Socialism in Chile," *La Voix du Peuple* (September 18, 1964), JPRS, *TICD*, No. 655.

"The Perfect Jorge Arrellano," *El Pueblo* (July 8, 1967), *JPRS, TICD*, No. 990.

"The Peruvian Communist Party Down the Path of Mariátegui," *Bandera Roja* (October, 1966), JPRS, *TICD*, No. 910.

POLITICAL COMMITTEE OF THE CENTRAL COMMITTEE OF THE PERUVIAN COMMUNIST PARTY. "The PCP and Secret Work," *Bandera Roja* (January, 1967), JPRS, *TICD*, No. 962.

"The Present Situation of the Argentine Communist Party," *Est et Ouest* (May 15–30, 1966), JPRS, *TICD*, No. 857.

"Present Situation of the Colombian Communist Party," *Este & Oeste* (December 1–15, 1965), JPRS, *TICD*, No. 806.

POWELL, RALPH L. "Maoist Military Doctrines," *Asian Survey* (April, 1968).

"Regarding the Fifth National Conference of the Peruvian Communist Party," *La Voix du Peuple* (October 7, 1966), JPRS, *TICD*, No. 903.

"Regional Committee of Lima," *Bandera Roja* (March 4, 1966), JPRS, *TICD*, No. 829.

"Reply to the Opportunistic Clique of the False Ecuadorian Communist Party," *Politica* (March–April, 1967), JPRS, *TICD*, No. 984.

"Resolution of the National Commission of Controls and Cadres of the Peruvian Communist Party," *Bandera Roja* (March 4, 1966), JPRS, *TICD*, No. 829.

"Resolution on Organization," *El Pueblo* (November 5, 1965), JPRS, *TICD*, No. 788.

SHEN-YU DAI. " 'Sugar Coated Bullets' for Latin America," *Current Scene* (December 23, 1961).

"Split in the Colombian CP," *Est et Ouest* (October 16–31, 1965), JPRS, *TICD*, No. 776.

"Statement of the Political Committee on the Existence of an Anti-Party Group in Our Ranks," *Unidad* (August 15, 1964), JPRS, *TICD*, No. 650.

SUÁREZ, ANDRÉS. "Castro Between Moscow and Peking," *Problems of Communism* (September–October, 1963).

TRETIAK, DANIEL. "China and Latin America: An Ebbing Tide in Trans-Pacific Maoism," *Current Scene* (March 1, 1966).

———. "China's Tough Brazil Nut," *Far Eastern Economic Review* (April 15, 1965).

———. "Mexican Traders," *Far Eastern Economic Review* (May 28, 1964).

———. "Mao, Castro and Khrushchev," *Far Eastern Economic Review* (November 7, 1963).

"Unity Is the Guarantee of Success in Our Struggle," *Pravda* (January 19, 1965), in JPRS, *TICD*, No. 695.

"The Unity of the Communist Movement and Anti-Imperialist Cohesion," *El Siglo* (April 9, 1964), JPRS, *TICD*, No. 603.

Yu Chao-li. "The Great Significance of the Victory of the Cuban People's Patriotic Struggle Against U.S. Imperialism," *Red Flag* (May 5, 1961), in *SCMP*, No. 262.

PERIODICALS

Asian Survey. 1964–1967.
The China Quarterly. 1961–1967.
Chinese Communist Affairs. 1966–1967.
Current Scene. 1961–1967.
Far Eastern Economic Review. 1959–1967.
Global Digest. 1966–1967.
Hsin-hua Yüeh-pao (New China Monthly). 1962–1965.
Peking Review. 1959–1967.
Problems of Communism. 1963–1967.
Shih-chieh Chih-shih (World Knowledge). 1959–1966.

NEWSPAPERS

Hsinhua Daily News Release.
Jen-min Jih-pao (People's Daily).
The New York Times.

PAMPHLETS

Lin Piao. *Long Live the Victory of People's War!* Peking: Foreign Languages Press, 1966.

Li Tso-peng. *Strategy: One Against Ten—Tactics: Ten Against One*. Peking: Foreign Languages Press, 1966.

Mao Tse-tung. *The Chinese Revolution and the Chinese Communist Party*. Peking: Foreign Languages Press, 1959.

SHAO TIEH-CHEN. *Revolutionary Dialectics and How to Appraise Imperialism.* Peking: Foreign Languages Press, 1963.
UNITED STATES INFORMATION AGENCY, Office of Policy and Research. *Communist Propaganda Organizations and Activities in Latin America During 1966.*

TRANSLATION SERIES

Joint Publications Research Service. *Translations on International Communist Developments.* 1963–1967.
United States Consul General. Hong Kong. *Current Background.* 1959–1967.
——. Hong Kong. *Survey of China Mainland Magazines.* 1959–1967.
——. Hong Kong. *Survey of the China Mainland Press.* 1959–1967.

MISCELLANEOUS

MOZINGO, DAVID. "Peking and Hanoi." Paper read before the University Seminar on International Communism, Columbia University, New York City, N.Y., February 15, 1967.
STRONG, ANNA LOUISE. *Letter from China* (February 28, 1968).

RADIO BROADCASTS

Bogotá Correspondent's Dispatch in Spanish to NCNA.
La Paz Correspondent's Dispatches to NCNA Peking.
La Paz Radio La Cruz del Sur.
Lima Correspondent's Dispatch in Spanish to NCNA.
Peking NCNA Domestic Service in Mandarin.
Peking NCNA International Service in English.
Tirana ATA International Service in French.

Index

INDEX

Castro, Raúl, 155
Chang Kuang-tou, 15, 21
Chang Yeh, 142, 150
Chao Yi-min, 24
Chelen, Alejandro, 249
Ch'en Yi, 148
Chile: trade relations with China, 20-22; *see also* Chilean Communist movement
Chilean Communist movement: pro-Soviet orientation of, 247; establishment of Spartacus group, 247; early organizational efforts of pro-Chinese group, 248-50; response of pro-Soviet forces, 250; expulsion of pro-Chinese militants, 250-52; pro-Chinese analysis of international and domestic situations, 252; relations with Trotskyites, 253-54; pro-Soviet denunciation of Chinese splitting activities, 254; pro-Chinese rejection of peaceful road, 254; establishment of Chilean Revolutionary Communist Party, 254-55; denunciation of neutralism in Sino-Soviet dispute, 255; on stages of revolution, 255-56; adoption of strategy of people's war, 256; praise of Cultural Revolution, 256
Chilean Revolutionary Communist Party: establishment of, 254-55; stand taken in Sino-Soviet dispute, 255; on stages of revolution, 255-56; adoption of strategy of people's war, 256; on the Cultural Revolution, 256
China-Brazil Cultural Institute, 12
China-Latin American Friendship Association, 19, 25
China Peace Committee, 260, 267, 270
Chinese Revolution: stages of, 46; Mao on need for distinguishing stages, 46-47; tasks during first stage, 47; nature of state during various stages, 48; Mao's contribution to theory of state, 48-50; premature transition to second stage, 50-51
Chou En-lai, 27, 148, 259
Chu Chi-tung, 11, 18
Chu Teh, 27, 88, 126, 259

Chu Tu-nan, 19
Class analysis, 38-45; Chinese evaluation of Brazilian classes, 196-98; by Communist Party of Brazil, 200-201, 205; by Peruvian Communist Party, 212-14, 215, 217; by Colombian Communist Party, 236-37; in Dominican Republic, 268-69
Class struggle theory: Mao on need for class analysis, 38-39; enemies of the people, 39; policy of CCP toward landlord class, 39-40; national bourgeoisie as ally of proletariat, 40-41; policy of CCP toward national bourgeoisie, 41; petty bourgeoisie as ally of proletariat, 41; composition of petty bourgeoisie, 41-42; peasant as most dependable ally of proletariat, 42; classification of peasantry, 42-44; policy of CCP toward peasantry, 44-45; proletariat as leading force in revolution, 44-45; global scope of struggle, 45-46
Codovilla, Victorio, 270
Cohen, Arthur, 48, 50
Colombian-Chinese Friendship Society, 13
Colombian Communist Party: pro-Soviet account of split, 231; split in Communist youth movement, 232; formation of pro-Chinese Youth Union, 232-33; establishment of pro-Chinese party, 233-37; class analysis by, 236-37; on international issues, 238; denunciation of neutralist policy in Sino-Soviet dispute, 238; strategy and tactics, 238-39; rejection of peaceful path, 239; endorsement of Mao's theory of army building, 239-40; condemnation of Castroite deviations, 240
Communist Party of Brazil: origin of revisionism, 183; formation of pro-Chinese faction, 184; Grabois on CCP as vanguard of world revolution, 185-86; response to CPSU letter of July 14, 1963, 186-89; slowness of CCP in recognition of, 189-90; Chinese recognition of, 191; Duarte's at-

(314)

INDEX

Louise Strong on Debray's errors, 172; attacks by pro-Chinese parties on Debray's book, 173-80
Sino-Uruguayan Cultural Institute, 25
Solorzano Hernández, Gustavo, 16
Sorro Encalada, Pedro, 11
Sotomayor Pérez, José, 209-10, 220
Spartacus group, 247-51
Strong, Anna Louise, 172
Sweezy, Paul M., 104, 110-11

Teng Hsiao-p'ing, 206, 259
Toussent Jean, Alfred, 263-64
Trade relations: reasons for small volume of, 14-15; with Mexico, 15-16; with Argentina, 16-17; with Brazil, 17-20; with Chile, 20-22; with Cuba, 22, 165-67
Translations, 13-14
Tretiak, Daniel, 163
Tricontinental Conference, 164
Trotskyites, 253-54

Tung Pi-wu, 27
Turcios Lima, Luis, 283

Uruguay-China Cultural Association, 25

Vanguarda Revolucionaria Marxista, 249, 253
Venezuelan Friendship Society, 25
Vieira White, Gilberto, 231, 233, 236, 237

Wang Wei-chen, 11, 18
Wang Yao-ting, 18
World Knowledge Publishing House, 13
Wu Hsiu-ch'uan, 24, 190

Yon Sosa, 283
Yu Chao-li, 141

Zagoria, Donald, 130
Zamora Medinacelli Oscar, 226, 229

Studies of the East Asian Institute

The Ladder of Success in Imperial China, by Ping-ti Ho. New York: Columbia University Press, 1962.

The Chinese Inflation, 1937-1949, by Shun-hsin Chou. New York: Columbia University Press, 1963.

Reformer in Modern China: Chang Chien, 1853-1926, by Samuel Chu. New York: Columbia University Press, 1965.

Research in Japanese Sources: A Guide, by Herschel Webb with the assistance of Marleigh Ryan. New York: Columbia University Press, 1965.

Society and Education in Japan, by Herbert Passin. New York: Bureau of Publications, Teachers College, Columbia University, 1965.

Agricultural Production and Economic Development in Japan, 1873-1922, by James I. Nakamura. Princeton, N.J.: Princeton University Press, 1966.

Japan's First Modern Novel: Ukigumo of Futabatei Shimei, by Marleigh Ryan. New York: Columbia University Press, 1967.

The Korean Communist Movement, 1918-1948, by Dae-Sook Suh. Princeton, N.J.: Princeton University Press, 1967.

The First Vietnam Crisis, by Melvin Gurtov. New York: Columbia University Press, 1967.

Cadres, Bureaucracy and Political Power in Communist China, by A. Doak Barnett. New York: Columbia University Press, 1967.

The Japanese Imperial Institution in the Tokugawa Period, by Herschel Webb. New York: Columbia University Press, 1968.

The Recruitment of University Graduates in Big Firms in Japan, by Koya Azumi. New York: Teachers College Press, Columbia University, 1968.

The Communists and Chinese Peasant Rebellion: A Study in the Rewriting of Chinese History, by James P. Harrison, Jr. New York: Atheneum Publishers, 1969.

How the Conservatives Rule Japan, by Nathaniel B. Thayer. Princeton, N.J.: Princeton University Press, 1969.

Aspects of Chinese Education, edited by C. T. Hu. New York: Teachers College Press, Columbia University, 1969.

Economic Development and the Labor Market in Japan, by Koji Taira. New York: Columbia University Press, 1970.

The Japanese Oligarchy and the Russo-Japanese War, by Shumpei Okamoto. New York: Columbia University Press, 1970.

Imperial Restoration in Medieval Japan, by Paul Varley. New York: Columbia University Press (forthcoming).

Li Tsung-jen, A Memoir. Edited by T. K. Tong. University of California Press (forthcoming).

Documents on Korean Communism, by Dae-Sook Suh. Princeton, N.J.: Princeton University Press (forthcoming).

Japan's Postwar Defense Policy, 1947-1968, by Martin E. Weinstein. New York: Columbia University Press (forthcoming).

Publications of the
Research Institute on Communist Affairs

Diversity in International Communism, Alexander Dallin, ed., in collaboration with the Russian Institute, Columbia University Press, 1963. A documentary record of the issues agitating the international communist movement in the years 1961-1963.

Political Succession in the USSR, Myron Rush, published jointly with the RAND Corporation, Columbia University Press, 1965. A theoretical and historical account of the problem of political succession in the Soviet regime.

Marxism in Modern France, George Lichtheim, Columbia University Press, 1966. A historical study of French socialist and communist theory and practice since World War II.

Power in the Kremlin, Michel Tatu, Viking Press, 1969, was first published in 1967 by Bernard Grasset under the title *Le Pouvoir en URSS* and also in England by William Collins Sons and Co., Ltd., in 1968. An analysis of the shifting balance of power within the Soviet leadership in the 1960s.

The Soviet Bloc: Unity and Conflict, Zbigniew Brzezinski, revised and enlarged edition, Harvard University Press, 1967. Focuses on the role of ideology and power in the relations among the communist states.

Vietnam Triangle, Donald Zagoria, Pegasus Press, 1968. A clarification of the factors governing the relations among the communist parties and states involved in Vietnam.

Communism in Malaysia and Singapore, Justus van der Kroef, Nijhoff Publications (The Hague), 1967. The first book-length study of the communist movement in the Malaysian-Singapore region today.

Radicalismo Cattolico Brasiliano, Ulisse A. Floridi, Istituto Editoriale Del Mediterraneo, 1968. A discussion of the problems faced by the Catholic Church when it becomes actively involved in the struggle for social justice.

Stalin and His Generals, Seweryn Bialer, ed., Pegasus Press, 1969. An anthology of war memoirs from Soviet books, journals, and other writings which gives a picture of the Soviet military elite and of Stalin's role during World War II.

Marxism and Ethics, Eugene Kamenka, Macmillan and St. Martin's Press, 1969. The author examines both Marx's positive ethics of the truly human man freed from alienation and Marx's materialist critique of moralities as class-bound ideologies.

Dilemmas of Change in Soviet Politics, Zbigniew Brzezinski, ed. and contributor, Columbia University Press, 1969. A collection of essays which appeared in *Problems of Communism* in 1966-1968, discussing prospects for the Soviet political system.

STUDIES OF THE EAST ASIAN INSTITUTE

The USSR Arms the Third World: Case Studies in Soviet Foreign Policy, Uri Ra'anan, The M.I.T. Press, 1969. Using Egypt and Indonesia as case studies, the author analyzes Soviet involvement in the Third World.

Communists and Their Law, John N. Hazard, The University of Chicago Press, 1969. The author analyzes the Marxian socialist legal system and examines the implementation of policy by law in the communist world.

Fulcrum of Asia, Bhabani Sen Gupta, published jointly with the East Asian Institute, Pegasus Press, 1970. The author analyzes and documents the relations among China, India, Pakistan and the Soviet Union during 1947-1968.

Le Conflit Sino-Soviétique et l'Europe de l'Est, Jacques Levesque, Montreal University Press, 1970. The author examines the impact of the Sino-Soviet conflict on the relations between the U.S.S.R. and Poland (1956-1959) and between the U.S.S.R. and Rumania (1960-1968).

Between Two Ages: America's Role in the Technetronic Era, Zbigniew Brzezinski, Viking Press, 1970. The author projects the impact of technology and electronics on the political and social values of the United States, the Soviet Union and other "post-industrial" states.

Communist China and Latin America, Cecil Johnson, Columbia University Press, 1970.

FORTHCOMING BOOKS

Communism and Nationalism in India: M. N. Roy and the Comintern, John P. Haithcox, Princeton University Press.

The Tragic Experiment: Czechoslovakia 1968-1969, Ivan Sviták, Columbia University Press.

Parteielite im Wandel, Peter Ludz, translated and revised edition, The M.I.T. Press.

The Political Regimes of the U.S.S.R. and Eastern Europe, Michel Lesage, Presses Universitaires de France.